ALICE COOPER
WELCOME TO MY NIGHTMARE
DAVE THOMPSON

OMNIBUS PRESS

London / New York / Paris / Sydney / Copenhagen / Berlin / Madrid / Tokyo

Exclusive Distributors
Music Sales Limited,
14/15 Berners Street,
London, W1T 3LJ.

Music Sales Corporation,
257 Park Avenue South,
New York, NY 10010, USA.

Macmillan Distribution Services,
56 Parkwest Drive
Derrimut, Vic 3030,
Australia.

Every effort has been made to trace the copyright holders of the photographs in this book but one
or two were unreachable. We would be grateful if the photographers concerned would contact us.

Printed in the EU

A catalogue record for this book is available from the British Library.

Visit Omnibus Press on the web at www.omnibuspress.com

CONTENTS

Introduction

Back in 1997, shortly before the death of his former Alice Cooper bandmate Glen Buxton that October, drummer Neal Smith was shooting the breeze with his old friend when the subject of the Rock and Roll Hall of Fame came up.

The Alice Cooper band had only recently become eligible for induction; the 25th anniversary of their late sixties formation was celebrated in 1994, and there were precious few bands of that vintage that deserved induction more than the Coopers. Maybe it did take them two years to really pick up steam, but still the run of hit singles (and LPs) that blasted Alice Cooper through the early seventies not only remains peerless, it also includes some of the seminal rock anthems of all time.

'I'm Eighteen', 'School's Out', 'Elected', 'Hello Hooray', 'Under My Wheels', 'No More Mr Nice Guy', 'Generation Landslide', 'Billion Dollar Babies', 'Be My Lover' – you could stuff a greatest hits CD with the songs for which Alice Cooper are most renowned, and then you could stuff another with the songs for which they're best remembered: 'Dead Babies', 'I Love The Dead', 'Black Juju', 'Killer', 'Sick Things', 'Halo Of Flies', 'Hallowed Be Thy Name'.

Alice Cooper may not have been the heaviest band on earth but they still made everyone else look like lightweights, and the fact that the sainted heads of the Hall of Fame had not dragged the Coopers kicking and screaming into their marbled halls the moment that the group became eligible was... well, it wasn't even inexplicable. It was contemptible.

"The Rock and Roll Hall of Fame," laughed Buxton, "can kiss my Rock and Roll Ass."

"That comment stuck with me all these years," Smith smiled 13 years later. "So, about a year ago, I wrote a song about it..." and, as he worked towards the second album by his current Killsmith project, there seemed no reason on earth why he shouldn't include it.

Except one.

The day the telephone rang and it was the Rock and Roll Hall of Fame. The Coopers were in, and Smith was astonished. "I never dreamed in a million years that we would ever be inducted." And, as for 'The Rock And Roll Hall Of Fame Can Kiss My Rock And Roll Ass'... "Well, it was a good idea at the time but we'll see what happens. Nostradamus I'm not."

Killsmith is one of the most enthralling of all the myriad bands to have emerged over the past three decades-plus from the wreckage of the original Alice Cooper band. *Sexual Savior*, the band's debut album, was released back in 2008 and proved one of the most challengingly perverse records of Smith's career, a litany of thrilling riffs, thunderous chords, monster percussion and the kind of lyrics that could make an Anglo-Saxon blush.

This time around, things were a little more level-headed. *Killsmith 2*, Smith laughed, was "a lot more radio friendly than the first one. I got that off my chest, got all the x-rated words out. *Killsmith 2* is a lot more radio friendly but with the power of the first one. Just the way songs are written... catchier choruses. Twelve songs and they're all brand new, although I guess 'Kiss My Ass, Rock And Roll Hall Of Fame'... I guess I can't put that one on."

He continued, "I'm the most excited for the fans who have stuck with us for such a long time. Within the last 10 years, there's been petitions circulating and these people just can't understand why we weren't in there. I'm still amazed that, in 1973, we had the number one LP with *Billion Dollar Babies* and, to me, that was the peak of our career in terms of things happening out of the blue that we weren't even expecting. I didn't think it would ever get any better than that, and with the hesitation about us even getting a nomination to the Hall of Fame....

"I know Alice has wonderful fans, but the original band has wonderful fans as well. Their support has been strong and non-wavering over these many years, and I'm most excited for them. I think this is a great day for the fans, a great time for them." And the fact that the nomination itself was so overdue, in a way, only made it that little bit sweeter.

"The only time I actually got excited about the nomination was when I realised... I was very pessimistic that anything positive could come out of it, because it took 16 years to be nominated. And all the bands that are in there, I love, but I think there's been a handful of bands that have no place in there. You put them up against the Beatles, the Rolling Stones, the Who, Jimi Hendrix, Elvis Presley, the real monsters of rock and you wonder why they're there. So I was a little disillusioned with that.

"But then I started looking at the first time nominees, the bands that got in on the first nomination, and man, that was when I got excited. I thought if we were ever going to be nominated, and we ever got in, it would be amazing to get in on the first nomination. And that's what we did. In reality, it is a great thing and I am excited about it."

Especially pleasing, for Smith and for the band's fans, is the fact that it is the original band that is being inducted, and not Alice Cooper alone. That, after all, would not have been a shock – even at the peak of the band's success in 1972-1973, people were more likely than not to refer to Alice Cooper as the individual singer, the lanky, face-painted, snake-wielding freak whom his parents had named Vince Furnier, and allow the remainder of the band to lapse into anonymity.

No matter that Smith, guitarists Michael Bruce and Glen Buxton, and bassist Dennis Dunaway were as much a part of the act as their frontman; nor that the vast majority of the band's greatest numbers were at least co-written by one or other of them. To the public at large, Alice Cooper was Alice Cooper, and it's a misconception that history has clung tenaciously onto ever since.

Or maybe it isn't a misconception. For every band and every performer of note has that one transcendent moment upon which the remainder of their career hinges, and for Alice Cooper the man, and Alice Cooper the performer, that moment took place precisely 39 years before the Hall of Fame induction, at a time when both were more likely to be immortalised in a House of Horrors or Wall of Shame, than proclaimed an integral part of rock's DNA.

Hindsight and history's habit of creating neatly delineated eras from the tangled mass of rock'n'roll's chronology does not always agree but, as of spring 1972, what we now know of as glam rock was still an explosion awaiting ignition.

T Rex, Slade and the Sweet were all up and running, and the latter's recently acquired penchant for make-up and costume certainly placed them into a visual ballpark they shared with the other two. But three bands do not a movement make, no matter how successful they might be, a point that is pushed home even harder when one considers just how vastly different were the musical fields in which they operated.

The all-electric *The Slider* album was imminent but, until it was delivered, T Rex was still a rootsy folkadelic band with an eye for jamming Eddie Cochran riffs. Slade were a yobbish but well-disciplined hard rock band prone to covering Steppenwolf and Janis Joplin in and around their own foot-stamping material. And the Sweet were generally regarded as undiluted bubblegum, eternally beholden to the saccharine penmanship of the Chinnichap songwriting duo.

Yes, something was happening. Hindsight insists on it.

For the average 11, 12 or 13 year old, though; the generation that was just beginning to read the weekly rock papers, but whose world was largely still built around *Top Of The Pops*; who looked to rock'n'roll music as a means of delineating their adolescent obsessions, and maybe drop a clue or two about what being a teenager actually meant, 1972 really wasn't offering much more than 1971 before it. And scanning the upcoming release sheets for the next few months, it would require an astonishingly fine-tuned crystal ball to pinpoint the half a dozen forthcoming 45s that would convert a vague feeling of musical resolution into a full-fledged pop revolution.

There was another stab in the dark from a one-hit wonder named David Bowie; a no-hits veteran trying it on again as Gary Glitter; a long-running Ladbroke Grove hippy saga called Hawkwind; a new arty outfit called Roxy Music; perennial commercial no-hopers Mott The Hoople; a bunch of Mancunian sessionmen called 10cc; and what appeared to be the latest in a long line of American singer-songstresses, Carly Simon's kid sister or Melanie's mum, a chick named Alice Cooper.

Radio North Sea International, the offshore alternative to Radio One that crackled through the static of a late-night transistor radio, was championing the novelty charms of Edwina Biglet and the Miglets, but Radio One itself was still stuck on Nilsson's 'Without You'. And with the big three (again, T Rex, Slade and the Sweet) between singles, the summer yawned ahead like an anchorite's pyjama party.

But suddenly, things started to change. Bowie's 'Starman' was a sweet little song, half 'Over The Rainbow', half leftover hippy whimsy ("Let the children boogie" indeed), but it struck a chord regardless, especially after the already weird-looking Bowie appeared on *Top Of The Pops* and draped one arm across his guitarist's shoulders. Glitter's 'Rock And Roll' was a primeval stomp, all heys and yeahs and pounding percussion, an avalanche of sound that could not help but make you smile. Roxy were James Dean in space alien drag. Hawkwind whooshed and bubbled with a riff that tasted like acid felt – and so on and so forth till you reached Mott The Hoople, whose hit was written by David Bowie and the whole thing felt so circular that the future was inevitable. All the young dudes were carrying the news.

But it took Alice Cooper to tell us what that news really was; raven-haired Alice with her stage full of pets and her Barbie doll playthings, an all-American insert into an otherwise Anglo-based battlefield, her mascara so thick that her eyes looked like spiders, her long nose so hooked that pirates grew jealous, and her gender so bent by the weight of her name that it took an extra moment or two for all the pieces to fall into place.

Alice was a band, Alice was a man, and what was the news that she hastened to deliver?

School's Out.

That was what we'd been waiting for; that is what we needed to hear. All those other records were jigsaw pieces. Bowie waving behind-the-bike-shed explorations in our faces while pointing out that the opposite sex was only one of the role models available. Roxy declaring that clothes maketh man, but only if man makes the right noises first. Hawkwind brought the recreational chemicals, Glitter brought the liberation of spirit.

But it was Alice who kicked down the last of the obstacles, who tore down the strictures of establishment structure, who spoke of freedom and showed us how to grasp it. Other acts handed us the best bits of adulthood and told us to make of them what we could. But Alice formed the Department of Youth, and then handed out membership to everyone who wanted it.

What better start could there be to the long summer holiday?

Forty years later, it seems strange to still be harping on about that record, or even that era. Rock has moved on, Alice has moved on. But the challenge that the summer of 1972 set out remains as potent today as it did at the time, and all the more so if you ask yourself this. Has any six-to-eight week span in rock and pop history ever introduced an entire generation to so many bands, beliefs and cultural touchstones that remain, decades later, the iconic idols of so many people?

Not just a favourite band. We're talking something so far beyond mere favouritism that it borders on obsession. David Bowie, Hawkwind, Roxy Music, 10cc, Mott The Hoople – the kids who discovered them the first-hit-around have remained true to them ever since, and have been repaid by careers that are still relevant, if not resonant, today. And then, once again, there is Alice, who isn't only relevant and resonant, he is also still performing at the same peak of perfection that he ever was back then; still staging stunning shows that leave audiences wide-eyed with open-mouthed amazement; and he is still the ultimate childhood sweetheart, the schooldays ghoul-friend that you never forgot. And never really got over.

Oh, and still proclaiming that school is out because… well it is, isn't it? How could it be anything else?

Dave Thompson
Delaware, December 2011

Author's Note

Alice Cooper. Is it a man, is it a band, is it a brand name? Or is it all three? Writing this book, and then editing it afterwards, it became clear that some form of consistency was required. Therefore, the simple name Alice refers to the singer who first led the group that gave him his name, and then went out on a solo career. Alice Cooper, and variations of that (the Coopers, the Cooper band etc) refer, indeed, to the band.

And Vince Furnier is the guy who joins the two together, but whose own life and story only ever play out in the background of the world he co-created for the rest of the world's entertainment. For that reason, this book is not a biography of Vince Furnier. His life events play a role in it, of course; his background, his demons and his fascinations inevitably influence Alice and the Coopers. But Vince Furnier tells that story in his *Alice Cooper, Golf Monster* biography, and he tells it well, because that book was about the life he lived.

Welcome To My Nightmare is concerned with the life that he created.

Chapter One

Starry Starry Night

Walk the streets of suburban Detroit today and it's difficult to believe they ever bred a monster.

No, we should rephrase that. If modern America has any cottage industry at all, it is its penchant for turning out bogeymen, and that is a line of descent that reaches back into colonial times, when the Headless Horseman of Sleepy Hollow haunted the nightmares of the god-fearing Puritans, and the wicked witches of Salem, Massachusetts, danced with the devil and cursed their neighbours' cows.

A line drawn from there bisects some beastly horrors, and American culture has always raced to give them faces. Lizzy Borden with her axe may not have been the country's first serial killer (she was acquitted of the crimes, after all), but the rhyme that danced through the American psyche back when the Fall River slaughter was first uncovered…

Lizzie Borden took an axe
Gave her mother forty whacks
When she saw what she had done
She gave her father forty-one

… is as familiar today as it was back then, and has become the unspoken soundtrack to so many Hollywood blockbusters (not to mention B- and C-movie turkeys) that it's almost miraculous that there aren't Lizzie action figures to line up alongside your Freddies, Jasons and Leatherfaces.

The blaze of great horror movies that dominated the Depression-whipped thirties, those that followed in their footsteps through the Cold War fifties and those that erupted again during Reagan's eighties all bred their own singular terrors with which a nation of parents could either scare their kids to bed at night ("Go to sleep, or Michael Myers will get you"), or else rise up to screen the innocents from. The great comics scare of the mid-fifties, in which an entire industry was savaged by the powers of Right and Decency grew exclusively from the horrific scribblings of the EC Comics house and its manifold contributors, and we see just how far American values had shifted if we compare the fate of the fifties Crypt Keeper, lambasted in government and exiled from print, with that of his nineties equivalent – who was handed his own television series.

So yes, America has always bred bogeymen, but it is only in recent years that they have truly stepped out of fiction and the mass imagination, to literally clear the streets at night, and offer paranoia-struck citizens a reason to stockpile handguns. In the past, America's true bogeymen were cartoon characters and movie stars. Today, they are paedophiles, drug fiends and all-purpose serial killers. And few people scare their kids to sleep with them because they are just too real for comfort.

And too close.

So we walk, again, the streets of suburban Detroit and we realign the thought. It is hard to believe that these quiet streets bred one particular bogeyman, one who stepped out of fiction to become reality, but one who then transformed that reality back into entertainment, to shift in the course of little more than two decades, from Public Enemy Number One, to nothing less than family entertainment, a fun night out for every generation, and a touchstone for everything that is self-perpetuating about America's love of the showman.

In the seventies, Alice Cooper was Lizzie Borden, Freddie Kruger and the Zodiac Killer all bound up into one, with a dash of demonic possession for luck. Today, and for more than 20 years before today, he is PT Barnum, Buffalo Bill, Hefner, Hughes and Howard Johnson's, and Frankenstein. Everyone and everything that has ever asked what does America really want, and been able to answer that question successfully.

America wants spectacle, America wants excitement, America wants pizzazz. But most of all, America wants a bogeyman, and it has always been lucky in that respect. Because one always comes along.

In the mid-fifties, the bogeyman's name was Elvis Presley, and when Alice Cooper was a little boy, seven, eight or nine years old, that's who he wanted to be.

Rock'n'roll was still an infant at the time, even younger than its young admirer, and Elvis was the baddest of the bad boys who were driving polite society into apoplexy. It didn't help that he sang like a black man, at a time when even many American radio stations still exercised a colour ban, but his sound was only a part of the problem.

His hair was greasy, his lip was curled, he looked cruel and insolent before he even opened his mouth. And the way he moved! 'Heartbreak Hotel', Presley's first American hit single, entered the chart just a month or so after Vince's eighth birthday, beaming into a shaken nation's living rooms with the television cameras focused wholly on the singer's upper body to reinforce what the newspapers said about the rest of it; that he gyrated his hips with sexual abandon, and simply watching him move made impressionable young girls soak their seats.

In an age when television and the movies were still tightly controlled by decency laws that were formulated in the thirties, where married sit-com couples slept in separate beds, and even a kiss goodnight could send a teenager down the rocky road to degradation, despair and death by a thousand STDs, Elvis Presley was more than the first rock star. He was the first Shock Rock star as well, a man who mumbled when he should have talked, who sneered when he should have smiled, and who may have loved his momma, but who left a trail of broken hearts regardless.

Would you let your daughter marry the Pelvis?

Alice talks about Elvis in his autobiography, the wryly titled *Alice Cooper Golf Monster*. "I would stand in the mirror and imitate him. The sneer. The swivel hips." Even as a kid, he says, he was "a great mimic".

He probably was. He still is. But it was the mirror, not the mimicry, which he would grow to personify. The mirror that he raised to the world that wound around him, but whose ugliness seemed apparent to Alice alone. He admitted as much, too, when *Life* magazine journalist Albert Goldman confronted him about his stage show that had great swathes of responsible society up in arms, and much of irresponsible society enfolded in his arms.

"People put their own values on what we do, and sometimes those values are warped. They react the way they do because they are insecure.

They consider [what we do] shocking, vulgar... [but] people who are really pure enjoy it. If Edgar Allan Poe were alive today, he'd do the same things as we do."

Goldman agreed. "Confessing fantasies most people'd rather die than reveal, Alice Cooper became the scapegoat for everybody's guilts and repressions. People project on him, revile him, ridicule him. Some would doubtless like to kill him." But Alice simply cackled. "Of course we're in bad taste. There isn't anything in America which isn't in bad taste. That's wonderful, isn't it?"

Not that he necessarily considered himself to be tasteless. Nor even rebelling. As he frequently remarked on other occasions, he simply took his own pop cultural loves... B-movie horror films, spy thrillers and Hollywood, kitsch magazines and *Tales From The Crypt*, all the stuff that enthralled almost every kid growing up in the American Fifties... he took them and he mashed them together with the wave of teen fantasies that succeeded that era, the pop of the British Invasion, the pulp of Roger Corman, the freedoms of psychedelia, and then he kept on mashing. He lived the life of a Marvel Comics superhero for years before he became one, and a horror movie superstar for years before he became one of those, either.

A timeline of Alice Cooper's recent career would bullet point any number of achievements in the nineties and beyond, from writing a theme for *A Nightmare On Elm Street*, to writing a graphic novel with *Sandman's* Neil Gaiman, and onto musing on the possibility for running for elected office in his adopted hometown of Phoenix. And in every single instance, it was simply a matter of reality catching up with the dreams he'd created at some point in the past. Most celebrities live out their careers to the sound of ever-diminishing achievement, the deeper into the future they delve. Alice Cooper never fell into that trap, because he'd already predicted what would happen long before.

Of course he did. How could he not have? He was the bogeyman, after all.

Naturally Alice wasn't Alice when he started; wouldn't, in fact, become Alice until he was staring his twenties full in the face. To the friends and family who watched him grow, he was Vince, Vincent Damon Furnier (pronounced Fern-ee-ay) to be precise, a scrawny child born on Wednesday, February 4, 1948, and named for his Uncle Vince in the first part, and the writer Damon Runyan in the second.

It was not a great news day. The Detroit papers, like those across the rest of the American north-east, were dominated by the bitter weather that had been snarling travel and traffic since Christmas, and showed little sign of letting up. Across the oceans at the tail end of India, Ceylon was finally shrugging off British rule to become the independent nation of Sri Lanka, but that had little resonance in Michigan, and neither did many of the other big stories of the day.

The Supreme Court was preparing to rule on whether or not it was constitutional for religious education to be entered into the school curriculum (it was not), and the Democrat President Truman was fighting the threat of sundry Southern party members to secede and form their own breakaway party. The Soviet Union was rattling its sabres over what it saw as American attempts to divide Europe, militarise Germany and move against the Communist bloc.

But Detroit itself was booming as the city's automotive trade continued celebrating the return of the male workforce from the war, and America in general began to ease back into a peacetime that promised wide open vistas of opportunity and movement, both of them predicated on the motor car. A gallon of gas cost 16 cents, a new car hovered around the $1,200 mark. Wages were rising, inflation was falling. It was a great time to be alive; a great time to be an American.

Not such a great time to be the newborn Vince Furnier, though. In the 1976 autobiography *Me Alice*, he mourned, "I was born... in a hospital they call the 'Butcher's Palace' in Detroit and I was lucky I made it out of there because a lot of people didn't. They didn't do such a bad job on me, except that I was born with eczema, and infantile asthma." The former, he would overcome. The latter would become one of the driving factors in his young life, as his parents sought a climate that would not send their son breathless to the emergency room every time the barometer dropped.

Vince's family were a mixed bunch. On his father's side, the Furnier side, descent was traced back to the Huguenots, the wave of French Reformed Protestants who were persecuted out of their homeland at the end of the 17th century, and whose diaspora took them all across the globe. Some did not stray far; England, Switzerland, the fledgling Dutch Republic and Prussia all welcomed (or otherwise) the Huguenots to their shores. Others found their way to what is now South Africa, but what was then a tangle of fledgling territories still seeking their own identity from a confusion of English and Dutch overlords.

But the hardiest ones moved to North America, to another jumble of colonies that were searching for cohesion, but whose politics (if not their actual policies) already seemed to offer a haven from oppression. Vince's Furniers were among them, and they seem to have made a mark.

A seventh cousin of the Furniers, family tradition insists, was Marie-Joseph Paul Yves Roch Gilbert du Motier, the Marquis de Lafayette, the French-born aristocrat who fought for the republicans against the monarchy during the American Revolution, then effectively switched sides and fought for the monarchy against the republicans during the French uprising. A man of changing political convictions, then, but he was a feather in the genealogical cap that the young Vince never tired of. You could even see the family resemblance, he said, in portraits of the great man, in the sharp, high cheekbones and straggling dark hair that were family traits.

Neither was the Marquis the Furniers' sole claim to familial fame. Even closer in time and bloodline was Thurman Sylvester Furnier, an evangelist who went on to become the President of the Church of Jesus Christ. Thurman was Vince's grandfather.

One of 10 children born to a gardener, John Washington Furnier (1838–1923) and his wife Emma (1846–1910), Grandad Thurman was born in Washington, Pennsylvania, on April 21, 1888, and lived to the ripe old age of 85, long enough to see his grandson become one of the biggest stars of the American stage. As big a star in that field, in fact, as Thurman was in his.

The Church of Jesus Christ is one of the handful of churches that developed out of the Mormon church following the death of its founder, Joseph Smith Jr, at the hands of an Illinois lynch mob in 1844. To the outsider, it differentiated itself from its parent simply by truncating its name (the Mormons are the Church of Jesus Christ of Latter Day Saints). But a deeper divide, of course, separates the two.

The schism was caused by the bitter wrangling over who should succeed the fallen Smith. The Mormons elected Brigham Young, the President of the Church's Quorum of Twelve; the Church of Jesus Christ (whose members are resolutely not Mormon, despite adhering to its holiest tenets) followed Sidney Rigdon, the senior surviving member of the original church's governing First Presidency, and William Bickerton, one of Rigdon's first converts following the break.

It was Bickerton who organised the first branch of the Church of Jesus Christ in 1851, and who then led it to full incorporation in 1865. It was always a small church by many applicable standards; 150 years on, worldwide membership is estimated at a little over 12,000 folowers, with just 3,000 of those living in the United States. There were fewer still when Thurman Furnier was ordained a pastor on January 3, 1915, but his passage up the ranks was swift. In 1916, he became an evangelist, charged with taking the Church's message out of the pulpit and into the countryside, and on October 7, 1917, four months after he joined the United States Army, he was elected an Apostle.

Married now to Vince's grandmother Birdie, Thurman had two children, eight-year-old Lonson and six-year-old Vincent "Jocko" Collier, when he joined the army on June 5, 1917. A third son, Clarence, was born in 1918 and finally the future Alice Cooper's father, Ether "Mickie" Moroni Furnier, arrived on March 26, 1924.

By now, Thurman was working in the automotive industry; Detroit was America's motor city, and Thurman could not escape its grasp. He worked as a payroll clerk at one of the factories, but his religious beliefs were never far from the surface as he continued his rise up the Church hierarchy. Indeed, by the time he reached the pinnacle, when he was elected President on April 11, 1965, he had served in every position in the church.

It flourished, too, beneath his guidance, frequently being described at least as the fastest growing of the various offshoots from the original, and Thurman Furnier's eight-year Presidency played its own part in broadening its reach. How ironic it was, then, that while the old man's grandson remained silent about his own religious upbringing, on the other side of the century-old schism, a singing, dancing, Mormon family called the Osmonds, were proselytizing as furiously as they turned out hit records. For Vince, dinner at his grandparents' house must have been fascinating.

The Furniers were a close family, and when Mickie married a 21-year-old Tennessee girl, Ella Mae McCartt, in 1946, his folks were never far from view. Young Vince grew up listening to Uncle Jocko spinning yarns about the pool hall he'd started up using the winnings from his prizefighting days, and almost all of them turned out to be true. Nobody seems to remember why people started calling him Jocko, but the nickname stuck and if Ether hadn't christened his firstborn Vincent, Jocko himself might have forgotten his real name.

Mickie's oldest brother Lonson, too, had long since surrendered his birth name. He was now Uncle Lefty and he had long since left Detroit for a job at the Jet Propulsion Laboratory in Los Pasadena, home to both America's space program and the early years of its atomic development. But his nephew knew him well enough to remember him as a tuxedo-clad playboy whose California social life at least took him into hanging-out range of actresses Lana Turner and Ava Gardner. For a kid who knew nothing more of the world than he gleaned from the streets of Detroit, and his weekly visit to the Saturday morning movies, Lefty was glamour personified.

Then there were the cousins. Very early on, little Vince realised that the survival of the Furnier family name had been nailed to his shoulders, and his alone. Two years older than he, sister Nickie Ann was the first in what became a veritable sea of femininity, as Ella Mae's side of the family added their own offspring to the pot and left Vince with 13 cousins, "mostly girls". He would fulfil his familial duty, too. Although he would ultimately change his name by deed poll to Alice Cooper, he waited until his career was well established before doing so.

The past half century's worth of redevelopment has rendered Lincoln Street, where Vince grew up, almost unrecognisable. A ragtag of single family homes that stretched out from Turnbull Street, the neighbourhood now lies in the shadow of the monstrous John C Lodge Freeway. But the nearby Wayne University's Wayne State Stadium (now Tom Adams Field), home to the Wayne State Warriors football team, was just a walk away, while the predominantly Polish make-up of the family's neighbours brought an air of central European exotica to the very air he breathed. The older Vince needs only to imagine the scent of pierogi or roulade to be transported back in his mind to Lincoln Street. That and the sound of bat on ball.

If granddad's religion and his uncles' glamour were the high points of Vince's family upbringing, his outdoor life revolved around baseball in general, and the Detroit Tigers in particular.

The Tigers had represented the city since the side's formation in 1901, and their early years remain a legend as they fielded the now almost-mythical Ty Cobb, and ran up three successive American League

Championships between 1907 and 1909. Cobb retired in 1921, but the Tigers remained a powerhouse, taking the World Series Championship in 1935 and again in 1945, and being there-or-thereabouts for much of the time in between.

By the time Vince was born, however, even that most recent triumph was beginning to fade from the memory and, while the side could still produce the goods, and boasted the all-but unstoppable Al Kaline, following the Tigers through the fifties meant being doomed to disappointment year after year after year.

Vince and his father never gave up, though. If they weren't listening to the game on the radio, they were outside emulating (and often surpassing) their heroes, and when the boy grew too old to be content with playing one on one with dad, he gravitated towards the local pick-up team that represented Lincoln Street in a kind of sporting gang war with its neighbours. Away from the Polish enclave of Lincoln Street, Detroit's Irish, blacks and Italians had their own streets, their own teams, and baseball was their chosen battleground. Occasionally blood would be spilled, occasionally tempers would fray. But for the most part, internecine rivalries were taken out on the diamond, and Vince Furnier flourished. Might even, if the breaks had been right, have made baseball some kind of career.

But there was one drawback. His health, and the asthma that kept him balled up in his bedroom, breathless and streaming, almost as often as it allowed him outside to play. His frailties were particularly ruthless in the autumn and winter, and while his school friends were out in the inevitable snow drifts, Vince would be reduced to watching from the window, reeking of Vicks, or squinting over the plastic model aeroplanes and automobiles that he loved to build. And the only cure the doctor could offer, the only thing that might save the kid from a lifetime spent in sniffling suffering, was a change of climate.

Uncle Lefty spoke up immediately. "Come out to Los Angeles and stay with me." The family had already spent a season there when Vince was a toddler, and had seen the difference it made to the boy's health; they had put down brief roots in Phoenix too, and seen the dry desert heat affect an instant improvement. Each time, however, money worries drove them back to Detroit to endure another miserable winter. Never poor, they were never exactly wealthy, either; like so many families, they simply got by on what they had.

But in 1955, Mickie and Ellie Mae pulled Vince and Nickie out of Havenhurst Elementary School, and loaded them into the family's old Ford Fairlane for the 2,300-mile, 36-hour drive to California, an exploratory mission that would ultimately find them moving there for good. And when they got there, an older Alice reflected, he experienced a defining moment. "My first taste of the big time."

Lefty lived in the San Fernando Valley, an address that left little Vince unmoved until they arrived there and, amidst the palm trees, sunshine and greenery that are everyday Los Angeles, he discovered his uncle's swimming pool. He had never seen such a thing before, certainly not planted in the middle of somebody's garden, and there and then he made himself a promise that he still remembers today. One day, he would have his own swimming pool.

The Furniers made three or four trips back and forth between Detroit and Los Angeles, by which time the faithful Ford Fairlane had long since bitten the dust. Now they journeyed in an imported Ford Anglia, a tiny motor far better suited to the slow streets and short rides of its British homeland than to the wide open spaces of America. Cramped in the back, the kids entertained themselves as best they could; in the front, their parents just prayed for the journey to end. The day they made the journey for the final time, to take up permanent residence in the sunshine, everybody breathed a major sigh of relief.

They could not have known that their travels were by no means over.

Mickie, a trained draughtsman and electronic engineer, had already found work alongside brother Lefty at the Jet Propulsion Laboratory; Ellie took a job waitressing at Lawry's restaurant on La Cienega Boulevard, a fascinating slab of modernist architecture designed by Wayne McAllister (the eye, too, behind the first in the Marriott chain of hotels). Nevertheless, money remained tight, and home became a succession of the cheapest rentals they could find that were in striking distance of both work and school. One day Mickie returned home from a business lunch with Lefty and some associates, astonished at a bill that touched $30 – or, two weeks rent for the Furniers.

For Vince, the paucity of spending money was simply one more childhood challenge to be overcome with as much ingenuity as he could muster. Which, considering his tenders years, was considerable. "If I needed a quarter to get something I wanted," he told *Spec* magazine in

September 1974, "I would steal a dollar from my mother's purse, spend the quarter, and put the change in my sister's dresser drawer where my mother was sure to find it. I wasn't so stupid as to spend the whole dollar; I made sure there was money left over so my sister would be incriminated."

In Los Angeles as much as in Detroit, much of his money was spent on going to the movies. The golden age of American cinema was still going strong, still holding its own against the threat of television as the number one destination for families, teens or just kids out on their own, looking for a couple of hours' worth of budget-priced entertainment. It didn't even matter what was showing; at that age, in those days, a movie was a movie, and Vince devoured everything from the Rodgers & Hammerstein style musicals that lit up the screen in vivid Technicolor, through to the low-budget horror flicks that flickered for a week and were then shunted off to obscurity.

He recalled those days for *Famous Monsters* magazine in 1999, how every Saturday one local theatre or another would present a 10a.m.–6p.m. succession of horror movies. Eight hours of thrills for just 30 cents. "We would go to see *It Came From Beneath The Sea* or *It* or *Them!* or *It Came from Outer Space* or something like that, and I used to just look forward to that so much. I always thought of myself as being a pretty average kid, because... [the theatre] was packed with kids my age. It seemed like whenever there was a full day's horror bill, every 'normal' kid in Detroit was there watching them; I wasn't the only one. It was great! Going to the movies was a full day. If you came out and it was still daytime, well – you didn't really go to the movies. Even the local theatre had marble walkways and red columns and these huge Gothic chandeliers – and an usher who would wear one of those little box hats."

He was so fortunate, he realised later in life, to be a kid at a time when some of the greatest horror films of all time were emerging. But he was not afraid to look backwards as well. The theatre would often screen the old RKO and Universal classics from the thirties, and Vince drank them in too, filing every creature and creation away in his imagination, ranking the films by how much he loved them.

Some movies he fell in love with, others scared him half to death and he fell even harder for those. *Dracula's Daughter* was one favourite, but *Creature From The Black Lagoon* was the first one that sent him running out of the theatre in terror, the scene where the creature stumbles upon a hapless camper "and... pretty much takes his face off. I went running out of the theatre." But of course he went running back in again for the next day's performance, so he could find out what happened. Another unforgettable thrill was delivered by John Carradine's *The Unearthly*: "That creeped me out too, where big bald Tor Johnson had no eyeballs..."

But another influence was making itself felt on the family life, one that would impact on the adolescent Vince even harder than horror. Throughout their years in Detroit, the Furniers had regarded granddad Thurman's religious enthusiasms with respect, but distance. They weren't quite agnostic, but ask whether the family was Protestant or Catholic, and the answer would generally be a long silence.

Perhaps it was the physical distance that now lay between father and son; perhaps it was simply the search for something in life to hang onto that might raise them above the scrimp and save of everyday life. But shortly after the family arrived in Los Angeles, both of Vince's parents began attending the nearest branch of the Church of Jesus Christ, embracing the religion with a fervour that saw the entire tenor of their family life change.

Mickie gave up his three packs a day smoking habit, and removed all traces of alcohol from the house. He stopped swearing. The entire family would be in church every Sunday, Wednesday and Friday and, when Saturday rolled around, the youngest Furniers would be in church again, cleaning it for the following day's services.

Like his father before him, Mickie started moving up in the church ranks. He developed an interest in missionary work, out among the Native Americans whose reservations all seemed to have been planted in the most inhospitable corners of the American southwest, and who lived, for the most part, in a state of poverty that would embarrass the Third World. Mickie's mission took him into one of the most notorious reservations of all, across the state line into Arizona, to the San Carlos Indian Reservation, or Hell's Forty Acres as it was more commonly and perhaps accurately known.

Founded in 1871, the San Carlos reservation was home to half a dozen different Apache tribes, two thousand square miles that amounted to the tenth largest reservation in the country. Not all of it was desert; the vast and beautiful Ponderosa Forest is a part of the San Carlos Nation, but of course that brought its own dangers and hardships. There were no gaudy gambling casinos or cut-price smoke shops on the Native American horizon in those days. Families lived so far below the poverty line that an abandoned car was considered a happy home, and as each family inevitably grew, so would the car, extended outward into fresh "rooms" with cardboard, sticks and mud. A good wickiup, as these constructions were called, could withstand most of what nature threw at it, but still the Furniers could scarcely believe their eyes the first time they caught sight of one.

It was certainly a challenge for anybody minded to try and improve the inhabitants' lot in life, but Mickie threw himself into his calling. Less than two years after he uprooted his family for a new life in California, he announced that they were moving again.

They were heading north again, this time to Uniontown, Pennsylvania, close to the headquarters of the Church of Jesus Christ. There, Mickie continued to emulate his father's rise through the Church hierarchy, while furthering his studies at the church. Then, in 1949, the family returned to Arizona for a time, then back out to California, and then to Arizona one final time, just in time for Vince to enter Junior High School.

Except he didn't.

Mickie had landed a job at the Goodyear Aerospace plant in Phoenix, Arizona. He had found them a home in a nearby trailer park, and every weekend, the family would drive out to the reservation to do whatever they could for the people there. It was following one such visit, the July 4th weekend of 1961, that Vince, hitherto healthy as a horse, began violently throwing up.

Early thoughts that he had caught the flu were quickly dispelled; now his parents were asking whether he'd maybe been bitten by any one of the myriad poisonous critters that also called the reservation home. He was always grubbing in the dirt with the kids he met there; he could have been stung or bitten by anything from a scorpion to a black widow spider, to one of the 18 different species of venomous snake that Arizona is host to.

The boy shook his head. Nothing like that. Besides, his illness did not follow the course of such a calamity, and neither was there the telltale mark, somewhere on his body, that would suggest such an attack. What he could produce was copious quantities of a foul-smelling green vomit, and that was when his parents knew it was time to seek medical attention. It no longer even mattered that the ensuing medical bill would probably push them into debt for months to come.

13

Blood tests confirmed what the examining doctor suspected from the moment he clapped eyes on the boy, and no doubt everybody wondered how an 11-year-old boy could have suffered a burst appendix two days earlier and not been totally incapacitated there and then. Somehow, however, it had happened and now Vince's entire body was awash with peritonitis. Every internal organ had been affected, his very blood was thick with poison. When Vince's parents asked for a long-term prognosis, the doctor told them that there probably wasn't one. The boy maybe had a 10 percent chance of survival. If he was lucky.

Rushed into surgery, the doctors extracted four and a half quarts of poison from Vince's system, "enough... to flatten an army", the boy later bragged, but still he wasn't out of the woods. Every day when his parents visited, he seemed thinner than before and by the time his ordeal was over, their six-stone son had lost something like one third of his body weight.

He was physically altered, too. His spine had curved, and when he stood up, the beginnings of a hunchback were plain for all to see. Antibiotics had caused his hair to fall out. He looked as though a good wind would not simply blow him over, it would probably snap him in two. And it would be three months before the hospital would even consider discharging him. But he survived, and his parents' religious faith grew even firmer every time they looked at their own walking miracle, the boy who came back from the brink.

Clearly, they marvelled, God had great plans for their son.

Chapter Two

See My Lonely Life Unfold

In spring 1962, still scarred and scrawny from his hospitalisation, 14-year-old Vince Furnier resumed his school career, enrolling at Squaw Peak Junior High on N 34th Street, Phoenix.

He was still weak. At home, his mother fed him steak and liver to try and build him up, then packed him off to school begging him not to get into a fight. A simple blow to the stomach might just tear him wide open before the doctors had the chance to complete their work; a year on from the initial attack, Vince would return to hospital to be opened up again, this time to remove the scar tissue. The resultant scars reminded him of a shark bite he had seen in a magazine some place, so that's what he told people it was, a souvenir from his days spent surfing in Los Angeles.

He was not a shy kid. So many years spent moving house, and the incessant social life that revolved around his church activities ensured that it was easy for Vince to make friends, while eyes and ears that always aimed to stay one step ahead of the crowd saw him readily build a reputation as the class clown. But he could bend himself to study, too; he excelled at art and English, and the teachers seemed to enjoy him.

"I was a good student, and I did well at school," Alice wrote in *Spec* magazine. "I went out of my way to be charming and funny in the classroom. Not wise-guy funny, but nice funny. And I was known as a great diplomat. I could talk my way out of any fight, and I could talk my way out of just about any situation that came up."

He was also a peacemaker, defusing difficult situations in class with a well-timed joke or humorous remark, a gift that certainly placed him in the teachers' good graces – to the point where his extra-curricular entertainment value was often enough to win him a higher grade than his actual class work merited. "Maybe I was lucky, but I enjoyed school. I'm naturally competitive and I like performing, and I always found a way to work those qualities into my everyday routine."

Where Vince did differ from his school friends was in his social life, and the fact that he didn't really have one. His illness played a part in that, of course, but so did his family life. "Being the son of a minister, my whole social life was based around the church and the people who were connected with it. On Wednesdays, Fridays and Sundays there were church-related events, and that was my entire social life for years and years."

He didn't even care much about girls, even as he watched his friends begin to take their first hesitant steps towards the opposite sex. He was far more interested in building his model airplanes and watching the Little League baseball side.

He had moved on to High School by now, enrolling at Camelback High for a couple of weeks before transferring to the newly opened Cortez High, home to the state High School baseball champions. Of course Vince applied for a trial, and although it was no surprise to discover there was no place for him on the team, he later admitted to being crushed by disappointment.

His sporting ambitions would soon find a fresh outlet, however, and this time it was one at which he would excel.

High School brought out another natural ability, this time for drawing and painting, a talent that quickly allowed him to cross the unspoken barrier that traditionally exists between first-year freshmen and their elders. Now he was hanging with an art class sophomore, Dennis Dunaway, collaborating on visions that they had just discovered to be mutual. One summer break, he and Dunaway were hired to paint a mural. Hired, for money. "Now we both considered ourselves working artists," Vince reflected.

Vince and Dunaway were inseparable. Salvador Dali was a mutual hero, and so was James Bond, still a storybook character in those last years before his adventures hit the big screen. On television, the pair gravitated to the same kind of fare that obsessed them at the movies.

It was the heyday of John Zacherley's Shock Theater, a long running movie slot whose eponymous host appeared clad in an omnipresent undertaker's cloak. His wife, known only as My Dear, and his lab assistant Gasport, would be on camera too, stooging Zacherley through his introduction to that week's classic horror film, or even joined him in interrupting the movie, cutting away during random scenes to depict the trio in some unearthly situation. Vince and Dennis never missed an episode.

They were fans, too, of Freddy the Ghoul, broadcasting his own brand of horror-themed slapstick on local Phoenix TV every Saturday afternoon, and aloud, both boys would wonder precisely what qualifications you required to land a job like that. Imagine being paid to host old horror movies on television. "Even today," Vince continued in that *Famous Monsters* interview, "that would be a pretty cool job."

For now, it was enough to transfer his interpretations of his favourite horror moments into his school work. He got into the Dadaist and Cubist schools of art, he devoured comic books and he studied surrealism, then combined them all into his work. Sometimes, his art teacher would recoil at the sheer macabre nature of the boy's work, but there was never any questioning his technique or vision, and Vince's ideas began fermenting further. He would become an artist, not in any one field but across many, taking the myriad themes that his fascinations planted in his mind, and making his living from re-creating them in whatever medium that was to hand. Dunaway was alongside him every step of the journey.

Like Vince, Dennis Dunaway was a relative newcomer to Phoenix, Arizona. He was born on March 15, 1946, in Cottage Grove, Oregon, back then a tiny farming community to the south of Eugene. He was the eldest of four children, a clean cut kid – "classically coiffed", he called himself – but he was already something of a hero at Cortez High. The year before Vince arrived, Dunaway was a member of the High School's legendary "Undefeated" cross country team, and clocking his new friend's tall, thin frame, he and another runner, John Speer, moved quickly to recruit Vince to the same outfit. With coach Emmet Smith sharing their enthusiasm, Vince was in. As an artist and a sportsman, the missionary's son was slowly carving out his niche in the world of High School.

Vince still speaks proudly of his accomplishments as a long distance runner. One of the first freshmen ever to make Cortez's varsity cross-country team, he became a Letterman in September 1962; that is, one of the select band of proven athletic stars who earned the right to wear a sweater with the school's initial painstakingly hand sewn onto it by a proud parent. Even better, by his senior year, he was sporting no fewer than four stripes on his sweater, and that "meant a lot. The toughest senior guys in school usually had only two stripes, because they generally only lettered in sports during their last two years."

Vince was ultimately destined to take the school's 24-mile marathon record, adding to the accomplishment not only by achieving it in 105 degree heat, but also by being the only runner to complete the race. But home again, he was in the bathroom when the exertion, in the form of heatstroke, finally hit him. He collapsed to the floor, and though he was out cold for just moments, he awoke to find blood everywhere and his nose broken enough that its distinctive hook was now even more pronounced. It was the crowning glory to his athletic career, but it was also very much its last hurrah, too. Another fascination had made its way down the turnpike as Vince, Dunaway and Speer moved through High School, one that would turn the three boys' heads more thoroughly than any of their other interests.

Pop music had been a sickly beast for the last few years. Back in 1955, 1956, when Vince was mimicking Elvis in the mirror, rock'n'roll had seemed destined to rule the world forever. But it was a false dawn. Death (Buddy Holly, Eddie Cochran), imprisonment (Chuck Berry), shame (Jerry Lee Lewis), alcohol (Gene Vincent), religion (Little Richard) and the draft (Elvis himself) had seen to that.

Nothing had come along to replace them, either, and the kids had no alternative but to return to the healthy, traditional values of the years before the revolution; values that the music industry determined should be epitomised by songs about High School, about being true to your school and obeying your teachers, and – of course – falling in love with the girl or boy of your dreams whom you might kiss goodnight but go no further. And so was birthed a succession of spot-free adolescents with neat hair and sunny smiles whose (almost inevitable) lack of singing ability was either ignored or else totally buried beneath layers of candy-sweet backing vocals and string sections.

It was portrayed as Pop Music, but more than that, it was portrayed as a way of life. And the market was milked for all it was worth. In 1959 Tommy Facienda (a former member of Gene Vincent's Blue Caps) not only recorded a song called, quite simply, 'High School USA', he then rerecorded it 30 times. 'High School USA (Boston)', 'High School USA (Buffalo)', 'High School USA (Chicago)'... on and on around the country, devoting a version to almost every major city in the land. Almost. Phoenix didn't make the list, and maybe that dented the record's local sales a little. But no matter.

Every place there was a High School, the high school hits blared out across campus and any kid who turned up their nose at the noise, and thought leathers and grease were still the way to be dressed, well they were the bad boys and they always came to a sticky ending. The Shangri-Las' 'Leader Of The Pack', which smeared its eponymous anti-hero across the tarmac, tells that story.

At Cortez, Vince, Dunaway, Speer and a few more of their friends were paramount among the naysayers who threw their hands up in horror every time another fresh-faced imbecile started squawking on the radio, although they never really embraced the bad boy end of things either. Instead, their listening tastes moved towards the melodramatic end of the spectrum, the foreboding twang of Duane Eddy and 'Peter Gunn', the honk of Johnny & the Hurricanes, the moods of Henry Mancini, music that had little to do with the keening of the High School pack, but which whacked you over the head with something else, with a sense of adventure, of excitement, of drama.

Occasionally something would fall out of the hit parade and capture their imagination. Vince was a big fan of Dion & the Belmonts, the hottest vocal group of the dying doo-wop era, and a fan too of the Four Seasons, whose syncopated harmonies and ethereal falsettos took the Belmonts' sound to fresh epic lengths. He loved the sonic barricades that hemmed in each and every Phil Spector production, and every time he heard a Beach Boys record it took him back to Los Angeles and the life he could have lived had the family only stayed there.

A chart-topper for the Beach Boys in summer 1964, 'I Get Around' still transports him back there. "When I was a kid, that was the ultimate dream," Vince told *Metal Hammer* in 1994. "To have your own car, have your friends and just cruise the streets. There are certain songs that still stand up after all these years. You hear them on the radio and you just turn it up, really crank it. What I judge a song on is that if I get in the car and hear it on the radio, I turn it up. 'I Get Around' is one like that."

But that was all pop was for the early sixties, a succession of records, as opposed to artists, that made you want to run out and spend money. And then the Beatles arrived and everything changed, not just for Vince and the circle of his friends who fell so hard for the Fab Four moptops, but for American music in general. Suddenly pop was exciting again, and when the Beatles were followed by the Stones and the Kinks, Gerry & the Pacemakers and Freddie & the Dreamers, wave upon wave of British Invaders, all with their own take on a solid beat and a rhythmic heart, the winsome whining that preceded them wasn't simply pushed out of sight. It was trampled underfoot. Not for the last time in Vince Furnier's universe, school was out.

The Beatles crept into every facet of Vince's life. Training on the running track, he, Dunaway and John Speer would adapt the lyrics to their favourite Lennon-McCartney songs for the job at hand, and sing their hearts out as they ran around the track: "We beat you, yeah, yeah, yeah," or "Last night I ran three laps for my coach". They bought the records and clipped the pictures out of magazines. They lived for the group's US TV appearances and dreamed that they would come play in Phoenix... they never did, not in 1964, nor 1965, nor even on their final tour in 1966. But that did not lessen their local popularity, not with Arizona in general or the Cortez campus in particular.

Which was when Dennis Dunaway had an idea. The Annual Lettermen's Club Variety Show and Talent Contest was on the horizon, and Vince had already been given the task of recruiting the evening's entertainment. It wasn't going very well, either. As he put it in *Me Alice*, "Nobody had any talent. Nobody even deluded themselves." Vince had put up signs all over the school and, so far, just one budding talent had stepped forward, a would-be conjuror. Finally, "I called a meeting in the locker room before a track meet one day and asked for suggestions."

The first few weren't too helpful, things like dressing Dunaway in drag and having him sing 'I Enjoy Being A Girl', and then tumbling downhill from there. But then Dunaway himself spoke up, asking, "Why don't we all do it?" and the thought bubble just expanded from there. The first Beatles merchandise was already hitting the streets, Beatle wigs and Beatle guitars. What if the three of them… well four, actually; they had to find a fourth… donned a Beatles wig apiece? Their black track outfits could double for Beatles suits, topped off by the jackets that Vince was sure he could convince his mom to run up. They would carve guitars out of wood or cardboard, hire a couple of girls to set up a convincing barrage of screaming hysteria, and then lip-synch their way through their very own Beatles concert.

It was a brilliant idea, and it quickly became even better. Another of Vince's extramural activities found him working on the High School newspaper, the *Cortez Tip Sheet*, a four-page tabloid that kept the kids informed of what was going on around the campus. Vince's main concern was an op-ed column called "Get Out Of My Hair", based around the notoriety that developed not only from having cultivated the longest hair in the High School, but also from being on course for eight separate suspensions for his pains.

He wrote beneath the magnificent pseudonym of Muscles McNasal, but the best thing about the job was that it brought him into contact with kids who might otherwise never have crossed paths with a field and track Letterman. Kids like Glen Buxton, a hard smoking, heavy fighting, two fingers up to authority boy who spent more time with his guitar than he did with his schoolbooks, and who didn't care who noticed. One day Vince asked him why he was working on the *Tip Sheet*. "Because it's a great way to meet girls," the bespectacled, blond Buxton grinned, brandishing the camera that came with the post of staff photographer.

Glen Buxton was born on November 10, 1947, in Akron, Ohio. The second of three children, he was also a born troublemaker or, as he impishly put it, "a bit of a rebel. James Dean was the man, I was still a kid when he died [in an auto wreck in September 1955] but I discovered him a few years later and that was it, man."

First his hair took on the distinctive wave that Dean had thrust into a shocked society's face. He started smoking, and admiring fast cars. He chased girls and when the rest of his friends started worshipping rock'n'roll, he went one step further and positively deified it. He was 11 when he got his first guitar, a birthday gift that was contingent on him taking formal lessons, but of course they were simply a means to an end. He later laughed, "I never really got to grips with the stuff my teacher wanted me to learn, but I could play a really mean 'Johnny B Goode'."

The Buxton family arrived in Phoenix in early 1961, after father Tom was handed a transfer from his job at Goodyear Aerospace's Akron plant. Two years later, Glen entered Cortez High, a bad boy looking to be even badder "I met this guy named John Tatum, and we had a surf band together, then I met Vince on the paper and we started hanging, he brought in Dennis, and that was when we did the Beatles thing."

It was Buxton who suggested that, rather than mime their performance, they should actually try and play it. He and John Tatum could and would provide the melodic bedrock; their own band had already eased a few Beatles songs into their repertoire, and so long as nobody tried anything fancy, all the bass and drums needed to do was keep time behind the vocals. Vince had already declared himself the band's lead vocalist, so Buxton looked at Dunaway and another friend, Phil Wheeler. "Any questions?"

None. Wheeler was installed on drums; Dunaway took the bass. "Glen went with me to Montgomery Ward [department store] and we picked out this bass that was called an Airline bass," Dunaway told *Ink* in 2004. "I'd go over to Glen's house and we'd pick out the notes of our favourite songs."

They sought a name and someone came up with Joe Banana & the Bunch. It made them laugh, but they dropped it when they realised that only the accompanying motto, "music with a-peal", actually appealed to them. Besides, if they were aping the Beatles, they needed to be insects. They settled on the Earwigs, "after those little bugs that crawl into your ear", Vince reflected. "A type of water scorpion that smell bad when you step on them and they can crawl through your ear and infect your brain."

It was an apt description. Even with the best will in the world, nobody in the Earwigs could imagine that what they had in store for their audience would be much less of an irritant than that. Resplendent in the tracksuits and the synthetic Dynel wigs that proved easier and cheaper to obtain than the Beatles ones, they took the cafeteria stage and, having abandoned the idea of actually playing their instruments at the last minute, they waited while a friend cued up the record player.

They played three songs, then bowed out to the tumult of screams set up by the three girls they'd hired for the occasion. "Earwigs! Earwigs!" the trio howled, and the players left the stage convinced that any kind of cool standing they had ever had at Cortez was now dead and buried. "That," Buxton shuddered, "was the most humiliating experience of my life."

So it was one hell of a shock to the system when the big night dawned and, appearing 12th on a bill of 13 acts, the Earwigs found themselves finishing second in the competition. The following week, when the *Tip Sheet* was published, two of its very own staff members, Vince Furnier and Glen Buxton, were front page news.

Maybe it was the fact that they'd been so bad that they were good. Maybe it was because nobody could believe anyone would have had the nerve to put on a show like that. There were any number of reasons, and theories, for the success of the show. But the players didn't care. Everyone was talking about them, everyone was patting them on the back. For the moment at least, they were stars, and they loved every ounce of the attention. "People complimented me the next day for having the guts to do it," Vince recalled in *Me Alice*, "and girls started talking to me who never before would have anything to do with the skinny guy with the big nose from the track team. It stimulated my entertaining chemicals like never before. I got hooked on the limelight."

Phil Wheeler stepped back. It had been fun but he wanted nothing more to do with the Earwigs. For his erstwhile bandmates, however, that first taste of stardom was all it took. Recruiting their track buddy John Speer to the cause, the Earwigs were soon established as regular visitors to Buxton's home, rehearsing in the family garage. That, the guitarist's parents later recalled, was when "we realised it was getting serious".

The Buxtons were certainly accommodating. "We never objected to Glen bringing his friends home," Glen's parents told writer Patrick Brzezinski. "They were always welcome in our home. We were always interested in whatever he was doing." They even tolerated the noise, at least so long as it didn't disturb the neighbours, and the band was under strict instructions to wrap things up by nine each night. Jerry Buxton, Glen's mother, recalled, "It would start out fine but get louder as the practice went on. Sitting in the house, you could tell when the sound increased as the walls would start vibrating. It kept us running out, saying the same thing, 'Turn it down!'"

Rehearsals were· slow, as Dunaway and Speer learned to pick their way across their chosen instruments, while Vince continued working at moulding his voice into shape. But it was a sign of just how quickly the band were able to put their name about that, in October 1964, less than a month after the Letterman party, the *Tip Sheet* dispatched student Nancy Prince to interview the band.

"Speer and Vince and I were all on the track team last year," Dunaway explained, "and we used to make up words to Beatle songs to keep us in rhythm when we were running around the track. One day I stopped and said, 'Hey guys, let's get together and start a new singing group.' We saw Glen and Tatum playing guitars and asked them if they'd like to join."

A manager was procured, he continued, after they saw "this guy riding down the street on a bicycle one day so we yelled at him and asked him if he'd like to be our manager". Within 24 hours, Nick Sataslow "had a bunch of jobs lined up for us".

Entreating Vince's mother, clutching rough designs for their proposed stage wear, the Earwigs were soon resplendent in vivid yellow jackets worn over black turtleneck sweaters. Musically, too, they were marching forward. Despite the Earwigs' Beatlemaniac origins, the newly emergent Rolling Stones were the rock upon which the band was now being built, with Vince adding harmonica to his vocal duties in order to more accurately emulate Mick Jagger. Soon, the members were scouring the local record stores and radio airwaves in search of further catalogues to plunder. They were even beginning to write their own material, self-confessedly derivative, but that never erased the thrill of being able to announce "this is one of our own songs" from the stage.

"When we first started, we did nothing but the Rolling Stones, the Yardbirds, the Who and all the English rock bands that were an alternative to the Beatles," Vince told *Hypno* in 1996. "We wouldn't even do their hits, we'd do their obscure stuff."

He dismissed the other musical heroes of the day. The first time he heard Bob Dylan, for example, he simply laughed. He thought the nasal ragamuffin was a comedian and could not comprehend why so many people took him seriously. He told *Penthouse*, "He was singing about dogs falling off a cliff and things like that... I thought it was the silliest thing I'd ever heard in my life."

The band's musical brew was not, all concerned have admitted, always the most appetising, even after they started gigging out and about. The musicians were learning on the job, often stopping songs that were already in motion so someone or other could try again at a tricky riff or fill. In any other, larger, city, the Earwigs would probably have been squashed on sight. But they were not in a larger city. They were in Phoenix, a city where local live rock'n'roll was at a premium, even at a grassroots level.

The band played its first live show, booked for a sweet 16 party being thrown by a girl at school. According to Vince, they were the only guests who showed up. But slowly, things began to come together. They made themselves available for every school dance they could find, whether they attended the school or not; and at Cortez, they found work by arranging shows themselves.

The same month that the *Tip Sheet* article appeared, the Earwigs could generally be heard most lunch times and, when the end of the month brought the school's Pit & The Pendulum Halloween ball, the Earwigs were the house band, and they proceeded to bring the house down. They built a guillotine on stage and, while it was never intended to be anything more than a prop, the gasp of shock that arose from the audience as the band appeared around it was a memory they would one day return to.

They landed a residency at the Pizza Pub (without the guillotine), where they were paid with all the pizza they could eat, and that brought bookings at similar venues, ensuring that the Earwigs remained well fed if not well paid.

Parking lots were another favourite haunt. Another local band, the XLs, were in much the same place as the Earwigs (they too began life as a Beatles cover act), and so the two would stage Battle of the Bands competitions at the Christown Mall parking lot, with the afternoon's honours going to whichever group played the loudest. A decade later, several members of the XLs, including frontman Bill Spooner, would be touring the world as the Tubes.

Yet it wasn't all plain sailing. Local licensing laws meant that the bars were generally out of the band's reach and, even when they could get a booking, it would be without their frontman. Vince's dad was, considering his religious beliefs, surprisingly tolerant about his young son's musical activities, and even encouraged them to an extent. But there was one rule that could never be violated. Vince was not permitted to perform in any venue that served alcohol, and with his romantic life still bound up in parental strictures, his bandmates soon learned to amuse themselves by regaling their frontman with tales of their own booze-fuelled nights of sexual abandon. "Actually we were as sexless and sober as he was," Buxton later laughed. "But it was still really funny."

Clubs that catered to a teenage audience were springing up, though, as well as other venues where alcohol was not on the menu. And of all the local venues, the one that the Earwigs, like every other band in town, were most desperate to get a foothold in was the VIP Lounge (later the VIP Club).

The VIP was the brainchild of Jack Curtis, a promoter and booker who had been working on the local teen scene since the dawn of the decade, when the one-time entertainment columnist for *The Arizona Republic* newspaper opened Stage 7 at the back of the Phoenix Junior Chamber of Commerce building on N 7th Street in February 1961.

Initially he concentrated on local talent. The opening night was headlined by Ritchie Hart and the Heartbeats, a group whose name was redolent of the music in vogue at that time. Slowly, however, he began reaching out to more renowned, national, talent. B Bumble & the Stingers, the instrumental band best remembered for the novelty classical mutilation 'Nut Rocker', were the first "hit" band to play for Curtis; Jan & Dean and the Righteous Brothers, the Coasters, Bobby Vee and Del Shannon followed, while Curtis also branched out and began presenting shows at the larger State Fairgrounds.

Further Curtis clubs followed as the VIP Lounge was joined by a second venue, the Beau Brummel, and Dale Pitney, whose band the Motion was one of Phoenix's biggest attractions, still speaks admiringly of Curtis. "Jack was a true friend of Phoenix teens. He put together clubs for young people to go on weekends where they could hang out with kids their own age and listen to Phoenix bands play their versions of the latest hits. A lot of bands got their start at clubs such as the VIP. As Motion, we had the best times of our lives until life caught up with us.... college, marriage, kids and mortgages which replaced the fun of the sixties."

Nobody remembers how long it took for the Earwigs to even be allowed to audition for Curtis, and when they did finally get to tread his stage, their initial response was that they had failed dismally. Days, even weeks, passed, and they heard nothing from him. Then one evening, John Tatum was at the VIP on his own, watching another band entirely, when Curtis caught his eye – and demanded to know why the Earwigs had not been back in touch with him. He wanted to run them through a second audition, just to iron out a few things he thought they could improve on.

And so long as that went OK, he already had a date pencilled in for them to play.

In fact Curtis had just one reservation about the band. He hated their name. And so, it transpired, did the band members. They, too, had long got over the jokey soubriquet they had coined the previous year. No longer were they the Beatles tribute act that formed as a joke for a letterman party. Now they were the Spiders. And they looked like they were from Venus – or so the excitable K-LIF DJ hired to promote an upcoming Tucson show insisted later in the year.

"This Saturday night from eight until midnight and of course the admission is only one dollar… that's one buck for the swingest show and dance in Tucson, the Tribesmen and the sensational Spiders from Venus!"

The Spiders from Venus name would rarely, if ever, be invoked again, and it certainly does not appear on any extant posters or press coverage the band received. But six years later, English singer David Bowie would quite coincidentally christen his group the Spiders From Mars and, way out in some parallel universe where the Phoenix rockers never changed their name, the stage was set for a truly interstellar battle of the glam rock bands.

Chapter Three

Fresh Out Of Phoenix

Jack Curtis became the band's de facto manager. Learning that they had no transport, he bought John Tatum a car, a 1956 Chevy, and reminded the band they now had no excuses for being late to an engagement. Discovering that Buxton and Tatum both played through the same tiny amplifier, he shelled out for a second one. And, once he saw how quickly the group's performances were taking off, he began impressing upon them the importance of image; of giving audiences something to remember them by. Music, he impressed upon the musicians, was only half the battle. Kids could dance to music all night long and never even glance up at whoever was playing it. Give them something to look at as well, though, and they were yours for keeps.

The Spiders did not have the local stage to themselves, even after Curtis set about building them a stage of their own, a Spiders-only dais at the opposite end of the club to where bands usually performed, then decorated it with a vast spider's web. The Young Men, the Next of Kin, P-Nut Butter, the Red & White Blues Band, the Precious Few, the Motion and many more vied with the Spiders for local fame, but Vince and his cohorts always seemed to remain one step ahead.

They were, after all, a distinctive sight. Aware that their enthusiasm for playing still occasionally outstripped their abilities, they threw themselves into Tatum's visual stimuli. They started interspersing the music with madcap comedy routines borrowed (and then adapted) from television's then-popular Smothers Brothers. Long before anybody conceived of anything so fancy as a light show, the club's doorman-cum-snackstand manager Bob LaFollette was turning a hand-cranked strobe light while they played. And any money the band members earned was ploughed back into clothes; not costumes, because that idea had yet to strike, but still they cut a distinctive shape. Their sonics were pulled along in the outfits' wake.

Vince later told the UK magazine *Sounds*, "We weren't interested that much in the Beatles, but we were more interested in Jeff Beck's guitar sound like on 'Happenings Ten Years Time Ago', or the Pretty Things doing 'I'm A Roadrunner', all those early, really rotten, raunchy things. The early Kinks when they sounded like they were gonna break your eardrums."

'Lil' Red Rooster', with Buxton breaking out a mean slide guitar; a pounding 'Dirty Water'; a hypnotic 'Mona'; a blistered 'In The Midnight Hour'; blues-busting takes on 'I'm A Man' and 'Smokestack Lightning'; that was the fare with which the Spiders courted the hearts of Phoenix youth.

They worked up a solid slab of Rolling Stones covers that ranged from the sublime ('19th Nervous Breakdown') to the ridiculous (a hesitantly sung, but contrarily beautifully played 'As Tears Go By') and on to the comparatively obscure. 'Down The Road Apiece', 'Oh Baby, We Got A Good Thing Going' and a Mach 10 'Surprise Surprise' were all in their repertoire, and hissy tape recordings of the band's rehearsals, and a couple of fragmentary live tapes from 1965-1966 testify to their ambition.

In 2011, 45 years after those recordings were made, Vince laughed, "I'm [still] afraid to listen to the rehearsal tapes from high school," but he need not have been so nervous. By the standards and expectations of the day, the Spiders were a damned good garage band.

Vince's voice is pitched as close to the nasal whine of John Lennon as it can get and, while the sound of the band is more clatter than clarity, the random guitar lines that chime through their own 'Public Enemy #1' can be readily allied with any of the myriad basement recordings that the CD age has exhumed from the British end of the beat boom.

They powered through Chuck Berry with slathering élan, and if Vince could never emulate the bathos that Eric Burdon brought to the Animals' 'I'm Crying', he compensated with a gutsy growl that offered an animalistic counterpoint to the band's distinctive backing vocals. 'Baby You Know' offers another chance for Buxton to pull out his best Brian Jones-style solo, and a seething garage-choked take on 'Talk Talk' (a song that Vince would return to in a later lifetime) rocks with a sinister effect that points the band's sound straight towards the twisted Californiana of their future.

It was this solid grip on the Invasion that raised the Spiders above their peers, as Vince explained to writer Michael Delaney in 1971. "There were all these surf groups trying to break into long-haired Beatle music. It was so bad. The Byrds were the first to do anything that was original and then nobody knew which lead to follow. We used to do all kinds of obscure British stuff. Things like the Yardbirds and Moody Blues, the weirdest material that was coming over from Europe. It was an experiment in terror, I guess. There were all these groups trying to sound mystical and portentous and failing with each attempt. They tried to ape the Byrds and nobody can do that. We were ugly and couldn't get across with Byrds music... the band was excruciating."

By summer 1965, the highlights of the Spiders' repertoire were a pounding rendition of 'Why Don't You Love Me', by the minor league Merseybeat band the Blackwells, and a song they picked up from the latest Rolling Stones LP, a Bo Diddley-stylised version of Marvin Gaye's 'Hitch Hike'. It was this pair that Jack Curtis seized on that September, when he took the Spiders into Audio Recorders, a recording studio further down 7th Street, to cut what would become their first single.

It would be released on Phoenix's own Mascot label, a regional powerhouse that had been around since 1961. P-Nut Butter ('What Am I Doing Here With You'), Frank Fafara ('Only In My Dreams' and 'Golden One'), Roosevelt Nettles ('Mathilda' and 'Got You On My Mind') and Jim Boyd ('Don't Ask For More') had all scored regional hits for Mascot, rising up the K-RUX and K-RIZ radio charts, and 'Why Don't You Love Me' would deservedly soon join them, a solid reproduction of the "classic" British Invasion sound with Alice's harp and mannered "yeah"s dancing around an archetypal guitar solo, and a solid grasp on the song's ultra-contagious hookline.

In the wider scheme of things, the Spiders' version of the song was no more successful than the Blackwells', but it was hot in Phoenix, and when you flipped the 45, 'Hitch Hike' rode a neat (if brief) call and response vocal and a lead voice that might be an octave higher than anything Vince would later lay down, but was distinctive regardless. Vince was washing the car in the family driveway the first time he heard himself on the radio. "I couldn't believe it was me. It was... like meeting a twin."

The record's success inevitably raised the band's profile higher than it had ever been before. But it had more personal connotations for Vince. He was now involved with the High School sweetheart whom he still considers "my first real girlfriend". Debby Hickey lived in the same housing project as the Furniers, Country Gables, and the two belonged to the same swimming pool association. In fact that's where they met, dripping poolside one afternoon, and they wound up dating for three years. There was just one cloud on their horizon, Debby's mother. Vince told *Spec*, "[She] hated me because my hair was too long, [and] just kept making it more and more difficult for Debby and me to see each other. What a miserable woman. She just hated my hair."

Vince's response was to warn her that one day, he would be famous; one day, his band would be stars, and that she'd better be nice to him or else Debbie would lose out on it all. And he was convinced that the local radio fame of 'Why Don't You Love Me' bore him out. How he looked forward to rubbing the ghastly Mrs Hickey's face into his success; and how bruised was his ego when the woman simply brushed the hit aside as a meaningless irrelevance and carried on as before. "She couldn't care less. All she could see was my hair."

Away from the Hickey household, the Spiders continued their ascent. Jack Curtis' contacts landed them a spot on local television's *The Wallace And Ladmo Show*, an often lunatic variety show fronted by Bill Thompson (Wallace), Ladimir Kwiatkowski (Ladmo) and Pat McMahon. Broadcast by the independent KPHO-TV Channel 5 in Phoenix, the team spoofed the news, played skits and sketches, aired cartoons and generally created television mayhem in such fine style that the show remained on the air until as late as 1989.

The show's own musical troupe, led by another graduate of Jack Curtis' stable, singer Mike Condello, specialised in spoofs of the week's biggest hits and bands, and even spun off a selection of records of their own, including the spot-on Beatles parodies *Blubber Soul* and Commodore Condello's Salt River Navy Band. But more traditional musical talent, too, was welcomed and so were the Spiders. Their television debut accordingly arrived in early 1966.

Another, more unconventional, airing for the band arrived in the form of a few weeks spent performing in legitimate theatre, as New York actor and comedian Jan Murray brought the stage show *Bye Bye Birdie* to the Celebrity Theater. The Spiders played the Birdies, the backing band for singer Conrad Birdie (Murray), and the play's run gave them an early taste for just how demanding, and also how satisfying, it could be to cross dirty ass rock'n'roll with the disciplines of a fully choreographed stage performance. It was all a long way from Broadway, and further still from the deliciously lush movie musicals that Vince had grown up loving and learning every word to. But in the back of his mind, and his bandmates' too, a tiny seed was beginning to germinate, the desire not simply to play a gig, but to put on a show. A show with a story, a show with a plot. A show with a beginning, a middle and an end.

Their ambitions lay quiescent for the time being. Back at the VIP Club, a list of the bands for whom the Spiders found themselves opening is essentially a who's-who of the American tour circuit of 1965-1966. Them, the Lovin' Spoonful, the Animals and Peter & Gordon were just some of the names that passed through Phoenix, and most of them played either the VIP Club or, if a band was too big for that venue, the Arizona Veterans Memorial Coliseum, and the Spiders would open for them there. Indeed, the Spiders were the first rock'n'roll band to play that venue after it was opened up to that genre, opening for the Byrds in November 1965.

Perhaps the most memorable show the Spiders ever played, however, came the following September 4, when the Yardbirds passed through town. That was the night that the Spiders contributed their own piece of legend to the Yardbirds story.

For the Yardbirds themselves, their latest American tour was a chaotic venture, scarred by guitarist Jeff Beck's growing dissatisfaction with the life of a pop star, cancelled shows, and unimagined delays. But the headliners never forgot the night in Arizona where the opening act was a local band whose entire repertoire comprised Yardbirds songs.

Vince explains, "We were the house band, and we were opening for the Yardbirds. Now, when we opened for anybody else, we would do all our Yardbirds songs, so we went out there and suddenly we realised that 80 percent of our set was Yardbirds songs, and they were the headliners that night. I talked to Jeff Beck once, and he said 'I absolutely remember that, I remember this little group of kids doing our songs and we thought you did pretty good. You did a pretty good version.'

"Of course then they got up on stage and they were the Yardbirds and they destroyed us."

Beck's bandmates Chris Dreja and Jim McCarty, too, recalled the night. Vince continues, "I was interviewing Chris and Jim for my radio show and I was telling them about the time we opened for them while we were in High School and they said, 'Yeah, and you guys did all of our songs before we did, then we got up and blew you off stage.' I said, 'Yeah, you destroyed us,' but they said, 'But you did really good cover versions'."

Amid so much triumph, there was one cloud on the horizon. While the bulk of the Spiders were thrilled to be sharing a bill with the Yardbirds, and relished every opportunity to sit at the feet of the next beat-booming R&B band, Tatum's eyes were opened widest by the Byrds and the Hollies, groups whose use of and love for harmonies opened up vast new musical vistas in his mind, vistas that he knew the Spiders would never entertain. He was also aware that one of his own friends, the XLs' Bill Spooner, had a band that fit his musical ideal to the letter. The day in spring 1966 that Spooner mentioned he needed to add a new vocalist to the group's front line was the day that Tatum quit the Spiders.

It was not a move he reflects upon with any fondness. Three months later, the group broke up, but it was too late to return to the Spiders. They had long since replaced him with guitarist Michael Bruce, the sole applicant to the ad they had pasted up on a music store noticeboard.

Arizona through and through, Michael Bruce was born on November 21, 1948. Like Vince he was still attending High School, across town at North High, but he and the Spiders had crossed paths several times as they turned out in sundry Battle of the Band competitions, and invariably came up against either the Trolls (aka the Duels) or the Wildflowers, the bands that Bruce had led since he first seized control of his guitar.

The Spiders fascinated him, he admitted. They reminded him, he often said, of the gang members in *West Side Story*, the epitome of street fighting cool. But Bruce fascinated them in return. A Wildflowers single, 'On A Day Like Today' (backed by 'A Man Like Myself'), had already proven at least as successful as the Spiders' sole waxing, but there was one other thing that pushed Bruce to the fore. He had a van, and now that Tatum and his Chevy had driven off into the sunset, transportation was at a premium. Bruce later joked, "I think they wanted the van more than me."

He did not immediately throw his lot in with the Spiders. At no point did his new bandmates ever tell him that he was actually in the band; rather, they'd just tell him when the next gig or rehearsal was, and expect him to be there. Looking back, it was fairly clear that he did have the job, but Bruce remained uncertain enough that he never left the Wildflowers, either. He just adopted a stage name – the distinctly un-pseudonymous Bruce Michael – and continued to play and record with them, even cutting a second Wildflowers single, 'More Than Me'/'Moving Along With The Sun', before finally accepting that he was a full-time Spider.

Throughout the first years of the Spiders, Vince remained a paid-up member of the Church of Jesus Christ. His father was now a pastor, a skilled preacher who was destined eventually to become a church elder, and every third Sunday, the Furnier family would sit in the congregation while dad turned the full force of his rhetoric upon his flock.

How that congregation would stare as Vince took his own seat in the church, long haired and increasingly outlandishly dressed, and how the old ladies would tut and whisper as word spread of the boy's latest transgressions. How he had been suspended again from school, for refusing to get his hair cut. How poor Mrs Hickey was at her wits' end with daughter Debby's choice of consort. How he was seen out late at night by one person, or seen playing rock'n'roll by another. His name was mentioned on the radio whenever a local jock role-called the musicians responsible for the Spiders' first single, and that set the tongues wagging as well, because everybody knew that a career in rock'n'roll was the first step on the slippery road to Hell.

Everybody, that is, apart from Vince's father. Mickie Furnier may not have wholly approved of his son's choice of activity, and might have fervently prayed that it was just a passing phase before Vince embraced the church for the third generation in succession. But he was not going to put his foot down and tell the boy to stop, for the same reasons as his own father had never tried to force his religious convictions down his children's throats. The boy would come to his senses when it was time for him to do so. Until then, Vince was simply asked to remember his father's status and not to do anything to embarrass him. In return, Mickie came along to a few Spiders shows, and appeared to have a great time while he was there.

Meanwhile, the Spiders' fame continued to spread. They played their first out of town shows, and were introducing more of their own material into the set. A snarling storm of fuzz guitar called, appropriately, 'Don't Blow Your Mind', a song that had been a part of the live show since John Tatum was in the group, was completed, and Bruce and Dunaway came up with a solid R&B firestorm called 'No Price Tag' – two songs that the Spiders promptly earmarked for their next single.

They recorded at a small studio in Tucson, Santa Cruz Recording, which in turn boasted its own label, also called Santa Cruz. There, studio owner Foster Casey watched the band stumble through what some sources have claimed was a near complete album's worth of material, but just the two tracks would surface, to become a Phoenix chart topper that summer of 1966.

"Recording wasn't an easy chore for us," Vince confessed in *Me Alice*. They had no clear idea of what they were doing, or even supposed to be doing, and while the studio provided an engineeer, his concern was simply to get the band's sound down on tape. He had nothing to offer when it came to deciding what that sound should be. So, "We played our parts in unison and came up with a version of the song that sounded like we were all stuffed into a phone booth," and Jack Curtis did the rest, arranging for friends, family and VIP regulars to deluge the Tucson radio stations with requests for the record.

'Don't Blow Your Mind' eventually rose to number three on Tucson's K-FIF playlist. But the real thrill for the Spiders, and a shock for Vince's parents, came when they entered and won the latest Battle of the Bands contest. First prize – a trip to Los Angeles, then as now the centre of the American West Coast music industry. Make it there, it was said, and you could make it anywhere.

In fact that was not, and has never, been true. History is littered with the corpses of bands who reached the top of the pile in California, but who could never take that one crucial step across the state line and into the rest of the United States. As 1966 turned into 1967, however, and the Spiders realised that they had taken Arizona fame and fortune as far as they could, the city was boiling.

No less than San Francisco, half a day's drive up the coast, Los Angeles was seething as bands like the Doors, Love and Buffalo Springfield added their twopenn'orth to the burgeoning psychedelic scene, and clubs like the Whisky a Go Go, the Troubadour and Gazzari's flourished on the streets of dreams that the locals collectively called Hollywood.

The Spiders knew they were not yet ready to compete on the same level as those other bands. But they also believed they were as good as some of them and, having now opened for almost every major group of the era (at least those that bothered to journey through Arizona), they had long since proved they could hold their own with the best of them.

What they didn't have was proof of their prowess. Writer Paul Williams, reflecting in *Fusion* a few years on, bemoaned the paucity of written evidence of the Spiders' excesses of the age. "The only report tracked down of their early Arizona shows spoke of [Vince] leaning through a window sill held in his hands, wanking out some real psychedelic blather about leaning into the windows of yer mind."

Alice's memoir, however, includes a passing mention of meeting Jimi Hendrix, as he opened for the Young Rascals in summer 1967: "One cool hipster and a nice guy. He let us buddy around with him," (the same seemingly contrary billing played New York's Central Park in July), while Michael Bruce's autobiography recalls a night out in Chandler, just 25 miles outside of Phoenix, where a local redneck grew so tired of their performance that he flashed a switchblade in their direction.

"It wasn't that unusual for us to get chased out of town. We'd have bottles thrown at us, you name it." Gang loyalties in mid-sixties Arizona, he continued, divided strictly down Cowboy and Indian lines, and it was rare for the two to join forces. Until the Spiders came to town. "We had to stay inside the National Guard armoury because the Cowboys and the Indians had lined up outside, ready to beat the hell out of us." A new song, all minor keys and yearning sentiment, and suitably titled 'Nobody Likes Me', emerged from the experience.

Another night, Glen Buxton recalled, "We were playing for the greasy peoples, the beehive hairdos and the jocks, doin' a place in Tucson that held 2,000 people." He told *Circus* magazine, "It was back in the days when long hair was on women... and let me tell you, our hair was not short. We went dancin' in there and the places was crawlin' with greasers, and those guys were gonna kill us. There was about five guys lookin' at [Vince] goin' 'Ah'm gonna gitchoo outside an' Ah'm gonna beat the sheeit outa yoo.' I was the first one on stage and I'm practically shitting my pants cause I have to get all the way over to the other side of the stage, and I'm scared outa my mind, and they're all buggin' me, and there's this chick right in the middle.

"She's like this dirty, clap-ridden, pimply, braced groupie idiot that everybody hated, and I didn't even know that, ya know? And I go out feelin' like I'm walkin' the gauntlet and the chick goes, 'Play "Louie, Louie". Play "Louie, Louie".' And I go, 'Play "Louie, Louie", huh.' All this shit goin' on and I'm going to get killed and she's going 'Play "Louie, Louie".'"

Many bands would have been cowed by such experiences. The Spiders simply shrugged and vowed that next time, they would piss off even more people. "We had bruises all over out bodies from the foot-poles," Vince chuckled in an interview for the *Story Of Pop* encyclopaedia. "That's how much promoters refused to touch us. So we decided to go on stage and do anything that we wanted. Some nights we used to stagger on stage so drunk, I'd pass out at least three times during a set. Surprise... surprise, people dug it and quite often they used to come along just to see what would happen to us. I'd just stand in the middle of the stage and pass right out and the crowd would cheer. The band would pick me up, I'd get back together again – take a swig of this gawdamnawful cheap Ripple wine – and crash out once again."

What was it about the Spiders that incited such hatred? Their hair, their noise, their apparent disregard for those tenets of law and order that redneck society – itself traditionally perched on the far right wing of American politics – held dearest. Rock'n'roll was still an affront to great swathes of society back then, and the deeper into the American heartland you travelled (and Arizona was almost as deep as you could go), the greater the hatred of its creators.

The Spiders were not hated for who they were, but for what they represented, and besides, what were they doing prancing around like a bunch of fags on stage, when they should have been at an army office, signing up to go kill gooks in Nam? The United States had now admitted that its intervention in the east Asian civil war was something more than the advisory policing mission that had once been the official line, and was dispatching ever greater numbers of troops to the combat zone. Why, the rednecks wanted to know, were the Spiders not first in line to crush the rise of Communism?

The Spiders generally laughed at such questions, behind their interrogators' backs, of course. Three of the band – John Speer, Dennis Dunaway and Glen Buxton – were now attending college, generally regarded as the ultimate get-out-of-jail-free card when it came to donning fatigues and fighting for freedom; the remainder, Vince and Michael Bruce, were still at High School, but they had their own plans for further education in mind. Or at least, they did before Los Angeles appeared on their horizon.

Beginning in March 1967, the Spiders were making regular visits to Los Angeles, piling themselves and a slowly growing retinue of friends – roadie Mike Allen, manager Dick Christian and lighting engineer Charlie Carnel – into Bruce's van for the six hour straight shot down Interstate 10, and from the moment they first set foot on Hollywood Boulevard, they wondered why they had waited so long to take the plunge.

It was freak central. Every corner was littered with kids who, in the parlance of the time, had tuned in, dropped out and turned on. Every store seemed to be pounding out music, every breath filled their head with unknown doors and unimagined highs. Those first few days in Hollywood, the days that the band originally planned would be devoted to finding work, were instead spent simply imbibing the spirit of the city and comparing everything they saw to its nearest equivalent back home.

There was no competition. The shops were brighter, the girls were prettier, the locals were friendlier. In Arizona, having hair that went over your collar was regarded as a personal affront to every passing stranger. In Hollywood, the hair started at the collar and the Spiders looked positively bald by comparison.

In Arizona, the Spiders were the wildest thing on ten legs. In Hollywood, every band was wild, and the ones that were left behind were the ones that simply weren't wild enough. Right now, the Spiders fell somewhere in the middle and, as they window shopped through the thrift stores and head shops that lined the streets of Hollywood, and dodged the locomotive trains that still rumbled down the centre of Sunset Boulevard, their talk was full of the image changes that they could and would enact once they found a paying gig.

The problem was, every other band in town had the same idea. Audition nights in Arizona meant calling the owner of a club and asking if he would take a look at you. His answer would usually follow in the next breath. It was different in Los Angeles. The clubs in Hollywood held open audition nights, and you could tell when they were happening from the lines of musicians who started to congregate outside the venue that afternoon. "It was like a battle of the bands, every night every place we went," Glen Buxton sighed.

Neither was being at the head of the line any guarantee of being given a spot at the audition. Friends of friends of the club staff would call over, and be invited to queue-jump on the strength of a dropped name. Musicians would be pulled out of line because they looked so much better than the rest, or they might be told to go home because they looked so much worse. It was chaos, and that was only the start of it. Some clubs hit on the idea of charging the auditioning hordes an entry fee, and that took another bite out of a band's hopes and dreams. Others got sick of the police hassling them about blocking the sidewalk, and began demanding musicians sign up in advance for auditions – and then, again, cherry-picked their friends and their friends' friends from the lists.

But slowly, the Spiders were able to make themselves heard, scratching their way into performing at parties, or making themselves available for any of the many free concerts that were springing up, often in strict defiance of the law, around the city parks. One of the first, if not the first, took place in Griffith Park on March 26, 1967. Two nights later, the Spiders opened at Gazzari's, on the Strip, and that was how things went for the next few months. They would meet people and find friendly floors to crash on, or they would pile back into the van and sleep there as best as they could. But they were never able to put down roots because they always had to return to Phoenix. In fact some nights, the band would have time to do no more than play their set before having to leap back into the van and return to Phoenix, their brains still buzzing from the thrill of the show.

"I was very naive when I arrived in California," Alice told *Spec.* "I was like a lamb going into the slaughter. Coming from that church background I didn't have any idea about sex at all. We lived right there in Hollywood in the heart of the Evil Hill, the area between Sunset and Santa Monica Boulevards, just below the Whisky. I didn't even know what a homosexual was – I just thought everyone in the neighbourhood was fond of poodles. Finally, I caught on. You get an education living in California."

There was no shortage of willing educators. The Spiders found a crash pad, courtesy of one Doke Huntington, who worked as a private secretary to actor Tony Curtis. His home on Weatherly Lane, just off Santa Monica Boulevard, became the Spiders' home from home while they were in Los Angeles, and it was some time before the musicians finally realised why so many of Doke's more flamboyant friends spent so much time hanging around the house, just watching the young men hang out. But the revelation didn't shock them. They were in Los Angeles, after all, and after two or three trips out to the city, they finally made the decision they'd been talking about for six months or more. It was time to abandon Phoenix altogether and move to Los Angeles for good.

It was a fresh start all round. Mickie Furnier presented the band with a new van, a distinctive yellow beast that allowed Michael Bruce's old beater to finally retire. Another friend, likewise lit up with a Hollywood dream, agreed to accompany them as a roadie and lighting operator, handling the ramshackle collection of coloured floodlights that the group had recently invested in. And the Spiders became the Nazz, after ceaselessly spinning a recent Yardbirds' b-side, 'The Nazz Is Blue'.

The band knew the lie of the land now, and those first weeks in the city were dedicated to rehearsing for the next round of auditions that they knew they would be attending, and checking out the kind of bands they knew they would be up against. They would borrow ideas, or steal them if they wanted to, and then insert them into their own brand of stagecraft – an increasingly riotous act that set every participant, musician and onlooker alike, into almost perpetual motion, Vince prowling the stage like a B-movie serial killer, his bandmates the front line of a menacing street gang, and the audience pinned to the walls by the noise as the musicians selected their victims.

Their set was fast approaching the point where it was wholly self-composed. The occasional favourite cover would still surface, but often it was so mangled by the band's imagination that audiences needed to have it identified for them. Other songs were torn straight from whatever the musicians were reading or thinking at the time, headlines from the newspaper, speech bubbles taken from comic books, queer expressions they'd hear on television and earmark for future inspection.

Bruce and Dunaway gelled as songwriters, one bringing an instinctive grasp of melody and drama to the stage, the other digging deep into a macabre mind in search of ideas that made him shiver. 'Lay Down And Die, Goodbye' was unquestionably written in the thrall of the Yardbirds, its guitars a snarling echo of 'Happenings Ten Years Time Ago'. But the title made the Nazz's intentions clear and, as their repertoire developed, so did the rage with which they rocked. 'Everything Is Orange'... 'Mr Machine'... 'Travel Agent'... 'Animal Pajamas'... 'Wonder Who's Loving Her Now'. The music had cohesion and with it, the ethos that would become the band's raison d'etre. As Vince liked to reflect, "The hippies saw the future in [the Nazz] and it scared them to death."

Chapter Four

She Gave Her Mama Forty Whacks

"When we were starting," Vince enjoyed reminding people, "it was the time of the Doors, Buffalo Springfield, Love." Almost a decade later, in 1975, he told the *New Musical Express*, "We were competing against 20,000 other bands just in LA. We'd do things like 'auditioning' for three hours at a club, and then not being offered work: all people were really doing was getting us to play free at their club.

"We were starving, physically starving, and we were tired of being fucked around. So our attitude was, we're gonna make you look at us. We're gonna grab your attention."

One evening, hanging around outside the Gaslight, a club on Sunset Strip, Vince fell into conversation with a band called the Rainmakers. One of the myriad acts that had finally got a foot on the first rung of the local ladder, the Rainmakers had just scored a week-long residency at the Gaslight, and Vince told them he'd be sure to come down to lend his support. He'd bring the rest of his band along too.

They exchanged phone numbers and Vince went on his way, only to be stunned a few days later when the phone rang and one of these so recent acquaintances asked him a favour. The Rainmakers' guitarist had fallen ill and they couldn't make that evening's show. "Sorry it's such late notice, but could the Nazz fill in for us?"

They could and they did, and the wheels began to turn. The gig at the Gaslight became a regular event; so did shows at the nearby Hullabaloo. And it was within this sudden flurry of activity that they met Sherry Cottle, booker at the Cheetah Club, out on Venice's Pacific Ocean Park pier complex.

Sadly destroyed in the series of arson attacks that ultimately led to Ocean Park's closure in the early seventies, the Cheetah was modelled on the club of the same name in New York City, a 7,000 square foot dance floor surrounded by stainless steel walls. The Doors had played there, Janis Joplin and Blue Cheer, alongside almost every other significant band that called the LA club scene home. Not quite sure what to make of the Nazz, but blown away by their enthusiasm and wit, Cottle invited the band to audition for the Cheetah, and was sufficiently impressed to rebook them.

The Nazz made their debut at the Cheetah in early August, opening for the Doors at a concert marking the first anniversary (on August 3) of the death of comedian Lenny Bruce. Lenny Brucemas was guaranteed to pull an all-star audience, while the billing placed the Nazz immediately after the Butterfield Blues Band, a hard-driving Chicago blues rock outfit that many were then comparing to Cream.

There was no way they could fail.

To horrify.

It was a rout. With the lighting blaring and the amps feeding back, they hit the stage in a flash of noise and colour, and plunged straight into the theme from television's *Patty Duke Show*. They had, they assumed, rehearsed their set to perfection, every high and low exquisitely paced, every heartbeat choreographed for maximum effect. But very few people hung around to hear that. They cleared the Cheetah crowd in four songs flat.

Journalist Howard Bloom elaborated on the occasion for readers of *Circus* magazine: "They came out in chrome coloured suits with fringes, while fog machines spilled dense clouds around them and black lights triggered the phosphorescent glow of spinning wheels at the back of the stage. Then they thoroughly antagonised a crowd that had come for Jim-Morrison-style rock by giving it a mixture of Dionne Warwick tunes and science fiction songs about computers taking over earth. By the time they got into their fourth number, 7,000 Doors fans had fled."

Those that remained, however, made an impressive audience in their own right: Sherry Cottle, who was already planning the group's next appearance; Vito, the leader of the hippy choreography team Vito's Dancers; and three members of a loose aggregation of local groupies who went under the name of the GTOs – Girls Together Outrageously. Next to Cottle, they would become the Nazz's most tireless cheerleaders.

On August 22, 1967, the Nazz played the first of seven consecutive nights at the Cheetah, opening for the funk-driven Watts 103rd Street Rhythm Band. It was an absurd pairing, but Cottle knew what she was doing. Audiences might not like the Nazz, but their loathing was contagious. Word of mouth spread, "You have to see this band – they're atrocious," and sensing the groundswell of interest, Cottle established the Nazz, alongside the somewhat less controversial Chambers Brothers, as the Cheetah house bands. By early September, the Nazz were opening two nights for Buffalo Springfield, and Cottle was opening up her own home, a three-bedroom house on Beethoven Street, to the band members.

They were not the only musicians on the premises, though. Other groups shared Cottle's hospitality, including, for a few days in late October 1967, a visiting British band called Pink Floyd.

Still riding the British success of their debut album *The Piper At The Gates Of Dawn* and the attendant hit single 'See Emily Play', Pink Floyd were the epitome of the UK underground, at a time when it was still struggling to catch up with its American counterpart. Certainly three days at Winterland in San Francisco did little to impress the local freak community as the Floyd travelled without much of the lighting and stage effects that hallmarked their reputation, while frontman Syd Barrett was now firmly in the grips of the psychological malaise that would lift him out of the band and into rock legend before they even cut a new album together.

The band's management, watching Barrett's disintegration drag the group's reputation with it, was frantic, pulling out every stop to cancel the tour and bring the band home, but while they waited for their flights back to London, Pink Floyd made their way to Venice, and a memorable meal with the Nazz.

A decade later, Glen Buxton recalled, "Syd was a very strange person. He never talked, but we'd be sitting at dinner and all of a sudden I'd pick up the sugar and pass it to him. It was like I heard him say 'pass the sugar'. It was like telepathy. That was the first time in my life I'd ever met someone who could do that freely, and this guy did it all the time. He was definitely from Mars."

According to Vince, Barrett spent most of his time sitting silently in the kitchen clad in the same pair of crushed velvet pink pants. But the entire Pink Floyd made its way down to Gazzari's one afternoon to watch the Nazz audition for a regular gig there, and offered their own contribution to the proceedings by first dosing their housemates with marijuana brownies. Then it was down to the Cheetah Club, where the Floyd were making their Los Angeles debut.

"The Cheetah Club was the occasion that Syd decided his permed hair was too curly and had to be straightened before he could go on," Floyd drummer Nick Mason recalled, a tale that Glen Buxton confirmed with his memory of being sent out to a nearby drug store to pick up a tub of hair gel. Which Barrett proceeded to empty over his head. He stepped out onto the stage and, in the heat of the stage lighting, "it looked like his head was melting".

Those other denizens of the Cheetah, the Doors, became friends of the Nazz, even inviting them into the studio to watch as they recorded their second LP, *Strange Days*; while other groups found their own paths crossing with the Nazz, for better or for worse. In mid-November, the Nazz opened for Clear Light, a band widely touted as the next Doors, and the year ended with another run of Cheetah shows that took the Nazz right up until Christmas.

They squeezed out a new single. 'Lay Down And Die, Goodbye' became the first and only release on their own Very Records label. It sold a handful of copies to the curious, and a few more to the odd soul who wanted a souvenir of the frenetic live show, but that was not the point. It was true that the Nazz had yet to make a mark on any place outside of Venice, but still six months in California had established them way beyond their expectations, and they were not as loathed as they liked to make out, either.

Another Phoenix friend joined the family. Neal Smith was the band's roadie. Like Glen Buxton an Akronite, he was born in Rubber City on September 23, 1947 before his family transplanted to Phoenix. A Camelback High graduate, he played in a band called the Holy Grail and was first drawn towards the Spiders not so much by music, as by a sense of homesickness; he and Buxton bonded over their Akron past, and their friendship grew from there.

The rest of the band were not immediately taken with Smith. In fact Vince admitted in his *Me Alice* autobiography, "I always thought Neal

Smith was a jerk. I first saw him at a Battle of the Bands in Phoenix when he was the drummer in a rival band, the Surf Tones. Every group in that particular Battle of the Bands agreed to pool their equipment so each band wouldn't have to reset the stage after each set and lose the attention of the parking lot audiences. Neal… was the only musician there who was against it. He made all the musicians disassemble their equipment so he could set his drum kit on risers. Then in the middle of a 16-minute version of 'Wipe Out', he did a 14-minute drum solo."

Smith signed up as the Spiders' roadie at first, while still looking for a band of his own. He was already there, then, when they received their first and, so far, only taste of record company interest. A label called Sound Records came knocking, and Smith recalls, "[they] wanted to sign them, but they wanted the band to back up another singer." The Nazz refused. They had not come so far with Vince to drop him now. Either they signed' as a unit or they didn't sign at all. Their suitors took the latter option, only for the band to then discover they might be needing a new vocalist after all. Vince was off to Vietnam.

Drummer John Speer had quit the band by now, walking out in December 1967 after one disagreement too many, and remaining tight-lipped over the reasons for his departure ever since. Michael Bruce, however, remains convinced it was the pot brownies incident in the presence of Pink Floyd that did it. "He got really mad… [and] the next day he loaded his car and left for Phoenix."

His replacement, however, was already waiting in the wings. It was Buxton who pushed for Smith to be elevated from roadiedom to the band itself, and this time, it was Smith's love of firearms that swayed him. Buxton was toting a Derringer at the time and loved nothing so much as driving out into the desert to practise his shooting. Smith, on the other hand, had a Thompson sub-machine gun. With the rest of the band toting .22 rifles, shooting practice had just gone up another notch.

Smith slipped effortlessly into the vacant drum seat, bringing with him an education that had seen him play in orchestras and marching bands almost from the moment he could hold two drumsticks. And he was the first to learn that he would not be going to Vietnam, after one particular trip into the desert left him with a bullet wound in his foot.

Aiming for a rabbit, Vince instead hit his bandmate, and that was the end of Smith's military hopes. Particularly after Smith insisted he'd been trying to commit suicide at the time. In the eyes of the American military, it didn't matter if you wound up dead once they had their hooks in you. Just so long as you weren't the one who pulled the trigger.

His bandmates were not so fortunate. Contrary to what they all believed, enrolment at Glendale Community College was not enough to convince the military that the Spiders would be more of an asset to the home front than they would being cannon fodder on the front line. Buxton, Bruce, Dunaway and Vince all received A-1 classification, meaning they were considered both suitable and available for unrestricted military service. Now it was up to them to convince the army otherwise.

All four were still registered as residents of Phoenix, so it was to Arizona they returned, growing ever more fearful as the lights of Los Angeles receded into the distance. Yet they weren't despairing yet. They had a plan.

The Southern Comfort flowed the night before they were due to appear at the conscription office, and wardrobes were ransacked for the most outlandish clothing they could find. The idea, shared with so many other would-be draft dodgers, was to appear so freaky, outrageous and all-round undesirable that the Army would rather lose the war than recruit them.

At first, it looked as though their scheme would work. Dunaway was disqualified because of his appearance and the likelihood, apparent to even the most bull-headed recruitment officer, that there was no way he could be transformed into a lean, mean fighting machine. Not in this lifetime, anyway.

Buxton was sent packing and so was Bruce, after he suffered what looked like a complete mental breakdown while actually on the bus to boot camp. Which left Vince, his head still swimming from the alcohol, resplendent in a pair of gold lamé trousers, his hair a tangled mass that reached towards his lower back, a hippy, a horror, a degenerate mess. Yet he, it was declared, was precisely what the army was looking for, and he knew why as well. The recruitment officer was the same lunkhead who'd just stolen girlfriend Debby away from him (much to Mrs Hickey's relief), and who hated his old rival with a passion. Vince was told to go home and start packing. He was off to war.

It was pure chance that saved him. Chance, and the US government's decision to try and quell mounting criticism of the seemingly indiscriminate manner in which American youth was being harvested for the war. Shortly after Vince's 20th birthday in February 1968, but before he received his actual call-up papers, it was announced that the military was reverting to a practice that was last seen in 1942, drafting future conscripts by lottery. All pending inductions were placed on hold until the drawing took place on December 1, 1969.

The possibility of being sent off to war still hung over Vince Furnier. But he had about 18 months of freedom ahead of him in which to get on with his life. At the beginning of March 1968, the Nazz returned to Los Angeles with just one goal in mind. To become so huge that, if Vince did end up being hauled off to the war, it would become the biggest headline news since Elvis Presley was drafted. Because they would already be the biggest stars since him.

The little boy who used to swung his hips in the mirror was about to grow up.

The reprieve gave the band a whole new outlook. Like a dying man anxious to cram as much into the time that was left to him, the band turned everything up full blast; their look, their sound, their music, their attitude. And their name. Word had filtered through of another band called the Nazz, a Philly-based outfit led by one Todd Rundgren, and the fact that the Venice Beach Nazz heard the news long before their Pennsylvania counterparts became aware of them suggested that any attempt to hang onto their name was doomed. It was time for another change.

A handful of names was bandied around, including the distinctly memorable Husky Baby Sandwich. But the title that would soon be ascending to infamy was not granted by any earthly power.

Or so one of the stories goes.

The group was back in Phoenix now, returning home for the Christmas holidays and then staying on to build up another stash of cash, "a war chest", as Neal Smith puts it, of four to five thousand dollars, with which to finance their next assault on Hollywood. One night, road manager Dick Phillips invited the group round to his house, where his mother had set up a Ouija board. Immediately, an unseen force began manipulating the pointer, painstakingly spelling out a name that meant nothing to anybody. It was Alice Cooper.

They asked the board who she was. Its reply arrived with chilling deliberation.

ALICE COOPER IS VINCE FURNIER.

They could not allow the matter to rest there. Over the ensuing years, the band members and friends threw themselves into research, and soon a tale of supernatural fear and superstitious horror presented itself. Alice Cooper was an English woman, born in the 16th or 17th century, one of two sisters who were widely believed, or at least accused, of practicing witchcraft, at a time when the craft was a capital crime.

The authorities came for Alice's sister first, dragging her away in chains, imprisoning and interrogating her, extracting and believing the kind of confession that would not even pass muster as the script for a modern low-brow horror film, and then condemning her to death at the stake. Alice watched in terror as her sister burned, and she knew that she was next. Days, maybe even hours, before she was arrested, she committed suicide by poison. Vince, the Ouija board told the band, was her reincarnation. Or, perhaps, she was his. Driving back to Los Angeles a few days later, the band was involved in a highway accident that wrote off their van and came close to writing off the band as well. As they stared in disbelief at the wreckage of their transport and the broken gear strewn across the highway, the question came to every mind. What if Vince really had died in the crash? And what if Alice, the 16th century witchy Alice, had reanimated his corpse for her own wicked, vengeful purposes?

They had their story. Or one of them, anyway, because there would be a lot of others.

In an age when many of the biggest hits of the day seemed to be by wholesome female singer-songwriters, Joni Mitchell and Laura Nyro, Melanie Safka and so on and so forth, Alice Cooper was precisely the kind of name that would be attached to an all-American blonde folk singer. Wouldn't it be cool, Vince laughed, to draw in an audience expecting an evening of lightly strummed earnestness, and then hammer them with the full force of the Nazz?

"The name started simply as a spit in the face of society," he cracked to *Rolling Stone* in 1973, fully mindful of the fact that the magazine was one of those that had foisted such fare upon the public. "With a name like Alice Cooper, we could really make them suffer."

On other occasions, he simply mused on the "Baby Jane Lizzie Borden sweet and innocent with a hatchet behind the back" prettiness of the name. "There was something axe-murderish about Alice Cooper. It reminded me of Lizzie Borden. [It's] got a *Whatever Happened To Baby Jane* feeling to it. It was like feminine, but it wasn't feminine. It had some sort of ring to it, something disturbing."

And on others, he dismissed all those other tales and told what he swore was the "honest-to-God truth". And it is just as likely (or otherwise) as all of those other explanations. In 1975, he told *Circus*, "We were sitting there, we were still high school kids, and we were over at these girls' house. They were secretaries, and they wanted to be a band. They were called the Weeds of Idleness, and they really were sincere, but they were horrible. They worked as secretaries and they would really help us out. We would go there every night and they'd prepare us all this food. So, it was over at their house and we were sitting there saying, 'We got to find a new name'... and I said, 'We don't have anything to lose, let's do something that no one's going to relate to at all.' I could have said Jennifer Smith or Mary Truesdale, but it just happened that Alice Cooper came out. It was the very first name that came out too."

Further variations blossomed. "It is rumoured that Alice's real name is Vernon Harlipp," announced *Teen* magazine in November 1972. "Alice Cooper is his mother's maiden name and the family is distantly related to the late Gary Cooper. However, Alice refuses to comment on any of the above." And in late 1973, *Melody Maker* reported that Alice's childhood pet was a baby King Snake that he found in the garden one day. "[He] called the snake Alice, because it was the name of a little girl at Sunday School. It wasn't until it died that he found it was a man snake, after all. Vince was so upset as its death he cried for days, and there was nothing his mother could do to console him. [But] he never forgot that snake."

Glen Buxton, however, mused on a more prosaic influence, as Jefferson Airplane's 'White Rabbit' hit the charts and ignited a counterculture-wide fascination with English author Lewis Carroll's *Through The Looking Glass/Wonderland* tales. Alice, as the titular heroine of both those story books, was a popular name in 1967 and early 1968, as popular as another folk hero of the age, the Mini Cooper motor car, winner of the 1967 Monte Carlo Rally. The combination of two such powerful icons, the fantasy of psychedelia and the style of Swinging London, seemed irresistible to a bunch of self-confessed Anglophiles whose greatest thrill so far had been to meet Pink Floyd on their first visit to America, and whose own musical dreams remained locked solidly into the turbulent thrash of the British Invaders. They could as easily have named themselves Lucy Lotus.

But they didn't. They were Alice Cooper and Sherry Cottle sprang into action, designing new identities for the musicians, to be smeared across their press releases. Vince was sorted; he was Alice. But Glen Buxton became "a brooding figure of the past, a black knight once feared by many"; Dennis Dunaway was "an artist of the courts, painting the picture of history, knowing the colours of tomorrow"; Neal Smith was "a warrior king, born of power, bred in the stronghold of the gods" and Michael Bruce became a "poet of the streets, writing songs of centuries, a figure in the fields of tomorrow".

And where their identities went, their wardrobe would follow. Their hair was already reaching lengths that even the established long hairs of the day would have looked askance at. Now their costuming, already absurd and borderline bordello, began to echo the nomenclatural deception. Neal Smith's sister Cindy was the co-owner and designer at a Phoenix boutique; she became the band's official costumier, and while she worked on her first designs and outfits, the Coopers set their sights on a suitable scene in which to debut their new-found depravity. As Vince wondered aloud in a 2010 interview, "Why do we always have rock heroes? Why not a rock villain? I was more than happy to be rock's Darth Vader. I was more than happy to be Captain Hook."

A free concert was looming. The Nazz had a booking to play alongside Blue Cheer and the Nitty Gritty Dirt Band at the Earl Warren Fairgrounds in Santa Barbara, on March 16, 1968 – Michael Bruce's birthday. Delaying the declaration of their name change until they were actually on the stage, what happened next passed into both the band's folklore and local legend.

Alice told *Fusion*, "We've always been into liquor, but at that time it was almost the biggest thing in our act. We were into getting falling down drunk and then going out to play those long-ins, where you know everybody was really into the whole consciousness of this new dope scene and walking around saying 'groovy' and 'oh wow' to each other and making that particular social scene, which we never put down at all, it was just that we had our own scene, and right then our big thing was wine."

The problem was, "a lot of the kids were still at the stage where they were very puritanical about alcohol, and our main approach then was just to get as fucked up as possible and go play and see how obnoxious we could be. Just to create any kind of absurd disruption of that, what, sylvan sort of placidity we could. And it worked, it was great fun. People would walk around in circles saying, 'Wow do these guys suck, who the fuck are they?', and some would come up later and ask us why we were trying to bum everybody out.

"One other thing is that at the time our music was almost total noise, no real order at all, and lots of people didn't like that too much either. But we did, and we kept on, and every once in a while somebody would come up after we finished and say they really dug what we were doing, and we'd give 'em a swig of Red Mountain. Some of them were like intellectual types who tried to talk about atonality and chance music, but lots of times they were bikers who'd give us their wine or offer us some downs and tell us what a bunch of lames they thought all the hippies were. I think they really identified with the music we were doing better than anybody else, because it was so noisy they heard motorcycles in it."

All of a sudden, he smiled, "There was Alice Cooper. And people hated us. They hated us so much they came to see us. Even other bands hated us. Friends of ours started hating us. But they came to see us."

Chapter Five

Pretties For Frank

Without ever isolating an audience of their own, the Alice Cooper band had found a new way of making people talk about them – by alienating the people who did come to see them. At the festival, they determined to be the loudest band on the stage. Now they resolved to become the most colourful too, haunting the Hollywood thrift stores for the hippest women's clothing they could find, a kaleidoscopic blur of lamé and feathers, corsets and stockings. It was a look that their idols, the Rolling Stones, may have pioneered a couple of years ago with the video shoot for 'Have You Seen Your Mother, Baby', but for the Stones it was simply a gimmick. The Coopers were determined to transform it into a lifestyle.

Phoenix was already in their pocket. A local promoter, apparently enthused by both the band's name and following, had offered them naming rights to a club he intended opening, as a *Teen Gazette* article dated Saturday, April 6, 1968, declares. "The Valley's newest teen night club opened last night with Alice Cooper, formerly the Nazz, namesake of the club. The building, located at 5555 E. Van Buren, was completely redecorated, including wood panelling on the walls and pink crepe-like material draped from the ceiling of the lobby. With this combination, Alice Cooper is a sure winner."

Neal Smith recalls, "Somebody had this old country and western bar. They wanted to turn it into a rock bar and they said we could do anything we wanted to it. So we changed the name to the Alice Cooper Club and because they gave us carte blanche to do whatever we wanted, we painted the whole inside pink.

"We were so inspired by the S&M thing from Hollywood that we had whips and chains and handcuffs and all this crazy stuff everywhere, although in the west, whips aren't a big deal."

In fact the club remained open for just one weekend, two shows headlined by Alice Cooper and a third featuring the Music Machine, 18 months on from their Top 20 success with the Spiders' old stand-by 'Talk Talk'. "It may have stayed open a little longer," Smith concedes, "but we didn't play there again. Either way, it had a very short shelf life."

More and more of the band's time was being spent in Los Angeles. Not every venue that they approached for an audition got past the photographs that the band would hand over, and even once they'd convinced the club owner to book them, there was still an audience to win over – or not. But throughout the early spring of 1968, Alice Cooper slowly found their world expanding, through their own machinations and those of their most infamous fans.

Girls Together Outrageously (or Occasionally or Often, depending upon the mood) were an aggregation of Laurel Canyon groupies whose speciality was dancing together at various Hollywood clubs, clad only in skimpy white T-shirts and diapers, and revelling in the evocative identities that Tiny Tim had already conferred upon them: Miss Sandra, Miss Sparky, Miss Pamela (Miller – later to become a celebrated groupie and marry singer Michael DesBarres), Miss Cinderella, Miss Mercy and Miss Christine. Surnames were unnecessary; the girls' reputation was identification enough.

"We called ourselves the Laurel Canyon Ballet Company," recalled Miss Pamela and, one night at a Mothers of Invention show at the Shrine Auditorium, while Zappa was "wandering around after the show", she "made a point of slamming into him on the dance floor". They fell to talking and soon, with Miss Christine installed as Zappa's housekeeper, she was inviting her companions up to Zappa's home, actor Tom Mix's old mansion in Laurel Canyon, to entertain the other guests by singing and dancing to his Mothers of Invention records.

It was a great act, or so Zappa thought, and he was soon laying plans to incorporate the GTOs' routine into three of his own shows at the Los Angeles Shrine. There, *Rolling Stone* described their performance as "beautifully choreographed, and so what if one of the Mothers thinks they're astonishingly flat and can't carry a tune in a bucket?" The fact was, they brought further invention to the Mothers' performance, as well as offering the more testosterone-driven members of the audience a ready outlet for their most primal emotions.

Not all of the Mothers were thrilled by the girls' arrival into their world. Bunk Gardner recalled them as "vampirish, black lipstick, black mascara, black everything", and found them "a little bit too unattractive for my tastes". But Zappa's enthusiasm knew no bounds.

Neither did Vince's. He met Miss Christine at the legendary Cantor's Deli one night and, confessing that "I had developed a little crush on [her]", he began accompanying her to work, babysitting Zappa's two children, Dweezil and Moon Unit. And Miss Christine started talking to her employer about him, probably not making too much of an impression on a man who spent every day being told about one band or another, until she said the magic words. "Their name is Alice Cooper. And nobody likes them."

"Nobody at all?" Zappa asked.

"Nobody at all," Miss Christine confirmed.

The band had already started sending demo tapes and unsold copies of 'Lay Down And Die, Goodbye' out to various local record labels, but always to no avail. That was no surprise; every label in the city was already being deluged by young hopefuls, and even Jackson Browne's demos were binned by David Geffen before a secretary rescued them and forced him to listen. So Alice Cooper's failure to find an interesting label probably had less to do with the fact that people hated them than the fact that they had been lost in the stampede.

Zappa knew that, of course. But he also respected Miss Pamela's opinions and, even more pressingly, he was actively searching for new talent (if that was not too grandiose a term for his intentions) to launch the pair of record labels he had recently launched, Straight Records, for what he considered mainstream acts, and Bizarre Records, for the more avant-garde.

The GTOs were already on board and so was Wild Man Fischer, a paranoid schizophrenic singer-songwriter who Zappa discovered busking a clutch of fragmentary ditties on a Hollywood street corner. Captain Beefheart was on his way, and all three, Zappa knew, fit the manifesto he had already composed for the label, that it would "make records that are a little different… present musical and sociological material which the important record companies would probably not allow you to hear".

The additional presence of folky singer-songwriters Tim Buckley, Judy Henske and Jerry Yester did negate those intentions somewhat, but still Alice Cooper sounded like they might make perfect stablemates for the Straight catalogue. But the group did itself few favours when they finally got to meet Zappa himself.

"Frank was a guy that we understood," Alice explained in that *Famous Monsters* interview. "He was a Dadaist. He worked in surrealism and he worked in a lot of media in his music. And he was funny! He was making fun of hippies and making fun of politicians and the straight people – everybody was fair game to him. Very early in our career we found out who Frank was, and we listened to *Freak Out* and *Absolutely Free* [the Mothers' first two albums] and we just laughed because this guy is like the Spike Jones of rock'n'roll.

"We didn't really get into how good he was until after *We're Only In It For The Money* and those albums, when he really started playing guitar and we really started listening to the songs and how brilliant this guy was. But he was the only one that was interested in Alice Cooper."

Alice had already invited Zappa to come see the band at Cheetah's one night, and had grown accustomed to being brushed off. He refused to take no for an answer, however, and when he found himself at a party that Zappa was also attending, he determined to cajole the moustachioed maestro ceaselessly, wearing down his resistance. Finally, if only to shut Alice up, Zappa agreed to meet the band, uttering the words that would form the framework for one of the most infamous of all Alice Cooper legends: "All right. Come by in the morning and I'll listen."

And so it was that at 7p.m. on a bright Sunday morning in June, the calm of Zappa's sleep, and of Laurel Canyon itself, was disrupted by the sound of the Alice Cooper band, in full costume and full flight. Miss Christine had let them into the house and helped them set up their gear. Then, with the rest of the house still silent, they started playing.

Zappa appeared, bemused and bathrobed, clutching a cup of coffee that he had scarcely been sufficiently awake to pour. "What are you doing here?" he asked.

They told him; he groaned. When he said "in the morning", he'd meant later, much later. And when he said he'd have a listen, he'd been expecting a cassette. Not a live performance. But he allowed them to finish their short set, hummed and hawed for a moment to himself, and then asked the first two questions that came to mind. "Are you on drugs?" – no. And "Where are you from?" The moment they told him that they were from Phoenix and not some far-out corner of the traditional underground, he was sold.

"I'd understand if you were from San Francisco or the Village or England. But Phoenix? OK, I'll sign you."

It was as easy as that.

Zappa was never to become an Alice Cooper fan. He signed them for the pure artistic notion that, if he didn't, nobody else would, and because he thought that someone, somewhere in his fanbase might appreciate them. Later that day he called his manager Herb Cohen and told him to start drawing up a record contract and, having ascertained that the Coopers were also management-free, suggested that Cohen step in there as well.

A couple of gigs were arranged to keep the Coopers busy. Zappa had a show lined up at the Wrigley Field ballpark in south Los Angeles on June 27; the Grassroots and T Bone Walker were already on the bill, but Alice Cooper were slipped onto the foot of the schedule. And they were as bad as he expected.

Bunk Gardner told Zappa biographer Billy James, "They were pitiful musically, even embarrassing. But it was Theater of the Absurd and the kids loved it. Forget the music, it was the weird show that the kids loved. But I still cringed at how bad musically they were. I just didn't understand why Frank and Herbie signed them to begin with."

Zappa added the Coopers to another upcoming show as well, at the Whisky A Go Go in July, and that was the cue for the same venue to call the Coopers in for another gig, a couple of weeks before the Zappa gig, opening for the British blues band Ten Years After on June 24. And there, Straight Records set the tapes rolling, to record the earliest known Alice Cooper concert tape.

Twenty-five minutes on stage gave the band time to perform just eight songs, opening with the twisting time signatures and staccato riffs of 'No Longer Umpire' as an instant test of the audience's sensibilities; bleeding into the marginally more conventional 'Today Mueller', a song written about a girl they knew back in Phoenix ('who is a lot of fun'); and then into the first of their truly experimental numbers, a brief but brittle 'Ten Minutes Before The Worm' that took the two previous numbers' penchant for twitching and twisting round the rudiments of melody and transformed itself into a medley of madness.

Signature falsetto backing vocals soar; Smith's drums scream like electric guitars; and no sooner does one eccentricity close than another, Dunaway's 'Levity Ball', storms into sight, the most conventional song in the band's entire repertoire, and destined to remain one of the finest, particularly around the mid section where the band's love for Pink Floyd, who once spiked their brownies, was writ around its mock ending re-creation of Syd Barrett's 'Interstellar Overdrive'.

'Nobody Likes Me', that self-mocking relic of the Spiders old woes, lopes past on harmonies and flashes of a Bo Diddley beat; and then another thrash as 'BB On Mars' ("it's about this BB... on Mars") mutates the group's old beat-boom sensibilities into the kind of warp-speed demolition that sundry post-punk British bands would, a decade later, consider themselves very clever for concocting.

The band's subsequently publicised loathing of the blues does not stand comparison with 'Sweet Low, Sweet Cheerio', a song whose freak show lyric belies a quintessentially Quicksilver Messenger Service backing track, and makes a mockery, too, of the aspersions that were being cast on the band's musicianship elsewhere. And then it's into the closing number, a fiery 'Changing Arranging' that staggers in on a mood borrowed wholesale from Zappa's 'Who Are The Brain Police?', but quickly shrugs off those trappings to develop into another of the deceptively poppy little numbers that Alice Cooper tucked away behind the shock tactics.

It was a dramatic performance, devastating in places, and the audience response gives immediate lie to the ongoing insistence that Alice Cooper were the most hated band in LA. Neither was it a one off. In July, the *LA Free Press* caught them at the newly redecorated Cheetah Club's Bastille Day party, and described them as "showstopping" but, in truth, appearing more impressed by the venue's recent makeover. Gone, it celebrated, was "most of that obnoxious sheet metal which made one feel like the inside of a garbage can".

Another venue welcomed them through its doors, and introduced Alice, at least, to another piece of his own future. Located just off Sunset, Thee Experience was a new venture, operated by the same husband and wife team that had successfully run another club, Thee Image, in Miami, Florida, for the last couple of years. Even more excitingly, the Florida operation's house band, Blues Image, were now themselves based in Los Angeles, and guitarist Mike Pinera recalls a vibrant scene.

"Thee Experience really knew how to take care of musicians. Hendrix would be popping in, the Who, Jim Morrison was a regular, we had great bands there all the time. Alice Cooper became the opening band for the venue, so I used to see them every weekend. They had not yet made it, but they were on Frank Zappa's label and they were quite bizarre for that time. They were already putting the dark make-up under the eyes and they looked very far out and I remember the first time we played together, I invited them into the dressing room and shared our sandwiches and our coffee and stuff. Whereas the rest of my band, the Blues Image, they stayed away. They said, 'They're kinda scary man, just tell us when they're gone and then we'll come back'."

Already, however, it was apparent that Alice Cooper rose far above the reputation that their wardrobe and make-up had provided them with. Pinera continues, "What it stood for, the lipstick and the black stuff under the eyes and the lingerie, people didn't like that but nobody could deny it was a good band, and their originals were very well crafted. So some people hated it, but others loved them. There were bands that were equally as dark with their persona and their appearance, but they couldn't play worth the crap. Plus, Los Angeles was known then for all those guitar players with their acoustic guitars, doom and gloom and the end of the world, and it wasn't good. Los Angeles needed bands like Alice Cooper."

And Alice Cooper needed Los Angeles. For now. Having stepped away from the crush of Sherry Cotelle's Venice home, the band drifted across town to Watts, where the Chambers Brothers, the other house band at the Cheetah, put an entire basement at their disposal beneath their headquarters on Crenshaw Boulevard. There, Alice Cooper rehearsed for their biggest date yet, at the Newport Pop Festival, out at the Orange County Fairgrounds, on August 3. On an esoteric bill that sprawled from Canned Heat and the Chambers Brothers, to Steppenwolf and Sonny & Cher, the Alice Cooper band tore the afternoon to shreds with a set that defied all categorisation.

The following week they were back home in Phoenix to headline an event named for one of their own songs, the Levity Ball, and a week after that, in Los Angeles again, they played the second Brucemas Festival at the Cheetah, out on the beach with the Doors topping the bill. And in September, watching the Chambers Brothers rehearse for their next major gig, opening for Jimi Hendrix at the Hollywood Bowl, they were stunned when Hendrix himself walked in.

He remembered them immediately from their encounter the previous year, and shared their excitement at their upcoming record deal. With the under-age band members having all returned to Phoenix to get their parents to sign on the dotted line, the contractual paperwork was finally completed; Alice Cooper would sign to Straight the following day.

Hendrix was less enthusiastic about their plans to hand their management over to Cohen as well, though. Instead, he suggested they accompany him back to his hotel, the Landmark, to meet a guy that Hendrix himself had only just been introduced to, Shep Gordon.

New Yorker Gordon briefly outlines his career to that point: "I graduated from the University of Buffalo, and went to the New School for Social Research for a semester. And then to LA as a probation officer for a day." Now he was selling copies of the *LA Free Press* on the corner of Sunset Boulevard, and living at the Landmark because he had nowhere else to go. But he was also in the music biz too; together with his business partner, accountant Joe Greenberg, Gordon was the West Coast agent for the Left Banke, fellow New Yorkers who hit a couple of years before with 'Don't Walk Away Renee'.* And he was always on the lookout for fresh talent.

According to Vince, laughing at the story later, it was Janis Joplin who introduced Gordon to Hendrix, but only after she'd decked him when he broke up what he thought was a fight between her and some guy. Turned out that they were fucking, and Janis was just being noisy, but she apologised the next morning when she saw him by the pool, and Hendrix did the rest. His attempts to give the Left Banke a foothold in Los Angeles notwithstanding, Gordon did not have a moment's experience as a manager, but Hendrix shrugged his complaints away. "You're Jewish, aren't you? You should be a manager."

Gordon agreed. On the spot, Alice Cooper was signed to the newly-formed Alive Enterprises and the following day in Zappa's office, Gordon took control immediately. The proffered contract was for one LP, with options on two subsequent releases. He accepted that, and he nodded to Zappa and Cohen's offer of a $6,000 annual advance. But when Cohen announced that Straight would keep the band's publishing, Gordon swooped. They could co-publish. The band would keep 50 percent for

---

* Forty years later, Alice would recall the connection when he covered the Left Banke's 'Pretty Ballerina' for his *Dirty Diamonds* album.

itself. Later, he admitted that he didn't have a clue what publishing meant. But if Cohen and Zappa wanted it, then it had to be worth something.

"The record and concert business was innocent and exiting," Gordon continued. "Tickets were three, four and five dollars, and record companies helped to develop talent." The manager, on the other hand, was there to "try to keep a sense of reality in the individual artists, though hard to do. A sense of how lucky they are and how fleeting success can be, and to hold onto what works and be thankful, rather than jealous, greedy, angry. These are always the things that seem to break up bands as they start to get successful."

His own responsibilities were "manifold. But first and foremost to be the one person who isn't a yes man… tell it as it is… protect their money… build a highway to fame and fortune that they can travel down and warn them when they take a wrong turn in the road or their ego starts to blur their vision." And in return, he expected the artist "to show up on time and do their jobs".

Gordon didn't request, and has never accepted, a management contract with the band. Everything that he and Alice Cooper, individually and collectively, would do together was agreed on a handshake at best, including his 15 per cent share of the initial advance. He was already aware that he would be ploughing all of that, and more besides, back into the band; the $6,000 was not simply living expenses and play money, after all. It was intended to finance the recording of their first album too. A recording that Straight Records demanded be delivered to them within a month.

In the event, 12 of the 13 cuts intended for what would become Alice Cooper's debut album were taped in three days straight, the band locking themselves away in the studio to play and replay their regular stage set live, and then go through the tapes to find the best-sounding takes. The 13th song, 'Levity Ball', was lifted from the Whisky tapes (although loyalties to their favourite hang-out saw the eventual album claim it was the Cheetah) after a studio version resolutely failed to capture the same energies.

It was basic, it was rudimentary, it was a far cry from the weeks and weeks that other bands liked to spend agonising over their art. But Gordon knew, and the band agreed, that Alice Cooper was not an act that lent itself to perfection. What the record would deliver was what the group itself distributed, a hard, loud, fistful of noise, pounding into the listener's head forever.

Frank Zappa had originally intended to produce the sessions personally, but it soon became apparent that his vision of the group was very different to their own. "I remember Frank came to only one recording session for the... album," Michael Bruce told Billy James, while Alice told Canadian journalist Mike Quigley, "Frank wanted to produce us, [but] he didn't get the feeling that we wanted. Nothing on him, but he wasn't on the same trip. He started to, but we said we weren't happy with the feelings we got off the cut... the album now is more us than the other production that Frank did. I think he was trying to produce more of a... sort of a cheaper image."

Abandoned, too, was a mad Zappa scheme to press the album onto a series of five-inch "hip pocket" sized discs and package them in a biscuit tin, under the name Alice Cookies. Alice Cooper were essentially on their own. "Frank is too political," Alice shrugged to *Rolling Stone* the following year. "He takes himself too seriously. He acts like Hitler, and with that moustache he even looks like Hitler."

In Zappa's stead, another member of the Mothers, Ian Underwood, was delegated to oversee the sessions (he would be uncredited on the final record), but a few of Zappa's methods did survive the great man's departure. Neal Smith told Billy James, "Frank Zappa said he wanted the album to sound like a car driving past a garage while a band was playing. That was his goal, and I think he more or less achieved it. He had us set our amps around the drum kit so there was total leakage. We would run down the song, setting the dials on our amps and stuff, just trying to get a proper sound going that we could record and Zappa would say, 'We got a take'. We would be like, 'What, we didn't even play the song yet'."

Compensating for what they lacked in studio finesse by amplifying the theatricality, the Coopers bar-hopped deliriously from the infuriatingly unfinished 'Titanic Overture' that opens the proceedings by leaving even the most casual ear expecting something more, through to the beat band psych of 'Reflected', a song that would enjoy a renewed lease of life three years later when it was redesigned as 'Elected'.

Everywhere, the sounds of mid-sixties Stones, late period Pretty Things, off-kilter Beatles and a railroad disaster full of British Invaders was fed through the band's own world view and spat out as something that could almost have been tuneful if it had not been so skewed. Painstakingly, the band learned a handful of themes from James Bond movies, then learned them again played backwards. Hey presto, a new melody. They penned their first ballad, 'Come With Us Now', drawing on Alice's love of old

Burt Bacharach, and for a while they used it to open their set, a deceptive calm before the upcoming storm.

They sat and watched movies, then imagined how they might have sounded if Alice Cooper had written the soundtrack – 'Levity Ball' was their imaginary contribution to *Carnival Of Souls*.

Onstage epics were exaggerated, minor ideas were laid down as they stood. Two years later, Alice Cooper would sweep up a clutch of these snippets, including the mood-mangled 'The More I Want You To Know', and convert them into one epic medley, the behemothic 'Halo Of Flies'. Another loose sketch would one day become 'Dead Babies'. But in 1969, the vignettes were allowed to stand on their own two feet, a fractured feature of an album that felt like a roomful of mirrors had just been shattered, then reassembled with no care for cohesion. What better title could there be for such a creation, then, than the one they all agreed upon? *Pretties For You*.

"I like *Pretties For You* for its originality," Neal Smith told *Goldmine* in 2000. "When you create music that sounds like other music that's going on at the time, it becomes dated. On the other hand, when you do something that's different, it has a better chance of holding up over time. Unfortunately, when we went into the studio we were very green and we didn't know anything about the recording process."

Alice Cooper gigged on. In September 1968, they landed a booking in Denver, Colorado, opening for Steppenwolf. October took them to Philadelphia for a show with the MC5, played out in front of an audience of just 100 people. They landed a three-night residency at the Bank in Torrance, subverting the subtle rent-a-rock pop of Three Dog Night, and Zappa seemed to line them up to play every California show he was offered, including a two-night showcase at the Shrine that he devoted in its entirety to the Straight Records roster. *Pretties For You* would not be hitting the stores until June 1969, at the behest of distributors Warner Brothers. But there was no harm in getting the buzz going early.

Shep Gordon toiled furiously meanwhile, all but living on the telephone as he worked to book the band into every venue he could, no matter how far away it might be, or how askance the venue itself might feel. One of the first bookings he ever got for the band was at an army base in Colorado, the group billed as Alice Cooper & the Hollywood Blondes, and one can only imagine how the average military recruit responded when he discovered the true nature of Miss C and her playmates.

It was not at all unusual for the group to pile into the van and drive halfway across the country, just to fulfil a lone booking, but if they ever complained about the seemingly disproportionate effort that the journey required, Gordon had his answer ready. Too many bands became stars in their own towns, and were completely unknown every place else. Alice Cooper were spreading their name across the country, and no matter how far they had to travel to do it, if they could make one kid sit up and listen, then that was one kid who might buy the album. Or bring his friends to see them the next time they played.

Nobody doubted that it was Zappa's name, rather than the band's, that brought them the most work; sometimes Gordon only had to tell a promoter that Alice Cooper were signed to Frank Zappa's label and he had another date filled on his desk calendar. And when they weren't working, the band was in rehearsal, shut away says Alice in an empty building called Psychedelic Supermarket, named for but otherwise unrelated to the legendary club of the same name in Boston. From there it was just a short drive back to the Landmark, where Gordon had now installed the band members; and from there, it was just a short walk into the heart of Hollywood.

And it was Hollywood that created the Alice Cooper band, the materialistic hedonism of a city-within-a-city that was built upon the dreams of Mammon and Babylon, and which had fought so garishly for its own principles even as the rest of the world, or certainly the West Coast, seemed hell bent on reaching utopia. It was a dreamland, the home of the American movie industry, where the only currency that counted for anything was naked ambition. As Alice later remarked, no self-respecting rock star of the day would admit that they did it for the sex and drugs, the fast cars and flashy clothes, and even when Zappa's Mothers of Invention drew a line in the sand, titling their third LP *We're Only In It For The Money*, the confession was deflected by the sleeve design's deliberate parody of the Beatles' *Sgt Pepper*.

Alice Cooper, on the other hand, made no bones of the fact that they wanted to be famous, wanted to make money, and they didn't give a damn who or what they had to trample in order to achieve those ends.

They masked their backgrounds, their private lives, their inner selves. There would be no acoustic confessionals from Alice Cooper, even as the rest of Los Angeles lined up behind the ghastly sirens of James Taylor, Carole King and the rest of the singer-songwriter tsunami that swept out of Laurel Canyon to broadcast their neuroses to the world. Indeed, when history repeats the Cooper band's claim that they remained renowned as the worst band in Los Angeles, it is merely parroting the words of the louder rock critics, those who found in Taylor and co a solace for their own private demons.

To the kids who packed out four nights at the Whisky at the beginning of 1969, whooping and roaring through a performance that was now so tight that the crowd could barely breathe, the Alice Cooper band was neither a joke nor a sore thumb. It was liberation. It was freedom. It was a reminder that rock could still roll, and that nothing could slow it down, not even the theft of the Coopers' amplifiers from the back of their van one night in late January.

"The whole thing is a direct product of television and movies and America," Alice told Michael Quigley in a 1969 magazine interview that was swiftly co-opted for the band's own press kit. "Cause that's where America's based. That's where their heart is from the sex and violence of TV and the movies, and that was our influence. We weren't brought up under a blues influence. We were brought up under an electronics influence – the bomb (I'm not knocking the bomb, I think the bomb's a gas), but television has been the main influence for this generation, and that's why this whole thing is happening. You just let your lower self go, and then it takes on all these aspects of the society – the city with horns blowing, the people yelling things at each other, and the all-in-all violence and chaos of the city. Put that on stage with music, and that's what this is."

"The worst bill I ever saw was at the Whisky," shuddered guitarist Andrew Gold, one of the myriad young hopefuls whose own laid-back ways and tuneful songsmithery were riding the new wave of adult balladeering. "Linda Ronstadt was playing a week there [February 19-23, 1969] and Alice Cooper was opening. I couldn't believe it, nobody could believe it."

Ronstadt was still rising at the time, still working to shrug off her early folk roots in favour of the broader pop confections that would ultimately establish her as one of the biggest female American superstars of the seventies. Her debut album was awaiting release; most people knew her still as the voice behind the Stone Poneys. But a sizeable crowd would turn out anyway to experience what, even then, was widely regarded as the most beautiful singing voice in Los Angeles. And what they did get as an appetiser?

"This is a song called 'Ten Minutes Before The Worm'... this is 'Earwigs To Eternity'... this is 'Lay Down And Die, Goodbye'... this is 'Don't Blow Your Mind Like We Did Last Summer'." And every one, howled the hippies as they fled for cover, was distinguishable from its predecessor only because the band seemed to play a little louder each time.

Glen Buxton flashed an evil smile. "If we thought an audience needed something extra, if we knew before we went on that they probably wouldn't like us, we would start loud and then just keep inching up until by the end, we were deafening. Some bands start loud and they have nowhere to go, but it's like the guitar in Spinal Tap that goes up to 11. Mine went up to 20."

"People were walking out, leaving their drinks on the bar and just walking out," Gold recalled. "There were more people on the sidewalk outside than there were in the club, but you could still hear Alice Cooper, and I still say that the band wasn't even playing music by that point, they were just making a free-form noise with everybody screaming over it because they didn't care. They wanted to make their mark on the night and that's what they did."

Alice did not argue. "It's like an art experiment to see what you can do to make people react," he told writer Eve Rizzo that same year. "And what you can present in a certain way. Most of us were art majors in college for two years and the same philosophies hold true in art and music. Alice Cooper's specialities have no boundaries... whatever comes up, comes up... and we'll do it!"

Buxton however denied that the band ever abandoned their set in order to further enrage an audience. "We would never have done that. For a start it wouldn't have been fair to anybody who did want to watch us play. And secondly, we were already most people's worst nightmare, playing our normal set. Why would we need to be any worse than that?"

At the same time, however, the band did little to counter the rumours or, indeed, the criticisms that circulated around their performances, positively revelling in their reputation and even smiling indulgently when another group came along, the quirky sibling-led Halfnelson, that threatened to dislodge them from that roost.

Soon to emerge on a wider stage as Sparks, Halfnelson were fronted by the brothers Ron and Russell Mael and, by their own admission, they eyed Alice Cooper's reputation for a theatrical presentation with some awe. It was not, however, until the entire band went to a Coopers gig in the meeting room above the cafeteria at the UCLA that they realised just how much further they had to go.

Halfnelson drummer Harley Feinstein recalls, "We sat down on the floor right in front. At this time Halfnelson was in a very early stage in its development. We had talked a lot about the concept of adding theatrics to our live performances but I don't recall that anyone had come up with any specific ideas other than wearing some make-up and fancy clothes.

"The band took the stage, the stage lights went on and they started playing. We were thunderstruck. We had been saying, 'We need to do something theatrical' and Alice Cooper was already doing it 1,000% more than we could have possibly imagined. One of the young ladies in our entourage, Diane Cunningham, who was an intellectual artist type stated that she checked her pulse while 'Sun Arise' was playing and her pulse was beating precisely to the beat of the song. After it was over we just said, 'Wow could we ever be that amazingly good?'"

Sparks would, of course, come to grips with their ambition in the end. But for now, Alice Cooper had the field to themselves. "We were going out of our way to be obnoxious," Alice admitted to journalist Michael Delaney. "We used to get so drunk that we couldn't play. I'd wear a pink clown suit and go on stage and pass out after two numbers. I'd tell the kids to get lost and they would. They loved it but they left. I was so drunk. We were notorious for things we hadn't done. People were making things up about us and writing them down. They were taking Alice Cooper and making us into this anti-hero thing."

Besides, not everybody hated them. Journalist Eve Rizzo told *Scene II* readers, "Their sound can best be described as exciting... fast... loud – their set includes a variety of numbers – no single show is like another. Each performance is a surprise, due to their unpredictable use of costumes and scenery. Their costumes are absolutely gorgeous – all created by Neal's sister Homer Fudgecake!"

The album release drew closer. In March 1969, the Coopers played a festival at Speedway Meadows, in the shadow of San Francisco's Golden Gate Bridge, alongside Crazy Horse and the MC5. The following month, they were opening a string of arena shows for the Mothers of Invention. A tour was arranged, criss-crossing the country in the weeks before the album's release. Tentacles stretched as far afield as Ohio, Pennsylvania and

Chicago, and in June they reached New York City for the first time, a couple of the shows at the Felt Forum giving way to a residency at the Scene, entrepreneur Steve Paul's already-legendary hang-out on 8th and 46th Street in Manhattan.

There, the likes of Hendrix, the Doors, Iggy Pop and the Velvet Underground had already carved themselves into the local folklore; now Alice Cooper were to do the same with a string of five shows in six nights (they broke amidships for a gig in Philadelphia) that Glen Buxton recalled as "truly eye opening… because it was the first time we played to an audience that actually understood what we were doing".

New York and Los Angeles were more than the geographic poles of the American entertainment industry. Culturally, too, they were at odds, the one sunblissed and doped out, the other gritty and speeding. The Velvet Underground were a New York archetype, although even New York itself didn't realise the fact at the time; so was the poetic beat madness of the Fugs; so were any of the many bands that musically, lyrically and most of all physically kicked the California mantra of peace and love back into the hippies' smug, blissed-out faces.

Alice agreed. He told *Scene II*, "Every audience is a positive or negative one, depending on what you give them when you first go on stage. It's like a reflection. If you want to see it in the audience you have to produce it and they'll pick up on it and then it becomes like communication. The things up on stage is contagious. If you smile a lot, or if you see someone who's really happy up on stage or if you see someone who's apathetic, you're the same way. So it's up to the performer."

Alice Cooper played to their own every excess, and New York howled for more. "Alice Cooper, a musically driving and visually exciting act, had a strong first set at Steve Paul's Scene on June 12," reported the trade magazine *Billboard*, wondering "how much of Alice Cooper is a put-on", but essentially concluding that it didn't matter. With their "big sound" and "good solos", and the "wild ending" afforded by the showcased 'Don't Blow Your Mind Like We Did Last Summer', *Billboard* was seemingly predicting big things for "a wild group". And the magazine's voice would not be in the wilderness for long.

Chapter Six

They Kill Chickens
(Don't They?)

With their first full US tour kicking off in June, the band was still on the road as the first reviews of *Pretties For You* came in, a mixed bag that ranged from *Record World*'s insistence that they had taken "a cue from John Cage and Frank Zappa... for this package of strange, discombobulated sounds and songs", to the *Arizona Republic*'s somewhat puzzled contemplation of "music [that] is supposed to convey a happy, bright, optimistic attitude about life... in order to provide an alternative to all the social criticism and pessimism about the state of the world found in so much contemporary music."

The result, the paper's critic concluded, "is quite comfortably at home in the 'heavy psychedelic' category, whatever that means", and local feeling seemed to be more excited by the refusal of sundry local record stores to allow the album to go on display without a "censored" sticker to mask the flash of female undergarment that artist Ed Beardsley had included on the cover art. Zappa's original idea of releasing the album in a cookie tin seemed so old-fashioned compared to the controversy that the band was now embroiled within.

The tour was not only designed to promote the album, however. Indeed, close to a year on from its recording, the group had already outgrown it, and they readily admitted that, were they to be recording it today, *Pretties*

For You would emerge as a very different-sounding disc. They proved that in concert by extending and elaborating the best of the record and simply shunting the remainder to one side, occasionally incorporating elements of one song into the birth of another, and pushing ahead towards the second LP that Straight was already demanding.*

The tour was also a fact-finding mission, striking out into the unknown in search of a city that might prove more receptive to the Alice Cooper band than Los Angeles. Hollywood was home, but there were preconceptions there that might never be shaken, no matter how popular the band became elsewhere. Far better, Shep Gordon decreed (and the band readily agreed) to find a city that loved them from the outset; that could, in effect, become their own Cavern Club, a place to build and refine and build again, before an audience that was not constantly shouting out for 'Fire And Rain', and wetting its collective pants every time another solo troubadour washed up in town.

All summer long, Alice Cooper played the festival circuit, sprawling multi-band events in Toronto, New York, Eugene, Vancouver and Seattle, and each one a chance to view the industry's idea of the new decade's up-and-comers first hand.

In Seattle, they caught Led Zeppelin rising like Behemoth above the already anachronistic sounds of the Doors, the Byrds and the Flying Burrito Brothers. At the Toronto Pop Festival, they played the Varsity Stadium alongside Sly & the Family Stone, Blood Sweat & Tears and Al Kooper ("I can't believe I never realised how close our names were!" – Glen Buxton); in London, Ontario, they blew away even Keith Emerson's Nice, and left the local *London Free Press* drooling, "Alice Cooper... a light-popping, five-man rock group from Arizona... stomped on a metal satchel, speared the big bass drum, threw microphones and stands on the stage, drummed out all the violent motions of war, and died. It was a groovy scene. And it happened in London."

Everywhere, the unknown and unrated Alice Cooper played their set, usually close to the dawning of the festivities, and then hung around to watch everyone else, meet the musicians, mingle with the audience, and

---

* A new contract extending the original deal across two further LPs would be signed in October 1969, with the first of those discs to be recorded in November.

just get acquainted with what, in the parlance of the times, might be called "the local vibe".

"Often when we perform," Alice told *Cream* magazine, "people don't want to get close; they think they might catch a crab that had the clap or something. They're afraid they might understand a little. We get acid freaks at our concerts that get so tense they want to kill us or something. I remember one guy who was very big and muscular; he jumped on stage while I was doing my Errol Flynn act with a sword. I gallantly put the blade to his chest and he jumped off again. I was magnificent."

And then they reached Detroit.

Michigan in general, but Detroit in particular, felt like home from the moment they arrived there. For Alice himself, that came as no surprise. He was born there, after all, and had spent much of the first ten years of his life in the city. But had he even told the promoter that, before the group was introduced on stage as a home-grown phenomenon? He didn't think so.

On August 3 at the Mount Clemens Pop Festival, on a bill nominally headlined by Country Joe McDonald, John Mayall and Muddy Waters, local heroes the MC5 and the Stooges were already set to tear apart a field filled with blissed-out blues aficionados and leftover psychedelics. The Coopers simply took their intentions even further, announcing their arrival in town with a vibrant blur of vision, sound and outrage. Days later, Detroit's Eastown Theater took the band even closer to its heart and, by the time Alice Cooper returned to the city in October 1969, opening for the Who on their triumphant *Tommy* tour at the Grande Riviera, the decision to relocate the entire operation to Detroit had been made in every way bar the bus tickets.

Before that could happen, however, there was one more legend to hammer into place: a spot on the bill at the Rock and Roll Revival Festival in Toronto on September 13.

Destined, by virtue of film-maker DA Pennebaker's camera crews, and the rest of the day's near-mythic status, to become one of the most talked-about events in the early history of Alice Cooper, the Toronto Rock and Roll Revival Festival was, as its name suggests, originally intended as a showcase for a couple of returning old rockers. Chuck Berry and Jerry Lee Lewis were both scheduled to appear, with their own possibly dubious ability to draw the crowds supplemented by the addition of sundry bigger names to the bill.

Of these, the promise of John and Yoko Lennon with an all-star Plastic Ono Band was the carrot that drew most fans to the festival grounds, albeit one that was to prove somewhat divisive. After a short set of rock'n'roll oldies, Lennon essentially turned the set over to Yoko, who yowled and yipped her way through two free-form numbers that really did seem to go on forever. Even the band, led by a bemused-looking Eric Clapton, seemed less than enamoured by her capering.

The Doors were there too, and through their auspices, Gene Vincent, perhaps the greatest of all the fifties originals, and a man whose friendship with Jim Morrison is the kind of relationship from which novels are made, a twilight noir zone in which one broken rocker's Hemingway slurs up to the other's shattered Dylan Thomas, and they drink one another under the table.

Except Morrison was still firing on all cylinders at that time, hanging out at the Shamrock Inn on Santa Monica Boulevard, just enjoying being famous, with his own disintegration far, far off in a still unscripted future. So Vincent took on both of those roles for himself.

Jim Morrison himself summed up Vincent's appeal. "He was always doing weird stuff like jumping out of cars, breaking his body, and never seeing a doctor. We drank two bottles of bourbon a day. I don't remember the first time we met because I was trying to be drunker than he was. I was in the studio when [he] recorded 'Caravan', which is a very difficult vocal. Outside he was shaking like a leaf from all that alcohol in his system, but he went in and sang it in two takes and walked out completely sober."

It was Morrison who bartered, begged, and finally blasted Vincent onto the Toronto bill, and the initial idea was that the Doors would join Vincent on stage and give everyone a treat. Scheduling snafus ensured that it didn't happen like that, but Toronto was a triumph nonetheless, and not only for Vincent. It was a triumph for his backing band as well: Dennis Dunaway, Glen Buxton, Michael Bruce and Neal Smith.

It was the band's success at the Toronto Pop Festival earlier in the summer that nudged them onto the bill. Smith remembers, "We were beginning to get a reputation up there, which was why we were booked. And then we were asked if we'd back Gene as well, the Doors were supposed to do it and for some reason they couldn't, so we were asked and we jumped on it like a heartbeat.

71

"It was great. We were in rehearsals for a couple of days in somebody's basement in Toronto, Gene was there and he was a very, very cool guy, we got to know him really well, and of course he was a big inspiration for the Beatles and the Doors as well. Gene was one of the first people ever to wear black leather pants on stage and a lot of people followed that, like Elvis and of course Jim Morrison, and all the guys from the Doors were on the side of the stage watching the show because they were such huge fans of Gene's."

Indeed, by the time the set climaxed with a scorching 'Be Bop A Lula', half the crowd was in rapture, half was stunned into silence, and John Lennon was on stage, embracing his idol in tears. And the Cooper band was reeling from the sheer dichotomy of the afternoon. Right now they were conquering heroes, the unrecognised faces who pushed Gene Vincent to his greatest musical triumph in a decade. Less than an hour earlier, they were demons on the verge of crucifixion.

The Coopers' musical performance that day rarely receives any mention, and that despite a slew of semi-official live albums circulating of the show, most of which not only, laughably, completely misname the songs performed, but also add a couple that have nothing to do with either Alice Cooper or the festival – 'Ain't That Just Like A Woman' and 'Goin' To The River' were recorded by Canadian rocker Ronnie Hawkins in 1964!

But fine crunches through 'Fields Of Regret', 'Freak Out', 'Nobody Likes Me' and 'No Longer Umpire' are joined by a surprise leap back to a lyrically revised 'Don't Blow Your Mind', while a lengthy instrumental thrash looked forward to the renewed version of 'Lay Down And Die, Goodbye' that would soon be taped for the Coopers' second album.

Neal Smith recalls the band's stage show at that time. "We'd have the smoke bombs and Alice was ripping up the feather pillows, and Mike Bruce had some CO_2 canisters and would blast the feathers into the audience, and that was the finale of the show. It was," he understates, "very explosive." Tonight, though, all of that paled into insignificance alongside another onstage accoutrement altogether – a chicken. Well, a chicken, and the guy who thought it would be a good idea to bring a live bird to a rock festival, and then toss it onto the stage while Alice Cooper were playing. Alice threw it back – he thought it would fly away.

"I mean, they have wings, don't they?"

Instead, the audience ripped the bird to pieces, and the next day there was just one talking point in the press. That Alice had bitten off the bird's head and sucked out its blood. "After that," Alice said ruefully, "we had to check in with the Humane Society every town we played."

Four years later, he related the story to the *New Musical Express*. "Someone threw a chicken on-stage. I chased it around for a bit and finally gave it to someone in the front row. Now, if the chicken later died, I'm sorry. I don't know what happened. Next day, Frank Zappa came up to me and said, 'I hear you tore the head off a chicken and drank its blood'. And I said, 'Oh really?' But I didn't deny it. I love rumours."

In fact, Alice later claimed that the truth was even sicker than the rumours. In 1997, he told *Kerrang!*: "The first 10 rows of the audience were all the people in wheelchairs. The cripples tore the chicken to pieces...."

Of course, the headlines screamed louder than the truth. With Shep Gordon gleefully egging on reporters who came to his office for confirmation of the story, not quite confirming it but certainly not denying it either, Alice's onstage chicken sacrifice became one of the year's biggest stories, known even to people who might never otherwise have heard of Alice Cooper.

"There was a lot of cool stuff that happened that night," says Neal Smith, "that really gets overshadowed by the chicken incident. That was just a great sound bite for the press and the media. But the thing with Gene Vincent was really really cool and it was almost like a rite of passage for us."

It was also a passing of the flame. A decade earlier, after all, Vincent had been regarded as controversial, even distasteful, as he dragged his crippled frame onto the stage and made no attempt to disguise the lame leg legacy of a near-fatal motorbike accident. His own defence was that he was simply being himself, and he was; how much more distasteful would it have been for him to have hidden his disability away, as though it were something to be ashamed of.

Alice Cooper did not have a disability to flaunt. Not physically, anyway. But mentally? That was another matter entirely. Gene Vincent had a twisted body. Alice Cooper had a twisted mind.

Neither was it simply the gullible public and sensation-hungry tabloid hacks who were hooked by the Coopers' craziness. The Who's Pete

Townshend was so outraged when he heard the most distorted version of the chicken incident, and so unshakeably convinced by its veracity, that a couple of years later he included a reference to "bands that kill chickens" in the song 'Put The Money Down'. And when *Rolling Stone* interviewed him in 1982, and the conversation turned to stagecraft, his continued disgust would have been admirable if it wasn't so palpably, foolishly misplaced.

"I remember being horrified seeing Alice Cooper beheading live chickens on stage. And it didn't really redeem him that I had smashed guitars, y'know? Somewhere there was a line. I don't know whether it was because it was live, or because it was real blood. But the fact that he later went on to make some great records didn't redeem him either. He's sick, tragic, pathetic, and will always be that way. I'll say hello to him on the street, but I'll never tip my hat to him."

The fact somebody as intelligent and media-aware as Townshend should not only believe the hype, but actually convince himself that he had witnessed the crime with his own eyes, is a potent advertisement for the pervasiveness of Alice Cooper's growing reputation.

Yet the chicken incident would soon become just one in an entire litany of legends that hovered over Alice Cooper's head. Soon there were reports, according to writer John Grissim, of Alice "floating a weather balloon full of worms over the audience and popping it with a BB gun. Or tearing apart crabs and fish and throwing the pieces to the crowd. In Chicago he once terrified the Kinetic Playground by toying with a giant boa constrictor that had just eaten rabbit. He once shaved several cats (his own he claims) from the waist down, spray-painted them, and released them into the audience. One time in Vancouver, B.C., a naked girl ran onto the stage and was promptly incorporated into the act when the group covered her with shaving cream, added a bag of feathers and flagellated her with dead chickens."

One night, Alice reported incredulously, he was asked if it was true that he had set fire to a dog on stage. He did not deny it and, while the attentions of the animal welfare departments (not to mention the band members' own sensibilities) ensured that there would be no repeat of the chicken incident on stage, Alice Cooper used their reputation to their advantage anyway, rarely contradicting fans who passed on their own favourite tales of dismembered dogs and crucified cats, and throwing further gasoline on the pyre by incorporating an inflatable rubber rabbit into the stage show, and killing that instead.

Neither was it always a gratuitous act of violence. Sometimes, Alice insisted, it prevented trouble too.

The Sagnisaw Festival, on November 26, 1969, was already teetering on the edge of a full-scale riot when the Coopers took the stage. Presupposing the horrific security misjudgements that the Rolling Stones would make at Altamont Speedway just days later, the promoter apparently turned a blind eye to the local Hells Angels' insistence that they be placed in charge of the venue's security, and had already been beaten up by one group of bikers. Another posse had chained a girl to the back of a bike and dragged her around the grounds through the crowds. By the time Alice came out in his nightdress, singing "nobody loves me" in a little-girl-lost voice, the Angels were ready for blood.

They got it. As the rabbit appeared on stage and the band members started their own assault on its hapless form, the bikers leaped up to join them, beating and kicking and screaming for blood, while the musicians gathered around them to chant "kill it, kill it" to the rhythm of Smith's drums. By the time the bunny was finally killed, Alice laughed later, the bikers were so exhausted that they'd completely lost their lust for more gore.

Over 7,000 onlookers gave the Coopers a standing ovation and that, says Shep Gordon, was the night he knew that Alice Cooper was destined for stardom. Yet, no matter how heavily the likes of *Creem* magazine (itself based locally) and journalist Lester Bangs championed the city's favourite rock'n'roll sons, all admitted that it would take something like a minor miracle to ever push a Detroit act into the same commercial framework as a similarly placed New York or LA band.

There was a mood to Detroit rock, a feeling and a sense of purpose that simply didn't sit comfortably with the USA at large, and no matter how hard the likes of the MC5 or the Amboy Dukes pushed themselves round the country, they were never going to shake off the "Detroit band" appellation.

Alice Cooper recognised this and, for the time being, accepted it. Live performances were no longer about clambering over the heads of out-of-town headliners to try and get attention, because audiences had usually already decided where their own allegiances lay. It was about pushing yourself ahead of the other bands on the circuit, building the impression of rivalry between one group and another, and then going head to head in the Grande Ballroom, to see who would come out on top this week.

In terms of theatricality, nobody streaked ahead of the Stooges. Fronted by the lean, lithe Iggy Pop, and powered by a cocktail of anger, adrenalin and whatever drugs the ravenous Stooges could get their hands upon, the band thrived on notoriety, violence and action.

Away from Detroit, knowing critics would look spiffily down their noses at the Stooges and describe them as naïve, banal, brutal. But Pop was a born showman, and the Stooges were a riff machine programmed to destroy every time it hit the stage. Alice Cooper realised that the first time they opened for Iggy and found themselves wanting in every department. But it would not take them long to catch up.

"I don't expect people to understand our music right now," Alice told *Rolling Stone* in 1970. "Iggy Stooge is using his music and theatrics as a totality too. No one considers that the music behind him is the whole backbone of Iggy. They just look at him on the level of his stage act. If he didn't have Ron Asheton and the rest of those cats behind him it wouldn't be the same." Years later, he admitted that he hated having to follow the Stooges onto the stage. The audience would already be worn out.

The decision to relocate Alice Cooper to Detroit was not taken precipitously. In his all-encompassing history of the Detroit rock scene *Grit, Noise And Revolution*, author and DJ David A Carson notes how the Alice Cooper band only gradually infiltrated itself into the regional scenery as 1969 shifted into 1970. At the same time, however, the nature of the shows they played were ample testament to the speed with which the city accepted them.

Most of Detroit and, indeed, Michigan's most legendary sons ran across the band at one point or another, and most came away with very firm opinions of what they witnessed. The Frost's Dick Wagner, who would go on to become such an integral part of both the band's and the solo Alice's futures, first met the group on one of these visits, and ignited a friendship that survives to this day. Stooges guitarist Ron Asheton, meanwhile, recalled "some incredible nights with Alice Cooper, those guys really thought they could put the drink away, which isn't surprising given who they hung out with in LA. But then they came to Ann Arbor and it went up to a whole new level."

Musically, Asheton saw the early Alice Cooper as "a great rock'n'roll band looking for a reason to play great rock'n'roll. It wasn't until they started hanging out with the Detroit crowd that they really got a handle on what they wanted to do because that was where they finally saw what was possible. Los Angeles sucks you dry no matter how creative you are, look at what happened to us [the Stooges spent an extraordinarily unfruitful few months in LA in 1973], but Detroit won't let you rest, it won't let you sit still, and they came up here and they just caught on fire."

"We felt like fingers that fit into the Detroit glove," Alice agreed in *Alice Cooper, Golf Monster*. "The Stooges, MC5, Amboy Dukes, Bob Seger and now... Alice Cooper! We were in."

Checking into a succession of hotels, their residency usually dependent upon which establishment they owed the least money to, Alice Cooper leaped feet first into the local scene, musically and creatively. A close-knit scene with every band well aware of how it slotted into the local live jigsaw, Detroit recognised the Cooper band's suitability as swiftly as the band did, welcoming them not as outsiders trying to stick a finger into the city pie, but as rank outsiders like themselves.

Times remained hard. Countless nights as the band pulled into another cheap no-name motel, the musicians would flip coins to see who got the bed, who got the foldaway, and who got the floor. Medical problems would go unchecked and untreated until there was sufficient money in the kitty to pay for a doctor's visit, and the musicians were still more likely to self-medicate with whatever a fan or friend might offer them than sink hard-earned cash into filling a prescription. Not when it could better be spent on stage props.

The band's wardrobe continued to expand, formal stage costumes easing in around the thrift store tat that the band had previously relied upon. Alice picked up a strait jacket; Buxton picked up a silver shirt; at a time when so many other acts on the circuit were purposefully dressing down and casual, wearing nothing more extravagant on stage than they would when they were mowing the lawn, Alice Cooper journeyed back to the golden age of glitz and glamour, and the belief that, if you wanted to be treated like a star, you had to look like one.

Alice Cooper had cut their second album now, returning to the studio with producer David Briggs, soon renowned as the co-architect of Neil Young's sonic sculptures and laying down *Easy Action*, a set that was so many light years ahead of its predecessor that even their fans admitted it could have been a different band.

Only 'Still No Air' and 'Refrigerator Heaven' (a title that Alice alone would revisit in 'Cold Ethyl' five years later) looked back at the disconnected musical pastures of *Pretties For You*. Elsewhere, songs were formed and formulated now, ideas were harnessed and held down by something more than willpower alone. Yet there was something still missing; the sense that Alice Cooper may have shaken off their garage band past, but sonically they had yet to shake off the garage.

It is an extraordinarily varied album. 'Mr And Misdemeanour' opens the show, a swaggering rocker that blended the snarl that now took hold of Alice's vocal with a singalong melody that stepped straight out of *West Side Story*, while Glen Buxton lay down a guitar solo that was pure Doors in devotion. 'Below Your Means' might have stepped off the Pretty Things' *Parachute*, so seductively tight was it coiled, and later the Stooges were deliciously invoked by the pell-mell thrust of 'Return Of The Spiders'.

But the heart of *Easy Action* lay in the sheer diversity of the band's playing and material, a mood introduced by 'Shoe Salesman', a sweet semi-ballad that looked wistfully back at Pink Floyd's 'Arnold Layne' while dancing around a teasingly mischievous drug-induced lyric. 'Laughing At Me', too, caught the band in introspective mood, while 'Beautiful Flyaway' was the kind of maddening ditty that Paul McCartney might have grafted onto the Beatles' White Album. But the piece de resistance arrived with the album's conclusion, a seven-minute revisit of 'Lay Down And Die, Goodbye', all but unrecognisable from the two-year-old 45 as it drove back into Stooges territory on the heels of the same super-insistent riff that would, two years later, conquer the world as the Osmonds' 'Crazy Horses'.

Devoid of lyric until the song has just 30 seconds to go, this astonishing instrumental swerves and screams through any number of musical shifts and changes. But whereas the earlier Alice Cooper made such moves with their eye on keeping the audience guessing, this time the moods were exquisitely blended. Each passage in the performance bled from and blended into those on either side, creating a journey through musical space that might have had an eye on the old Pink Floyd influence, but did so with a very different goal in sight. For all their own denials, Floyd soundtracked a life spent getting loaded on acid. The Coopers sounded like they mainlined motor oil.

And so 1969 drew to a close with Alice Cooper looking at a new home, looking towards the release of their second LP, looking towards a future that seemed to dazzle with possibility. There was just one cloud on the horizon. The 18 months that had stretched ahead when the authorities first announced their intentions to hold a draft lottery were almost up. On December 1, 1969, Vince Furnier's fate, together with that of 850,000 other potential inductees who were born between January 1, 1944 and December 31, 1950, would be decided by the drawing of 366 blue plastic capsules, each numbered to represent one birth date, from a glass jar. The order in which the capsules were removed from the jar would determine the order in which young men would be called up.

The first capsule was pulled and the number, 257, was read off: September 14. Every able-bodied man born on that day, in any year between 1944 and 1950, was assigned the first seat on the war wagon. They might as well start packing now.

Next out of the pot, April 24. Followed by December 30. And then, February the four... teenth. Glued to the proceedings like everybody else in the country, Vince held his breath every time the hand reached into the jar. But that was his closest call yet and, the deeper into the night the proceedings stretched, the more he relaxed. Out of 366 possible numbers, his birthdate, February 4, was the 210th out of the pot, a figure so high that even the most pessimistic observer acknowledged that it amounted to an automatic deferment. But if he needed any reminder of just how random the process was, there was that heart-stopping moment at the very top of the show. If he had been born just ten days later, on St Valentine's Day with gruelling irony, he would have been considered A1.

Eighteen months earlier, dodging one draft-shaped bullet, the Coopers had celebrated by moving to Los Angeles. This time, they celebrated by leaving it. In May 1970, midway through another season of ceaseless gigging, the band officially took up residence in Detroit.

With *Easy Action* now on the shelves, Straight Records had handed them a May 1, 1970 deadline for their next album, an impossibility that was avoided only by Zappa's own plans to sell the entire American Straight operation to Warner Brothers. It was not, he insisted, the fact that the label had done little to recoup any of the money invested into it; Zappa's own workload had grown so heavy that he simply did not have the time or effort to give all the attention it required, and he had no intention of becoming an absentee landlord – one of the biggest complaints, of course, being levelled at the Beatles as they watched their Apple label subsumed into corporate anonymity.

Warners could not complain at the purchase price. Zappa put Straight on the market for a bargain $50,000, a fee which was utterly negated when one took into account the money owed to the label by the various artists on the roster. According to the Straight accounts, the Coopers were $100,000 in debt to the label – meaning that if they recouped even half of their debt, Warners wouldn't have spent a dime.

The deal appeared straightforward but sadly, it was not. The question of the band's publishing rights, 50 per cent of which remained owned by Zappa and Cohen, was somehow omitted or even overlooked in the shuffle. The ensuing lawsuit was to drag on for more than four years, and result in a serious blow to the Alice Cooper finances once it was finally resolved. For now, however, with the initial deal done and dusted, Alice Cooper found themselves with another six months in which to write and record their third album. And they were going to make every moment count.

The Coopers wrote furiously, but they were building not simply a new LP but also a new onstage persona. "It's not that we threw all the rule books out the window," says Neal Smith. "But we really had an open slate to work with. There were no preconceived notions. The thing about that group more than anything, and this is why I like to dissect all the musical angles about it, there was nothing from a musical background that couldn't inspire us. We were honing our theatrics, and what we wanted was a way to kill Alice onstage every night, a song to perform while we did it. And by the time we reached the third album, we realised that violence was around us all the time. We never focused on it, but we were thinking we should have an execution on stage."

While roadies Charlie Carnel and Mike Allen set about building the elaborate piece of stage gear they called the Cage Of Fire (an onstage box filled with plastic streamers that would be set ablaze for a dramatic but, sadly, highly dangerous and illegal spectacle), the band set to work on the song that would become the focal point for this climax, 'Black Juju'.

Nine minutes of drum and basics, 'Black Juju' is a primal chant, a silent scream, a lullaby for the sleeping dead, a reminder that bodies need their rest – until it's time to wake up, and the voice that calls for resurrection is one of the eponymous Cooper's most terrifying.

It was Dennis Dunaway who came up with 'Black Juju' in the first place. "He didn't get the nickname Doctor Dreary for nothing," Smith continues. "He was one of the main creators of 'Dead Babies' too."

At first 'Black Juju' was just an idea and a rhythm, pieced together while the Cooper band toured. "It was worked on in hotel rooms," Smith recollects. "We really didn't have a rehearsal studio, our rehearsal studio was the stage, so we sketched it out in hotel rooms on telephone books, and we all agreed it needed a heavy dark African percussion. I wanted to work on the percussion way beyond anything I'd done before.

"I was a percussionist. I learned all the rudiments early on and then went into orchestra, so my background was open to everything percussive, and one of my big influences was jungle drums, native American, African, raw percussion. I wanted it to be a big feature drum song, and it was the perfect vehicle. There's a lot of music that uses that tribal primitive vibe, but for me it was like taking Gene Krupa and putting him on floor Toms. Gene Krupa in Haiti."

The song would be unveiled at the band's first major festival date of the year, on June 13, 1970 at the Cincinnati Pop Festival.

Promoted by Detroit's own Russ Gibb and Michael Quatro, the festival was nominally headlined by such heavyweights as Grand Funk Railroad, Traffic and Mountain. Bob Seger, Ten Years After, Mott The Hoople, Brownsville Station, the Damnation of Adam Blessing and Zephyr also figured on the bill but today the festival is remembered for just two of its performers, who between them put on two of their most legendary performances.

Iggy Pop first. Topless and bedenimed, with silver lamé wrist-length mitts and a studded dog collar, he bemused the show's commentary team, headed by a former *Today Show* announcer named Jack Lescoulie. "Since we broke away for a [commercial break], Iggy has been in and out of the audience three times... we seem to have lost him, we're trying to get a light on him now... there they are..."

The camera closes in on Iggy as he accepts something handed up from the mass of bodies beneath him (the late Stiv Bators, vocalist with Cleveland's Dead Boys, always maintained that he was the responsible party), glances at it for a moment, and then proceeds to smear it across his bare flesh. And then comes what remains one of the most surreal pieces of commentary any rock performance has ever received. "That's peanut butter."

But there was more to come. 'Black Juju' fell halfway through the set this night, but was already a theatrical tour de force, Alice stripping off his shirt and draping his bandmates in white sheets, prowling the stage while they hung motionless… and then a cream pie soared out of the audience and caught him in the face.

The cameras caught it, too, just as they caught the peanut butter, and it was that moment of utterly unchoreographed insanity that ensured the Cooper band would join Iggy in the ensuing 90-minute TV broadcast (Grand Funk, Traffic and Mountain rounded out the programme); ensured, too, that their local, Detroit, stock rose a little bit higher as either the footage, or talk of the footage, became the number one topic of conversation.

Journalist Cub Koda, whose band Brownsville Station, was also on the bill, laughed. "That wasn't a music festival. That was a foods festival. Because first you had Iggy and the peanut butter, and then you had Alice and the cream pie. And I still cannot imagine what possessed anybody to bring a cream pie to a festival. Or how it remained intact until it came time to throw it." Like the chicken at the Toronto Peace festival, there was just something about Alice Cooper that prompted people to bring strange things to a concert.

Suddenly the Alice Cooper band was hot. But old reputations are hard to shake and, when *Rolling Stone* caught the band at Max's Kansas City in September 1970, the legend that they remained the band that people loved to hate was not going away.

Journalist Elaine Gross's opening lines captured the antipathy that still faced the band. "'You suck!' shouted the drunk kid,'" and her observations could have been drawn from any one of a hundred earlier shows. As could Alice's response.

"'Yes, I do,' replied Alice Cooper, laughing. Alice proceeded to crouch down on the stage and began chanting softly into the mike, 'Suck, Suck, Suck.' But the kid really hated Alice, and like a perfect straight man screamed, 'You still suck!'" Until, finally tiring of the aggravation, Alice motioned to security who led the heckler away."

And that, perhaps, was the biggest difference. In the past, Alice Cooper played to audiences and suffered whatever that audience had to offer them. Now they were big enough to control the environment. The crowd was still encouraged to get out of control. But only for as long as the Coopers remained in control.

PORTRAIT OF THE ARTIST AS YOUNG VINCE FURNIER.

ALICE'S HIGH SCHOOL YEARBOOK PHOTO. SPLASH NEWS

ALICE FRONTING THE CORTEZ TRACK TEAM. SPLASH NEWS

AN EARLY PICTURE OF SPIDERS PLAYING LIVE.

ALICE IN 1969 - GETTING READY TO OFFER SOME *PRETTIES FOR YOU*. GETTY IMAGES

HE EYES HAVE IT! MICHAEL OCHS ARCHIVES/GETTY IMAGES

ALICE COOPER IN FULL *KILLER* MODE, 1971. LEFT TO RIGHT: DENNIS DUNAWAY, ALICE, NEAL SMITH, MICHAEL BRUCE AND GLEN BUXTON. BETTMANN/CORBIS

THE ALICE COOPER GROUP FLEX THEIR *MUSCLE OF LOVE*. GEMS/REDFERNS

ALICE AND GIRLFRIEND CINDY LANG. TIM BOXER/GETTY IMAGES

ALICE AND HIS PARENTS MR AND MRS ETHER FURNIER. DAILY MAIL/REX FEATURES

A POSED STUDIO PORTRAIT OF ALICE COOPER NAKED WITH HIS SNAKE. RB/REDFERNS

ALICE AND THE BAND WITH THE LONDON TRAFFIC-STOPPING POSTER, 1972: NEAL SMITH, ALICE, MICHAEL BRUCE, DENNIS DUNAWAY AND GLEN BUXTON. MICHAEL PUTLAND/ GETTY IMAGES

ABOUT TO APPLY HIS MAKE UP. TERRY O'NEILL/GETTY IMAGES

ALICE IS EXECUTED ON THE FIRST EUROPEAN TOUR, OCTOBER 1971, COPENHAGEN, DENMARK. JØRGEN ANGEL/REDFERNS

ALICE COOPER AND HIS BAND WITH FLO AND EDDIE AT A SEX SHOW IN COPENHAGEN, NOVEMBER 1972. JØRGEN ANGEL/REDFERNS

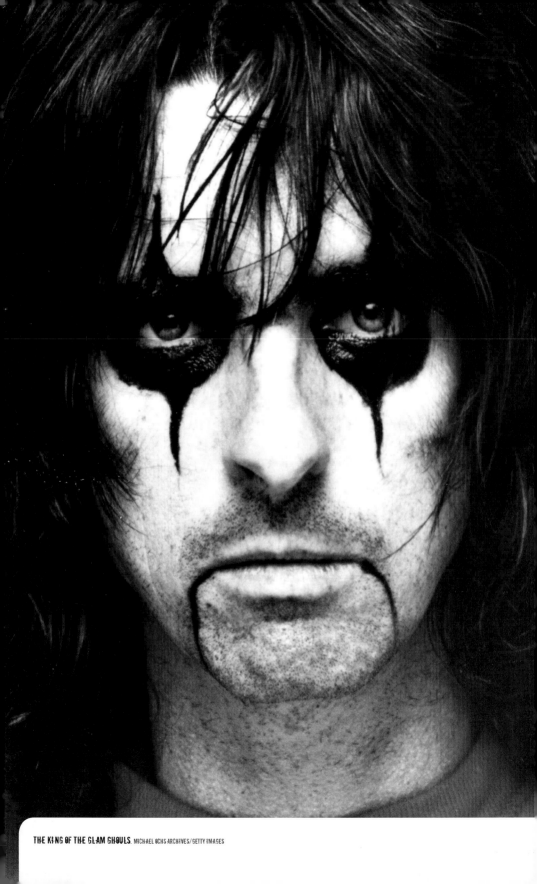

THE KING OF THE GLAM GHOULS. MICHAEL OCHS ARCHIVES/GETTY IMAGES

Yet no matter how stage-managed the act was becoming, still the group remained beyond the pale for many observers, and not only among their public. Their peers, too, continued to view the band with suspicion.

On August 25, 1970, Alice Cooper arrived in Washington DC to take part in one of the summer's most ambitious touring oddities, a mobile festival called the Medicine Show Caravan Show.

Schemed and financed by Warner Brothers, the Medicine Ball Caravan Show was initially unusual in that only one of the bands featured on the bill, Stoneground, actually played every show on the itinerary. The true stars of the enterprise were the Hog Farmers, a gaggle of 150 or so hippies-and-co who travelled across the country, seemingly setting up random concerts wherever they touched down. The musical acts, who included the Mothers of Invention, the Youngbloods, BB King (who replaced the original headliners, the Grateful Dead), Doug Kershaw and Delaney & Bonnie, simply dropped in and out as their own schedules saw fit, with Alice Cooper's involvement restricted to just this one single performance, in DC's L'Enfant Square alongside Sageworth And Drums, Hot Tuna and the ubiquitous Stoneground.

Frank Zappa, whose summer 1970 Pauley Pavilion show was one of those that the Hog Farmers descended on, was less than complimentary about the venture. He condemned "the hiring of fake hippies ($10 a day, 10 days, $100 to 'Get out there on the psychedelic bus and promote this groovy movie'), and then send[ing] a bunch to... concerts... to pass out crappy little leaflets." And Alice Cooper, too, found the venture more trouble than it was worth.

The problems began the moment Alice Cooper arrived at the venue, to discover the Hog Farmers did not want them to appear. "They hassled us more than anybody ever did," Alice told *Rolling Stone* a few weeks later. "'We don't like them, they're theatrical. We don't want them to go on. They might break our microphones.' And we said, 'What are you talking about? Warner Brothers hired us to go on this thing'."

What they were talking about was a gig back in May in San Francisco, with Alice Cooper sharing the bill with the Stooges and the Flaming Groovies. Alembic, the company providing the PA for the Medicine Ball, had been working that show too and, according to the company's records, the Coopers were responsible for trashing three expensive microphones.

The company did not want to see a repeat of the carnage, and was prepared to enforce its stance in the most dramatic way possible. Alembic was also responsible for recording the concert for the souvenir movie and LP that Warner Brothers intended releasing. If it refused to roll the tapes, there was nothing anybody could do about it.

Alice Cooper would not back down either, though. They had been booked to play the concert, and they intended playing it. Journalist John Grissim, documenting the tour for the book *We Have Come For Your Daughters: What Went Down On The Medicine Ball Caravan*, continued, "The argument is heated and personal, but in the end the necessity of the moment produces a stalemate."

"We had to get the Washington police to let us on," Alice told *Rolling Stone*. "And then [Hot Tuna] came up and told the people who were running the PA to let us play. 'We dig them, and they'll use our equipment.' So we went on and used [Hot Tuna's] equipment, and had the crowd standing. It was really incredible."

Alice Cooper took the stage and, true to his threats, Alembic's Bob Mathews unplugged the 16-track. But nobody noticed and nobody cared. Clad in a pretty frock and a silk scarf, Alice commenced the burlesque grind that always announced his intentions, and began slowly to strip down to a black body stocking, "a gaunt-vindictive horribly anaemic wicked witch straight out of the Wizard of Oz," shuddered Grissim, but of course the movie was only just beginning.

François Reichenbach, filming the event for the intended movie, was spellbound. Grissim again: "As Alice vamps and swirls, Francois likewise weaves in unconscious counterpoint, shouting instructions to his crew, pointing, gesticulating, clasping his hands, and beaming with unalloyed delight. Alice begins his finale with an eerie hypnotic ritual, removing his necklace to swing an amulet back and forth, repeating, 'Sleep. All bodies need sleep,' with the cracked voice of an old woman while the music takes on clockwork syncopation. The stage falls dark save for a single spot on the amulet."

'Black Juju' had reached its appointed spot at the end of the set now, and while the planned execution was still in the wings, it was a shattering climax regardless. Still crouching in the dark, still holding every eye in the place in his grasp, he reached slowly down to the stage, to where a single dazzling spotlight had been secreted between the monitors.

His fingers groped for a moment for the switch, as Neal Smith's drums continued the clockwork beat. And then the spotlight flashed on and as the audience reeled back in dazzled shock, Alice was screaming "wake up!" and the band hit the riff that powers the song, a theme that restaged the Missa Luba's 'Sanctus' in the heart of a voodoo swamp.

Grissim again. "The stage is engulfed in a rainbow wash of flashing lights as Alice reaches for a large pillowcase full of chicken feathers and throws it out at the crowd... the flurry of feathers is carried back by the breeze to surround the chicken-feather flinger in a small blizzard. At this instant the crescendo reaches a crashing tonic chord that Alice punctuates by aiming a flare gun into the sky and launching a pyrotechnic rocket that explodes in a dazzling shower high over the square. That's Alice Cooper – and at 9:40 P.M. that's the show."

Chapter Seven

Loving It... To Death

A lice Cooper landed a cameo in Carrie Snodgrass' new movie, *Diary Of A Mad Housewife*, splintered visions of the band thumping through a cover of Steppenwolf's 'Ride With Me' while feathers billowed out around them. They intended it, Buxton said, to remind the movie's producers that they'd wanted Steppenwolf to begin with, only for the 'Born To Be Wild' hit makers to demand too much money. Reflecting on the very different trajectories that the two bands' careers would soon be taking, Buxton simply laughed. "That's why we went into 'Lay Down And Die, Goodbye' at the end. Because we weren't Steppenwolf."

The movie would be in the cinemas just around the same time as the band began work on the next album.

Given the choice of every label in the land, Alice Cooper would not have gone with Warner Brothers. The company had ambition, that was for sure, growing from a marginally successful offshoot of the better known movie studio to become a key asset within the newly conglomerated Kinney empire of entertainment, art and parking lots. But it also had its fingers dancing in musical pies that were anathema to the group. The singing-songwriting self-flagellator James Taylor was Warners' big star that year, and it was clear from both the music press and the label's own projections that it was his brand of mood and melancholy that road-mapped the future which Warner and his brothers anticipated embracing.

Alice Cooper, on the other hand, was simply another of Frank Zappa's playthings, picked up along with the rest of the Straight label catalogue, because the price was too good to pass over, and Glen Buxton growled, "Warners didn't have a clue what they wanted to do with us. Shep Gordon went to see them one day and the first thing they asked was whether Alice was going to keep the band around now there was such a big market for solo girl singers. They thought they'd picked up the new Melanie or Joni Mitchell or something."

Alice laughed, as he always laughed when such tales were relayed back to him; he knew how people still saw the name on the bill posters and thought it was a folk singer, and he knew what a shock they got when they found out otherwise. Shep Gordon laughed too, and he delivered the same response to this latest slab of corporate ignorance that he gave for every other stupid question. He simply smiled, nodded, and wrote another name in his mental notebook. One day, Alice Cooper would make all of these idiots eat their own words. In fact, they might already have been doing so, pushing the first shards of scorn back down the critics' throats with the same loving care as Alice fed mice to the stage show's latest acquisition, one solid stone of pure boa constrictor named Kachina.

This latest addition to the band's visual arsenal was inspired by the fan who appeared backstage at a show in Tampa, Florida, with a snake of her own. Alice jumped when he saw the beast, reacting with instinctive fear at the sight of the passive, coiled creature but then, he told his autobiography, "I thought, 'Hmmm, if I reacted that way to a snake, other people will too'." Plus, it fit the image. "If I were to pull out a three-inch worm on stage it would be a nine-foot python by the time it made the papers," he mused once. "After I heard that, I went out and got a python." In fact, Kachina belonged to Neal Smith, but the distinction was lost on the media. From now on, she was Alice's snake.

Introduced to the performance during the version of 'Is It My Body' that stretched far beyond its vinyl counterpart (and which incorporated elements that would later become 'Halo Of Flies' as well), Kachina swiftly became so familiar through photography and, later, television appearances that it was soon difficult to recall precisely how shocking, and indeed terrifying, her earliest live appearances were. But band and roadcrew alike recall entire rows of the audience recoiling in shock, and when the little girls at the front started screaming, it was not post-Beatles hysteria. It was fear.

Gordon picked up a copy of the *New York Times*. There, beneath the headline "Boy Girl Alice puts on a freaky show", writer Mike Jahn wasn't simply reeling from the band's New York Town Hall show, he was positively salivating over it. "On stage, the lead singer of a rock band, a young man named Alice Cooper, has taken off his silver jump suit to reveal black leotards and panty hose. Now he has a live boa constrictor and is wrapping it around his arm...."

Newsweek had already labelled the band "Dada Rock", and writer Lorraine Alterman was such a vociferous fan that she was already wondering what might happen if, one night, the constrictor constricted Alice. ("That's too much to hope for," replied fellow writer Henry Edwards). Now, the tale of Alice's charming snake antics were spreading even further afield. Suddenly everyone wanted to see what it was all about.

The Andy Warhol circus came out on their side. Every time the Coopers ventured into Manhattan, the Factory would disgorge its own retinue of brightly coloured he-she denizens in the direction of the venue, to see and be seen, to pose and be posed. Nightly, too, rumour insisted that this was the night that Warhol's whip dancer supreme, Gerard Malanga, would join the Coopers onstage to strut stuff with Alice. He never did, but the Coopers' act flagellated the dance floor regardless.

"We act as a mirror," Alice shrugged in that *New York Times* story. "People see themselves through us, [and] many times they react violently because they don't like what they see." Other times, however, they simply didn't like the group.

Certainly Jack Richardson, the Canadian producer who had nursed the Guess Who to hit status, seemed desperately unimpressed when Shep Gordon offered him the chance to produce the band's next album. Gordon had been in Toronto, killing time while he waited for the promoter to pay up for Alice Cooper's performance at the Strawberry Fields Festival. He knew Richardson's name, so he stopped by the producer's Nimbus Nine offices and deposited on a desk whatever Alice memorabilia he had on his person – the two albums and some promotional photographs that left the watching Richardson aghast.

Richardson knew rock, and he handled it well. But he was strictly traditional in his tastes. Raised on the show bands and pop of the pre rock'n'roll age, he had been working in advertising at Coca Cola when he opened his first studio. The Guess Who, the band that would ultimately spin off US million sellers Burton Cummings and Bachman Turner Overdrive, were both his first rock experience and his most lasting; the only other band of true note he had worked with were ultimately of no note at all, RCA half-hopers Noah.

He had no interest whatsoever in Alice Cooper. But, and he threw this out as much to try and get rid of his visitor as for any other reason, there was a kid in the office who might be.

A year younger than Alice, Bob Ezrin had been working as Richardson's odd-job studio lad for the past couple of years. He was not an especially prepossessing character, but he had an ear for arrangements and grandiose notions, and Richardson essentially let him find his own way, working with visiting bands on their material, suggesting sonic effects that might further their vision, and just generally making himself useful. Right now the boy was in class, studying record production at the Eastman School of Music under tutor Phil Ramone. But when he gets back….

Ezrin told the *New Musical Express*, "I went up to the office one day and everyone was in hysterics. The cover of *Easy Action* was laying around, and we were all really straight guys y'know. I mean, I was never really that much into rock 'n' roll. I had arrived at it more or less through things like Simon & Garfunkel. Anyway we put on the album and just broke up laughing. We didn't know if Alice Cooper was a guy or a chick and eventually it became a standing joke around the office that if anyone messed up that week, [they'd] be forced to go and work with Alice Cooper."

Apparently Ezrin had messed up. "I wasn't interested in the least. I hated the record, but [Shep Gordon] made my life such hell with his persistence that I reckoned that I'd go and see 'em just so they'd get off my back. So I went to meet them at Toronto. I walked into their hotel and... these five guys – everyone of 'em is a faggot, every one of 'em and they're all after me. I can tell.

"The road manager is a faggot, the roadies are faggots. I'm sitting there in my blue jeans, with my short hair, shaking inside, man, and here's this guy Alice Cooper – his hair is stringy and down to his shoulders, his pants are so tight I can actually see his penis through the crotch – they're slit at the side. He's talking with a slight lisp. I just could not handle it. Anyway they said, 'We're great and we want a producer'. Finally we parted company and I was like so relieved. It was such a horrendous experience – I was such a straight guy before all this started – and I just forgot."

He was soon given a brutal reminder. With Gordon still begging Jack Richardson to give the band a chance, Ezrin was dispatched to the band's Max's Kansas City show to see what he thought, not only of Alice Cooper but of a few other bands who had crossed Richardson's desk recently. "[I] followed the searchlights to the club and suddenly I was in this dark den of spandex, spider eyes and black fingernails," Ezrin recalled. Alice had recently taken to positively smothering his eyes in arachnoid mascara, borrowing the imagery from the Alvin Ailey dance troupe, but already he had made it his own. There is a difference, after all, between seeing a clown cavort behind a bizarre blur of make-up, and a six foot serial killer, and if Ezrin didn't know that when he first walked in, he quickly found out.

He settled into the table that had been reserved for him at the front of the stage, and then almost leaped out of it again as the band appeared on stage in total darkness and, to the accompaniment of three vivid orange flashes, launched into their opening number, 'Sun Arise'.

With Alice's face perched just two feet away from Ezrin's.

Afterwards, with the band off stage and the audience sat in shellshocked astonishment, the friend who Ezrin had brought along for the ride asked, "What the fuck was that?"

"I don't know," Ezrin slowly replied. "But I loved it."

He tried to analyze his enthusiasm. Musically, he said, the band was terrible. But for the first time in his life as a music lover, he realised that didn't matter. It wasn't their ability he was buying into. It was their presence. "It wasn't about 'being good'. It was about 'being.' It was the complete integration of the point of view and the personality into the presentation. The songs, the antics, the theatricality – they were Alice Cooper. In a world of T-shirts, beards and jeans, they were so refreshing and energising."

Back in Toronto, Ezrin added his voice to Gordon's continued exhortations; he had, in fact, already promised the group that they had a producer when he met them backstage.

Yet despite his enthusiasm, he was also very cautious. Untried in any position beyond Richardson's assistant, Ezrin had ideas and ambitions far beyond the glorified tea boy that the group originally thought he was. In fact, he would demand a lot of evidence to convince him that the Coopers weren't a shambolic garage band with a nice line in snake-handling.

Moving to Detroit, Ezrin booked into a cheap motel and invited the band over to play him their ideas for the album. One song from their live show stuck in his mind, a sprawling piece that he thought was called 'I'm Edgy'. The next time he heard it, in rehearsal, it sounded like an organ recital with a madman screaming over the top of it. It was actually 'I Wish I Was Eighteen Again', which they cut down to 'I'm Eighteen', but that's how many minutes it seemed to last for on the tape they played him.

Dennis Dunaway told *Goldmine*, "Before we hooked up with Bob Ezrin, we had a tendency to try and force too many ideas into one song, and as a result it wouldn't have any continuity. Ezrin was able to take those ideas and say, 'OK, wait a minute. Let's focus on this one thing and let that other thing fall by the wayside.' He was like a director, which was extremely important for us. Ezrin came along at a time when we were ready to go in a more acceptable and less abstract direction."

Neal Smith: "After our first two albums failed to launch us into Rock Stardom, we desperately needed a hit single. The summer of 1970, all five members of Alice Cooper were writing brand new songs in a much more commercial vein. Michael Bruce came up with the original idea for a new song celebrating the awkward teenage transformation from adolescence to adulthood."

"The tapes were horrible," Ezrin shuddered. "And I mean, horrible! They said, 'We like this sound. Can we get it in the studio?' I almost threw up."

Instead he set to work. His job, as he saw it, was to transform what the band was doing on stage into something that could succeed on vinyl, an art that they had neither perfected nor even considered in the past. His abilities as an arranger were crucial, but so was the vision that fired those abilities.

It was Ezrin who essentially locked the band away in the barn that they used for rehearsals, out near Pontiac, Michigan, and kept them there for as long as it took (Alice remembers it being seven months, although his autobiographical chronology is notoriously unreliable), rehearsing whenever they were not on the road, and pushing each musician towards the personal peaks that he felt, or at least hoped, they were capable of reaching.

For Alice, that meant teasing out a distinctive singing voice, one that would be recognisably Alice the moment you heard it, in the same way, he explained, as you know it's Jim Morrison when you hear him sing, or Lennon or Elvis. Right now, Alice simply sang; he had a voice, and he had a style, but he did not have an identity. Ezrin wanted people to know it was Alice from the moment he opened his mouth.

The same went for the rest of the band. Stop listening to your heroes to see how they play their instrument; listen to yourself. And slowly, over the course of their imprisonment, it made a difference. Essentially, he had them unlearn everything they had ever known, and then relearn it properly.

'Black Juju' and 'I'm Eighteen' aside, the band had just two songs primed for the next album as they marched into the RCA Studios in Chicago. The first was that brooding, pulse-beating throb through 'Sun Arise', hauled from the tuckerbag of Australian entertainer Rolf Harris. Live, it had been the Coopers' traditional show opener for most of the year; on vinyl, however, it became the show closer, the promise of a new day coming to chase all the darkness away, but delivered from a place that was even darker still.

The other was 'Is It My Body', their response to the growing acclaim they were receiving on the road at a time when so many people remained convinced that the entire thing was just another of Frank Zappa's crazy japes. But Ezrin remained unimpressed.

"Bob was a classically trained pianist," explained Buxton, "and that was what he wanted to bring to us. No, not us. He wanted to bring it to every thing he worked on. As far as he was concerned, he was the artist, he was the creator, and we were just the guys who would let him get on with it. He wanted to be Phil Spector; he used to talk about the Bob Ezrin Sound, and we would sit there and crack up, this little kid with short hair and sticking-out ears going on about all the ideas he had for us, and what we would sound like when he'd finished, and finally Michael turned around to him and said..."

"Bob, you know we're not Procol Harum." Michael Bruce laughed at the memory. "Essentially, Bob thought much of the music wasn't melodic enough. [So] he started working out all these classical parts for the songs. I'd say to him '... You can't put stuff in the music that's not us. We're a live rock'n'roll band who eat little babies. We're real treacherous and spooky...'"

"And he was making us sound like 'The Long And Winding Road'," Buxton shivered. The Beatles' *Let It Be* finale was just six months old as

92

the Cooper sessions got underway in September 1970, and the revisionist suggestion that the combination of Phil Spector and the Fab Four was anything less than genius was one that had still to enter the popular consciousness. Rather, the blending of Lennon/McCartney's craft with Spector's wall of sound art was still rebounding off the walls of pop genius, drawing comparisons that would have left the true Old Masters open mouthed with amazement. "They were pop songs with strings," Buxton said. "And people were treating them like the second coming of Beethoven. Which is why we wrote a song called 'Second Coming'. To see how far Bob Ezrin would go before he finally got the joke."

He never did, but Bruce admitted he didn't need to. "Bob worked really well on 'Second Coming'. Alice had the initial idea based around this line he had, 'Time is getting closer, I read it on the poster', and Bob then added the piano piece." A really pretty piano piece, bitter-sweetly tinkling beneath a lyric that itself seemed to pose more sad questions than arrogant answers, but also a line that fed into one of the minor songwriting controversies that the Cooper band would never escape from.

The band was in the studio recording the brief piano interlude that segues into 'The Ballad Of Dwight Fry'. A girlfriend of the band's, a lady named Monica, was on hand to provide the lost, spectral sob of "mommy, where's daddy?" that sets the mood for the song, and Ezrin was playing the accompanying piano part. As he finished, engineer Brian Christian walked over and told him "That was really beautiful."

"Thank you," said Bruce, interrupting. "I wrote that."

"And the whole room got real quiet. Bob never went out of his way to tell anyone I wrote that piano part. I mean, I only played it every fucking night live."

'The Ballad Of Dwight Fry' was, and forever will be, one of the Alice Cooper group's greatest accomplishments, and one of Alice's own greatest performances – recorded, Bob Ezrin decided, with the singer lying on the studio floor, with metal-framed chairs creating a cage. His cries of "I've got to get out of here" followed naturally from there.

Dwight Frye himself was the Kansas-born actor whom the Hollywood media nicknamed "the man with the thousand watt stare", a hyper-intense, hopelessly handsome star who might have become a matinee idol had he only chosen his roles a little more carefully. Instead he became a touchstone for every aspiring horror film star of the age, a reputation that was defined by his portrait of Renfield in Tod Browning's 1931 *Dracula*, and then enhanced every time he stepped in front of the cameras.

Fritz in the first Frankenstein movie; the halfwit Herman in 1933's *The Vampire Bat*; Karl in *The Bride Of Frankenstein*, Frye was the man that Hollywood turned to when it needed a convincing lunatic. And when Alice Cooper needed one of their own, they turned back to their own love of Hollywood schlock and disinterred Frye (misspelling him Fry) for their own ends.

Alice recalled his introduction to Frye for *Famous Monsters*, watching Frankenstein and then reading the credits as they rolled at the end. "And then it came up 'Dwight Frye', and I said 'What a great name! That's the kind of name you can write about.' So the song was really meant as a tribute to this guy – this great actor who played the lunatic so well. There was a magazine when I was like 10 or 12 years old called *Dig*, and their mascot, looking over every page, was Dwight Frye. You could just see his eyes and hair as he would be looking over the page – he was sort of like their Alfred E. Newman. I used to get my allowance and I'd go down to the store and buy *Dig* magazine and *Famous Monsters Of Filmland*.

"So, there was a weird, wonderful connection there. He was always, to me, by far the most psychotic of any character in all of those old horror movies. He was this little shaky guy that was just – I mean, everything he said sent shivers down your spine. Even some of the voices I use – some of the Alice voices, like in 'Steven' and in 'The Awakening', were patterned from the Dwight Frye voice – that 'heeee-heeeee-heeee' laugh of his – I always though that that was one of the scariest, most demented voices ever."

The song that bears Frye's name would share those qualities. 'The Ballad Of Dwight Fry' is an epic, a fable of dislocation and instability that journalist Amy Hanson once memorably described as "the most convincing glimpse into the mind of a mad man that rock'n'roll has ever set to music."

The most convincing ever to appear on stage, too, as nightly a nurse would emerge from backstage, leading a straitjacketed Alice behind her. Neal Smith: "We brought our version of Dwight Frye to life when Alice appears on stage wearing a straitjacket and makes a Houdiniesqe escapes from its restraints. The recording was helped along the way with Bob Ezrin's classical musical influence and an atomic bomb explosion!"

"If 'I'm Eighteen' was the commercial side of Alice Cooper, then 'The Ballad Of Dwight Fry' was the darker, more theatrical side of our group," Smith continues. "Most bands are influenced by others bands. But in Alice Cooper's case, we were also influenced by old Hollywood moves, horror movies in particular. The original 1931 *Dracula*, with Bela Lugosi, one of my favourites, featuring the insect-eating character Renfield, a lost soul and disciple of Dracula's. Renfield is played by actor Dwight Frye. Hence the name and direction of our song."

Alice would perform the song bound, thrashing and crashing uncontrollably while his bandmates taunted and kicked out at him. As a commentary on the state of mental health treatment in America at that time… "Well, we all knew what went on in those places back then," said Buxton darkly… it was cruel enough. But as a reminder of how society in general treats those that it considers less powerful, it was brutal.

Eric Carr, later to become drummer with Kiss, recalled the song's impact. "You have to remember what it was like in America in 1970. Shit man, we were living in fear. In total fucking fear. Vietnam had torn the country apart, you were for the war or you were against it, and it didn't matter how loud we were against it, if you were for it, you had the guns, you had the tanks, you had the bombers, they were all on your side and we all saw what happened if you stepped out of line."

On May 4, 1970, a National Guard unit deployed at Kent State University in Ohio opened fire on an anti-war protest, killing four students and wounding nine in what was the clearest and most direct statement yet that the rule of law was not going to be disrupted by peaceful protest – or anything else.

Carr: "It was unbelievable. Can you imagine the outcry in America… the American government… if that had happened in any other country? Gunning down unarmed students because they didn't agree with government policy? The strong taking out the weak, not because they posed a threat but simply because they were different. That's what Alice was reminding us. That it didn't matter how harmless something was, and Dwight Frye in the song, he was completely harmless. So they kill it because it's different."

Under normal circumstances, and by any other band's musical standards, 'The Ballad Of Dwight Fry' would have been the new album's crowning glory, a piece de resistance that the entire record spent its time building towards. Alice Cooper, however, had different ideas, and here Bob Ezrin leapt to their side. Privately he continued to doubt the band's musical abilities, even after they proved themselves eminently capable of composing music that his own ambitions could seamlessly dovetail into. But even he confessed that when they pulled something majestic out of the hat, there was nobody who could stand in the same room. That something was 'Black Juju'.

Remaining a work in progress until it progressed into the studio, 'Black Juju' now stood as the latest in a line of songs that testified to the band's love of Pink Floyd. The percussive pattern that wove through 'Black Juju' owed much to the title cut from the Floyd's second album, *A Saucerful Of Secrets*, and Michael Bruce's keyboard line that gave the song such additional eeriness had a similar genesis. "Dennis Dunaway got real upset because my organ part was similar to 'Set The Controls For The Heart Of The Sun'."

He wouldn't shut up about it either, especially after *Rolling Stone* picked up on the similarity in its review of the finished LP, and suggested that "the Coopers may yet have to answer to the Floyd in court". They didn't; bands were a lot slower to demand legal recompense for perceived borrowings and influences in those days. But still Dunaway worried and, finally, Bruce snapped.

"Come on Dennis, we are all big Pink Floyd fans. So what – we got caught on that one."

Neal Smith refutes the entire story. "Believe me, Pink Floyd's name was never mentioned while we were writing the song. We knew Pink Floyd, we hung out with them, I loved *Piper* and *Saucerful*, but we never ever sat down and said let's sound like somebody. In all the years we were together we never wanted to sound like somebody else, we wanted to be us.

"There was tons of music always around, and I still chuckle when I hear Pink Floyd and 'Black Juju'... I guess if you dissect any song, you could find something but drum wise, there's nothing anybody ever did that sounds like that. When I think of that song I think of Dennis, he was a unique bass player and his vibe, the dark side, it fit in with 'Hallowed Be Thy Name' and 'Second Coming', a dark religious cult thing. Years and years later, somebody asked me what was the relationship between 'Hallowed' and 'Second Coming' and I said I don't know... and I wrote them both. It never dawned on me that they were linked together. Plus,

I wrote the lyrics to 'Hallowed' in like five minutes. It's one of those things that just happened but it fit on that album really well."

'Hallowed Be Thy Name' nevertheless occupies a very special place in Smith's heart, as one of the few songs he wrote for the band "that came out exactly as I wrote it. Even the guitar solo! I sang it to Glen and he played it as I sang it. I actually tried to sing 'Hallowed Be Thy Name' on the album, but it really didn't work out."

It would, however, afford the band another legend, as a gig somewhere in the American south introduced them to a large white cross that just happened to be lying backstage. Of course Alice couldn't resist it and, that night, as the band played, Alice draped the cross across his back, outstretched arms holding it in place, and affected his own passion. It was just bad luck, Michael Bruce later laughed, that one of his aunts, and a very religious aunt too, happened to be at the concert.

What the band could not have known as they put the finishing touches to the LP; what nobody could have realised as they continued to laugh off the Alice Cooper band's cartoon theatrics, was that a lot was about to change. And all they needed to do was shave five years off their own lives. On February 4, 1971, Alice Cooper celebrated his 23rd birthday. But according to the lyrics that now screamed from every radio, hurtling off the single that Warners had just pulled from the completed session tapes....

… he was 18.

According to Alice, one of the first DJs to begin airing 'I'm Eighteen' with any regularity was a Missouri-based youngster named Rush Limbaugh, destined, in later decades, to become one of the American right wing's most vociferous pit bulls. He was not alone for long, however. Radio latched onto 'I'm Eighteen' with a grateful passion, responding instinctively to its strut and roar, seeing in the Cooper band's volume and snarl an antidote to everything that 1971 had thus far threatened to smear across the pop scene, the army of would-be James Taylors and surrogate Carole Kings marching to capitalise on the enormous successes those artists were riding; the crop of record company hopefuls aiming to step into the shoes of the recently sundered Beatles; unappetising candies from the bubblegum factories… the first glimmer of the Osmonds and the incipient Partridge family.

Across the ocean in the UK and Europe, Marc Bolan and T Rex were commencing their dizzying rise up the chart with 'Hot Love', the song (or, rather, the TV performances) that history has decreed marked the birth of glam rock. Surviving footage of 'I'm Eighteen' is the argument that threatens to burst the Bolanic bubble; in satin and tat, make-up and long hair, the Alice Cooper band not only conform to, they blueprint every visual hook, line and sinker that glam would now lay claim to. The difference was, they did it in a country that had no interest in glam, no sense of the sexual shockability that hallmarked Britain's early seventies. America seized on the violence that was bound up in the Coopers' appearance; the sense of society teetering on an edge of decay and degeneracy but, most of all, destruction.

It is a divide that has forever separated British and American rock'n'roll; in Europe, an artist's image is constructed (by the public and media, if not the artist itself) around its capacity for sexual shock; in America, it is built around anything but. At least if you want to succeed. David Bowie conquered Britain by claiming to be gay; in America, he was a faggot weirdo until he dropped the make-up, stopped the talk, and started making disco records. Sweet, prime purveyors of British glam were pushed as a hard-rock combo in the States, and Marc Bolan scored his only US hit before the majority of the country had ever had the chance to take a look at his wardrobe.

And all of this was not because the United States had anything against sex itself. It just liked violence better.

Alice Cooper looked violent.

"I think we were the start of glam," says Neal Smith. "Dennis in 1968 was totally dressed in silver. It was a time when there were people trying to figure out all kind of categories to put us in but we were definitely the forerunner of theatre rock. The Doors had some dark stuff, Jimi [Hendrix] had some dark stuff, but nobody ever put it together on stage. When we started off, there was nobody doing anything except playing on a flat empty stage.

"The lighting... we were the first ones to come up using big-time theatrical lighting; most of the time it was just the spotlight and whatever there was in the auditorium. Pink Floyd spearheaded it and of course there was a lot of psychedelic light shows in the sixties, but they still weren't using theatrical lights and it was being done in a very different way.

"We were the ground-breaking band of theatrics and there's really not a lot of physical support of that beyond still photographs. We did a live trilogy. I know on the album it's 'Second Coming, 'Dwight Fry' and 'Sun Arise', but we started the show with 'Sun Arise', that was the beginning; there were a couple of diff versions but we started with that, and then the 'Ballad' led into 'Black Juju' near the end of the show, and after that, we really started getting our stage legs on creating a show."

In 2010, he reflected, "Alice talked recently about how he puts a show together and it's exactly the way the band was doing it, we'd have the light opening, then we'd have the big theatrical centre section and then it turned heavy, and then the finale, the end of the show would always be the big piece. Instead of going out there like some bands and blam, blasting all the way through from beginning to end, we sort of built it. All the stuff he does today is almost exactly the same as we used to do, and that's great. It was a formula that worked for us. It doesn't work for everybody, but we were trying to do a theatrical piece and take the audience on a bit of an excursion, and I think it worked out. 'Black Juju' was the first time that it really worked out for us."

Everything had come together now. Early experiments with the cage of fire had failed; instead, the band had a life-size and lifelike electric chair constructed for their use, and every night Alice would be dragged across the stage, strapped in and fried. And it was not to everybody's taste.

"The advance publicity for Alice Cooper almost turned my stomach," author and journalist Albert Goldman confessed. "The pictures showed a kohl-eyed queen, cadaver face framed in a rat's nest of teased black hair, camping it up with a whole warehouse of lurid props, everything from a boa constrictor to an old-fashioned mission-oak-and-leather-strap electric chair.

"The advertising copy was the usual 'I can't see anything wrong with it' palaver about 'contemporary theatre' and rock as 'total experience' and the wondrous fact that we all have male and female traits. After surveying the whole hyped-up spiel, I concluded, 'If that's where it's at, who needs it?'"

But he was converted, as so many others were. "Then I saw the show and ditched my preconceptions."

Goldman's article, published in *Life* magazine in July 1971, fascinates because it is one of the few articles in the mainstream US media to actually nail what lay behind Alice Cooper. "The moment Alice sidled across the stage – in a black leotard zipped down to his navel – I recognised that he/she/it was thoroughly professional. Every provocative move and theatrical flourish was carefully calculated and precisely performed. Far from being a freaky aberrant, Alice was a shrewd operator intent on translating to the fagged-out rock stage some perverse excitement of the Andy-Warhol, Sado-Masochist, Low-Camp Drama and Cinema."

To the rest of the media, and therefore the public at large, everything that Goldman claimed Alice wasn't, they continued to believe – and in many cases hope – he was. They wanted him to carve up chickens and set dogs on fire. They wanted him to impale babies on pitchforks, and money on swords, and they wanted him to be dragged to the electric chair by two cops, and fried in front of a room full of people, all howling with the bloodlust of a Tyburn Tree tribunal. They wanted to believe, in that same way that every idol incites belief, that he really was as degenerate as he seemed to be. And why? Because that is what being an idol is all about; pinpointing your audience's darkest deepest fantasies, and then bringing them to life.

The death of Jim Morrison, lifeless in a Parisian bathtub that July, added further impetus to the band's momentum. Morrison himself had grown bloated and disillusioned in recent months, a corpulent shadow of the man he once was, but he remained the epitome of revolution as it evolved out of the miasma of psychedelia. Without him to spell dissolution aloud for an audience searching for meaning in music, and with Marc Bolan's UK fame yet to translate to America, the road was clear for someone new to drive down.

The act "create[s] tension in the audience", Alice told the UK magazine *ZigZag* in 1971. He admitted that the group's props were contrived, "but they're perfectly contrived. They're like, abstractly, surrealistically contrived. There's no real reason for the electric chair. There's no real reason for the feathers at the end, except for the tension of the orgasm. Everyone can relate – they can relax at the end. After all the tension, they go 'Ahhhhhh, finally!'"

Only once did Goldman's eye falter as he reached deeper into the crowd psychology in search of the soul of Alice's audience. "What gets everybody uptight with Alice Cooper is the sacrifice he makes of shame. Confessing fantasies most people would sooner die than reveal, he becomes a scapegoat for everybody's guilts and repressions. People project him, revile him, ridicule him and some would doubtless like to kill him. At some stage, he knocks out the young boys with the daring of his act and the rebelliousness of his image. After all, the ultimate rebellion of our time is the simple refusal to be a man."

Yet there was never any suggestion, once past the name, that any member of the Alice Cooper band, least of all Alice himself, was homo-, or even bisexual. That was Goldman's own psyche talking and, within six months of that article's publication, David Bowie would have seized upon that same notion and brought it to life. Alice Cooper, on the other hand, gave the impression that they would have stomped anybody who dared suggest such a thing, and they had the Women's Lib pickets outside concerts to prove it.

"Yeah, I did the whole trip with that," Alice told *ZigZag*. "We got picketed in New York and everything... Women's Lib hates us – they think rock lyrics are discriminating against women." And Alice Cooper was not about to disavow them of that notion. "I said I think that women should be used as sex objects. I think that's what they're best at. Very honestly, I said I don't think it's any insult because that's what their main purpose in life is – being sex objects. I mean, what's wrong with that... they can still run a corporation and be a sex object. I think that Women's Lib is pretty much a combination of horny dykes, which is cool. I like horny dykes... there's nothing wrong with that."

The new stage show fell into place, set to go out on the road as Warner Brothers released the group's third album, originally set to be called *Honest Alice*, but soon suitably retitled *Love It To Death*. Controversy, of course, had already dogged its genesis, as Warners took an eyeglass to the sleeve photograph that the band insisted was the record's front cover, and spied a teeny-tiny weenie poking out from Alice's fly. Of course it was merely his finger, poked through the opening just to see if someone would notice, and the band made no major outcry when a revision was suggested. Word of the controversy just added to the album's pre-release desirability, and the so-called censored cover became an emblem of the group's taste for outrage. An outrage that was growing every time they stepped on stage.

'I'm Eighteen' reached number 21 in the US; *Love It To Death* peaked at number 33. Neither, then, set the world on fire, and a second single in the summer, 'Caught In A Dream', foundered at a lowly number 94. It was in concert that Alice Cooper were wining and dining ever growing battalions of believers, still taking every gig they were offered (for a healthy $1,500 a night), and then taking the audience as far as they could. A journey that

Alice insisted, again to *ZigZag*, ended in the kind of rebellion that not one of rock's more storied protest acts had even touched.

"['Eighteen'] worked because people really liked it – they got into the whole idea of being 18... the frustrations. It's sort of like an updated version of 'My Generation'. We're drawing 10 times as many people [as we used to]. And when all those kids are coming to see us, then going, 'Wow, I think I'll go home and put on some of Mom's eye make-up'... and their dad's a cop..." His voice trailed off. Fame was not all, after all, about dealing with the faithful. It was about confronting your foes as well.

The *Love It To Death* tour kicked off in Pittsburgh at the end of March, and then continued almost without a break until the end of August, at which point the group would return to the studio to cut their next album, and then pack their suitcases and hit the road in Europe.

Everywhere they played, the venue sold out. Groups they had once only marvelled at from afar were now opening for them: Black Oak Arkansas, Canned Heat, Steppenwolf and Spirit. They shared bills with Black Sabbath and Led Zeppelin; they took Detroit's own Amboy Dukes on the road with them for one clutch of shows. Alice even began growing accustomed to having to follow Iggy Pop on stage, after the Stooges were added to a few midwestern bills. But the boot was firmly on the other foot now, as Stooges manager Danny Fields recalled.

He told Iggy biographer Paul Trynka, "Iggy's supposed to be on stage; you're pulling a needle out of his arm and there's blood squirting in your face. Meanwhile Alice Cooper and his band are adjusting their false eyelashes and powdering their noses in the same room. And I'm thinking 'these Alice Cooper guys are not as good as this band, but they're pros.' That was sorta the metaphor – both bands are playing for $1,500, and there's one that looked poised for stardom. And one poised for the floor of the bathroom."

"Every night when we went out there, we could feel the excitement going up a notch," Glen Buxton recalled. "There were nights when the place was going wild before we'd even stepped on stage so when we did it was like a riot was kicking off. Even when we were opening for somebody else, we knew we had nothing to fear because we just grabbed their audience and took them with us. It was like the headliners were opening for us, and they'd just been put on last so the kids could have an early night."

The first major concert ever attended by late guitar legend Randy Rhoads was an Alice Cooper gig, at the Long Beach Auditorium. His sister Kelle Rhoads told writer Thom Hazaert, "I can't tell you the impact this had on my brother. I told him, 'We're gonna go see Alice Cooper in Long Beach.' So him and [friend] Kelly Garni and me, Kelly Garni's mom had to drive us, we were just kids. And we went down and we saw Alice Cooper touring for the *Love It To Death* show, and… after Alice Cooper was done, my brother just turned white, and he was just staring at the stage, the concert was long over. And I think what happened that day was a light went on, and he got the idea that he could do this too. That was where I pinpoint him going, 'I can actually make this my living. I can really do this. This is what I want to do. This is all I have to do.' And I think that July 11, 1971 was when that happened for him."

"I hated playing on bills with Alice Cooper," Spirit's Randy California shrugged. "The kids didn't even care about the music. They bought their tickets to see Alice get killed. How could any other band compete with that?" And they were kids, too. Without ever deliberately targeting what modern marketers would call a specific demographic, it became apparent very quickly that Alice Cooper's primary audience was caught in the region of 12 to 15 years of age. Maybe, Alice reasoned, it was because their minds were more open; maybe it was because their social consciences were less developed, or maybe it was because teenaged boys really get off on twisted shit. They're the biggest audience for horror movies too. But Alice was complaining.

"We went to the Fillmore East the other night and all the audience kept screaming was 'boogie,'" Alice sniffed to *Rolling Stone*. "Or the blues. How many times can you lose your baby? And jams. All those lame jams. Unless you're somebody like Mike Bloomfield who really knows the technical aspect of it, most of the jams you hear are stereotyped. The people who dig groups like Ten Years After now are going to be washed up in two years. They're just going to be like old married couples."

Alice, on the other hand, represented the future.

Neal Smith: "The timing was right and that was key. I think a big part was the element of the band coming out of the Vietnam era; there were a lot of times when music is exciting but I think in turbulent times it is more so. There were so many huge elements going on, gay rights, the women's movement, black power, Vietnam, there were so many things happening and there was so much music. I don't think there has ever been a more exciting time."

Chapter Eight

School's Out For Killers

Shep Gordon headed a team that was pushing Alice hard and fast. "Like most commerce, music is a team game," he would state a few years down the line. "Jon Podell* has been Alice's agent for 35 years, placing Alice in the right halls with the right opening acts. Pat Kingsley, Caroline Pfeiffer and later, Lee Solters did the press; in Alice's case, this was probably the most important aspect because it drove his career more than radio. The other significant player was Bob Ezrin, who was able to take that rebellion and transform it into hit records."

Right now, however, the greatest role was played by Warner Brothers. "The record company was very significant because it financed a lot of our schemes," said Gordon. "Things like wrapping *School's Out* in panties. They didn't understand Alice, but they believed in us and, with a bit of pushing, allowed us to do our thing."

Love It Do Death was just a couple of months old and already Warners were demanding a new album, something for the Christmas stockings of every kid who stood and howled at the concerts. The whole time they were on the road, then, the band was writing furiously. 'Halo Of Flies' had already made it into the live set, a furious improvisation built

---

* Jonny Podell was the son of Jules Podell, a noted speakeasy operator during Prohibition who went on to manage and finally own the famous Copacabana night club in New York.

around a handful of songs left unfinished in the past, but towering over such unpromising origins thanks to an inspired lyric and an even more ferocious performance from Neal Smith.

Centred on a drum solo that still conjures images of giant spiders dancing in the desert, "'Halo Of Flies' was pretty simple," the drummer laughs. "We wanted all these fucking people who'd been saying for years and years and years that we couldn't play... 'what are you talking about?' So we had all these little pieces of songs laying about that went back to *Pretties For You*, and by the time of *Killer* they were even more obscure, so we put them all together into one song and it was just a great song."

But other numbers were falling into place alongside it; taut, concise rockers like 'Be My Lover' and 'Under My Wheels', the western epic 'Desert Night Thing' (eventually recorded as 'Desperado'), the makeweight but mauling 'Yeah Yeah Yeah' and 'You Drive Me Nervous', and finally, the two songs that could come to crystallise the Alice Cooper band's reputation for all time, 'Dead Babies' and 'Killer'.

Neal Smith recalls, "'Dead Babies' is another successful collaboration written by all five members of the band. The original idea for this song came from Mr. Black Juju himself, our dark side, Dennis. This was maybe the first true shock-rock song and was written to be controversial. But listen to the lyrics closely. It's about killing babies yes, but by parental neglect. 'Dead Babies' really opened the door for us theatrically. On stage a swashbuckling Alice flaunts a sword held high overhead, that's piercing a blond baby doll. While all around him are female mannequin body parts scattered over the stage."

Dennis Dunaway told *Goldmine*, "We often talked about having a 'germ' for a song, or an idea. And if a germ didn't develop, it would fall by the wayside. In the case of 'Dead Babies', it originally had a verse that didn't work, although I thought the chorus was great. I was very adamant about bringing the chorus back in. It so happened I had a bass line from a jam that was a completely separate idea, and one day I came in and suggested we try fusing the two ideas together. Nobody wanted to do it at first, but I finally talked them into it."

Still the band were not sure, but outside of their rehearsal hall, that big old barn on the outskirts of Pontiac, a captive audience, literally, was listening to their efforts and applauding this new song with gusto. A prison farm belonging to Oakland Prison abutted onto the Coopers' land and, when the band threw open the doors on the hottest days of the year, every sound they made could be heard by the working jailbirds. Who would then let the band know how they felt about it with either silence or applause. 'Dead Babies' received a standing ovation.

Returning to the RCA Studios in Chicago, recording *Killer* was as straightforward as *Love It To Death* had been protracted. Again Bob Ezrin produced, and again he introduced his own subtle flourishes to the band's basic roar. Alice laughs when he recollects Ezrin first suggesting the addition of oboe and cello to beef up some of the bass lines, and how the band waited, boiling with trepidation (and the chance to mock his efforts of course) as the producer keyed up the tape.

But it worked, just as Ezrin said it would; and so did another of Ezrin's personal touches, drafting guitarist Rick Derringer into the studio to handle two particular guitar parts; Glen Buxton was having girlfriend problems, and simply wasn't learning his parts quickly enough. So Ezrin found somebody who would, and simply smiled as Derringer walked into the studio, spent 15 seconds tuning his instrument, then laid down precisely the sound that Ezrin was looking for. And if the watching Coopers learned a little lesson in professionalism that day, all the better.

And so *Killer* came together as a classic combination of a band that knew the sky was the limit, and a producer who dreamed of flying even higher. Plus it packed the most photogenic cover star of the year, the smouldering eyes and patient smile of Kachina the constrictor.

Certainly the media was hypnotised. *Killer*, proclaimed Lester Bangs in *Rolling Stone*, "is without a doubt the best Alice Cooper album yet and one of the finest rock'n'roll records released in 1971. It brings all the elements of the band's approach to sound and texture to a totally integrated pinnacle that fulfils all the promise of their erratic first two albums, and beats *Love It To Death*'s dalliance with thirties flick 'spooky' cornball riffs by the sheer sustained impact of its primal rock and roll jolt.... This is a strong band, a vital band, and they are going to be around for a long, long time."

Alice alone made his first excursion to Europe in June 1971, flying to London for three days of press receptions prior to a longer tour in the autumn. It was a busy schedule, and one that got off to a bang, Warners' UK office declared, the moment the plane touched down on English soil and it was discovered that the old lady seated next to Alice on the flight was dead, and not fast asleep as people had assumed. The story was an invention, of course, the first of many that would shock the UK press over the next couple of years, but that didn't stop Alice from playing along with it. Natural causes were the culprit, but wouldn't it have been funny, he smirked, if he'd painted a couple of fang marks on her neck?

Most of Alice's time was spent in hotel rooms and record company offices, talking to the media. But his schedule also allowed time for some sightseeing and shopping, including a visit to a Kings Road boutique whose owner, and customers, would in later years become as notorious as Alice Cooper; under the new name of Sex, the little store at World's End would unleash the Sex Pistols on the world. Right now, however, Let It Rock catered for London's Teddy Boy community, the leftover fifties rockers who still littered the streets in decades-old fashion, and glared menacingly at anyone who passed by.

Malcolm McLaren, the store's co-owner (with partner and designer Vivienne Westwood) recalls, 'All the visiting Americans used to come in because they couldn't find clothes like ours at home, so Alice came in, nobody knew who he was at the time, or not many people anyway, but he introduced himself and bought some leather trousers, some tops... and he signed an album cover to put on the wall. Somebody stole it a few months later, but we always had Alice on the jukebox after that." And that jukebox would play its own part in the Sex Pistols history, when Johnny Rotten auditioned for his future bandmates by miming to Alice Cooper's 'I'm Eighteen'.

The trip was a well-marshalled exercise, one which first necessitated the waiting Anglos to be bombarded with the imagery that the American media was already familiar with. Brian Blevins of the UK magazine *Cream* warned, "audiences are likely to see some or all of the following: pigeons and chickens (quite warm and alive) thrown into the audience, followed by a whirlwind of feathers torn from a pillow; the massacre of a watermelon with a hammer, with juice and pulp gushing over the floor; the use of crutches and brooms and inflatable toys, smoke machines and a huge inventory of other gadgets and gimmicks; and physical fights among the members of the group.

"The musicians... will wear narcissistic shiny silver jumpsuits, dresses, a straitjacket, leotards or anything that fits, most of it made with loving care by Cooper's mother. Sometimes they will play music...."

Now that music was to be heard in concert. Despite the singer nursing a vicious dose of flu, Alice Cooper's UK debut finally arrived in November, with a late-night warm-up at the Mayfair Ballroom in Birmingham, out of sight of prying critics and out of reach, too, of many of those who were waiting to see the band.

Britain had been divided over the Coopers' worth long before their plane touched down. Word of their outlandish stage show had encouraged more than one publicity-hungry Member of Parliament to suggest that the group should be banned from visiting, while Alice insists that a ban actually came into force, "because of urban legends... 'Alice Cooper worships the dead and is cruel to animals'."

In fact, with the guile that so many record companies are capable of tapping when it comes to awakening interest in a new musical import, the ban and many of the outraged quotes were strictly for show, hyper-active minds in the press office calling their favourite contacts at the music and daily press, and passing on a story that might have been dreamed up in a meeting only an hour before.

If the Birmingham debut was low key, however, two nights later brought a baptism of fire as Alice Cooper launched into two shows at the London Rainbow, a converted cinema in the north London corner of Finsbury Park that had been hosting rock concerts (as the Astoria) since the mid-sixties.

The first of these, on November 6, 1971, saw them opening for the Who as part of a three-day event reopening the venue; they were a last minute addition (the lightweight rockers Quiver were the "official" opener) and, although an audience tape exists of the Alice Cooper band's performance, it cannot be said that they attracted much attention. It was the following night's show that drew all the eyes, as Alice Cooper headlined the venue, billed above former Bonzo Dog Doo Dah Band mainstay Roger Ruskin Spear, and Arthur Brown – himself no stranger to theatrical rock outrage and, in terms of a tempestuous career arc, even more of a role model to the Coopers than that.

Best remembered for the 1968 chart-topper 'Fire', Brown was blessed with one of the fullest voices in rock, capable of shifting in seconds from satanic whisper to blood-chilling scream, but his influences were American soul and R&B, shot through with jazz, lengthy improvisations and even four or five minute comedy skits. "It was the beginning of the underground," Brown remembers. "There was Soft Machine, ourselves, Pink Floyd, Marc Bolan was just starting out, and we were the sort of people they'd send out to places where there wasn't an underground and we'd carve the way. Sometimes people would kick our gear down the stairs because they objected to our music, sometimes they'd accept it."

They accepted it within the fertile atmosphere of London's prime underground nightclub, UFO, and it was there that Brown's imagery coalesced. Drummer Drachen Theaker recalled, "It was a wild act, but it wasn't that wild musically. We were just an R&B group underneath. What made it psychedelic was Arthur's acting ability, and the fact that [organist Vincent Crane] and I just overplayed to death at gigs. We made a hell of a noise for two people!"

Two period views of the Crazy World sum them up. First, journalist Charles Fox, writing in the *New Statesman*: "...there is a sinister element... one which recalls the smell of seaweed and the rattle of spades and pails. For somehow Arthur Brown contrives to be both the malevolent Punch and – in drag, with grotesque wig and flowered gown – a psychedelic Judy."

And now, author Nik Cohn: "... he was one long gangling skinny streak, complete with haystack black hair and great staring eyes and an elephant's nose. And when he came on, he was wearing Sun God robes, a science fiction mask, the Bug-Eyed Thing, and his head was on fire."

Got that? His head was on fire. Not his hat, not even his hair. His head. And though it eventually transpired that, actually, it was his hat, and occasionally his hair as well, still the effect – as Charles Fox continued – was "disconcerting, even faintly perverse".

The focus of the Crazy World's act shifted after Brown came up with 'Fire'. Part Biblical horror, part bad trip, 'Fire' was the cue for Brown's "crown" – originally a vegetable colander with a candle stick attached, but later developing into a considerably more elaborate helmet – to burst into flames.

'Fire' went on to top the charts throughout much of the civilised world, establishing and maybe even typecasting Brown as the God of Hell Fire. Certainly, he was never able to repeat its success, but the fire dance became one of the most famous routines in rock theatre. And now here was Alice Cooper, vying for a crown that Brown must surely have believed was his forever.

By 1971, Brown's live set had progressed far beyond a simple blazing hat. Caught on film at the Glastonbury Festival earlier in the year, with his new band Kingdom Come, Brown appeared surrounded by burning crosses, in and around which he would dance and flare, while unleashing those unearthly shrieks from the depth of his soul. Indoor venues were somewhat more safety conscious, and that included the Rainbow, whose own history included the night Jimi Hendrix torched his guitar on stage for the first time. So Brown contented himself with scaling things back, and crucified himself instead.

Beat that, Alice Cooper.

No problem, replied Alice and *Melody Maker* journalist Michael Watts sadly reflected that, "The kids who've never heard of Arthur Brown and Lord Sutch, and to whom the Stones and Zappa are an obsolescent fact of life... [have] discovered a new hero in Auntie Alice. Just wait till their moms and dads learn more about him, till they realise he chops up babies and is hanged on stage. Just wait till they start asking questions in the House about this 'undesirable American performer'."

Alice certainly shrugged away accusations that he was indebted to Brown. "I thought he was really good, but he wasn't really an influence. He probably has the greatest vocal range ever, but he was using his fantasy as I use mine. His was fire, mine was guillotines and babies," and it would be another 40 years before the two could truly be compared side by side, when Brown was special guest at Alice's Halloween 2011 show at the Alexander Palace in London.

Two hours into a show that had already seen him guillotined, Alice stood back while Brown was readied for his performance, face-painted in a twisted parody of the Yin and Yang symbol, robed and crowned and then ignited, to unleash that unearthly shriek once more. By which time, of course, it didn't even matter who had done what first or best. This was rock theatre in the hands of its two greatest exponents. Just like it had been, four decades earlier.

Then what about Screaming Lord Sutch? He, too, had a nice line in theatrical costuming and notions, and it seems almost petty, four decades removed, to recall the way the British press lined up to throw what were, in truth, very passing local fancies into Cooper's face, as though he deliberately sat down and thumbed through the last 10 years' worth of Anglo music papers, in search of past heroes to callously rip off. Yet it happened, and Sutch himself was not above poking fun at his new adversary.

"I was wearing white powder and black around my eyes in 1959," he told America's *Hit Parader*. "Alice Cooper has a nice act but I was doing that exact same thing 10 years ago. The only thing different is the sound of the music. I did everything that Alice does now. I used to do swords and axes and have the make-up on. I actually saw a picture in one rock magazine that I thought was one of my stage shots – but it turned out to be Alice. He was wearing top hat and tails, which is what I wore to promote the Lord Sutch image."

Interviewed some quarter of a century later, however, Sutch laughed at attempts to belittle Alice Cooper by pointing out his own precedents. "I borrowed from Screaming Jay Hawkins. He borrowed from… whoever. It goes on and on, and everyone takes something from someone and runs with it. Yes, Alice did a lot of the things I used to, but so what? He did a lot of things I didn't, and he entertained a lot of people by doing so. To be truthful it used to make me mad when I'd read about people putting him down for ripping me off, because it reminded me of how I felt when they said the same things about me."

The other big difference, of course, was that Alice had a sharp manager and a big record label behind him, but Sutch must have been very annoyed the week after the Rainbow concert.

"Alice Cooper gave a most moving performance at London's Rainbow Theatre on Sunday night," *Melody Maker*'s Chris Welch declared in his review of the show. "She made me want to move right out of the theatre; out of the rock business; out of the country. But I only got as far as the conveniently placed fountain in the foyer, where it was better to vomit than over the packed, wildly cheering audience." And his view was not an isolated one.

No less than in the United States, Alice Cooper divided as they conquered, slicing the waiting audience neatly between those who saw shock theatre as a welcome adjunct to a regular show; and those who believed it was the music that mattered, and that any attempt to do more was simply hyperbole and flash. *Melody Maker* clearly fell into the latter camp, at least for now. "America's greatest industry is packaging and its finest culture is advertising," snarled Welch. "Alice Cooper is crescendo and finale in gift-wrapped emptiness. Buy now. But your values cannot be refunded."

Elsewhere, minds were less closed to the chaos. "It was one of the best shows yet seen [at the Rainbow]," remarked the *International Times*, the hyperbole dimming only when you remembered that Alice Cooper was just the second band to headline the place since its name change. "The glamorous drag prince from America came to town and tore the place up. Perfectly structured singles rolled out from *Love It To Death*, a rocking razzamatazz in gold and silver lamé, like a scene from *Beyond The Valley Of The Dolls*.

"Further adventures with a straitjacket and electric chair followed, keeping the audience bewildered. The suffering was so sham it was surreal.... As music, it's not half bad, as showbiz it's riveting and as trash it is absolutely incomparable."

The view from the paying customers, too, was expansive. Martin Gordon, who in years to come would play bass for that very same Sparks band who once wrestled Alice Cooper to be Los Angeles' most hated, recalls the show vividly. "I saw Alice Cooper for the first time on November 6, 1971 at the Rainbow Theatre in London's Finsbury Park. It was my first experience of rock theatrics. The stage darkened, and a single spotlight fell on the stringy figure on his knees at the front of the stage. Alice (for it was he) was viciously bashing a hammer on the floor, and the syncopation (thump thump, thump thump) resolved itself into the Aussie ballad beloved of sheep-shaggers the world over – 'Sun Arise'. Alice sang the opening verse alone in the spotlight. With a flourish, the stage lights went up and the band crashed into the chorus. What a moment... it was revelation!"

They were, he laughs, a "gang of ruffians who stepped into the Rainbow Theatre spotlight; impossibly skeletal bassist Dennis Dunaway, swaggering guitar duo Michael Bruce and Glen Buxton – not people I wanted to meet in a dark alleyway. Or even a well-lit alleyway, come to that. It was *West Side Story* brought to life."

A similarly warm welcome awaited elsewhere on the continent, as Alice Cooper filed away shows in Denmark, Holland, Switzerland and Germany, where they shot a sensational "I'm Eighteen" for local TV's *Beat Club*.

There was a star-packed party in Paris, France, where guests were invited to attend dressed as actress Raquel Welch – another symbol, of course, of American packaging at its finest. Charlie Watts, Bianca Jagger and Alain Delon were among those who showed up (sans costume, sadly), but the star of the evening was Omar Sharif who, according to a report in *Express* magazine, "came as Raquel in the part of Myra Breckinridge. But he looked more like Groucho Marx. A lot of people came as Raquel in the part of *Kansas City Bomber*. You've never seen so many well-built ladies on roller skates in your life. They caused chaos."

The real Raquel, incidentally, was not invited.

French television got in on the act, airing captivating clips of 'Is It My Body', 'The Ballad Of Dwight Fry' and 'Black Juju', and providing future historians with one of just two widely circulated video souvenirs of the Coopers at their peak (the other was a few grainy black-and-white excerpts shot at a club in Asbury Park that same year). The snake and the straitjacket are both in evidence, and no matter how uninviting the venue, or tiny the stage, still Alice Cooper behaved as though they were visiting royalty, and not an American cult with a nice eye for dress-up.

'Black Juju' is relentless, scarifying and scabrous, hypnotic even before Alice begins the hypnotism, and if the electric chair routine relies more on bright lights and a slump of the shoulders, still Alice's revival is as intense as it is insistent, Smith's drumsticks beating clockwork behind the singer's sibilant demands... "rest, rest, bodies need their rest". And then, "wake up!"

The Cooper band bade farewell to the UK with one final performance, on television's *Old Grey Whistle Test* rock show and, almost exactly 40 years later, Alice sat down with one of the show's regular hosts, disc jockey Bob Harris, to reminisce. "Coming from Arizona, where we watched *Shindig* and *Hullabaloo*, and every week there'd be a new band from England and we'd sit there as kids and go 'Wow, we'll never get over to England, a little bar band like we are.' And we finally got [there] and it was a huge deal being on British television playing rock'n'roll."

They lived up to their own dreams. Four decades on, the version of 'Under My Wheels' that was turned out that evening remains a staple of rock television viewing, to the point of standing in as a proxy music video for the song. Their other performance, a brittle 'Is It My Body', while an entertaining offcut from the recording, catches Alice chatting away to the snake who had been hired for the occasion (Kachina was left at home to avoid customs hang-ups).

"You'd make a great wallet," he kids her, before making his way back to the dressing room he'd been assigned to, set at totally the opposite end of the studio to the rest of the band's. Which itself was so strange that finally, he asked why. Because, came back the reply, it was official BBC policy to have separately located rooms for male and female performers. "Your name is Alice Cooper, after all."

London marked the last time the *Love It To Death* stage act would be performed. A new show had been designed, centred on a life-sized working gallows built at Warners' movie lot and, following a couple of warm-up gigs in Saginaw, Michigan, December 1, 1971 saw the Academy of Music in New York become the scene of Alice's first ever onstage hanging.

"When we first did the hanging stunt, it took them three days to get me on the gallows," Alice admitted to *Melody Maker*. "'Alice, we've really got to hang you now' they kept saying...."

He was right to be nervous. On more than one occasion the gallows malfunctioned, and on one night they failed him completely. "What happened was, the rope suddenly broke during that part where I get hanged and I came crashing down on my knees at the back of the stage. It was a really bad fall. Apart from the initial shock and massive rope burn on my neck, I honestly thought that I had dislocated my neck and broken both my legs."

"Alice Cooper's new production, *Killer*, had its premiere performance here... and, just as expected, it went well beyond spectacular," swooned *Circus*. "Alice has always been more famous for his gaudy theatricality than, quite unjustly, for his music; but face it, any rock and roll act that offers a full scale hanging, complete with dense clouds of manufactured demon-fumes, more death-cult vibes than the Manson Family, and a super-heavy simulation of an artillery bombardment is not susceptible to mere musical analysis."

The speed with which Alice Cooper's reputation rose from "worst band in Los Angeles" to one of the hottest bands in the country was not purely down to their theatrics, of course. Less than three weeks into the American dates, a hissy tape recording of the St Louis show became one of the year's most celebrated bootleg albums, legendary enough to merit inclusion in the band's own *Old School* box set 40 years on, and a prize glimpse into the sheer musicality of the onstage experience. Behind the scenes, meanwhile, Shep Gordon and his team – which now included a quick-witted in-house PR called Ashley Pandel – worked tirelessly to ensure the band was never out of the headlines, backed up by a Warners press office that could not believe its own luck.

Too much of the label's home-grown output remained locked into a world of sensitivity, where the most outrageous headline imaginable probably revolved around the guitarist changing strings on his guitar, and where even James Taylor had wearied of constantly talking about the private life that his songs had made so public. As he finally snapped to *Rolling Stone* at the end of the decade, "They pick up on the mental hospital, family stuff, try to invent some category of rock that I belong to, or perhaps they pick up on my drug problem. [And] it gets to the point sooner or later when you start to think about your kids: 'What does your daddy do for a living?' 'He plays the guitar and he talks about his drug problems.' It's embarrassing to read the drivel that comes out of your mouth sometimes….."

Alice Cooper had no such conflicts. Adopting former Rolling Stones manager Andrew Loog Oldham's oft-repeated insistence that any publicity is good publicity, the band revelled in their notoriety. An idea only needed to sound like a good one for it to be pushed into play, and a rumour only needed to be more outrageous than the one before for it to be confirmed by a grinning band member, confident in the knowledge that it would be a headline the following morning. Alice Cooper was not simply a publicist's dream. The band was a tabloid journalist's dream as well.

No story was considered too outrageous. The old lady dying on the plane was one; an entire audience being treated for shock was another. Back in Michigan, it was reported, they shot a commercial for indigestion tablets – they played your stomach before you took the cure. "As the… circus pulled into the next city," Alice recalled in his autobiography, "there were four or five new fables of gore and excess awaiting us… incredibly imaginative rumours, and I could only shrug and say 'that's a good one. I haven't heard that one yet'."

"It got to the point," Glen Buxton mused, "where we didn't even need to open our mouths any more. We just let the rumour mill go wild, then reap the benefits. As far as the kids were concerned, there was nothing we would not, or could not do; if it was sick and disgusting and cruel and outrageous, then one of us had done it, and the rest had probably helped."

Rolling Stone witnessed the birth of one such fable, sitting interviewing Alice when the phone rang. "That was Shep," a grinning singer reported after he had hung up the phone. "Telling me about a page story in the

Charlotte News that said 'Girl Sickened By Rock Show'. She had to be taken out of the theatre when she saw us do 'Dead Babies.' Isn't that neat? So they did a big story on her."

Now that story was winging out on the wire services and, the following day, it would be all over the country, log-jammed with all the other exaggerations, rumours and outright lies. How the ASPCA was still monitoring the group's shows to ensure that Alice did not bite off any chicken's heads. How their concert in Atlanta went ahead only after they gave their assurances that there would be no gallows, electric chairs or feathers on stage. How a groupie girl broke her back trying to eat herself out for the band's amusement. How Glen Buxton shot an over-amorous gay fan, and then Alice fucked the bullet holes. Nothing was too outrageous, nothing was too obscene, and the more the media questioned the band about their degenerate lifestyle, the more that degeneracy would be thrust into the spotlight.

"You just haven't been in Virginia long," asked a newsman in Roanoke, VA.

"No, I haven't been in Virginia about a week," replied a straight-faced Alice. "She left for the coast."

Or...

Have you ever studied witchcraft?"

"No, I'm not into organised religion."

A lot of the tales that the band members heard about themselves would become enshrined in legend by the band's own songwriting. Much of the subject matter broached across 1973's *Billion Dollar Babies* LP was based on the group's own supposed lifestyle, from the rumour that swept British playgrounds that Alice's father had once been a dentist who was struck off for operating without anaesthetic, to the worldwide belief that the Coopers' favourite groupies were the dead ones, and that every time they hit a new city, roadies would be dispatched to undertakers and cemeteries to round up that evening's post-performance entertainment.

Even the true stories somehow twisted into fables. One night in Knoxville, Tennessee, Kachina got loose in the hotel suite and, according to legend, was last seen vanishing down the toilet bowl and into the city sewers. A search of the building certainly failed to find her and, while Alice was last seen heading into a pet store, where a replacement reptile, Yvonne, was purchased for $40, Kachina was alleged to be roaming the drains of Knoxville. Yet she reappeared a week later, nestling happily in what had been her former master's bed, and it's hard to imagine who was the most shocked by her discovery. Singer Charlie Rich, who had booked into the room that Alice had vacated? Or Kachina, to find herself suddenly cuddled up with a country and western singer?

Kachina found a new home with one of the hotel's employees; Yvonne, meanwhile, proved herself to be just as cool a trouper as her predecessor. At least once she'd started eating; for a long time, she simply refused her food. Finally, a vet suggested she be force-fed a rat. Or, according to another variation on the story, a groupie.

The stories emanating from the band's tour bus were legion, then. But the fables really kicked into overdrive once the band bought its own home, the newly christened Alice Cooper mansion in Greenwich, Connecticut.

In a small town better known for the homesteads of Rita Hayworth, Nelson Rockefeller and Bette Davis, the band had taken over the 40-room mansion that crowned the Galesi Estate, built in the thirties by a Broadway producer, and once fabled for having every wall covered with mirrors. The room at Number 17 Hill Road included a chapel, a ballroom, a library and a secret passageway that led to the kitchens, to allow the serving staff to pass discreetly through the building, all spread out across 15,000 square feet of living space.

"It's a dead ringer for a Vincent Price film set," *Melody Maker* mused. "It incorporates the unmistakable style of a man with money and a sadly demented mind. In the dark hallway lurks Alice's... Electric Chair, and next to that the skeleton of a pin-ball machine...."

Rolling Stone picked up the tale. "The band moved in and stocked Skippy Crunchy [peanut butter] in the kitchen, stocked artillery in the cupboards, tacked swastikas on the ceilings, installed a sauna bath over there and over here... in the middle of this vast, airy gymnasium-sized ballroom cluttered with beat-up amplifiers and trash... a man hangs from the ceiling, high above the Xmas tree. His plaster face tells you nothing."

But a friend of a friend who has a brother who knows somebody who works there, he could tell you a lot....

Occasionally, Alice would put a brake on a particularly repugnant rumour. Like the one that suggested he rehearsed for the stage act by dismembering the runaway kids who would turn up at the mansion, wanting to meet Mr Cooper, or training them to dismember one another.

He told *The Story Of Pop*, "We do it strictly for the audience. We're their outlet. We aren't condoning violence, we're relieving it. Just because I hack the head off a baby doll doesn't mean some kid has to run out and re-enact that situation with a real child."

At the same time, though, he admitted, "I never get repulsed by an audience's behaviour. In fact, I often think that it's real healthy. When I'm down on my knees hacking that baby doll's head off, I imagine that the girls out there, screamin' for the bits, would secretly like to change places with me. To be quite honest, I think I'm doing an artistic thing on stage… something that's never been done in rock until I came along. Not only am I giving them music, but also an image for them to think about."

The *Killer* tour wrapped up with a grand party and a prizegiving ceremony, as the band received their first ever gold disc. Rising to the very fringe of the Top 20 in America, the album had notched up sales of over half a million in the US in a matter of months, and it was a sign of just how quickly it had done so that the commemorative discs themselves were not actually ready in time. Instead, band and boa gathered in the office of Warners Executive VP Joe Smith to be presented instead with gold pressings of Jimi Hendrix's *Rainbow Bridge* soundtrack.

At the same time as it celebrated the triumph, however, Warners was growing impatient. In less than a year, Alice Cooper had grown from a tax loss for Frank Zappa's label into one of the highest-grossing live acts in the country. Yet that gold disc marked the sum of their achievement. 'I'm Eighteen' was routinely described as a hit, but it never cracked the national Top 20, and the two singles that spiralled off *Killer* had fared even more poorly. 'Under My Wheels' made number 59, 'Be My Lover' climbed 10 places higher. Now, with all the promotion in the world, *Killer* was resolutely stalled at number 21.

Nobody was yet saying out loud that Alice Cooper had found their commercial level and were doomed to remain there for the rest of their lives, a great concert act that never made the push onto the next level, but even Neal Smith looks back and admits, "We were climbing the charts all through the heartland of the USA. Unfortunately and unbelievably we were still not able to crack the Big Apple on the East Coast or LA on the West Coast. We were being rejected by the two largest music markets in America. The powers that be thought Alice Cooper was just a fluke. The music world also thought we had a theatrical rock show that overshadowed our questionable musical abilities."

There was, the band agreed, just one way to stop the sniping. "We desperately wanted to write a rock anthem that not only would get airplay in the US, but also in England and Europe as well."

Work on the band's next album was continuing as they toured *Killer*, but whereas that album slipped seamlessly into place around the indisputable epics that devoured almost half of its running time, the new material was proving harder to bed down, both in the live show and around any kind of LP-length statement.

Having exhausted, they thought, the theme of crime noir horror that was the overriding mood of *Killer*, the band worked now on a loose premise of juvenile delinquency. Ears lent to the material that was stockpiling, however, saw little in the shape of a single, much less a hit and much, much less an anthem. It was, Smith, admits, "crunch time". And that was the impetus that Glen Buxton was awaiting.

Alice had had an idea. One night as he watched a rerun of the forties TV hit *The Bowery Boys*, he was struck by one particular piece of dialogue, one character turning to the other and declaring, "Hey, Satch, school's out!"

The expression was old-time slang; it actually means "stop taking things so seriously. You're not in class now." But you could also take it literally, and that's where Alice's mind was wandering. What if school really was out?

Smith continues, "Glen came up with the intro and guitar riff for the ages and 'School's Out' was born. It was one of the most successful collaborations written by all five members of the band," while Alice was quick to tell *Melody Maker* about one further contributor. "We worked with Bob [Ezrin] like Elton John with Bernie Taupin. It's more than a producer/group thing. He's a genius. When we wrote 'School's Out' we never reckoned on strings and that. But Bob put them in – strings and horns. He made them just tasty. They haven't taken a thing off the hard rock approach. You see we've hit a level now that people know our music – they know it's Alice Cooper, and can only be Alice Cooper."

Looking back from decades into the future, Alice described a communal spirit that infused not just the band, but the entire record label. It was as though everybody knew rock history was about to be made, and they all wanted to be there to watch. In 2000, he told *Live Daily* writer Don Zulaica, "When we did 'School's Out', the president, vice president, head of A&R at Warner Brothers, everybody was at the recording studio at 2:00 in the morning, talking about lyrics, the tracks, the concept. They were so involved in the career building of Alice Cooper, they wanted Alice to do 20 albums with them. That's when a record company was a record company."

"And the rest as they say was rock'n'roll history," Smith concludes. "We got the national and international airplay we were looking for…" – and the summer of 1972 had the song that would define the era, not only in the USA but this time, across the globe. 'School's Out' soared to number one in the UK; number seven in America, and the band that Warner Brothers once worried might never break out of the cult bag was suddenly the biggest group on the planet.

Bar the Osmonds.

"Now there was no doubt Alice Cooper was for real," Alice celebrates in his autobiography. "Our remaining detractors had been silenced for good."

'School's Out' dominated that summer; soundtracked the summer holidays. Just as the band knew it would. The first time they heard the finished mix back in the studio, and maybe even before that, they knew there was no way they had not written a hit… not created their own 'Satisfaction' or 'My Generation', or any one of those songs, so rare in an artist's career but so crucial to the legend of rock in general, that will forever be an anthem. And in interviews around the release of the record, Alice expounded on his own reasons for creating the song.

"Pupil Power is a great thing," he told *New Musical Express*. "So long as it has some kind of constructive purpose. I've noticed that the kids today are a lot smarter than when I was a kid. Personally speaking, I feel that if a kid can take care of himself then he should be encouraged to do so. It makes him more of an individual… it gives him more confidence and eventually makes that person far more self-assured. Believe me, I am in total sympathy with many of the kids in what they are forced to endure under the present education system."

The notion that institutionalised education and institutionalised prison amounted to much the same thing was scarcely a new one. But Alice voiced it anyway. Touring through the songs that made up the new album, he told *Circus*, "'Luney Tune' and 'Public Animal No. 9' are like a combination of being locked up in school and being locked up in jail. One line says, 'Hey, Mr Blue Legs, where are you taking me', which is the policeman, and another says, 'Hey, Mrs. Cranston, where are you taking me,' which is the teacher. What's the difference between being locked up in school and being locked up in jail?"

And then there was 'Alma Mater', a paean to Buxton's school days and, in particular, "the time we took that snake and we put it down little Betsy's dress. Now I don't think Mrs. Axelrod was much impressed." As journalist Howard Bloom mused in *Circus*, "It seems Mrs. Axelrod took umbrage at Glen's misuse of her laboratory reptile back at Cortez High School and tossed Buxton out of the bio class. Little did she realise that one day the lad would get a loud and final revenge... in song!"

The band stretched its wings. In his autobiography, Michael Bruce explains, "There was a side to the band that was sort of beatnik or jazz-like. Dennis used to say that if he had a club, he would call it The Blue Turk. It was just one of those things we would talk about, and whenever we were in New York we would get into that beatnik, back-alley frame of mind. There were all these sides to the band. There was a psychedelic side and a hard rock side and a beatnik/blues side – and of course a comic side. 'Alma Mater', 'Slick Black Limousine', 'Public Animal No.9', those were things we sort of picked up from The Beatles, like little skits. There were all these sides to the band, which I felt would have allowed us to go on and do a lot more recording and a lot more records."

The theme of the album allowed greater elaboration. In the past, Alice Cooper had appeared to be on the side of the bad guy, the killer, the madman, the delusional loser. Now they were on the side of youth, as it fought to find a voice in an adult world, and leave aside the fact that 'School's Out' was almost callously preaching to the converted, it also became precisely the soapbox that rock'n'roll had always proclaimed itself to be.

"Say we don't care about politics," Alice told *Rolling Stone*'s Timothy Ferris. "And say MC5 does. They go out of their way to free John Sinclair and all this stuff, and they're actually doing something political. But we are also doing something political, on the fact that a policeman doesn't want his 16-year-old kid coming home with eye makeup on. That's politics. That is going to hurt a policeman more than hitting him on the head with a brick, because the lump is going to go away after a while, but the policeman is still going to be thinking, 'Oh, my kid is a gaf.' That gets into politics there."

Naturally the single 'School's Out' pulled the album of the same name in its wake, and that despite there being more commercial traction in the album's packaging – an open-up school desk, with a pair of paper panties folded inside – than the music itself. *Rolling Stone* was especially harsh: "Not all of *School's Out* is… rock. A good half is Broadway or movie soundtrack music, which is consistent with Alice's vaunted theatricalism. But in an album which so obviously panders to the whole fifties rock mystique – rock as social protest – such material is especially confounding. On the evidence of *School's Out* with its debt to Leonard and Elmer Bernstein, its plotting, its sound collages, Alice Cooper is more closely allied with the Emerson, Lake & Palmer wing which parades kitsch as art than with the furious monomania of Black Sabbath. This stuff is as bad for high-school kids as it is for their parents."

Especially once the Federal Trade Commission got wind of the panties and, presumably after conducting exhaustive tests, declared that they were a fire hazard and that the album could not be released in that form. As 10,000 copies of the album were shelved while the panties were replaced, nobody ever came forward to answer Alice's bemused question, when he first heard the news of the FTC ruling, and the incendiary properties of the giveaway panties. "What sort of person," he asked, "would be lighting a match down there anyway?"

Probably because he already knew the answer; the same sort of person who would commission a cannon as part of his latest stage act, and volunteer to be blasted out of it, every night on stage. *Melody Maker* caught an early glimpse of the band's proposed new stage show and raved, "It's going to take the form of a Broadway spectacular – ten dancers, a choreographer, a pit orchestra, lavish backdrops, and touches of *West Side Story*. And of course, the cannon."

That delight, sadly, was still on the shelf as the band continued touring through the spring and summer of 1972. A return to the UK was scheduled for mid-March but cancelled when the hosting venue, the Rainbow again, closed its doors once more. It would be the end of June before a new show could be pencilled in, and Shep Gordon decided to play one of the biggest gambles of his life.

The previous November had seen Led Zeppelin stage a couple of shows at London's Wembley Empire Pool which, since the demise of the *NME* Pop Poll shows of the mid-Sixties that were headlined by the Beatles and Rolling Stones, had been used largely for indoor sporting events and ice-skating. Now, the likes of T Rex, David Bowie and Slade were taking Led Zep's lead in edging British rock out of theatres and into exhibition halls, either the Empire Pool or the more cavernous Earls Court. Without even appearing aware of the promoters who warned him that an unknown American act was never going to fill such a place ('School's Out' was still awaiting release at the time), Gordon booked Wembley's Empire Pool. Alice, he was willing to bet, would triumph there.

It was a close run thing.

They had America sewn up. As Shep Gordon details, "A great deal of the image was calculated to have parents hate it. This always drives their children to it. The essence of Alice and what he wrote about was rebellious and my job was to present that image in a concise and shocking way that would reach parents and get them incensed and tell their children not to go see Alice because he is disgusting. It drove the kids to Alice by the millions."

Even the panties, replaced by FDA approved fireproof pairs, would create a stir. Dan Reed, programme director at Philadelphia's WXPN Radio, was just 11 when *School's Out* was released but, having already been drawn to Alice Cooper by *Killer*, he was among the first in line to buy the new LP when it hit the stores. Or, at least, have his mom buy it for him. What a surprise for Mrs Reed, then, when she walked into her son's bedroom a few days later and found Dan and some friends happily passing the panties back and forth between them.

What are they? she wanted to know. What are they for? Where did you get them? And, when Dan told her they came free with a record, she demanded to know which record.

"The one you just bought me," Dan innocently smiled.

"Mom freaked out."

Yes, America was Alice's. Britain, however, was a tougher nut. Journalist Chris Charlesworth, then on the staff of *Melody Maker*, recalls, "One of the greatest rock publicity stunts ever was stage-managed by the great Derek Taylor. Derek, of course, was the Beatles PR back in the day but in 1972 he was the 'special projects manager' at Warner Brothers in the

UK, and Alice Cooper was among their biggest acts at the time. He was coming to [Britain] and playing Wembley, and the concert was only half sold out. Big embarrassment.

"So Derek rented a huge, like 18-wheeler flat-bed open truck and stuck an equally massive two-sided poster (like a roadside hoarding) with Alice naked on it apart from his snake hiding his manhood, and ordered the driver to drive up and down Oxford Street, Regent Street, Piccadilly all day, round and round the West End. And then – killer move – the truck broke down (the driver did it deliberately) right at Piccadilly Circus at 5pm rush hour. Chaos. Traffic blocked everywhere. Huge jams. Cops furious. TV cameras come down, the Alice poster is on the news. Concert sells out. Derek's a hero."

And he continued to be one. It was during this same visit that Taylor booked Chessington Zoo for an Alice party. Guests bussed threre from London were met at the gates by female Warners staffers clad in skimpy schoolgirl uniforms and bearing endless trays of alcohol. First, guests were given the run of the zoo's in-house fairground for an hour or so, then led to the big top tent that was also a Chessington fixture, for a full circus performance.

Charlesworth continues, "High wire, animals, clowns, the lot, masses of free booze flowing all the time, topped off by a stripper or two which prompted several pissed and/or stoned partygoers to join in, including the schoolgirls, until there were about 20 naked and semi-naked people in the ring, schoolgirls in their underwear, men and women dancing together, whereupon some cops arrive and threaten to arrest everyone (especially Derek, who had probably tipped them off) unless everybody puts their clothes back on and go quietly to their coaches and back to London."

The following day, the newspapers had just one story on their mind. "ALICE COOPER ORGY SHOCK – Naked guests riot at VIP party for US shock rocker!" Of course, Taylor had been sure to invite a lot of photographers.

Further headlines tumbled from the press. The *News Of The World* declared Alice Cooper to be "the weirdest rock'n'roll band [ever] to invade Britain". *The Sunday Telegraph* described Alice as "a cross between Rasputin and Bela Lugosi, or Tiny Tim after tip-toeing through deadly night-shade, or Dracula risen from the grave once too often." And television watchdog Mary Whitehouse, never one to miss an opportunity to get in on the act when subversion was in the air, urged her National Viewers' And Listeners Association to call for 'School's Out' to be banned before it incited every schoolkid in the country to rise up against formal education.

Despite such acclaim (or maybe because of it – the music press could be very contrary when it felt like it), the old guard in the UK media did their best not to be impressed. Michael Watts, a *Melody Maker* scribe who could take at least some of the credit for ushering both Roxy Music (who opened the Wembley show) and the simultaneously rising David Bowie onto the scene of '72, chided "[Alice Cooper are] the gross product of a rancid teenage sub-culture, a musical horror movie for an audience weaned on the stream of horror flicks shown around the clock on American television. It's boloney when *Life* magazine portentously states that Alice 'becomes the scapegoat for everybody's guilts and repressions.' A horror movie is a titillating experience, and titillation is what Alice Cooper is all about."

Titillation and, of course, yet another good old-fashioned dose of controversy. In August 1972, a Pennsylvania evangelist named Rod Gilkeson announced a national crusade to save American youth from the "perversion and violence" being espoused by this "ambassador of Satan". He was talking about Alice.

American youth responded by pushing 'School's Out' even higher up the chart.

Chapter Nine

Have You Ever Had Gas Before?

The cannon was a no-go. But not because it was too dangerous. It wouldn't work because it didn't work. The idea was for Alice to be loaded into the cannon, given a moment to let himself out of a side door, and then the fuse would be lit and a dummy would fly across the stage into a waiting net. It looked good, too, in rehearsal.

But the first time they took it out on stage, with 20,000 kids watching and holding their breath, the dummy simply flopped halfway out of the barrel, and hung there like a lump. Finally Alice himself pulled it out of the cannon, and kicked the dummy off stage. The next day, he laughed, the cannon was sold to the Rolling Stones. Nobody mentioned that it was faulty. But violence, and death, remained a key element of the show, with the new album's "Street Fight" interlude taking on cinematic proportions.

It was not a gentle routine. On a stage strewn with garbage, Alice was forced to defend himself against four marauding street toughs, whom he would ruthlessly dispatch with his switchblade. And when it was first introduced, the musicians did their best to pull their punches and get away without any bruising. It swiftly became apparent, however, that it wasn't going to work like that; that it looked too fake. So the punches and kicks grew harder and harder, and the only concession to pain that they made was, they tried not to hurt Alice too badly.

Still he acknowledged to *Sounds*, "I get beat up, the other guys get beat up. When I fall down the stairs I get hurt. But I know that's what the kids want – I'm actually killing myself for the audience. You're spitting at death, defying pain. I don't really like pain at all. I would rather be killed in a car crash than get badly injured, because that would be hell, and dying might not be."

But he frequently came off stage nursing more than the occasional cut or bruise. One night, Alice said, he broke a rib. Another night, he broke three, and on another occasion, two knuckles were cracked. And the only consolation was, none of these injuries hurt at the time. "I didn't feel it," he continued in that *Sounds* feature. "But when I got off stage I went 'YEEAAAOW, OOOOAH!, that hurts!' It's just that you have so much adrenalin up there, you just do not feel it. When you step on that stage, it's my responsibility to destroy that audience. You have to stare at everyone in that audience and realise that you have got to have more power than any one of them. I assume responsibility of Alice Cooper. People are paying five dollars to see the show, and I kill myself to make sure it's right."

Yet something had changed. The mood of the presentation had shifted, the moral of the story had warped. Unable, in the time allowed them, to work up a completely new stage show for the *School's Out* tour, and with the cannon so regretfully mothballed, the band was still presenting the basics of the old *Killer* show; "modified to exclude infanticide and replace it with a knife-fight", as *Record Mirror* put it. And that was the cue for an interesting reversal of fortune.

In the past, as Alice was led to the gallows (or, before that, the electric chair), it was as punishment for some truly heinous acts, and though his audience never stopped adoring him, it could take solace from the knowledge that the monster was getting what it deserved. Hacking up babies deserves the death penalty.

This time around, though, the monster was a monster only because he took four lives. The fact that the four deserved what they got; that Alice, fighting for his life against a gang of street toughs, was the hero of the piece, not the villain, seemed to have escaped the choreographers, but it did not evade the audience. Night after night, as Alice was dragged to the gallows, and the audience was exhorted to reprise the chant "Hang him! Hang him!" that had been one of the most chilling moments of the old *Killer* performance… they didn't.

"The execution took on a kind of crucifixion atmosphere," mused *Record Mirror*. "It wasn't a baby-murderer they were hanging this time, it was their Alice. There was very little cheering or shouting at all as they dragged him to the gallows, and the thunder and lightning effects as he dropped through the trap seemed like a scene from one of those giant scale Hollywood bible movies. I don't know what reaction I expected from the audience – cheers or screams or what – but the feeling of really heavy tension in the darkness was very impressive."

Such grey shades of morality were, of course, seldom debated as the spectacular continued to make it way across the stages of the western world; indeed, asked about his own intentions for the stage show, Alice's eyes were now set on a venture that had exercised the band's imagination since the days of *Bye Bye Birdie* back in Phoenix. Throughout the summer of 1972, Alice talked incessantly about *Alice At The Palace*, a Broadway musical that was apparently scheduled to open at New York's Palace Theatre in October.

"It is my intention to progress into total environmental theatre," he told *New Musical Express*, "where nobody can get away, for the simple reason that they are part of the concept. As far as this show is concerned we'll probably just do it for a week and then depending on the reaction we will either take it on the road or sell it to a touring company."

He told *After Dark* writer Henry Edwards, "We figured that Broadway has never seen real rock. *Hair* wasn't rock. Our show is going to be a rock and roll combination on *Hellzapoppin'* [the 1941 dance spectacular that remains a benchmark for Hollywood choreography] and *Dracula*."

Neither did the ambition halt there. Casting around for a suitable director, the name Michael Bennett came up, the Toby Award-winning director of *Follies*, itself one of Broadway's biggest recent smashes. "If you're going to do the best thing on Broadway," Alice laughed immodestly, "you might as well get the best person!" And asked whether Bennett was already a fan, Alice laughed again. "[He] hadn't seen us but he'd heard a lot about us. I guess we have a lot of notoriety!"

Five years Alice's senior, Bennett had been choreographing Broadway productions since 1966. *Promises Promises*, in 1968, was his first major hit; *Company* and *Follies* followed, and his greatest success, *A Chorus Line*, was still to come. But, as Alice said, Bennett was already regarded as one of the sharpest choreographers around, and though he may not have had much to do with rock, he had at least worked with pop; *Promises Promises* was built around a score written by Hal David & Burt Bacharach, arch purveyors of some of Alice's own favourite songs.

"I went over to Michael's apartment and we talked a lot about it. Michael said that the kids are alienated towards Broadway and parents are alienated towards rock. We'll have parents bringing their kids and kids bringing their parents. We're going to lock the doors after the audience comes in. That will separate the men from the boys! We're also going to have dancers and people planted in the audience. We're trying to get a lot of Palace-type vaudevillians to be in it. Not the dead ones. We don't want to dig them up. But you'll be seeing us with people you'd never expect to see us with. We're trying to get the Three Stooges."

He was even intending to hire his own chauffeur, after discovering the old man had played "the Guy in the Straight Jacket" in *Hellzapoppin'* back in 1934, and that opened up another ambition, to try and reunite as many members of the original *Hellzapoppin'* crew as they could.

Ambitious though it was, however, the stage show was just one of so many projects occupying the band and their management's minds that summer. They talked, too, of a movie that would combine documentary, slapstick, performance and improv into one sprawling mass of disconnected madness. Ultimately imagining, perhaps, a cross between Frank Zappa's *200 Motels* and the Monkees' *Head*, he outlined one scene to a scoop-hungry *New Musical Express*.

"A guy comes out of a party in a Holiday Inn room. He's really starving, it's five in the morning, and room service is closed. Now you know how people leave the food they didn't eat on tables outside their rooms? Well, this guy sees this piece of cake with only five bites taken out of it; really delicious looking cake. So he starts eating it and it's really good.

"All of a sudden the door opens and there's this old man standing there with blisters bleeding all over his mouth, and he gasps 'don't eat the cake.' Then he falls over dead. The guy runs to his room and desperately rinses with Listerine. It ends right there and goes into something totally different."

Other scenes would take place in a psychiatrist's office, a graveyard, the wild west and even a fully appointed Hollywood film lot, the band tuxedo'd and wigged to perform a slick and slippery 'The Lady Is A Tramp'. Live footage would be pulled from a pair of shows in Texas in April 1973, and mayhem and chaos would rule the day, as a thwarted movie director teamed up on a tandem with a bearded Valkyrie to pursue the band across the globe. They escape on the back of a stolen elephant, to the strains of 'Halo Of Flies', In short, it was everything an Alice Cooper movie should be

And the gigs kept on coming, so many and so time-consuming that *Alice At The Palace* was soon shunted backwards, postponed from October 1972 to an unscheduled berth in the new year, and then abandoned altogether, lost beneath a stadium schedule that kept the band on the road until the beginning of September; allowed them six weeks off to enjoy a vacation, and then sent them back out on tour once again, with a few dates in the US and then a longer swing through Europe. And while they gigged, the new single emerged to prove that 'School's Out' was not a fluke. It was called 'Elected' and, although long-time Alice watchers knew it was essentially a cunning rewrite of their first album's 'Reflected', to the rest of the world and the waiting media, it was their most audacious effort yet.

The US Presidential elections were literally just around the corner; the country would be filing out to vote in November 1972, with Richard Nixon running for re-election to the most powerful gig in the world. And there was Alice, saying he wanted to run too. For the new party, the third party, the wild party. And what was his platform? Well, he knew that the world was in a sorry state, he knew that people had problems. And he couldn't care less. In other words, the hidden subtext behind every party political bullshit broadcast ever delivered was placed on open display, and the worst thing was, Alice still seemed more trustworthy than the goons we always wind up giving the job to in the end.

Alice traced the song back to its genesis; explained how 'Reflected' had simply been a rerouting of the notion that they had now returned to. 1968 was an election year as well, and Alice suggested writing a song called 'I Shall Be Elected'. But somehow, smiled *Circus* magazine, "a political tune didn't fit in with the whips, chains and bloody nightgowns they were toying with, and they buried the idea". Now it was back, accompanied by a hilarious short film of the band cavorting with chimpanzees and cash, and providing the election season with its most engrossing campaign film yet.

Sadly, the joke was lost on many people; America took its elections very seriously in those days, seeing the role of President as something more than merely a stepping stone to an overpaid career on the speaking circuit and a sinecure at the head of a multi-media corporation. No matter on which side of the political divide an observer stood, a song that essentially mocked the entire process, and questioned the fidelity of the candidates as well, was not something that could be comfortably broadcast too often. 'Elected' foundered at number 26 in the States, an undeserved fate for such a dynamic single, and neither was that a statistical blip. In terms of Top 10 45s, the Alice Cooper band would never score a true follow-up to 'School's Out', but by now, they didn't even care.

"We'd done it once, we'd made our mark," Glen Buxton shrugged. "Even if we'd released a dozen more number one singles, none of them would have had the impact of 'School's Out', so people would have said we were failing anyway. So we didn't worry about it. Besides, America was about the only country where we didn't keep on having hit singles, because the albums were far more important."

'Elected' climbed to number four in the UK, and John Lennon leaped aboard as a fan. "[He] told me that 'Elected' was his favourite record at that time," Alice told *Classic Rock* in 1999. "He said that he'd listened to the song nearly 100 times, but then at the end of the conversation, he said, 'Of course, you know that Paul would have done it better!'"

And the single might have done better, too, if Alice's latest British visit had not been confined to just one show in Glasgow, where *Disc*'s Caroline Boucher proclaimed that, while "Alice still isn't the ultimate in showmen, it was the best gig I've been to since early Led Zeppelin".

Three rows of trashed seats at the front of the Greens Playhouse testified to the power of the show; and Boucher spared a kindly thought, too, for the opening act, a duo that had been close to the Cooper camp since their days with Frank Zappa and Straight Records, the incredibly well named Phlorescent Leech & Eddie – aka Mark Volman and Howard Kaylan, the former front line of the Turtles, more recently the backdrop to the Mothers of Invention, but most incredibly of all, an integral part of the sound of T Rex at its most potently successful.

Their performance, a combination of coarse visual humour and sharp vocal harmony, had absolutely nothing in common with Alice Cooper's high-camp hard-rock dynamism. But they set the stage for the headliners exquisitely, and anybody with an ear for the duo's own recent musical history knew that they were fortunate to be in their presence.

It was Flo & Eddie's effervescent harmonies that rose above Marc Bolan's trademark sound to push T Rextasy to its sonic peaks and, across the run of hits that stretched between 'Ride A White Swan' in 1970 and

131

'Solid Gold Easy Action' in 1972, Flo and Eddie could rightly proclaim "every major hit single he had revolves around us. We said that to Marc, every day of the week. There never was a time when we didn't remind him that we had hit records before him and, if he hadn't brought us in, he'd never have had a hit of his own. We always brought that down on him, and it just made him laugh."

Kaylan explains, "There's a certain intrinsic whining quality to that kind of backing vocal, that I believe came largely from our time with [Zappa]. We were singing those notes all our lives, but there was a certain nasal-ness, a whininess to it, that came from singing those parts with a little tongue in cheek-ness. 'Hot Love', in particular, has a swaggering, fake sassy; it's us pretending to be chicks, with every bit of the gris-gris-gumbo-ya-ya that we could muster. It's almost mocking and it should be, because it's guys. It sounds like two 300lb guys in tutus, daring you to lift their skirts."

With their Zappa commitments over in early 1972, Kaylan and Volman immediately inaugurated their own career as Flo & Eddie, with the Alice Cooper shows geared around the release of their own debut album. Yet their presence, first in Europe in late 1972 and then as the opening act throughout Alice Cooper's 1973 US outing, marked an ominous crack in the world of Alice Cooper, as Howard Kaylan recalls.

"At that time, Alice was trying to insulate himself from his own group and keep the name for himself after his manager, Shep Gordon, said, 'You're the band, you don't need the guys.' He abandoned them more or less, and ended up taking us to his press conferences even though we were just the opening act. He liked having us around as confidantes and sidekicks."

A divide was forming. Michael Bruce snapped, "Alice was doing articles and interviews, and he would talk about everything in the world except the band. I think that was bothering a lot of members of the group. Management... tried to keep Alice isolated from the rest of the band, and I think that's what eventually led to Alice leaving. He was just in a world apart." A world that saw him spending more time with his celebrity friends than he ever did with his bandmates; and allowing them, too, to gatecrash that most sacrosanct of environments, the recording studio.

Howard Kaylan recalls nights in London when producer Tony Visconti "would just roll tapes and he's got hours and hours of tapes of us just sitting in the studio as high as kites, going off on everything, singing Presley and show tunes. There's one night where the two of us, Marc [Bolan], Alice [Cooper], Ringo [Starr], Harry Nilsson and Klaus Voorman wound up together at Morgan Studios and stayed up all night and did nothing, just got bombed and sang anything that came to mind, and recorded it all. It's just incredible. You're holding your sides."

The notion that a sundering of the Alice Cooper band was not only possible, but distinctly plausible, was one that raised itself in rumour more and more as 1972 gave way to 1973. It was no secret that Glen Buxton's health was giving way, lowering his input and impact imperceptibly, and years later even he would admit, "I was becoming the Brian Jones of the band" – a reference to the so-called Golden Stone's slow decline into incapacitation across the last couple of years of his time with the band.

But there were other concerns too: Bob Ezrin's belief that Alice's loyalty to his bandmates was holding his musical career back; Shep Gordon's growing insistence that so far as the public was concerned, the only difference between promoting Alice Cooper the band and Alice Cooper the singer was how many ways the money had to be split. And, of course, the media was now so accustomed to deferring to the singer when discussing Alice Cooper that the musicians themselves began, for the first time, to feel themselves sublimated behind Alice's larger than life persona. A mood that was not helped when Alice pushed himself even further forward than he already was.

"I take care of most of the ideas for the theatre part of it," he told *Teen* magazine. "[I] write the lyrics, handle the interviews and the whole image of the group while the rest of the guys take care of the music." But when he added that his chief influences were "a little bit of James Bond, a little bit of Barbarella and the rest from Burt Bacharach", and applied that to the Broadway pizzaz that had certainly Fred Astaired its way through much of *School's Out*, it was easy to wonder just how much of the music "the rest of the guys" really did have a hand in.

Occasionally a journalist would attempt to correct the misconceptions. But rarely was it pointed out that the band's songs were often a group-wide effort; nor that the rest of the band still called their singer Vince. Because when Alice Cooper went Christmas shopping in New York, and Alexander's department store stayed open just for them, nobody even mentioned the gifts that Bruce, Dunaway, Smith and Buxton bought for their friends and family. Not when they could document Alice's purchases: a sable fur coat, 22 rag dolls, 10 Blue Meanie dolls, 20 packs of playing cards and 57 original motion picture soundtracks from old Humphrey Bogart and Bela Lugosi films. And when Yvonne the snake curled up on a Monopoly board, Alice bought it for her.

Writing for the band's next album, meanwhile, continued apace. 'Elected' was already lined up for inclusion; so was the lacklustre 'Hello Hooray', a song composed by Canadian Rolf Kempf, and already successfully covered by folk songstress Judy Collins. Oddly positioned as a single in the new year, a ferociously vaudevillian retelling of the song was borne to number six in the UK (35 in America) on the strength of reputation alone; and so was 'No More, Mr Nice Guy', a song title that had already seen service the previous year, on the sophomore album by that other bunch of Los Angeles misfits, Sparks.

Discovered, with a certain serendipity, by the man responsible for Alice Cooper changing their name from the Nazz in the first place, a now solo Todd Rundgren, Sparks were still a far cry from the lean, mean hit machine that would take the UK charts by storm in 1974. Indeed, if they had any musical antecedent, the first two Alice Cooper LPs came close – there was the same sense of artistic endeavour over musical prowess; the same eye for a quirky tune over a memorable melody; and the same utterly left-field approach to anything even remotely approaching commerciality. Rundgren produced their eponymous debut album; James Thaddeus Lowe, the former Electric Prune, handled *A Woofer In Tweeter's Clothing*, and he later admitted that it was the failure of that album that pushed him away from the music industry.

Few people understood what he meant. Again, as with the early Alice Cooper, it would take lashings of hindsight and a major retrospective reappraisal for the first two Sparks records to even begin attracting the attention they deserved, and ironically it took the same remarketing approach to do so. In early 1973, *Pretties For You* and *Easy Action* were bound together as a budget-priced double album titled *Schooldays*; a little over a year later, once their own hits started rolling, Sparks' first two albums were likewise repackaged, and ears were finally opened to the final track on *Woofer* – 'No More Mr Nice Guys'.

Joseph Fleury, the band's fan club secretary and, later, manager, recalled, "Alice Cooper originally contacted us to ask if they could borrow a lyric

from one of Ron [songwriter Mael]'s other songs, 'Beaver O'Lindy'...
'I'm the girl in your head, the boy in your bed.' We politely declined,
and the next thing we knew, they just took the title from 'Nice Guys'
without even asking." Today, there would probably be a lawsuit, because
that's just the way the music industry works. Back then, vocalist Russell
Mael merely, wearily, sighed, "Well, at least somebody discovered this
song and made a buck or two out of it," but he surely smiled wryly when
he realised he probably wasn't alone in feeling that way. The Monkees'
'Tapioca Tundra' probably checked its own reflection every time it heard
'Alma Mater', from *School's Out*.

In truth, neither Sparks nor Alice Cooper could truly take the credit
for coining the phrase, which had been a part of the vernacular for years
already; and besides, the two Mr Nice Guys were wholly unrelated
in lyrical terms, as Alice regaled his audience with a catalogue of the
complaints he faced from straight society as he went about his business.
Still it was an anthemically self-aggrandising slice of bad boy mythology,
and its dip to a comparatively lowly number 10 in Britain was at least
masked by another Top 30 berth in America.

What all three singles had in common, however, was a sense that
whatever Alice Cooper were planning for their sixth album, it would be
a far cry from the studied darkness of *Love It To Death* and *Killer*. They
were brighter, they were cleaner, they were sharper. There was no sense
of menace any longer, complained a handful of critics, and no sense of
danger. It was as if Alice Cooper were cleaning up their act. *School's Out*
had already hinted at that with its studied insistence on placing style above
substance – its eternal title track notwithstanding, only 'My Stars' truly
slipped into the kind of musical milieu that *Killer* and *Love It To Death* had
so relentlessly made their own, the guitars that slash, the vocal that snarls,
and the melody that is as lethal as both of them. And what became *Billion
Dollar Babies* would prove even more studied, even more slick.

And it would become their biggest LP yet.

The most commonly circulating demos for *Billion Dollar Babies*, spread
across a bootleg that has been around since the late seventies, are, in fact,
the quadrophonic mix of the finished LP, replayed with one or more of the
four channels muted. The band members admit, however, that the portraits
it paints are not far from the actuality, and that the album's contents arrived
in the studio lacking only Ezrin's vision and sheen. An early take of 'Sick

Things' eschews all but a fractured guitar fuzz and shattered keyboards, as Alice intones the lyric with a lasciviousness that is positively palpable. The album's undisguised rockers, 'Raped And Freezin'' and 'Generation Landslide', rock even harder; and its most scarifying sequence, the Rodgers & Hammerstein in Hell of 'I Love The Dead' (a song, incidentally, that Michael Bruce found too macabre for even his tastes), is all empty spaces and guitars that sound like flies, buzzing around the cadavers' eyes.

And while they laboured on that, more new music emerged. Early in the new year, Alice Cooper were voted top in three separate sections of *New Musical Express*' then-prestigious annual readers' poll in the UK. They responded, Alice told writer Roy Carr, with the need to "give something in return – something positive and direct. Unfortunately, there wasn't time for us to play a concert in Britain because we're up to our necks preparing the new stage show for our three-month American tour. So we got real drunk one night and said, 'Hey let's send them a record'.

"But we didn't want to send something already on the album, or due for release very shortly. It had to be something new and exclusive. We'd always thought that it would be a real goof to do an Elvis-type thing. Yer know, all grease 'n' echo... a real boppin' rubber-legged knee-trembler. Well it so happened that Dennis (Dunaway) had written 'Slick Black Limousine', which was that sort of song, but there was no room on the new album for it and we'd already fixed up the next single. So we laid down the backing track at the mansion and put the vocal on when we were in London."

Ominous, however, was his insistence that Alice Cooper was expanding. "I don't always wanna be known as Alice Cooper the snake charmer. I want to expand the whole Alice Cooper idea. I want Alice to be a lot of other things."

For 'Slick Black Limousine', he was portraying "Alice Cooper – greasy rocker". But the new album, he was suggesting, would have even more varieties in store. And so it turned out. *Billion Dollar Babies* was, of course, a triumph, musically, lyrically and commercially. It topped the chart on both sides of the Atlantic, and positioned Alice Cooper, however briefly, among the biggest-selling acts on the planet. Yet in terms of the band's own musical development, and to place the Coopers amid the cinematic allegories that they held so dear, it is a Technicolor Hollywood epic which swamped its black-and-white B-movie predecessors only in terms of budget, casting and special effects.

The songs were nasty, but they were gratuitously so, a cut and paste of the very best rumours that had hallmarked the band's reputation in the past. Male rape, necrophilia, homosexuality, BDSM... dentists.... All filed into place on an album that could, and maybe should, have been a facile rejection of all the things that had made Alice Cooper such a vital commodity in the first place. But it succeeded all the same, buoyed not only by the sheer lavishness of its presentation; not only by the incredible momentum that had built up around it but because, like 'School's Out' (the single, not the album), failure was never an option.

As usual, Bob Ezrin took charge of the production, and the handful of cynics who still argued that Alice Cooper was a below par garage band who'd had a few lucky breaks, could take some satisfaction from the legends that circulated around its creation, and particularly, the lengths they would be forced to go to to camouflage the disintegration of the player whom even the band's detractors acknowledged as probably the best musician in the group, guitarist Glen Buxton.

"Glen [is] still real tired," Alice excused him. He told *Rock Scene*, "Glen can't drink any more – and he used to drink two bottles of whiskey a day! He's completely changed now... he's so tranquil, so laid back. It's pretty weird to see someone who used to insult you for nine or 10 years to be like that! He's so polite, it's just not him!"

Yet his kind words disguised real suffering. Buxton was falling apart, physically and emotionally. Drink and drugs played a part in his collapse, of course, but there were so many other triggers that even his friends gave up documenting them, or even trying to work out which ones were true, and which were just another flower on the grapevine of rumours and "a guy who knows them told me..."

There was the night, early on in the band's career, when his entire luggage, including every shred of ID he had ever owned, was stolen from the hotel – the shock of discovering himself, however temporary, with no means whatsoever of proving who he was transcended the simple calamity that it would prove to most people, and manifested itself as an absolute psychic shock.

There was another night, in an unnamed town on an undated tour, when an unidentified whisperer saw him reduced to emotional ashes by the demands of an especially twisted groupie.

And another one when the resolute (intolerantly so) heterosexual who, for reasons he could never fathom, was a magnet for every gay guy in town, went home with the hottest chick backstage, and never said a word about what had transpired when he saw his bandmates at breakfast the following morning. So they never said anything either, and they certainly never mentioned that someone else had told them that the chick was a dude… and an under-age one too.

Every band has those moments, every band has those experiences. But not every musician is equipped to deal with them, and whether or not any of the rumours were true, the fact is, Buxton was not one of those who could.

Without ever speaking publicly of the drinking and drugs that were taking such a toll on their guitarist, or the stress that he was trying so hard to combat but which only grew worse the more he self-medicated, Alice and the band made little attempt to hide their concerns for Buxton's future, not only as a musician, but as a living, breathing soul. Hospital visits were becoming a regular occurrence; on his most recent stay, he had part of his pancreas removed.

Buxton's own removal from the band would be a gradual process; he would remain a random spark in both the recording and touring process through until the end of the group. But Michael Bruce recalled the chaos that surrounded the quixotic Buxton's departure. "Alice and Neal and I went to Glen and asked him to step down. We were still gonna let him come to rehearsals or do whatever he needed to do. We wanted him to get help, and we were still going to pay him whatever he was earning. But he refused. He was really stubborn. That caused a lot of problems, and I think it did make it easier for Alice to walk. It was easier for him to leave the whole band than it was for him to stay and add another player."

For now, Buxton was still holding it together, at least on stage, if only because of the adrenalin combined with whatever else might be coursing through his veins gave him the necessary jump start. But in the studio, his only contribution to the finished recording was the sound of a guitar self-destructing in "Sick Things," and Mick Mashbir, a Phoenix guitarist who had played with Bruce and Smith back in the early mid-sixties, was already waiting in the wings, an auxiliary guitarist in the live show, ready to step to the front line at a moment's notice. As the *Billion Dollar Babies* sessions moved on, so Mashbir found himself called more and more often to step inside Buxton's boots.

There was a problem, though. Mashbir knew the material, he knew the musicians. What he didn't know was the studio, and the early sessions at the mansion were so chaotic and so unproductive that even Ezrin was at the point of giving up; abandoning work until the band was in a better state of mind or, better still, until Glen Buxton returned.

But there was no time for that. Instead, they decided a change of scenery was required, shifting across the ocean to London and booking immediately into Morgan Studios. The bulk of the album was recorded there, with Mashbir the reliable fingers on the frets throughout. To the world at large, however, he not only remained anonymous, he might as well not have been there at all. When 'Slick Black Limousine' fell out of *New Musical Express*, and the critics gathered to praise the slide guitar that shone through it, that ought to have been Mashbir's finest moment, because of course he played it. Instead, he mourned, Buxton was handed a Golden Microphone Award, and compared to Eric Clapton.

Worse would follow, though, as additional plaudits for the album's guitar work were spread even further afield.

Any number of special guests were filing through the studio doors. The cast of characters that Tony Visconti caught on tape one night was back, along with Donovan Leitch, the sixties singer-songwriter superstar who loaned some distinctive vocals to the song 'Billion Dollar Babies'; Family bassist Ric Grech, who recorded a couple of jams with the band, but never found his way onto an actual song; Marc Bolan, who dropped by one day with Flo & Eddie, and dipped a few guitar riffs into the stew; and Keith Moon who, from all accounts, set up his drum kit and then fell asleep.

Dennis Dunaway refuted many of the legends. "I think Donovan was the only one. It's too bad we didn't get more. It would have been great to have backing vocals from Flo & Eddie, but I don't think they're on there. And Harry Nilsson had an incredible voice. It's just unfortunate that it was uncontrollable because he was drinking so much. You couldn't get anything done when he was around. He would just fall across the mixing board and knock all the faders out of whack. But then he would stumble out into the studio and sit down at the piano, and his voice and what he was playing would sound incredible. I was like, "I can't believe this guy. Why doesn't he just stay there and play and sing for the rest of his life?'"

A few more jams did make it onto tape, but there was little in the way of out-takes or extra material for history to get excited about. The band was so well oiled at that time, the demands of their career so painstakingly choreographed, that they knew exactly what they were going to play long before they got into the studio. Yet there were two players who did join the band in the studio, whose contributions would be preserved on the finished record, and whose presence would, in fact, change the dynamic of Alice Cooper forever.

Steve Hunter was born in Decatur, Illinois, 1948 a musical prodigy even as a child who picked up the guitar when he was about 12, and crash-coursed every American guitar band he could lay his ears on, before turning his hand towards the British Invasion.

Hunter formed his first band at High School – the Weejuns were named after a favourite shoe. From there he joined the Light Brigade, alongside future Rufus keyboard player Ron Stockert, pounding around area nightclubs and bars on the same kind of circuit as the Earwigs and Spiders were suffering in the southwest, and subject to the same deprivations: the five sets a night engagements that barely paid the cost of the beer that kept the players hydrated, the long drives into the middle of nowhere to play a dance that nobody told you had been cancelled; and so on.

Yet he was attracting attention already, a wild guitarist whose grasp of flash led many to compare him with the young Jeff Beck, and in 1971, Hunter moved to Detroit to join the Mitch Ryder band, at that time one of the toughest gigging bands in the land. Ryder was certainly a ferocious performer, with enough hits behind him to ensure a healthy live schedule, and Hunter fit easily into that regimen, both on stage and in the studio – where he met, for the first time, the man with whom his career has forever been linked, producer Bob Ezrin, as he spread his wings outside of his commitments to Alice Cooper.

The Ryder band split in summer 1972, but Ezrin and Hunter remained in touch. The producer had long talked about pooling the talents of a few favourite musicians as a kind of house band to accompany him on future production gigs and, over the next three years, that pack would both record and tour with Lou Reed (*Berlin* and the epochal *Rock'n'Roll Animal* live album) and Peter Gabriel (his first, self-titled, post-Genesis effort).

It was at an Alice Cooper session, however, that Ezrin first saw this particular dream come true. "Steve Hunter played on a lot of *Billion Dollar*

Babies. He's my favourite guitarist and if you listen, there's just no one else who could have played lead on 'Generation Landslide' or that solo in 'Sick Things' but him."

Neither was Hunter the only guitarist added to the brew. Last time around, tiring of watching Buxton struggle with the chord changes that made up *School's Out*'s 'My Stars', Ezrin brought in another young player he had earmarked for the session team, ex-Frost guitarist Dick Wagner.

Wagner, too, was still reeling from the loss of his band at the time. Detroit born, Wagner had guided the Frost through three stellar albums, 1969's *Frost Music* and *Rock And Roll Music*, and 1970's *Through The Eyes Of Love* before they broke up. Wagner moved on, relocating to New York and forming Ursa Major, who toured with Alice Cooper on a few dates of the *Killer* tour, and whose 1972 debut album was another Ezrin production. But the band split, also that summer, and Wagner, too, followed the producer's dream. Now he was both playing and co-writing with Ezrin and, according to the producer, it was they who wrote what would become *Billion Dollar Babies*' most dramatic piece, the finale 'I Love The Dead'. "Alice threw some lyrics in," Ezrin told *New Musical Express*. "[Then] they bought [Dick] out."

At the time, it was still too early for anybody to see any genuine portents of the future, let alone the Cooper band's ultimate doom, in the simple juxtaposition of a producer and his two pals in the studio with the group. But the seeds of the Alice Cooper group's eventual destruction, sewn the previous summer by the first half-heeded whispers, were flowering nonetheless.

They were nurtured by alcohol. Alice himself was drinking heavily now, rarely seen without a can of Budweiser in the hand, and his bandmates were indulging appetites of their own. Glen Buxton confessed to having allowed great swathes of his most successful year to be blotted out by one excess or another, and observers around the band's inner circle all point to their own favourite crop of anecdotes to reveal the sight and sounds of a band that was... not out of control, because there were very few nights when a Cooper show passed off with anything but complete audience satisfaction.

But off stage and backstage, the sheer weight of money, fame and opportunity that had showered down upon them could not help but turn heads, crush inhibition and, however fleetingly, fill everybody with the belief that anything was possible, and everything was theirs for the taking. When Neal Smith became engaged to a statuesque blonde model called Babette, an oceangoing vessel was hired for the party and the guests taken on a night-long sail around Manhattan, offshore being generally acknowledged as the best place to indulge unobserved in fabulously hedonistic behaviour. When the ship finally docked at dawn the bleary-eyed revellers were each given hand-stitched custom white T-shirts to mark the event.

Behind such fun and games, tensions were beginning to gnaw at the band. All five band members were still contributing songs to the group but increasingly, it was Alice's that were the first to be seized upon by Shep Gordon and Bob Ezrin, the self-appointed deciding vote when it came to choosing material. In some ways it was understandable; alongside the relatively sober-minded Michael Bruce, Alice was the group's most prolific writer. But was he the voice of the band as well as its face? That was the question that exercised his colleagues; that and the growing gulf in the band members' personal income, as the songwriters soared into six figures a year, while the musicians remained locked in the lower-mid fives.

The very act of recording changed. Once the entire band had been in the studio together, watching and listening as the parts came together. The four musicians still worked like that. But Alice was no longer with them now, preferring to record his vocals alone with Bob Ezrin, as though he was somehow above his bandmates. Or maybe, as Glen Buxton mused later, "He thought there'd be less distractions if we weren't around, and maybe he was right."

When they did come together in the same room, the band's schemes were as grandiose as they had ever been, only now they had the money to actually carry them out. Well, some of them. Early plans for *Billion Dollar Babies* to be packaged with a free dollar bill inside each copy of the record, as a thank you to the fans, were scrapped when the Warner Brothers bean counters pointed out precisely how much money such a gesture would cost, before the dollar itself was even factored into the price. Instead, a still costly, but more rational, fake billion dollar bill was inserted into the packaging, slipped inside a sleeve designed to resemble a green snakeskin billfold.

Billion Dollar Babies emerged one of the most elaborately packaged albums of an already extravagant year. David Bowie's *Aladdin Sane* and Emerson, Lake & Palmer's *Brain Salad Surgery* bookended a year that saw the LP designer's art raised to fresh heights of extravagance, but still *Billion*

Dollar Babies stood out, with its cut-out bubblegum cards, a functional money clip, and a vivid inner sleeve photograph of the babies rolling in dollars. The outer sheen could not help but communicate itself to the music within.

Yet still Neal Smith confesses, "I'm still amazed that in 1973 we had the number one LP with *Billion Dollar Babies*. To me, that was the peak of our career in terms of things happening out of the blue that we weren't even expecting."

They knew, of course, that the album would be a hit. They hoped it would be bigger than *School's Out*. But in an age when no more than a dozen albums, and sometimes less than that, were ever likely to top the American chart in a year; and with the likes of Elton John (*Don't Shoot Me, I'm Only The Piano Player*), Led Zeppelin (*Houses Of The Holy*) and Pink Floyd's already perennial *Dark Side Of The Moon* all there or thereabouts, what chance did Alice Cooper truly have of bucking the statistical odds?

But in its first week of release, in mid-March 1973, *Billion Dollar Babies* became Warner Brothers' top-selling album, and having entered the *Billboard* chart at number 98, the following week it was number 18. Seven days later it was number 10, behind three previous album chart toppers (Elton, Carly Simon and War), and the flukish triumph of the *Deliverance* soundtrack. And then it was a two-horse race, Alice duking it out with Diana Ross and the immortal soundtrack to *Lady Sings The Blues*. But even Ross' initial supremacy only delayed the inevitable. On April 21, *Billion Dollar Babies* topped the American chart. A year later, with Shep Gordon proving as shrewd a financial investor as he had become a business manager, Alice was on the cover of *Forbes* magazine, headlining an article on "The New Millionaires".

"There I was with the hat, cane.... that was the best," he told *Kerrang!* in 1989. "I have it framed and on the wall, it meant so much, because we really hit the heart of America. Before that I'd been in *Rolling Stone* a few times, the cover of every major rock mag numerous times. But after *Forbes* I'd step on to a plane and they'd say, 'Excuse me Mr Cooper, you must be in first class'... and I never, ever sat there! I was always at the back, drinking too much. So they'd sit me next to these grey suits who'd ask me if I could sign their copy of *Forbes* for them.... because it was their bible. That was when Alice really had arrived."

And the rest of the Coopers were stuck back in coach.

Chapter Ten

Can't Think Of A
Word That Rhymes

The band hit the road as slickly choreographed as ever, but with an eye on the slickness more than the choreography. "We change it a little bit every night," Alice told *Rock Scene* magazine. "It really depends on what people throw on stage. Like if someone throws a baseball hat on stage, that'll change my whole way of moving around." Recently, they had seen a flurry of sex toys, vibrators and dildos, appearing amid the nightly rain, "so I'm still inventing things to do on stage. I get excited by the music, I really like it. By the time we get to New York at the end of the tour, the show will have really developed. It'll be so smooth."

Not everything that landed on stage was welcome, however. Violence was becoming commonplace at gigs, both in the audience and in the audience's reactions; as though the challenge that Alice Cooper had once thrown down, of appearing the biggest, baddest, meanest machine in town had drawn from the audience a need to be even bigger and badder. And meaner. By the mid-point of the tour, Neal Smith once said, the musicians were seriously considering wearing football helmets on stage.

Fireworks became an occupational hazard, including several that came close to doing serious damage. Massive M–80s exploded on the stage in Canada; another night, a smaller but potentially equally deadly firecracker landed in Michael Bruce's hair and it was fortune alone that ensured it was a dud. In Seattle, Alice was hit by a flying bottle. In Chicago, Neal Smith was struck by a dart.

Logistically, too, the tour was a nightmare. With Shep Gordon declaring it one of the highest-grossing tours in rock history, ticket sales in excess of 800,000 grossed some $4.5 million across 56 nights – a million or so less than Three Dog Night claimed their 1971 workload accrued, but they did not need to factor in the sheer cost of the extravaganza. Joe Gannon, a stage and lighting designer who had previously worked with Tiny Tim in Las Vegas and Neil Diamond in New York produced a *Hollywood Squares*-like set that weighed eight tons, soared 25 feet into the air and cost $150,000.

The tour covered 28,000 miles in the US alone, and featured around 70 press conferences in front of some 2,000 journalists. The band travelled aboard the Starship, a chartered four-engine, 48-passenger jet; their equipment was carted aboard two trailer trucks capable of holding 40 tons of stage gear.

A dentist's chair, a surgical table, 14 bubble machines (and 28 gallons of soapy water), 400 pints of fake blood, 2,800 spare light bulbs, 6,000 mirror parts, 23,000 sparklers, elevated risers for the band members, mannequins and statues, a succession of props and costume changes... "It's definitely more Alice Cooper stylised than ever before," a gleeful Alice boasted to *Circus* that May. "It's Alice Cooper theatre at its most intense."

There were other changes. A new snake, Eva Marie, was introduced for the sibilant 'Sick Things'; Yvonne had passed away in February and Alice guiltily confessed that it took him three days to realise, until the smell tipped him off. Neal Smith's sister Cindy was recruited as a dancing (and oddly orgasmic) molar, to accompany *A Clockwork Orange* star the Amazing Randi, in his role as the demon dentist, through the nightmarish surgery that accompanied 'Unfinished Suite'; on and on rolled the innovations, and the madness did not stop when the show was over.

A so-called party budget of $31,000 was allocated, and kicked off with a champagne luncheon in New York's West Village for 48 invited guests, who were then flown to Philadelphia for a cocktail party, a concert at the 19,500 seater Spectrum, another cocktail party (this time on a boat), a luxury hotel and a champagne breakfast. One-third of the budget was blown that night.

The most sensational change, however, was in the nature of Alice's death. He was back killing babies again, driving his sword through its hapless body and then impaling blade and babe alike between the legs of the little mite's momma. But when he came to pay for his crimes (to which necrophilia could now be added), the gallows had been retired, to be replaced by a guillotine, again manned by the Amazing Randi.

Alice told Rob Mackie of *Sounds*, "People said after the hanging, 'What can you do next?' so we did the guillotine, which is an extremely dangerous thing. That guillotine weighs about 40 pounds, and if the safety device didn't work, it would be all over. Be a great show but you could only do it once. I need that incentive, to know that I'm actually doing something death-defying for the audience."

Caught on camera in the still-gestating movie, there are few images more iconic, or indicative of the age, than a grinning, sweating Alice leering through the guillotine's frame, snarling his love of the dead, before he joins their ranks himself.

Originally, the blade was set to stop falling about a foot from Alice's neck, giving him plenty of time and space to wriggle out of the contraption while the audience's eyes were glued on Cindy Smith, lofting a severed dummy head from the basket. As the show was refined, however, so was the safety margin. Soon, the blade was halting no more than four inches away from him, "and I learned the art of timing!" he told *Famous Monsters*, "If I didn't get out of the way, that 40-pound blade could have very easily broken my neck or cut my head off for real."

The problem, he confided to *Rock Scene*, was, "Once you're in the guillotine, you can't get out. One time nothing happened, and I almost died... of humiliation!! Finally, I said, 'HEY – get me OUT OF HERE!' You know, that blade is razor sharp, and it weighs about 40 pounds!! If it didn't go right, it could cut my head off – really. It's far more dangerous than the hanging, because all that could happen with that was that if the rope broke you would get a rope burn." There was a catch in the apparatus designed to stop the blade from falling the full length of the frame.

"But if that catch doesn't work... Phewwwwwwww!" He shuddered. Every good magician knows that with the guillotine ... there's always the one time..."

And according to *Melody Maker*, whose New York correspondent Michael Watts was among the witnesses to the Philadelphia opening, that one time happened on night two of the tour.

Having long since abandoned its earlier, loftier disdain for the entire circus, *Melody Maker* opened its coverage of the tour by publishing a mock obituary of Alice, a hilarious spoof that declared, "The rock world today mourns the death of Alice Cooper who was accidentally killed last night when the safety screws failed on the guillotine he uses in his act.

"The singer, dressed in black, had just stabbed a plastic doll and was being led to the guillotine by mock-executioner, the Amazing Randi... mouthing the refrain 'I love the dead before they're cold' as his head was settled on the block. The audience was totally hushed. Then... the heavy knife blade fell unexpectedly quickly and Cooper's head jumped two feet into the air and then landed in the basket."

That was on March 17. By the following day, all hell had broken loose, with a caller to one of the other music papers, *Record Mirror*, asking for clarification of a story he had heard on the radio, that Alice was killed in a highway accident en route to a gig.

A call to Warner Brothers' UK office should have dismissed it, but it too seemed to be both in the dark and labouring beneath a welter of worried phone calls. The BBC, whose monopoly on British radio at that time suggests it would have broadcast the original story, denied having said any such thing, and was fielding its own torrent of calls. And over at *Melody Maker*, things were even more chaotic as staff fielded "a fierce onslaught of phone calls – more than Osmondrama or Cassidymania produced... 'Is he dead? Is he really dead?' was the breathless question every *MM* reporter had to face on picking up a phone. On telling grief-stricken fans that [Alice] was in fact not dead, and that [the obituary] was a piece of intelligent 'send-up,' *MM* staff faced a barrage of sometimes obscene remarks....

"After two solid days of this, it became blatantly obvious that a large section of *MM* readers had swallowed the article down the wrong hole."

The paper's mailbag groaned along with the telephone system.

"Could you please, please tell me if Alice is really dead. You stated that Cooper had been killed. If this is not so could you define the article's meaning" – from a reader in Cheltenham.

"I'm very sorry, but I don't share your sense of humour. Fancy saying that Alice had been killed. Do you realise how many hearts you've broken. I couldn't have been more heartbroken had one of my own family died" – from Julie Varley, of Wallasey, Cheshire.

And from Alice Cooper himself, "Gee, I wish it was all true! I lost $4,000 to Glen at blackjack last night. I could have died! Am I alive? Well, I'm alive and drunk as usual."

By the following week, the hoax had been put to bed, and another inquest began into just how complicit Derek Taylor and his UK Warners team had been in perpetuating it. As week turned into endless week, however, Alice himself admitted that if the guillotine didn't get him, sheer exhaustion might.

"I started this tour when I was 25," he said. I'm 43 now and we are still touring," he told *Circus* magazine. "The airplane looks like a flying three-month party. The whole back of the plane is covered with naked pictures. There's about six card games going on at once. Everyone's screaming and getting drunk at six in the morning. In Jacksonville, Florida, we had two days off and ran a 48-hour poker game in my room. When it was over, there were broken chairs, beer bottles and torn sheets all over the floor. You would have needed a steam shovel just to clean the room."

There was talk of taking the show to Las Vegas and Alice still held out hopes for Broadway. And he continued to inveigle himself into new arenas of influence. Two years earlier, around the time of *Killer*, the artist Salvador Dali was quoted as saying he'd like to design an album sleeve for Alice Cooper. Instead, he created a holograph titled *Le Brain* of Alice Cooper, a clear glass cylinder in which floated the 3-D image of Alice's head, topped with a tiara.

But a new foe, too, had arisen, the face of public decency. Alice had always run up against criticism of his act, and the larger he grew, the louder that criticism became. In November 1972, Alice Cooper were booked onto the maiden edition of ABC TV's weekly *In Concert*, sharing the billing with Seals & Crofts (!) and attracting complaints before the program even hit the airwaves.

Shot at Hofstra University on September 21 1972, it was a stupendous broadcast, kicked off by a glitter-panted Alice pouting and preening through 'I'm Eighteen', tearing off his shirt as he teetered on his heels, and the guitars howled dissolute around him.

His reprobate bandmates get in on the act, racing him through a gritty 'Gutter Cat' then battling through a brutal 'Street Fight', the onstage action purposefully courting the objections as bodies fell, sirens wailed and suddenly there was Alice, stalking the stage unrepentant and rabid, eyes wide and gait unsteady, confessing 'Killer''s crimes into the camera and not even blinking as he was led off to the gallows.

Only as the dry ice billows and the death march begins does he realise his fate, declaring his innocence and fighting the inevitable. But his heartbeat will halt before the beat of the drum, and before a purple-robed priest who awaits his confession, the killer is killed. Then he bounces back for a screaming 'School's Out', delirious and defiant, taut and triumphant, and climaxed with an orgy of feedback, bubbles and a stage in ruins. Even the normally staid television audience was on the edge of its chairs, and in homes all across America, kids turned round to look at their shell-shocked parents, knowing that their every worst nightmare had come true.

All across America, that is, except in Cincinnati, where the local ABC TV affiliate WPRC-TV station refused to air the band's half-hour segment of *In Concert* altogether, and showed an old episode of *Rawhide* instead.

"We were so proud of that!" Alice celebrated years later. "It's important to get on television, but it's even more important to get thrown off television!"

Now, *Circus* reported, the freaks were truly coming out of the woodwork. And they all seemed to wear the badge of authority.

"In Shreveport, Louisiana, Alice walked cheerfully down the steps of his plane only to be met by a grim-faced sheriff who promptly growled, 'Ah heerd about choo killin' them chickens, an' ah heerd about choo slippin' them posters 'tween you legs lahk they was your you-know-what. Yew do anything that ah even theenk is lewd, and ahm gonna slap yew in jail so fast yer ears are gonna fall off.' That night Alice stood on stage as if he were frozen in place. Only his mouth and his vocal cords moved. 'I couldn't even touch a manikin,' he says, 'or he would have slapped me behind bars. I was scared. Just plain scared.' In Memphis, the same thing happened all over again."

Over the ocean, however, an even greater menace than a local sheriff had emerged, as plans for Alice Cooper's next UK tour came up against the formidable twin towers of Leo Abse, Member of Parliament for Pontypool, and eternally vigilant TV watchdog Mary Whitehouse and her National Viewers and Listeners Association. Alice Cooper, Abse declared, was responsible for "the commercial exploitation of masochism" and, as such, was not the kind of entertainer that Britain should be welcoming.

"Cooper is peddling the culture of the concentration camp," Abse told the *Daily Mirror* newspaper during a presumably otherwise quiet news week in May. "Pop is one thing – anthems of necrophilia are another."

His act "is an incitement to infanticide. He is deliberately trying to involve these kids in sadomasochism."

Neither could Abse be accused of mere intolerance. Ferocious in his support of the repeal of Britain's anti-homosexual laws back in 1967, he also let it be known that his wife employed a man servant, John Barker, who also worked (under the pseudonym Justin Dee) as a drag artist. So this was not simple prudery at play.

Neither would anybody have suggested that, as is so often the case, Abse was simply trying to deflect the public gaze away from any other current affairs, and it was surely sheer coincidence that Abse should launch his attack on Alice Cooper on the same day, May 22, as one of his colleagues, Lord Lambton, resigned from office after being photographed in bed with a prostitute. Rather, Abse was simply reacting in the same manner that any caring parent would respond, after being shown pictures of Alice Cooper by his presumably terrified children, and resolving that no other little Britons should be forced to witness such depravity or horror.

It was the duty of Home Secretary Robert Carr, Abse declared, to deny Alice Cooper an entry visa to the United Kingdom. Diplomatically, Carr responded that Cooper would need to apply for one first. No Alice Cooper tour had been booked or even discussed.

Alice was never formally barred from the United Kingdom; never did have an entry visa revoked for fear that he might transform a nation of law-abiding teenagers into snake-handling baby killers with a taste for masochism. But a full year after Leo Abse brought his name into Parliament, Alice found, suspicions did linger.

Flying into Heathrow in March 1974, he told *MM*'s Chris Charlesworth, "I showed my passport to the customs… and the next thing I knew I was taken aside and kept for an hour while inquiries were being made. It seems that trouble with Leo Abse had caused my name to get among the list of undesirables. In the end they let me in, but that MP caused plenty of trouble. I'm thinking of dedicating my next album to him and his daughters who brought the matter up in the first place."

He continued, "I've never been busted or had any drug convictions. I'm not a revolutionary who preaches communism and yet I'm placed on the undesirable list all the same." He had even recently donated his time and image to a public information film warning young people to stay away from narcotics. "I said, 'If I catch you taking drugs, I'll come around and bite your puppy's head off'." Needless to say, "[that] got me into even more trouble".

But he was right to protest. For a couple of years now, Alice had told visiting journalists that he was more *Leave it To Beaver* than Polanski's *Macbeth* when it came to his private life; and it was no secret that domestically, he had been settled with the same girlfriend, model Cindy Lang, since they met on the *Killer* tour. Now, however, he seemed determined to come out of the respectable closet, declaring himself a convert to golf, that so-super-staid sport with which – although it was initially no more than a source of media humour and jokes – he has since become almost as synonymous as he is with rock'n'roll. It is a theme that dominates his own autobiography, his struggle for acceptance by his peers on the course lightened by the fact that he already had fame and fortune, but significant all the same.

It is golf that he would later credit with helping him through the hard times that were to come, certainly as he came to battle the twin demons of alcohol and a commercial downturn in the late seventies. Yet it could also be argued that it was golf that helped cause that downturn in the first place, as kids who had so far grown accustomed to viewing Alice Cooper as the hydra-headed embodiment of every nightmare they had never had, suddenly saw him revealed as something else entirely.

Image, as any artist who has ever succeeded... truly succeeded... in creating a larger than life persona will tell you, is a bitch. It requires careful nurturing, regular feedings and it demands to take on a life of its own. And it will reward its owner with untold riches.

But the mask cannot drop for a moment, because even the tiniest chink in the armour lets in the daylight of reality. And the more egregious that reality appears, the more at odds with the image itself, the harder the artist will need to work to keep the fans on board.

Golf was not the reason for the Alice Cooper band's so-precipitous decline. People did not band together to burn all the albums the first time they caught wind of Alice stalking the golf course in wide grin and denims, after going a round with Bob Hope, Groucho Marx or any of his other new showbiz friends.

Neither could you blame such intemperate comments as Alice blithely informing *Cosmo* that the best thing about his fame was "the bread I get from records and concert appearances", another remark that was apparently designed purely to sink his old image of being a ghoul for the sake of ghoulishness. Hell, they weren't even fazed when the UK teen mag *Jackie* caught up with Alice and found him relaxing in his hotel suite with his mother and pet puppy, coming on for all the world like an elder Osmond on day release. Or when mom punctured his pontifications about school by turning around and chiding, "You worked very hard, dear. I don't remember you not liking it too much." She turned to the writer. "I guess he just says things to make you laugh. He always liked to make people laugh."

And so he did. He joked about going head to head with boxer George Foreman, and boasted that the band had spent a staggering $32,000 on beer in the past year. He bragged, too, about his intake. "I used to drink a case a day, now I'm down to three six-packs." In other words, he was a typical all-American kid doing all-American things.

"Off stage, I'm the nicest guy in the world," Alice confirmed to *Hit Parader* that summer. "And it's so difficult for people to handle. What they don't realise is that it's really a 'Jekyll and Hyde' kind of thing. Sure, when I'm performing I become totally decadent. A depraved animal. I suppose you could say that I'm the 'new streamlined Frankenstein'. But, the truth is that once I come off... I'm really Ozzie Nelson."

None of these matters, individually, could be said to have snatched away the cloak of invincibility that once draped Alice Cooper; none of these things sent the kids in search of new nasties. But people did stop believing in what they saw on stage, and they also stopped insisting that what he sang about was real.

At the top of the pile in summer 1973, headlining one of the most extravagant and costly tours the United States had ever seen, Alice Cooper had reached a plateau and, while Alice himself now says, "I am happy with the fact that [we] got as far as we did," hidden within that remark is the acknowledgement that they had also got as far as they could. The only way to go now was down and, in an ideal world, the backstage machinations that were still gnawing at Alice to strike out on his own would have been raised a notch once the tour was over.

Instead, Alice was allowed to remain loyal to his bandmates, so that together they could discover that their day was soon to end. Indeed, they were still celebrating the final calibration of figures from the tour, everything from the cost of nine cases of beer a day for 96 days, through to the final expenses of $3.5 million. But in July 1973, *Circus* reported the first public airing for the tensions that were tearing the band apart, as Ashley Pandel*, head of Alice Cooper's promo team, declared, "They're going to pull back from the public life and do just one tour a year. The rest of the time they'll probably do things on their own. Alice would like to get further into motion pictures. Mike Bruce wants to do a solo album. Dennis Dunaway is into art and will spend more time painting. And no one knows what Glen Buxton will do. He'll probably go to a casino and try to win it."

Take that remark at face value, and it was ominous enough; not so bad that "Cooper band split" headlines started to appear, but certainly enough to cause Warner Brothers to make a few unhappy noises and, perhaps, point to a contract that demanded a second album before the end of 1973. So the retreat was cancelled. Work was still under way, said Alice, on the proposed Alice Cooper movie, and he was confident enough to start tossing around some working titles: *Hard Hearted Alice* (also a newly composed song title), *Muscle Of Love* (ultimately claimed for the band's next LP) and *Pelvic Thrust*, the latter drawn from a lyric in a new stage play Alice had seen in London, and fallen head-over-heels in love with, *The Rocky Horror Show*.

And, as for taking 12 months off, he admitted that he seriously doubted whether the band could survive even half that long out of action. "After two months, if we don't get back on stage we'll get so restless we'll go crazy. We'll probably all rent a jet and check into a Holiday Inn... for old times' sake."

And, of course, there would also be a new album.

Neal Smith: "After the overwhelming success of the *Billion Dollar Babies* album and tour, we returned to our Connecticut mansion to recuperate and begin thinking about writing songs for our next album. I, like Michael and Dennis, was always writing songs. After that tour, I was in a very melancholy mood and started composing some new songs, one of those songs was the original version of 'Teenage Lament'.

* Pandel would shortly leave the Cooper team to set up his own independent New York-based PR company, The Image Group, retaining Alice as a client, then quit the PR game altogether and, with his brother Carl and one other partner, open Ashley's, a bar, restaurant and disco on 5th Avenue at 13th Street which overnight became the hang-out of choice for all involved in the NY music business.

"None of us ever knew for sure if our songs would make it to the next album," he continued; for now, they were just stockpiling material. Yet *Muscle Of Love*, the final Alice Cooper band album, ranks as one of the most disappointing LPs ever released by a proven top act. Even today, with so many more decades of crumbling heroes and one-trick ponies to wave their own dreadful wares in its face, *Muscle Of Love* stands as an album of such supremely ordinary material that even Alice has all but disowned it. Or, at least, passed the buck onto his bandmates by insisting in his autobiography, "There were a lot of compositions where I basically felt like I was going, 'Okay, if you guys really like it that way'."

From the brutally juvenile humour that gave the album its title, through to the frankly boring cardboard box packaging that somebody, somewhere, thought would look good in the record racks, but which didn't actually fit in them, causing much confusion on the front lines of retail, *Muscle Of Love* was as drably utilitarian and workmanlike as the photos of the offstage Alice that were now beginning to show up everywhere. The all-American beer-drinking boy who used to be a monster, but he's all right now.

There were all manner of reasons for the album's failure, all kind of excuses. The most pronounced, however, were behind the scenes. Glen Buxton was not involved in the record's creation at all, and neither was Bob Ezrin, away with Lou Reed and taking Steve Hunter and (for the most part) Dick Wagner with him.

Jack Richardson took over, an older hand who had maybe not had a crash course apprenticeship in how to make an Alice Cooper record, but who could scarcely be condemned for a lack of experience. Now in his forties (he was born in 1929), Richardson might have turned down the opportunity to directly produce *Love It To Death* and *Killer*, preferring a more hands-off "executive producer" credit. But the Guess Who's success was based on his abilities, and so was that of country rock heroes Poco. He had produced fine middle-of-the-road albums for Gypsy and Hope, and he and Ezrin were blooding a new producer, too, Jack Douglas. An engineer by trade, Douglas had already worked with the Coopers on *School's Out* and *Billion Dollar Babies*. Stepping up a notch was the most natural thing in the world.

Unfortunately, he just would not have the materials to work with.

"It was a little bit different working with those guys," Smith explained. "Bob would help us with our arrangements, like he cut 'I'm Eighteen' down to three minutes, he crafted the songs and did the arrangements and I think great producers do that, they find the great hooks." Richardson and Douglas, on the other hand, simply recorded what the band presented them with. And it was not enough.

At different times over the years, Alice has tried to make light of the situation. Relaxed and casual, *Muscle Of Love* dispensed with all of the fascinations that had hitherto marked out an Alice Cooper album, and delved instead into what he described as "love, American style". Lyrically, indeed, there was much for the band's teenaged audience to get excited about as Alice led them by the hand into a world of fairly undisguised sexuality. The miscalculation they made was in thinking that the kids wanted Alice Cooper to teach them the facts of life, no matter how salaciously it might be done. Mom and dad did that, big brother or sister, or the kids behind the bike shed at school. Alice Cooper, on the other hand, was there to teach you the kind of stuff that the rest of the world cannot show, how it feels to kill yourself, the taste of blood and the smell of fear.

It was bad enough that he played golf in his spare time. Now he was putting his balls around on record as well.

"*Muscle Of Love* was just more of a laid-back album," said Alice in his attempts to defend the record. "We weren't doing any sort of horror on it. We just thought we'd sit back and make the album we wanted to, a fun album that didn't have any kind of concept. Usually we pressure ourselves into an image… the diabolical, notorious Alice Cooper. This time we thought we'd just sit back and have fun."

But what sort of fun was it really? Disco was just beginning to flex its muscles in the rock marketplace, and the first rock artists were beginning to pay attention. In London, David Bowie was in the studio with the Astronettes, cutting an album that (although it would not be released for close to two decades more) already predicted his own headlong dive into soul later in 1974. Marc Bolan was working with girlfriend Gloria Jones and backing singer Sister Pat Hall to transform the old sound of T Rexstacy into something gospel tinged and black. A lot of artists who really should have known better were making similar nods towards what really did seem like commercial expediency, but Alice Cooper should have been immune. As Neal Smith says today, "I can't get around disco, because there was nothing danceable about our music."

He elaborates. "The Rolling Stones did 'Miss You' and I think because they had an R&B background, Charlie and Bill laid down a great groove and it was 100% Stones all the way." Alice Cooper, on the other hand, delivered 'Big Apple Dreamin'' a tribute to a favourite night club in New York City. And even Smith admits, "It was definitely very danceable. That was the closest we got to disco"; and for many ears, it was too close.

Perhaps no song better illustrates the depths to which the band's creativity had sunk than 'The Man With The Golden Gun', written after the producers of the James Bond movie franchise invited Alice Cooper to submit a possible theme tune. Last time around, Paul McCartney and Wings had hit hard with the theme to *Live And Let Die*, ushering in what was widely proclaimed as a new age of rocking themes for the world's best loved super spy.

"Can't you just see the words 'Albert R. Broccoli and Harry Salzman Presents...' crawling across the screen?" a pink sailor-suited Alice challenged *Rolling Stone* as the song was being recorded. "*Live And Let Die* was the largest grossing film of [1973]. James Bond lives!"

Alice Cooper did a good job, turning in a performance that was as inspired as any other past Bond theme, and a good few later ones too. But the sense of urgency and immediacy that once kept Alice Cooper ahead of all comers was gone. Rather than slam down the song in record time, and have it on the producer's desk by breakfast, they took their time, deliberated, dawdled. And while they did so, the Bond crew got tired of waiting and went with a contrarily grisly offering from one time beat boom darling Lulu.

Yet timing was not the only reason for the song's eventual failure. Neal Smith confesses, "'The Man With The Golden Gun' is the one song, of all the eight albums we did, where I just wasn't happy with the basic track. It was supposed to be a contender for the Bond movie and all the parts were there, but it just wasn't as crisp as it should have been. I was happy with the drum part I played all the way through every album, apart from that one song."

Once upon a time, every member of Alice Cooper would have fought against mediocrity, no matter how much his bandmates seemed to scream in favour of it. That is why time spent listening to the demos that eventually became *Love It To Death*, *Killer* and, in particular, *School's Out* is so enlightening. You can hear the tension crackle between the musicians, you can hear their brains whirring and their minds turning the material over, looking for each and every way they can find to take a song to the next level.

The music that comprised *Muscle Of Love* did not enjoy that progression. There is no mistaking the demos for their studio counterparts, but it's rough edges, rather than rough sketches that characterised them, with even the lyrics sounding close to their finished form. True, 'Muscle Of Love' was originally titled, with somewhat greater subtlety, 'No Respect For The Sleepers', while the growing tensions within the band itself saw Neal Smith step out of the shadows to perform 'Baby Please Don't Stop', and make a great job of it too. But it didn't help; the song was canned at demo stage (he would later re-record it for his *Platinum Gods* solo album) and one of the best songs of the period was lost to Alice Cooper.

Muscle Of Love "is just so loose", Alice told *New Musical Express*. "That's what I wanted – a live-effect in the studio. I like mistakes. *Billion Dollar Babies* was too slick; it was so theatrical it lacked guts. So I thought back to my favourite Rolling Stones album – which was *December's Children* because it had mistakes all through it. *Muscle Of Love* doesn't have obvious mistakes, but there are a lot of dirty edges. In fact it even has a dirty stain on the cover."

Big deal.

"The song 'Muscle of Love' was the new direction of the band," Smith explains. "It was a really tough song. 'Hard Hearted Alice' I liked. But 'Crazy Little Child', I hated that song. Even when we were doing it, I was like 'why the fuck are we doing this? It makes no sense'." He turned his nose up, too, at the one song that did seem to offer a ray of light into the rentaday rock of the rest of the album, the teenage lament of 'Teenage Lament 74'. And it's ironic that he feels that way, because he was the one who wrote it.

'Teenage Lament 74' was written, he says, as a successor to 'I'm Eighteen', although it swiftly took on a whole different identity. "It was too sweet. 'Teenage Lament' was my song, I wrote it and I don't like it. I just can't believe it was chosen for the single. It changed a little bit from when I first wrote it, it came off OK, but I like the dark macabre stuff... it was just a weird thing, it was one of my songs hanging out when we were putting songs together and it developed, but it wasn't one of my favourites. Personally I was surprised that 'Teenage Lament' was chosen to be the first single off the album. 'Muscle Of Love' was my first choice for single."

He continues, "The band rehearsed the song and Alice did a rewrite of the lyrics, which was his job. The song got better and better." A reasonably promising portrait of disaffected youth was suddenly transformed into a genuinely affected slice of rock balladeering. Plus, Alice's opening line about his gold lamé jeans sounds far better than the original complaint that he had "no money in my jeans". After three years of non-stop hits, whoever was going to believe that?

So far, so good, then. "But," Smith continues, "while the vocals were being recorded, it was decided to add some female background vocals to the song. Not just any female singers, but an all-star line-up that included the Pointer Sisters, Ronnie Spector and Liza Minnelli.

"Now I loved our theatrics, I loved our outrageous stage shows, I loved my monster drum sets and I loved my wild clothes, but I am a purist and didn't like outsiders singing on our records." To his mind, that was the end of the song.

Yet what an appropriate release it should be. No matter that the accompanying promo film could as easily have been applied to almost any other song on the album, as the band stepped back to the golden age of the Keystone Kops and horsed around in prison break drag, the song was a glorious slice of adolescent angst that hit the UK record shops at much the same time as David Bowie ('Rebel Rebel'), Marc Bolan ('Teenage Dream') and the Sweet ('Teenaged Rampage') were all delivering what could likewise be considered their personal iconoclastic valedictions to the glam rock movement. In summer 1972, these same artists had sounded the clarion call for teenaged revolution. In spring 1974, they lay down the placards and went home.

Alice agreed. He told *New Musical Express*, "It's about a kid who's growing up today who doesn't want red hair, or glitter on his face, or flashy clothes, but he has to conform because it's a social thing. If I were a kid now, I'd rebel and go the other way. That's how the whole Alice thing started, only it became accepted. This poor kid is just stuck in the middle. He doesn't want to look like David Bowie or Alice. The song features the return of the individual." It was, he insisted, his favourite track on the album and he was vindicated when 'Teenage Lament 74' reached number 12 in the UK.

But there was no doubt that it was a farewell.

Ever loyal, *Circus* described *Muscle Of Love* as Alice Cooper's "latest and most shocking LP ever", and Alice played along by outlining the concept that lay behind it. "We did *School's Out* as a nostalgic look at the fifties. When I got the idea for *Billion Dollar Babies* it was just a series of songs. I wrote all those lyrics in one day, and the concept was right there in the lyric content... 16-year-old American kids driving Rolls Royces. *Muscle Of Love* is interested in urban sex habits."

"Sex openness is really healthy," he continued elsewhere. "In two years it's not going to be bi, homo, or lesbian sex. Sex is just going to be sex, and I'm preparing the kids for future shock."

Sadly, however, what promised to be the most shocking song of all never made it to the recording studios, the sad tale of a lonely housewife "who falls in love with her dishwasher detergent. Her husband's at work. She squeezes the bottle and white stuff comes out the top and goes into her dishpan. That's how Madison Avenue designed it. It's real sexual. Unknowingly, the lady falls in love with the bottle and sleeps with it." Perhaps equally unknowingly, that outline becomes an analogy for all that was wrong with the album. They had fallen in love with their own packaging, and forgotten the human (or, one might joke, inhuman) element within.

Certainly good reviews were at a premium, with perhaps the most vicious job of all delivered by Los Angeles scenester and record producer Kim Fowley, savaging the disc in *Phonographic Record*, calling for the immediate return of Bob Ezrin and aligning his absence with so many other critical partings. "When the Coasters lost Leiber & Stoller, they failed; when the Beatles lost Epstein, they failed; and when the Rolling Stones lost Keith Richards (think about it) they failed!"

He growled at the inclusion of the disco song; slammed 'Crazy Little Child' as "Alice's Leon Russell neo Randy Newman opus," and pounded 'Woman Machine' as "sexist slop. Shep Gordon is a genius. Bob Ezrin is a genius. Alice Cooper is a genius. But *Muscle Of Love* isn't... genius.... The LP by Queen on Elektra tries harder than *Muscle Of Love*. Buy it instead." How odd that Fowley should be among the co-writers with whom Alice would begin working on his next album.

The band toured *Muscle Of Love*, but the outing was short and generated few headlines. *Melody Maker*'s Chris Charlesworth, now the paper's US editor based in New York, was on board for part of the tour, flying out from La Guardia with Shep Gordon to Madison, Wisconsin, where snow covered the ground: "Shep gave me an Alice medallion to wear," he recalls. "It was a big, chunky piece of jewellery. The actress Cybill Shepherd was also accompanying Alice, covering it for some up-market magazine. We interviewed Alice together in a hotel suite, and for a moment I thought she and Alice were an item but they weren't. Each morning, on the Starship, we were all given a bag of vitamin pills by his road manager, Dave Lieberman."

Charlesworth also remembers that Dick Wagner was playing guitar in the wings. "It was the first time I'd ever encountered a situation where there was a hidden guitarist that the audience couldn't see. No-one tried to hide this from me... it was regarded as perfectly normal but I remember thinking how outrageous it would be if, say, the Who or Led Zep had a guitarist in the wings covering for Townshend or Page... unheard of! And the Cooper band was aspiring to the same level. I remember talking to Michael Bruce and he seemed a bit pissed off about it. Glen Buxton was obviously somewhere else entirely."

Live recordings from the tour, back-of-a-barn type tapes for the most part, show how easily a handful of the new songs slipped into the repertoire, but it was only a handful, as though the band had already conceded defeat; knew that they would never be able to replace the existing stage highlights, so they didn't even try.

It was as though a world had ended and the last people to know it were the people who created it. Other musical fascinations had arisen; and other preoccupations too. Alice made his non-singing television debut in a lightly supernatural TV movie called *The Snoop Sisters* and, after it aired, claimed to be receiving around five new scripts a week to consider. No doubt they took his mind off the unfolding catastrophe.

A show in Binghamton, New York was cancelled because the city fathers refused to allow Alice Cooper to play there; another, in Tampa, was canned because of unexpected winter weather. In Toledo, a rain of fireworks forced the band to walk off the stage, while seven carloads of police were called in to quell the 8,000 strong crowd. Eva Marie, Alice's latest snake, passed away. A projected European tour was cancelled.

And if Alice required any evidence whatsoever that the public appetite for gore had surpassed even his greatest achievements, it came with the monstrous success of the movie *The Exorcist* – a film that some folk were saying might never have enjoyed such popularity without the Coopers to prime the pump, but which had taken their vision of cinematic horror to hitherto unimagined heights. As journalist Caroline Coon put it when Alice arrived in London for a three-day promotional visit in March 1974, in the same week as *The Exorcist* opened in London, "Alice's reputation for daring to be more diabolically disgusting than anyone else on any legitimate stage in the word, took something of a knock."

People threw up during *The Exorcist* and left the theatre in fear of their lives, or at least their immortal souls. Cases of demonic possession were being reported or, at least, claimed, at a rate that was probably unparalleled since the Middle Ages. Membership of the Catholic Church was certainly soaring. Weakly, Alice Cooper's supporters argued that they had got out of the horror business just in time, and that that in itself proved their artistic worth, but again, the band's fans didn't want them to be worthy artists. They wanted Alice to take on *The Exorcist* face to face, and ram the old demon's green puke and bloodied crucifixes straight up where the sun don't shine.

And what did they get instead? Alice meekly proclaiming, "We're not any more violent than most TV cartoons, comics or Grimm's fairy tales, except that we are three-dimensional. As far as I'm concerned, anybody who takes me seriously on stage is really sort of weird, because I'm not taking me seriously. I'm doing a role just like Bela Lugosi acted Count Dracula. He didn't go around biting people in the throat when he was off stage. I only take horror to the point where it is entertaining. I hear that *The Exorcist* prevents people from sleeping. I don't think I've ever horrified people to that extent."

Three years earlier, such a blasphemy would have burned his tongue out.

Disillusion kicked in. In May 1974, a Canadian coroner reported back on the apparent suicide of a 13-year-old boy, found hanged from a length of hemp in his bedroom closet. According to *Rolling Stone*, "The boy's father told the inquiry that his son's experiment with execution dated from his viewing an *In Concert* show aired in Canada in March in which Alice did his staged demonstration of do-it-yourself death with a gallows and a hangman's rope." Yet even the threat of a new plague sweeping the nation, and hordes of teenagers ending their lives in a slew of Alice Cooper "Hanging Parties" did not dispel the threat of imminent redundancy.

Yes, a boy died and that was a tragedy. But that was nothing compared to the trail of terror that had haunted *The Exorcist*. The mysterious fires that broke out on set. The string of deaths – anywhere between four and nine – that struck the movie's crew and cast. The night watchman at the studio, the guy who set up the ice machines that froze the climactic exorcism scenes, one actor's father, one actress's grandfather. The fact that after the movie reached Georgetown, the Washington DC suburb in which it was set, the local death toll rose. The number of heart attacks allegedly suffered by the movie's audience. The lightning strike that destroyed a 400-year-old cross during the movie's Italian premiere at the Metropolitan Theatre in Rome. Alice had admitted that his whole schtick was a joke. So his audience looked elsewhere for teenage kicks, and you could probably bet your life that the devil doesn't play golf.

Circus broke the news. "In what may turn out to be the career move of the century, the world's favourite ghoul may give up a career of rock for TV and films. Why? The answer lies in a club and a golf ball." An entire interview was given over not to Alice's music, but to his love of the sport; his growing skill, the fact that he could now comfortably beat Norman, the bodyguard who first introduced him to the game.

"Keeping his mind on the ball, and off his usual worries about record albums and concerts, Alice regards the golf course as his sanctuary. The golf course is the only place he positively will not sign autographs. Although his best score so far is a humble 94, he aspires to become a scratch golfer, and may one day retire from rock and roll to become a pro. That one day may just be around the corner. After all, the most thrilling moment for the rock and roll star in the past few years happened on the golf course, when he hit his first birdie on a par three. He said it was more thrilling than his first gold record."

The following month an era came even closer to its end when the Alice Cooper Mansion in Greenwich, Connecticut, was destroyed in a fire. The band had largely moved away six months earlier, and nobody was on the premises when it happened. But still a lifetime of memorabilia was lost, and with it, Alice's own most tangible links with his past. By the time he and long-time girlfriend Cindy broke up, in the midst of this tumultuous period, even Alice had to admit that it was time to move on.

ALICE WITH PHOTOGRAPHER DAVID BAILEY POSING WITH BABY LOLA PFEIFFER WEARING COOPER STYLE EYE MAKE UP AND BAND MEMBERS WITH MACHINE GUNS. THIS WAS THE PHOTO SHOOT FOR THE COVER OF *BILLION DOLLAR BABIES* IN 1973. TERRY O'NEILL/GETTY IMAGES

ALICE WITH PAMELA DES BARRES AND RODNEY BINGENHEIMER. MICHAEL OCHS ARCHIVES/GETTY IMAGES

ALICE AND IGGY POP AT THE WHISKEY-A-GO-GO IN LOS ANGELES. JAMES FORTUNE REX FEATURES

ICE ON STAGE AT THE LOS ANGELES FORUM. JAMES FORTUNE/REX FEATURES

ALICE WITH HIS DRINKING BUDDY BERNIE TAUPIN, CIRCA 1975. FIN COSTELLO/
REDFERNS/GETTY IMAGES

ICE ON THE GOLF COURSE. REX FEATURES

ALICE AND WIFE-TO-BE SHERYL AT THE STEVEN WYNN GOLDEN NUGGET CELEBRITY
SOFTBALL GAME IN LAS VEGAS, NEVADA. BRAD ELTERMAN/BUZZFOTO/FILMMAGIC

THE HOLLYWOOD VAMPIRES - ALICE WITH KEITH MOON, IN LA IN 1976. DAILY MIRROR

CLUTCHING A NEWLY AWARDED GOLD DISC, ALICE MEETS QUEEN ELIZABETH II IMPERSONATOR JEANETTE CHARLES. LEFT TO RIGHT ARE PETER SELLERS, RICHARD CHAMBERLAIN, LYNSEY DE PAUL AND PETER WYNGARDE, DURING A RECORD COMPANY PARTY IN THE UK, SEPTEMBER 1975. EXPRESS NEWSPAPERS/GETTY IMAGES

ICE SHOWS OFF HIS GOLF SKILLS TO FELLOW GUEST, ACTOR PETER FALK AND HOST MIKE DOUGLAS ON *THE MIKE DOUGLAS SHOW,* CIRCA 1977. MICHAEL LESHNOV/MICHAEL OCHS CHIVES/GETTY IMAGES

CE ON THE 1975 *WELCOME TO MY NIGHTMARE* TOUR. CHRIS WALTER

ALICE'S *SCHOOL'S OUT FOR SUMMER* TOUR 1978, WITH GUITARIST JEFFERSON KEWLEY. CHRIS WALTER

FROM THE INSIDE, L-R DICK WAGNER, ALICE, WHITEY GLAN (OBSCURED), PRAKASH JOHN, STEVE HUNTER. CHRIS WALTER

CHARLEY WEAVER

ALICE APPEARING ON US TV'S *CELEBRITY SQUARES* 1975.

ALICE AND CASSANDRA PETERSON DURING THE 26TH ANNUAL GRAMMY AWARDS IN LOS ANGELES. RON GALELLA LTD/WIREIMAGE

ALICE ON *THE MUPPET SHOW* DAVID DAGLEY/REX FEATURES

Chapter Eleven

Welcoming The Nightmare

He really wasn't saying anything he hadn't said before, but it was Vince, not Alice, who gave the scoop to *Penthouse* all the same; Vince, not Alice, who distanced himself from the past, and Vince, not Alice, who was now looking to the future.

So far as the world at large was concerned, Alice would remain the celebrity. Of course he would. But from hereon in, the line that divides the public celebrity from the private individual was not so much drawn in the sand, as painted in vast neon swathes across the page. He had always thought of Alice in the third person, but now he talked of him in that way, too.

"Alice has a personality all his own. He doesn't want to be involved with anything established, anything traditional. I play baseball, and I play golf, and I listen to Burt Bacharach, and I watch TV, and I drink beer. Alice doesn't do any of those things. When it comes right down to it, Alice will not be involved with anybody except Alice. He's too far apart from everybody else, and that's his rebellion. He refuses to be like anybody in that audience or anybody on that stage.

"Trying to talk about Alice [is difficult]. Alice is such a different person. So individual that I can't talk about him, because he lives totally on spontaneity. Me, I'm Ozzie Nelson off stage. I'm 'Hi, guys, wanna go see a movie?' That's me, because I try to be so far away from Alice. I don't even want to know him. We don't stay in the same house!"

Maybe there had been a time when Vince Furnier and Alice Cooper tried to share the same body, back in the first flurry of success with 'I'm Eighteen'. But Vince got out fast. "I was kidding myself. I wore black leather and drank two bottles of whiskey a day. This is the honest-to-God truth. I was in a VO coma - a Seagrams VO coma - I was actually in a coma for days at a time. I started believing I had to be Alice all the time till I realised, 'What am I doing this for? They may be killing Alice with alcohol but why do I have to go, too? Why am I involved? I don't even know him that well!'"

It was not a distance that he would always maintain. There would be moments over the next five years when Vince truly believed that whatever spirit possessed Alice, be it an English witch, a self-destructive drive, or simply a total lack of will power, owned him as well. But for as long as he could remain in control, he would, and when the strings that held the Alice Cooper band together were cut, so were those that bound Vince to Alice.

Because they had been cut, irreparably and irrevocably, and the only question that nobody can answer, not even the principals in the now unfolding play, was when the blade touched down.

Was it when they said goodbye at the end of the *Muscle Of Love* tour, and finally embarked upon that year off, knowing that Warners' demand for fresh vinyl would be sated by a much deserved *Greatest Hits* LP?

Was it when Michael Bruce sat down with Shep Gordon one day and told him he wanted to make a solo album, brushing away the manager's warning that to do so could spell the end of the band?

Was it when Alice turned around and cut his own solo record, and proved what Gordon and Ezrin had been telling him all along, that a solo Alice Cooper was just as strong as the five man version?

Or was it when the five sat down and finally carved up the empire between them?

All of the players have their own firm belief, and they have lived with those feelings for long enough now that they are unlikely ever to relinquish them. Tales abound of deals that were reneged upon, and agreements that were bent if not broken; of promises unpromised and ideas unrealised; of behind the scenes manoeuvring and front page headline manipulations; and the only thing that can truly be agreed upon is that they all have the right to disagree. Because there is no single truth to be found. Just a series of events that ultimately added up to one inescapable fact.

Bruce was not alone in nurturing solo ambitions. Neal Smith, too, would take advantage of what they both fervently believed was a mere hiatus in the band's career, and while Bruce's *In My Own Way* was ultimately released in Germany alone, the drummer's *Platinum Gods* went unreleased for now.

Alice, too, was stirring, although his very first solo project would pass by almost unnoticed.

Canadian songwriters Steve Hammond and Dave Pierce had invited him to participate in a planned rock'n'roll stage musical, *Flash Fearless Versus The Zorg Women Parts Five & Six*, a sci-fi themed epic designed to pick up on the recent success of *The Rocky Horror Show* in London, by realigning *Rocky's* paean to old-time B-movies as a tribute to the episodic radio serials that once held the western world enthralled. Indeed, we join the adventure five parts into the action, with hero Flash and his crew already in the grip of the evil Zorg army.

Grandiosely packaged with a comic book outlining the action as it was relayed in song, the ensuing album was essentially a lure for theatrical producers to step in and bring Flash Fearless to life. But Chrysalis Records picked up the vinyl rights and three months in the studio saw the team, abetted by producer John Alcock, reach out across the universe for participants.

Alcock brought in his own most regular client, John Entwistle, who in turn invited along bandmate Keith Moon. Elkie Brooks, Robin Trower vocalist James Dewar, Black Oak Arkansas' Jim Dandy, Steeleye Span's Maddy Prior, the Moody Blues' Justin Hayward and more piled into the proceedings. But Alice was the headline attraction, stepping out to perform the two songs, the album's opening cut and first single, 'I'm Flash' and 'Trapped'.

Recorded in New York City with Bob Ezrin (who also handled Jim Dandy and Keith Moon's contributions), the two songs were delivered in classic Cooper style, but it did not help. The tidal wave of interest that the album's cast was expected to arouse simply did not materialise. The single flopped, the album did little better, and the entire shebang effectively faded from view until 1981, when the slightly retitled *Captain Crash Versus The Zorgwomen Chapters Five & Six* opened at Richmond's, a small theatre on Santa Monica Boulevard. Skewered by *Variety* ("an uninvolving space adventure spoof that tries desperately to be clever... but never even comes close"), it closed scant days later, forlorn and forgotten. Alice barely mentioned it again.

In fact, it is perfectly feasible that he didn't even remember it. Alice and Moon were partners in another venture around this time, an informal drinking-come-hell-raising club that also embraced a clutch of fellow hard drinking celebrity musicians – Ringo Starr, Harry Nilsson, Mickey Dolenz, Bernie Taupin and, occasionally, John Lennon among them – and which christened itself the Hollywood Vampires.

"I was always the life of the party," Alice confessed to *Classic Rock* magazine in 2011. "If I felt good by just having enough alcohol, if I could stay on this golden buzz from the time I woke up till the time I got to sleep at night, I'd be fine." The Vampires ("the Rat Pack with teeth," he once quipped) offered him that buzz and even today, a secret loft at the back of the Rainbow Bar & Grill in Los Angeles contains a plaque that honours its most celebrated coterie: "This is the lair of the Hollywood Vampires." "It was expected of us," Alice laughed, "to be the last one standing."

He did not drink like some of his friends. Moon and Led Zeppelin drummer John Bonham, he marvelled, could sink 36 brandies in a row, and still be back the next day. Like he said, he was content to simply maintain the buzz, and he didn't even register the fact that every day, the buzz required a little more fuel to get it going. This was just a way to spend time, to have fun, to unwind, and besides, it wasn't as if he was too drunk to work. In fact, one of the greatest ideas he ever had was conceived at the peak of the Hollywood Vampires, and the fact that he pulled it off so brilliantly more than outweighs another fact that is somewhat less palatable. He almost killed himself in the process.

Welcome To My Nightmare was to be the most extravagant and costly venture Alice Cooper (and that is the band, not the individual) had ever attempted. Every cent Alice had earned so far would be ploughed into the venture, and when he first broached the idea among his bandmates, he knew he was stepping onto shaky ground.

They listened, he has said, as Alice, Shep Gordon and Bob Ezrin outlined their ambition but they were also balancing the cost of the outing in their heads; lining it up against what Alice insists was the seriously defeatist attitude creeping into their heads. The relative failure of *Muscle Of Love* had seriously dampened the musicians' enthusiasm for extravagance, he claimed, and so had the rise of Kiss, a band that had little to offer in the form of musical competition, but whose stage show – financed by the seemingly bottomless pockets of Casablanca Records – was allegedly devouring as much money per show as the Coopers spent on an entire tour.

That, of course, was an exaggeration. But only in real terms. Visually, Kiss were a powerhouse of flame and levitation, of noise and explosion, and no matter that their records were almost stultifyingly dull retreads of whatever old riffs the band members could come up with, Kiss were playing venues after one LP that it took the Coopers three or four years to visit.

"We couldn't believe that Alice wanted to go out head to head with Kiss," Glen Buxton said. "That band had so much money behind them, it was like shooting an elephant with a pop gun." He wasn't impressed, either, by what he heard being outlined for this new Alice Cooper show. "It was visual but it was also very Halloween, whereas Kiss had a full armoury behind them. Dancers dressed as spiders against a guitar that shot out fireworks. I just couldn't see it working."

Alice was less in awe of the so-called competition. He told writer Mark Brown, "When I first heard about Kiss, I read a thing that said, 'Well, if one Alice Cooper works, four Alice Coopers ought to work.' That was basically the idea - to put four Alice Coopers together. And it worked. We never really did the same thing. They were much more pyro. Alice is more intimately scary, creepier, more Broadway-ish than Kiss. Kiss is more comic book."

Kiss, however, were not the issue. It was the future direction of the band that they needed to determine, and Alice's version of that discussion was straightforward enough. Two decades later, he told writer John "Shooter" Harrell, "The two albums before *Muscle Of Love* were huge hits, and we mutually began to think that the time was right for Alice to change – but in opposite directions.

"I had no doubts and thought that now that the door had been opened, we should make this even bigger, but they thought we should scale down. They said that because we were Alice Cooper, we would do just fine even in jeans, boots, and T-shirts. I said that was suicidal."

Yet his own vision was scarcely less suicidal either, sinking every penny into a project that had no guarantee whatsoever of succeeding.

Muscle Of Love had dented their confidence, but beyond that, so had the failure of so many other attempts to take what amounted to a theatrical production onto the road. The very same summer that Alice Cooper were discussing the nightmare, David Bowie had set off around America with what amounted to a full Broadway production, as he toured his *Diamond Dogs* concept album. The critics generally hated it, his own band all but mutinied, and audiences were none too impressed either. Finally Bowie abandoned the whole thing halfway through the outing, packing up the stage sets, sending home the dancers and boxing all the props. In terms of their American profile, Alice Cooper was a lot bigger than David Bowie. But their audience was just as fickle.

Alice was unperturbed. "I've often been asked why I fired the original band," he mused to *Classic Rock* in 1999. "Well, I never fired the Alice Cooper band, the truth is they fired themselves. After *Muscle Of Love* had finished, we hooked up to make another record and everybody wanted to do their own albums. Dennis wanted to sound like Pink Floyd, Mike wanted to be James Taylor, I don't know what Neal wanted, but none of them wanted to continue with theatrics... That was such a blow to the stomach for me. I mean, are you kidding? I said that we'd run the gauntlet of all that criticism, we were bloodied but not beaten and yet we'd got to the top of the mountain and now they didn't want it any more? No way! For me it was time to take it to the next level while we had everybody's attention."

Reawakening all of the ambitions he had once placed around *Alice At The Palace*, he drew up a list of his requirements. Just like before, dancers, props, costumes, choreography, everything needed to be perfect. But whereas Alice at the Palace needed simply to find a home and then bring the audience to it, *Welcome To My Nightmare* would go out and visit the crowds. "It's easy to say you want to do a show on Broadway," he mourned to *Rock Scene*, "but the unions... God! Is it a problem. Shep had to go and wear a suit and tie to meet with them, they thought the kids were going to come in and tear up the seats – which they might have done, I don't know. We couldn't use any of our own road rats – we would have to use all union people, it just got ridiculous." Touring *Welcome To My Nightmare* would allow Alice to handle things his way.

But that was not the whole story. There was another reason why Alice and Shep were so willing to gamble everything on this new venture, one which dated back to the days when Warners purchased the Straight catalogue from Frank Zappa, and back further still, to the contract negotiations with Zappa and Herb Cohen themselves.

For three years now, the publishing dispute that first raised its head around the time of *Killer* had been winding its weary way through the corridors of America's legal system, but finally a judgement had been arrived at. Interviewed by *Goldmine* in 1990, Michael Bruce explained, "Shep had lost two-thirds of the publishing in a lawsuit – all the way up to *Billion Dollar Babies* – so he was basically faced with starting over." *Welcome To My Nightmare* was the point from which he would begin.

Alice agreed, telling writer Russell Hall, "Shep asked how much money I had, and I told him he knew [the answer to that] better than I did. It turned out I had about $400,000 and he had about $400,000, so we put all that into the project. Our thinking was, 'If it works, it works, and if it doesn't, then we'll start all over.' We did everything we could to make sure it would be either the biggest success – or the biggest failure – we ever had."

The financial risk was huge, then, but there was also a safety net.

Neal Smith: "There was a loophole we had put into our contract [with Warners]. When the Beatles released *A Hard Day's Night*, it was on United Artists instead of Capitol, and that was because they had a loophole saying if they did a soundtrack they could find another record company to release it. So we had the same thing in our contract. Shep got it into the Warner Brothers contract and we wanted to use it for the same reason as the Beatles. Because you can get a huge advance [from a different label] if you ever do a soundtrack [whereas your own label would simply pay the same rate as usual]."

It was a smart move, too. The band's own movie, the long-mothballed (and newly retitled) *Good To See You Alice Cooper*, was finally ready for release, and Smith, Dunaway, Bruce and Buxton were all expecting that to be the project which triggered this clause. Instead, Smith remembers, "Alice used it on *Welcome To My Nightmare*. He used that clause on his own for his solo project, which was probably the first step towards pissing everybody off."

Even before recording began, Gordon was in negotiation for one of the American television networks to pick up the nightmare for broadcast, finally settling upon ABC. (It would be broadcast on April 25, 1975.).

And a record label proved just as easy to find. In the United States, it was Atlantic Records who stepped in with the riches Gordon was looking for; in the UK, it was Anchor Records. Both were willing to pay handsomely for the honour of having Alice Cooper on their label, and while Warners (and his increasingly estranged-feeling bandmates) howled in horror at Alice's perfidy, Gordon put the deal in place. Alice's ambitions went up another notch. A soundtrack album needs a movie to soundtrack. He got to work scheming that as well.

In March 1974, the team of Alice, Bob Ezrin, Dick Wagner and songwriter Alan Gordon (author of the Turtles' 'Happy Together', among others) decamped to the Bahamas to write and demo new material, and Ezrin admitted the entire process was a producer's dream. He had earned plaudits aplenty for his work on Lou Reed's *Berlin* album, a set that was as quixotically orchestrated as it was depressingly dramatic – legend insisted that when Reed asked for the sound of children crying, Ezrin went home and told his own kids that their mother had died, and then taped their screams. And though both Reed and Ezrin have since denied that, the tenor of the album was such that the tale remains a touchstone of *Berlin*. *Welcome To My Nightmare* might not be able to boast a similar legend, but it would be no less intense for all that. Only this time, it was entertainment, not excoriation that Ezrin strove for.

There would be moments of supremely sinister sonics. 'Years Ago' and 'Steven' haunt with their calliope-like accompaniment, and Cooper's voice twisting to that of an 11-year-old boy. And the necrophilia of 'Cold Ethyl' rocked as dangerously as any of the old band's more straightforward three-minute thrashes, drawing its own share of brickbats after esteemed US agony aunt Ann Landers got to hear about it.

"It was so over-the-top that it had to be funny," Alice told *Rue Morgue* in 2000. "Ann Landers wrote a big article about 'Cold Ethyl' and in it she said, 'How dare Alice write this?' I wrote her back and said, "Dear Ann: if there's an enormous rash of necrophilia that happens in the next year because of this song, please let me know. 99.9 percent of the rest of us know it's a funny song!'"

There was a nod back to the mood of 'School's Out', as 'The Department Of Youth' took a cock-eyed look at Cooper's own teetering place at the top of the rock tree, and acknowledged the fickleness of fandom. With a promo film shot against a scrapbook of photos and newspaper cuttings,

Alice was the ultimate leather-clad rocker, the epitome of the spirit of rock, the ghoul we elected to make sure school stayed out. And he knows it.

"We've got the power," the kiddy choir cries, and when a triumphant Alice asks who gave it to them, you know what he's expecting them to say. The Billion Dollar Baby, of course. Instead, they answer "Donny Osmond", because the kids from the far side of the Mormon divide were at the top of their game then as well, and all Alice can answer is "what?"

And there was a ballad, 'Only Women Bleed', which was destined to become one of Alice's best-loved, and most covered, songs ever, and that despite not really having much to do with the nightmare, or even with Alice himself. The title was lifted from a misheard piece of dialogue on the television, the melody was something co-writer Wagner was doodling one day. But they were born to be together.

Cut with the Toronto Symphony under Ezrin's expert hand, Alice (with Wagner) had not only written his first solo hit, he had also penned an international smash. Two years later actress and singer Julie Covington (a star of the original *Rocky Horror Show*) took 'Only Women Bleed' to number 12 in the UK.

There were teething troubles, of course. Despite having the nature of the nightmare already formulated, Alice admitted that it was the most straightforward songs that came first, 'Department Of Youth' and 'Only Women Bleed'. These first two tracks were recorded, and then writing resumed. 'Years Ago', the first of the album's most crucial thematic numbers, slipped out. A trip to Rio De Janeiro spawned the rambunctious 'Some Folks', with its deliberate nods towards Peggy Lee's 'Fever'; a visit to Paris unearthed 'Cold Ethyl' ("I guess I ate too many garlic snails," Alice quipped.)

It was September before the writing was over, and drummers Johnny Badanjek and Whitey Glan, bassists Prakash John and Tony Levin and keyboard player Josef Chirowski could line up for sessions that shifted from New York's A&R and Record Plant to Jimi Hendrix's Electric Lady, and up to the Toronto Soundstage, each one lending its own staff to the proceedings. And Steve Hunter was there of course, teaming up with Wagner to provide the album with what remains a headline performance quite apart from Alice's.

Throughout Lou Reed's recent *Rock And Roll Animal* tour, the pair had developed into a sensational double guitar attack, duelling wizards whose work on the ensuing Reed live album was already being talked of in the same kind of tones that accompanied the legendary Jeff Beck/Jimmy Page-fired Yardbirds of late 1966. The difference was, while Beck and Page rarely meshed in the manner that their subsequent reputations suggested they should; and while that line-up of the Yardbirds would pass with little more legacy than one fiery 45, Hunter and Wagner pulled it off every night. "Steve did a lot of ghost work for everybody," Alice confirms. "Ask Steve Tyler about Steve Hunter and Dick Wagner, and he calls them the dynamic duo because they are the best tandem guitarists in America."

At first, Alice wondered how it would feel, stepping into the studio without the familiar safety net of Dennis, Neal, Glen and Mike surrounding him, and looking back he admits, "It was a shock. But at the same time. I was surrounded by incredible players, Dick and Steve and Prakash and Whitey, these were all guys who were really good players and they were all stage players too, so I understood immediately."

Bob Ezrin's Eastmans' mentor Phil Ramone dropped in; so did the crown prince of Hollywood horror, Vincent Price, whose role as "the curator" presaged his work on Michael Jackson's *Thriller* by eight years. And around this battalion of brilliance, Cooper and Ezrin worked the songs into the shape of the concept – a child struggling to awaken from the darkest nightmare they could envisage. 'The whole thing,' Alice explains, 'is done on the level of a Peter Pan."

Price's involvement was an especial thrill and, talking to *Hit Parader* the following year, Alice remained as excited as he was the first day they met. "We were sitting around for him to come into the studio and expecting him to be dressed all in black, you know. He comes in and he's wearing a Hawaiian shirt and purple stripes pants. Everyone is going 'That's Vincent Price!?' Then he goes in and he does this really Edwardian dramatic reading and it scares the hell out of you. Then you look at him and you just have to start laughing, because he looks like Ronald McDonald. I really get along with him, we are very good friends."

Auditions were under way for the dancers who would accompany Alice through the depths of his nightmare and play their own part in its unfolding. Four spots were up for grabs, two male, two female, with the eventual victors being signed to a one-and-a-half year contract that incorporated a world tour, a television special, stage appearances and even the possibility of a movie.

Some 3,000 dancers turned up on the day of the female auditions, including one who did not even know who Alice Cooper was. Raised in Pasadena, California, Sheryl Goddard studied ballet until she was 16, when she switched to jazz. In 1975, she was attending Citrus College in Azusa, California, when some friends suggested she audition for the Alice Cooper stage show, and she went along as much out of curiosity as ambition. "I knew about Bach, not rock," she told *Phoenix Home And Garden* 15 years later. "I had never heard of Alice Cooper. I thought I was auditioning for some blonde, female folk singer."

Yet "the skinny little ballerina" as Alice described her years later, got the job and she also remembered the first time she ever touched her new employer, while teaching him how to stretch for one of his own dance routines. "I hurt him. He told me to never touch him again." Before long they were an item, a state of affairs that caused some unpleasantness with Alice's ex, Cindy Lang, who threatened to sue him for 'palimony'.

With the cast now complete, attention turned to the television special, shot at a video studio in Toronto early in the New Year.

Over the course of five days, with a full team of musicians and dancers adding to the $20,000 cost of simply getting the proceedings on film, 11 songs were performed for the cameras, painstakingly retelling the story of the album for a project that was so revolutionary that nobody even knew what to call it.

Rock video was not even a minority interest in early 1975; would not be envisioned as a commercial contender until the end of the year brought Queen's 'Bohemian Rhapsody' extravaganza. A few artists had used film in the past, Alice Cooper among them, but generally as nothing more than a means of promoting their latest single without having to tour the world. But you had to reach back to the Beatles' *Magical Mystery Tour*, in 1967, to find a comparably album-sized venture, and that was the role model Alice was aspiring towards.

Alice explained his plans to *Record Mirror*'s Martin Lang, "The idea is to put on a musical nightmare. And not only will there be the film and the album, but we're also going to put some of the scenes in the new stage act. There's plenty of room to work with so we're going to make it as much fun as possible, and with Vincent Price in the thing it can't fail to be.

"I look at it as a formula, a fun formula. We always work in total concept. So *Welcome To My Nightmare* is going to be... well if you really think about a nightmare it's totally absurd, a *Hellzapoppin'* experience. Lyrically, the LP is on a nightmare level, where it jumps around but at the end it leaves you like you went through somebody else's nightmare, you went through Alice's nightmare. It introduces a new character, this guy Steven. I don't even know him yet, but he's frightening as hell. He's a nice little kid but he keeps going back and forth and you never know where he is. He's part of the nightmare. It's fun, it's a fun type of horror show."

Reflecting from further afield, as he prepared the album's *Welcome 2 My Nightmare* sequel in 2011, Alice continues, "*Welcome To My Nightmare* was a very classy album and a very creepy Alice. It was a very rich sounding album. Bob [Ezrin] brought that to it; it had a very rich sound to it, it didn't have the normal rock instrumentation that we'd always used, except for 'Cold Ethyl' and songs like that, those were pure Alice raunch songs. But even 'Welcome', the theme, was – wait! It's almost jazzy, and it still worked, and I think as long as it's Alice singing it, the audience allows me to go in some weird directions."

The album was complete, the TV special was in the can. Now it was time for the stage show. Over $250,000 was earmarked for the outing, beginning with another Joe Gannon extravaganza for the basic set. A towering cyclops was constructed, first to menace Alice during 'Steven', and then to be beheaded. Producer-director-choreographer David Winters, a choreographer on *West Side Story*, was hired; and so were four professional dancers who, Alice delightedly insisted, had been "thrown out of Las Vegas for indulging in lewd activities". They hadn't, but it was a great story.

As for the skyrocketing costs, he simply shrugged. "I don't really care whether the thing comes off commercially, as long as it's entertaining. There's going to be things in the stage act that kids have never seen before."

There were close to five months of rehearsals to negotiate. The Disney studios were commissioned to construct the stage set and accompanying props. Fresh backing tapes needed to be recorded to ensure the seamless reproduction of the music onto the stage, and elaborate choreography was required to allow each night to run as close to clockwork as possible. And once all of that was in place, there was still the business of the tour itself.

The itinerary was enormous. Over 70 shows were ultimately lined up around the album's release, an exhausting routine that saw Alice scour the

United States before moving onto Europe in the autumn; he could not, then, have been faulted if he breathed a sigh of relief when he learned that a proposed swing through Australia had been cancelled after the government weighed up his potential impact on the country's youth.

"I am not going to allow a degenerate who could powerfully influence the young and weak minded to enter this country and stage this sort of exhibition here," huffed the responsible minister, and so the likes of the young Nick Cave and Jim Thirlwell, just two prime examples of upstanding Aussie youth, were deprived of the opportunity to catch a show that had been happily broadcast on American TV. "The head of Australian immigration has called the new show obscene," Shep Gordon sniffed. "He said that Alice eats live chickens on stage... he says that Alice has a tendency to drop live hornets on his audience... and he said that Pat Boone wouldn't let his daughter see Alice's show."

That, apparently, was the big one.

"There's nothing lewd in this show," Alice insisted in an April interview with the *Chicago Tribune*. "I believe in suggestion. I don't do it. I suggest it. I don't even use animals in the show, other than myself. It is not an attempt to shock anyone. It's just entertainment."

"It's just like a cheap Japanese horror movie," Gordon concluded, and that was an excellent comparison. Footage from the television special was projected onto a backdrop which had been sliced horizontally so that Alice could suddenly and unexpectedly burst through it, his arrival cleverly synchronised with the image of him that was being projected until the exact moment he emerged. The costuming, though excellent, was deliberately exaggerated for the back row of the auditorium; the stage sets were grotesque and over the top; the dancers cartoony and comical even before they donned the glow-in-the-dark skeleton suits (left over, perhaps, from the *Good To See You Again, Alice Cooper* props; Alice himself wears one in the graveyard scene).

Even Steven's toy box dwarfs the boy himself, and still the nuances of the performance itself, the expression on Alice's face as he watches his toys bash one another over the head, for example, were not truly visible until the *Welcome To My Nightmare* concert movie, shot in London towards the end of the jaunt, finally arrived.

Unlike the spiders who emerge for 'Devil's Food', and dangle and dance through one of Wagner and Hunter's now-patent guitar duels, the new album did not devour the entire set. A few older hits were scattered through the show, not necessarily to the concept's advantage (how jarring for little Steven to suddenly declare that he's 18), but effectively regardless. Still there was no denying the show's coherence, nor that of the nightmare concept itself, and no matter how often Alice, or any other performer for that matter, has attempted to conceive a similar convincing concert performance, *Welcome To My Nightmare* remains the closest that rock has yet come to staging a full blown costumed narrative production.

Support throughout the American leg of the tour was provided by another Detroit rocker, Suzi Quatro, as she attempted to translate her UK success to an American audience, and she looks back on the outing with undisguised glee.

"We were all on the same aircraft for 75 shows," playing everything from poker and blackjack, to staging dart gun fights in their hotel, "using mattresses as cover. It ended up in the corridor. Alice peeked out to see where I was, and I shot him right between the eyes. He had to wear a bandage and also wore my T-shirt on stage out of respect." Later, when he discovered Quatro would be celebrating her 25th birthday on the road (on June 3), Alice arranged for the entire touring party to fly down to San Antonio to see the Rolling Stones.

The two bands gelled. "Alice's show was such a contrast to mine. I was just straight rock'n'roll, he was theatre. But we worked well together, and it was so well presented. The dancers and the props, and such a good band. Plus two members [Alice and Wagner] from our home town Detroit. It was like Old Homes week."

A handful more shows also saw the package joined by a young British band, label mates at Atlantic Records, the Heavy Metal Kids, named not for the musical genre, but for a William Burroughs creation. Drummer Keith Boyce recalls, "We played some US shows with Alice, and then when he came to the UK, we were on the bill again. It really was special. I think we watched the show every night for weeks, and never got tired of it. Likewise, Alice would watch our show from the wings most nights. By now, Alice was a solo act and I think he could see that we were very much a band, and a gang much as the original Alice Cooper were. I think Alice dug that."

Today, a tour of that size, and an album of that magnitude, would afford its creator at least a couple of years respite before being despatched to cut his next LP. In the mid-seventies there was a very different work ethic, with artists routinely contracted to produce a specified number of records within a strict time period, usually at a minimum rate of one a year. Alice had kept abreast of the contract's demands with the *Greatest Hits* album, but the decision to take *Welcome To My Nightmare* to a rival record company, even if it was a part of the same parent organisation as Warner Brothers, did not sit well with the bureaucrats. The nightmare was still on the road, in fact, when the label stepped forward with a nightmare of its own.

Deliver a new album, or we will sue you. And it wasn't only Alice who received the notice. The entire Alice Cooper band were hit with it too – and why? Because, like Dunaway, Bruce, Buxton and Smith, Warners viewed *Welcome To My Nightmare* as a one-off solo project, after which the band would reconvene for business as usual. And Alice had offered no indication to the contrary.

Push, as the old saying goes, was about to become shove.

Chapter Twelve

Can't Sleep, Clowns Will Eat Me

Two years had elapsed since the Alice Cooper group last came together in the studio, but Bruce, Dunaway and Smith did not need any reminders of where their strengths lay. All three had been writing steadily in the months, not only accruing material for their solo albums, but with a new Alice Cooper album also firmly in mind. Buxton, awash in a nightmare all of his own, seems to have been happy to allow the others to get on with things, though the door would always remain open for him to reassume his role when he felt able to contribute.

Meeting up at Smith's home in Greenwich, Connecticut, they began working through the songs they had to hand, and creating anew too. Musically, all were solid; lyrically they were more or less sketches, the same as they always had been. It was Alice's job to write, or at least refine, the lyrics, and it was at that stage, too, that an underlying concept would be nailed down.

The one they already had going was a strong one, though. Among the biggest Hollywood hits of the past year was *Rollerball*, a futuristic sporting fantasy in which armoured speed skaters fought to the death. A theme that played loosely around the same ideas began to suggest itself, the notion that Alice Cooper had already broached two of America's greatest fascinations, sex and violence; it was time they investigated the third, the country's ingrained love of sport.

Neal Smith: "We wrote the music, and Alice would have written his own lyrics. Alice comes in and that was his job; he would have taken the song, rewritten the lyrics and I'm sure they would have gone in a whole different direction. We had great songs on there, some great ballads – 'Rock Me Slowly' was a great song, but that could have become 'Go To Hell', for all I know."

It could have. But it wouldn't. As the band's sessions progressed, so it became increasingly evident that Alice was a no show.

Not that he ever said so. Dunaway told *Goldmine*, "We couldn't really talk to Alice. People would screen our calls and tell us that they would get the message to Alice." It took an age, it seemed, before Alice himself let them know what was going on. He was working towards that required new album himself, using much the same musicians and team that he employed on *Welcome To My Nightmare*. The band... the old band, the group he had grown up with and without whom he might still be attending track meets in Phoenix... was over.

Outrage, shock and disbelief. Smith speaks for all three players when he recalls the last time the team's future was threatened, back in Los Angeles in 1967, with a local record label, Sound Records, gagging to sign the band – but only if they dumped their vocalist. "They stuck with Alice. They always stuck with Alice. But when things turned around, he decided to go out on his own. I can understand that from a business standpoint but it's interesting to this day, our back catalogue still sells more than all four of us put together. It goes back to the old adage of the singer not the song, but all I know is when Jimi Hendrix left the Experience it wasn't the same thing. I still loved Jimi Hendrix, I thought he was great... But he was not *as* great."

Work on the new album was halted. Suddenly there were more pressing matters to attend to. Smith continues, "When Alice said he wasn't going to come back, there were all these logistical problems because we all owned the name Alice Cooper, and we had to work that out."

The spectre of legal action arose, but Smith shot it down. "It could have been the biggest lawsuit in rock history, but it would only have made a lot of lawyers rich, and made us all hate each other, and I didn't want that because we were all best friends. And I said, 'You know what? Every band breaks up, even the Beatles, and every band has to come to an end, and I'd rather do it when we were at the top rather than grind it into the ground.'

You can't force someone to make a record that has any substance or feel to it if they don't want to. Either we're in there 100% emotionally or we're not." Alice was not, so a new arrangement needed to be agreed upon.

Alice would remain Alice. "Part of the settlement was that we all still own part of the name to this very day. Alice kept going and we all agreed to that, and to this day we all honour that. We encouraged Alice to become Alice."

Finances were sorted out. Shep Gordon had long since housed the band's earnings in a corporation, Alice Cooper, Inc. When the band broke up, the corporation was dissolved, and the money was distributed to the five shareholders.

And the band looked to the future, too. "We also agreed that we would take the name of our biggest album, *Billion Dollar Babies*, and we incorporated that name and we used it as our band name." And while Alice, Ezrin and company set off in one direction, to record what would become *Goes To Hell*, the newly minted Billion Dollar Babies headed in another, to record *Battleaxe*.

Management fell into place, a demo tape was circulated. Warners, perhaps surprisingly, passed on it, but perhaps unsurprisingly, too. They too had never seen Alice Cooper as much more than one man and a band, and they already had the one man tied down. What did they need the band for? Billion Dollar Babies ultimately signed with Polydor and, sadly, everything went downhill from there.

With guitarist Mike Marconi joining the band from Smith's solo sessions, and keyboard player Bob Dolin to complete the soundscapes, the hugely ambitious *Battleaxe* was recorded with producer Lee Decarlo at the helm, and swiftly swung out as a hard rock masterpiece – so much so that one can only imagine how magnificent it would have been had Alice worked his own magic on its contents. But the problems started early and they simply didn't stop.

The first became apparent the moment the record hit the stores – or, more accurately, the moment the needle hit the vinyl. Mixing the album, the opening 'Too Young' was simply pushed too far. Two shots of sonics, the "dada da boom boom", were mixed so high that the stylus literally popped off the record. A quarter of a million copies of the album had been shipped and sold, but the complaints flooded in and so did the returns. It didn't matter that Billion Dollar Babies were about to launch their maiden tour. The record was withdrawn from sale while a fresh remix was hurriedly effected (Jack Richardson handled the duties), and the group was on its own.

The album stopped selling. The wait for the remix, Smith mourned, "took all the momentum of the original release and slowed it down. And then some other things that shouldn't have happened did happen, and we realised that it was no longer the Alice Cooper machine we used to have. We were trying to reinvent the wheel and do the best with what we had, and there were just some things that happened that were very unfortunate."

The band's timing was perfect. Kiss were at their commercial peak, riding the Bob Ezrin produced *Destroyer*. Cheap Trick were rising. The Death to Disco campaign was gathering speed, the New Wave was around the corner. America wanted to rock again, and Billion Dollar Babies had the hardest hitting show of all.

Smith: "We spent hundreds of thousands of dollars on the theatrics. It cost us a lot of money and it was a great show."

His enthusiasm remains undiminished, even today. "I had hydraulics under my drums, and I did one solo where I went up at a 45 degree angle; I was strapped to my seat and all the drums were strapped down and I played the solo like that. But then at the end of the show, from underneath my riser came a full size regulation boxing ring, with my drums raised behind it. Then Mike Bruce came out dressed as a modern gladiator with a battle axe, which was a guitar with a big axe on it, then Mike Marconi came out with another one; one was green, one was red and they started battling to the death.

"On either side of the stage, there were these 15 foot high thermometers, marked out in million dollars, and every time you dealt a blow, that would be a million dollars, and the death blow, when you got your opponent on the floor, you'd go over and get the battle axe itself, which was this huge blade like something out of a science fiction movie, with a really sharp blade and Mike would lift it up and put it between Mike Marconi's arm and torso, right into the ground, and then blood would fly everywhere and then the thermometer would go to a billion dollars.

"And all the while this was going on, it was like Emerson Lake & Palmer, Dennis on bass, myself on drums and Bob Dolan on keyboards, and we would play the 'Sudden Death' piece from the album, which was a great jazz-rock fusion kind of song; we did a long version of it which was really, really amazing, so we pushed our musical boundaries. Then we'd have the smoke and the lightning, and we'd come back out, Mike Bruce had a bottle of champagne and we did the song 'Winner'; we squirted the champagne, the confetti would come down, and then we'd do 'Billion Dollar Babies' or 'School's Out'. It was really a great show, but unfortunately we couldn't take it more than four shows.….."

Management problems. Promoter problems. Record company problems. And, finally, tour problems. Four shows into the outing, gigs in such midwest Cooper strongholds as Flint, Pontiac and Muskogee, everything ground to a halt.

"And that was it. We'd put a lot of energy into it and one thing led to another. We needed certain things to happen for this to continue, and a couple of them fell out of place. Maybe we shouldn't have gone out with such a big, extravagant show, but that takes the fun out of it. That's what we were about and that was the show. It was a lot of energy, plus it was an emotional time for all of us because there had always been the hope the group would get back together and this was us acknowledging that that wasn't going to happen. We tried very, very, hard to do it and we were pumping tons of money into it and you just reach a point of how much more...."

Billion Dollar Babies disbanded, but if Alice had assumed that fortune would smile any brighter on him, he too was in for a rude awakening.

Shep Gordon defends the decision to shatter the band. "The manager needs to understand the root popularity of the artist, and help him manifest projects that get that across, and can be financially successful." *Welcome To My Nightmare* had done both of those things, and done so with such panache that it was no wonder Gordon and Alice believed the band was no longer necessary.

What they had perhaps forgotten, however, is that a band is more than a bunch of guys who hang out with the singer and take away their own share of the income. A band is often also an organic part of the singer's whole, a sounding board and a source of inspiration, a creative hydra whose input is based not only on current requirements but also shared experience.

Alice re-created that to some extent by surrounding himself with a new team of regular players, and of course Bob Ezrin and Shep

Gordon both offered a degree of continuity. But though they shared his life and many of his likes, they had never shared every one of the experiences that made Alice into the performer he now was; and no matter how remarkable their own suggestions might have been, often they were only suggestions. As a band, Alice Cooper had always done what they wanted to, and five heads are always more headstrong than one. Alone, Alice still looked to his surroundings for guidance. But those surroundings had changed completely, and the new album would be cut in their image.

Welcome To My Nightmare was still on the road when Alice was obliged to turn his attention towards a new LP. With tongue possibly firmly implanted in his cheek, Alice opted to call it *Hell*. It was, he explained, envisioned as a sequel of sorts to *Welcome To My Nightmare*, with that album's protagonist, Steven, now being told a bedtime story. So *Hell* (or *Alice Cooper Goes To Hell*, as it would ultimately emerge) follows its titular hero into the underworld, where he gets into a fight with the devil over who is the coolest ghoul.

The possibility that hell is itself a disco is never far from the surface; indeed, it is one that Alice has often returned to, as 2011's 'Disco Bloodbath Boogie Fever' testifies) and when Alice realises that he is effectively trapped in Hades, he always seems aware that he has one chance to escape – to sing the kind of pretty song that neither the devil nor most disco dancers could tolerate. He chooses 'I'm Always Chasing Rainbows', a song made so achingly immortal by Judy Garland, and he makes his escape, although he knew he was taking a chance – with his listeners' tolerance, if not the Prince of Darkness'.

"We did it... I said let's do it the way Alice would imitate Eddie Cantor," Alice laughs. "That's part of Alice. There's something about that old vaudeville that seeped into Alice." But was it likely to seep into his audience's consciousness too? That was a question that time, and record sales, alone would answer.

The sessions were rushed. 'I'm The Coolest' was intended as a duet between Alice and actor Henry Winkler,"the Fonz" of television's *Happy Days* fame, and negotiations developed far enough for Alice to abandon attempts to line up a replacement on the off chance that Winkler should back out. Which he did, ultimately declaring that taking on the role would leave him typecast forever in the role of a wisecracking supercool soda pop dude – something, presumably, which another few years of filling that role on one of America's most popular television shows would not do. Alice wound up performing the song alone.

Other corners were cut. The cover photo of Alice, distinctively green-fleshed, was actually cropped from the inner sleeve of *Billion Dollar Babies*. In the past, Alice Cooper had been a byword for extravagance. This time around, the whole thing reeked of cost cutting, and as he looked at proofs of the cover itself, Alice could only have sighed and remembered a night in Las Vegas, a year or so before. Elvis was there and they had gone up to his hotel suite – where the King of Rock handed the Lord of Evil a handgun, and told him to point it at him.

It was not the first time they'd met. "I got to know him and consider him a friend of mine," Alice told *Get Rhythm* magazine in 2001. "He invited me over one night and we talked for a real long time. That would be back in about '72 when he looked real good, he was like the Elvis we all like to remember."

Now, however, Alice was less certain. But you don't argue with Elvis, so he took the gun, aimed it... and his world turned upside down as the karate-mad Presley threw him over one shoulder, then planted his foot on Alice's throat. The gun was out of reach, Elvis was laughing down at him, and all Alice could think was, "Wow, what a great album cover this would make".

Better than this one, anyway.

Billboard's review of spring 1976's *Goes To Hell* was encouraging. "Very similar in overall concept to [*Welcome To My Nightmare*], even down to the sequencing of hard rock and ballad cuts. *Hell* is at least the equal of its predecessor, with an even more ambitious storyline. Alice keeps moving towards becoming the James Joyce of commercial rock surrealism."

Privately, Alice would have argued that he was on top of the world. A little over a year after the couple first met, he and dancer Sheryl Goddard were getting married; in March 1976, the pair were wed in a ceremony presided over by the fathers of both the bride and groom. Both were ordained ministers.

But the album and, indeed, the accompanying tour, was doomed. According to one former label staffer, Warner Brothers had yet to forgive Alice for taking *Welcome To My Nightmare* elsewhere and, in a show of corporate vengeance, had quietly decided to allow the new album to sink or swim on its own merits. That may or may not have been true. But the promotional outlay certainly seemed less lavish than in the past, and when Alice lined up a summer tour to promote the record, two dozen dates spread between late June and early September 1976 scarcely hinted at the kind of workload he normally accepted. Further evidence of straitened circumstances was revealed when he talked of holding the theatrics back, of presenting a straightforward rock'n'roll show and eschewing even the one sequence in the album that could have matched any past excess, a boxing match with the devil.

There were other tensions too, pressures that had less to do with Warners and more to do with Alice himself. The drinking that he had always treated as such a joke, just one more factor in the creation of the All-American Boy, was worsening, nobody doubted that. But in the past, it had not affected his professionalism. Now, that seemed less guaranteed, and while Suzi Quatro laughingly recalls him as "a functioning drunk", she also acknowledges, "I was definitely aware that he drank all the time. The good thing was, though, he was not an aggressive drunk."

No, he was a depressive one, and there was more than one occasion on the *Welcome To My Nightmare* tour when bandmates and entourage alike suspected Alice was simply going through the motions.

Part of this was simple boredom with the sheer weight of choreography, timing and organisation that the tour demanded, and a growing impulse to simply kick the set to one side and put on a blistering rock'n'roll show. But another part, a bigger part, was his sense that performing simply got in the way of more important pursuits. Like drinking.

His appearance changed with his personality. No longer gaunt and hook-nosed, Alice was suddenly pale and puffy. More than one cruel observer suggested that the reason for digging out an old picture for the *Hell* album cover was because a recent one would have been too horrific. There was not quite an embargo placed on photographing the star, but the opportunities to do so were certainly being limited.

He stopped eating and started vomiting blood instead. And it really didn't matter to him if Warner Brothers set up any interviews or not, because he wasn't doing them. "I was like Howard Hughes," Alice told *Creem* in 1979. "I didn't want to see anyone. I just locked all the doors and tore the phones off the wall."

And now he was being sent back out on the road.

A band called the Hollywood Vampire Orchestra was finalised from Alice's now regular field of musicians, and rehearsals were set to get under way. And then on June 10 1976, just two days before he was due to kick-start his first rehearsals with the band (and 20 days before the opening concert, in Halifax, Nova Scotia), Alice collapsed.

Rushed to the UCLA hospital, he was held overnight, but the diagnosis was simple. He was suffering from anaemia. Two weeks of rest was the minimum he required. Two months would be preferable.

The tour was cancelled. Ticket sales, which in any case had scarcely been dramatic, were halted and refunds were issued. And the same doomsayers who had picked up on the rumours about Warner Brothers' reluctance to push the new album now had another piece of scuttlebutt to chew upon, the possibility that Alice was simply retaliating against his label's bitterness. And *Goes To Hell* could go to hell.

There were a few bright spots. Plucked from the album as Alice's next single, in the hope that its sonic similarities to 'Only Women Bleed' might strike gold once again, a single of 'I Never Cry' reached number 12 in the US. A *Midnight Special* TV performance was shot and broadcast in August 1976, and that helped inch the album into the American Top 30. And the following month, Alice was a guest host at the televised *Rock Music Awards*, where he faked a breakdown midway through the performance, declared he could not "do this any more" and then grabbed a girl, seemingly at random from the front row of the audience, and ripped her clothes off.

Beneath, she wore a black leather cat suit; and behind them, the stage erupted into the raw roar of 'Go To Hell'. Staged and hokey it might seem in retrospect (all the more so after both U2 at Live Aid, and Bruce Springsteen on his 'Dancing In The Dark' video, reduced the surprise to mere mundanity once the eighties rolled around), but at the time it was stellar television. At the time, it proved that Alice was still on top.

But without a tour and a concerted media campaign, and compared with past excesses and successes, 1976 had come and gone and left Alice Cooper essentially running on the spot.

Running, and drinking, and mourning the loss not of his status at the top of the American rock tree, but of the inflatable shark that lived in his swimming pool. Fire, which had already consumed his home in Connecticut, had erupted at his new home, the mansion he and Sheryl owned in Hollywood. According to news reports, it was neighbour Ringo Starr who alerted the fire brigade, but when Alice returned home, it was to discover that he had not only lost a portion of his home. Someone had also stolen the prop from the movie *Jaws* that he'd been gifted by director Steven Spielberg.

He needed help. And, for a moment, he thought he had found it.

At 42 years of age, Doctor Eugene Landy was the shrink to the stars. His much-publicised relationship with Brian Wilson of the Beach Boys saw to that, and when Alice first engaged him, it was in the belief that if the doctor was good enough for the man who wrote 'Good Vibrations', he was good enough for Alice.

A clinical psychologist, Landy specialised, he said, in what he called the dysfunctional lifestyles of the rich and famous, the urges that intense fame and dazzling spotlights seemed to bring out in them. "For some reason, I seem to be able to relate to them," Landy told *Rolling Stone*'s David Felton. "I think I have a nice reputation that says I'm unorthodox by orthodox standards, but basically unique by unorthodox standards."

He was also, by his own admission, "outrageously expensive", $90 an hour when that was more than double the going rate of the average shrink. But Landy was not average; and he did not measure treatment time in hours. Years were more his style; he admitted to *Rolling Stone* that he saw Brian Wilson's treatment requiring at least that long.

His background was certainly unconventional. A High School drop-out, Landy nevertheless graduated Los Angeles State College with a degree in psychology in 1964, before collecting a Masters and a PhF from the University of Oklahoma. Back in LA, he published the first authoritative lexicon of hippy slang, *The Underground Dictionary*, and then set up his psychiatric practice in the early seventies, using word of mouth and a growing reputation to lure the first stars into his orbit. Actor Richard Harris and television host Rod Serling were both numbered among his satisfied clients, he said, and now Alice Cooper was about to join them.

Landy did not work alone. His team of seven also included a psychiatrist, Sol Samuels, physician David Gans, and a nutritionist named Nancy, all of whom worked in concert to address a patient's ills. Drugs and alcohol were deemed off limits, diet was regulated and a healthy workload, built in Alice's case (like Wilson's) around songwriting and recording, was decreed.

But while Alice placed his trust in Landy, others in his circle – beginning with wife Sheryl and manager Shep Gordon – were less impressed, a situation that grew increasingly tense as Landy's treatment continued and Alice not only showed no signs of recovery, but offered little to suggest that he was even aware of the treatment. His social life continued as before; so did his alcohol consumption; and so did his decline.

He kept that aspect private, of course, throwing himself into every opportunity to work that arose, as if he realised that the more he kept moving, the less his detractors would be able to pin him down. There would be no descent into a booze-soaked silence for Alice; he took a role as a singing waitress in *Sextette*, an oddball comedy that co-starred Mae West and fellow Hollywood Vampires Keith Moon and Ringo Starr, and he was working towards a new album as well, a rapprochement with Warner Brothers of course, but also one that would – as per Landy's instructions – focus his energies away from the self-destructive tendencies that had delineated his stage persona in the past, and present a whole new face to the world.

And on paper, it appeared to be his most solid characterisation since the days of *Killer*, a hard drinking (of course), harder boiled private detective named Maurice Escargot, a direct descendent of the Mickey Spillane type PIs who once dominated detective fiction, or the sea of sleuths whose adventures filled the B-movie theatres and serialised radio shows of the forties and fifties.

It was an intriguing proposition, even if the concept itself was never to be fully embraced. *Lace And Whiskey*, as the album was titled, took its name from the (fictional) paperback novel that was photographed on its cover, the self-styled "outstanding murder mystery of the decade". But once inside the disc itself, *Lace And Whiskey* was less about the detective and more about his lifestyle, a swaggering hard man bent on living life to its alcoholic full – an autobiographical twist that Cooper would tease into even sharper focus with the declamatory 'I Never Wrote Those Songs', distancing himself even further from the Alice of old; and 'My God'.

"It's a concept... that has nothing really to do with the music," Alice agreed to *Circus*. "The whole concept is in the packaging of this one – a sort of *Farewell My Lovely* type of look." And as for Maurice Escargot, he was as real to Alice as the arch fiend of old, and just as unreal too. "It's just another character. You write the music, and all of a sudden you say 'Who do I have doing this song?' And a character is always a sort of whim in your mind anyway – somebody that you kind of want to be. The thing with Maurice is that he's a real Clouseau character. And that has always been somebody I've wanted to be kind of."

Working as usual with the Ezrin/Wagner/Hunter team, with Ezrin and Wagner his collaborators on every song, *Lace And Whiskey* seemed determined to eschew the formula laid down by its two predecessors. True, *Lace And Whiskey* was once again debuted with a ballad single, this time the genuinely affecting 'You And Me'; but elsewhere, 'Ubangi Stomp' allowed everybody to rock out with an absolute lack of self-consciousness, while the smirking 'Road Rats', a paean to the road crew that had helped keep things rolling for almost a decade now (ever since the Spiders first earned enough money to hire someone else to haul their gear for them), would gain fresh impetus when it became the basis for the movie *Roadie*.

There was one song, however, whose inclusion Alice would forever regret, to the extent of personally demanding its removal from the proposed track listing of the *Life And Crimes* box set more than 20 years later. '(No More) Love At Your Convenience', he condemned, was "our attempt to make fun of disco. That song was really, directly, a satire. He lines all the people up in the disco and mows them all down like the St Valentine's Day Massacre, and they keep coming out of the grave. They won't die, and at the very end you have that guitar coming in, the rock guitar overwhelms the disco part

"So, 'Love At Your Convenience' was a satire. We wrote it as a satire. Unfortunately, we weren't clever enough to let the audience know it was a satire. It was like Kiss doing 'I Was Made For Lovin' You', it was a total disco song and once in a while I think it's OK for an established band like Alice or Ozzy to do something that is totally away from what they do, but still do it in their style. It's a very end-of-disco bloodbath; there's a whole Broadway thing that comes in there, it was almost something out of *West Side Story*, almost something out of *Guys & Dolls*."

Today, Alice readily admits that the schmaltz is simply a part of his DNA; "Bob [Ezrin] and I can't get away from that. It's there, so I say bring it out. The overlapping vocals that are so Broadway but it makes sense, and I think it's a signature of Alice. I don't try to change that; I say

'There, let it be what it is'." But it did not work on the album, as ears instead simply flipped the satire on its head and accused Alice of going deliberately disco; of selling out; of losing the rock.

With so much else percolating around it, it was ironic that the key to the album, and indeed to much of Alice's own personal musical iconography, lay in a song that wasn't even listed on the original LP sleeve.

A magnificent lyric and a fabulous melody, both bolstered by the inclusion of America's most stirring anthem, 'The Battle Hymn Of The Republic', 'King Of The Silver Screen' was another paean to the golden age of Hollywood starlets and, again, Broadway musicals. Only this time, they are seen through the eyes of an overweight construction site worker who dresses as a starlet in the privacy of his own home, while plucking up the courage to let his workmates know the truth.

Which is something that Alice may not have physically done, but which he agrees is something he identifies heavily with. "It was something that was always there. I never stepped out and intentionally said 'I must listen to old Broadway songs', but I may be the only straight guy in the world that knows all those old Broadway tunes. I listen to *A Chorus Line* and musically and lyrically I go, 'This is so good.' And of course I know it sounds gay, but musically I have to admire it and there are parts in there that I would love to have written on an Alice level.

"I can move into that world and dissect those parts and bring them out, and the great thing is that Bob Ezrin is the other guy who is straight and knows those tunes and he'll say, 'Yes, we can do that, somehow inject that in here and make it work.' We do a lot of hard rock but every once in a while, we'll drift into a song that only I would do."

'King Of The Silver Screen' meets that qualification head on. At its core, it is a straight comedy piece; over-think it, and it could be a reflection on the glam era that was now a historical artefact. But more than that, it is a statement of intent; of one man's need to shake off the personal and emotional straitjacket into which society and his peers have tied him, and admit who he really is beneath the bluster. Alice was exhausted; but more than that, he was tired of being Alice. 'The King Of The Silver Screen' was his way of laying his deepest emotions bare.

The old beast was not dead, of course. Take the new album out of its sleeve and a sheet of paper falls with it, an invitation to enrol in the Alice Cooper Fan Club, emblazoned with the words Join Or Die. "I'm only asking," the accompanying message assured readers. "But you'd better listen because you might not like the alternative."

He began planning the new tour, talking up a three-act performance that commenced with a solid burst of oldies, led into a sequence based around the last two albums, then hit the finishing line with the new material. And in June 1977, with Doctor Landy now an intrinsic part of the tour entourage, the show hit the road in America. It was Alice's first US outing in two years and ticket sales were as brisk as they ought to have been. But once-loyal supporters were unconvinced. The name on the ticket was Alice Cooper's. But the show was something else entirely.

A dynamic set had been put together, of course. With Alice terming himself (and the tour itself) The King Of The Silver Screen, a giant television set was positioned in front of the band, while a host of costumed props ran riot around it; giant spiders, machine-gun toting roosters, a vampire and cannibals. Short, specially shot movies were projected onto the television KAKA TV commercials for ear-odour remedies, movie previews for *The Family That Ate Their Dog*, and "coming soon" trailers for *Police Gynaecologist* and *Celebrity Neurosurgery* – fantasy television shows that would not be out of place on a 21st century schedule, but which seemed the height of gauche tastelessness in 1977.

But *New York Times* critic Robert Palmer caught the show at Nassau Coliseum on July 21, a little short of the midway point through the tour, and declared it "a case of the tail wagging the dog. The theatrical elements that Mr. Cooper introduced into arena rock – and theatrical means the full panoply of Hollywood and Las Vegas show business, from the lights to choreography to elaborate costuming – have swallowed up his music."

The opening 'Under My Wheels', with Steve Hunter and Dick Wagner locked seamlessly together, was a phenomenal way to start the show, that was undeniable. But "it provided a high point that the show did not reach again. Cooper's brand of Detroit hard rock has taken a back seat to his contrived theatrical gestures. Once the early hits had been dispensed with, the band settles into playing anonymously behind the huge television screen. There were no more musical sparks, and the show seemed dead; Mr. Cooper could have been walking through it in his sleep."

Alice would have argued the point; would have pinpointed so many aspects to the show that equalled and even surpassed the notions he had pushed forward before, and in terms of spectacle he was correct. The difference was, in the past, his shows had been continuous, building the sense of menace and magnificence from the moment he set foot on the stage, to the climax that would inevitably dispatch him from it.

It was the tension that had gone, that and his once infallible sense of pacing. The first third of the set dispensed with the early seventies favourites; the mid-riff looked back at *Welcome To My Nightmare* and *Goes To Hell*; which meant the new material, the unfamiliar material, fell at the end of the show, baffling the audience with songs they didn't know, when they should have been up on their feet for the hits.

True, the set-closing 'King Of The Silver Screen' was a spectacle, the battle hymn howling out over fireworks, pyrotechnics and enough noise to deafen the most doubting heart. But still you could not escape the impression that it was just one more in a series of stock rock statements, well-rehearsed vignettes that flowed from one to the other, but which were more or less interchangeable with one another. There was no drama now, no mounting fear or anticipation. Just a string of clever moments, and Alice knew it. He just did not know what to do about it.

Turning the crystalline concision of 'School's Out' into a 20-minute showcase for the musicians' virtuosity wasn't his sharpest move ever, either.

Off the road at the end of The King Of The Silver Screen outing, Alice knew he was tapped out. Exhausted. A wreck. But where could he turn? The doctor had left the building. One dispute too many with Shep Gordon ended with the manager attacking the quack with a baseball bat – because Landy *was* a quack, a fraud and a charlatan who would wind up being forced to surrender his licence to practise psychology in 1989, before a court barred him from having any contact whatsoever with even his most famous client, Brian Wilson.

Alice escaped Landy's clutches a lot earlier, and with a lot less expense, than the Beach Boy. But he was also no nearer an end to his own struggles, and the worst part of that was, he just could not bring himself to admit it to himself. Which made Shep Gordon's insistence that he pull himself back onto the horse for a string of dates in Las Vegas all the more galling. In his autobiography, Alice recalls saying "no" to Shep Gordon for the first time in their relationship. Then he hung up the phone.

Gordon rang back minutes later. This was not just a regular show, he explained. This was the proverbial Offer You Cannot Refuse, courtesy of the Mafia hoods that allegedly then controlled great swathes of Las Vegas. Still Cooper refused. Back and forth they went but of course, showman Alice was always going to trump sad, battered, beaten down Vince. Warner Brothers was owed another album, and once again it was threatening legal action if it wasn't delivered on schedule.

Two nights at the Aladdin Hotel in Las Vegas gave the label what it wanted – a live album titled, unimaginatively, *The Alice Cooper Show*, and which wandered fairly haphazardly through the repertoire with no more pizzaz than its birth pangs suggest.

The album remained a sore point more than a decade later. Alice told *Kerrang!*, "When I did that album, I was so out of it, so sick. I'd been touring for five years solid. I was at my alcoholic peak! After a binge that had lasted for three years, I couldn't possibly get any more in my body to get myself up. The stage show never suffered, but when it was all over I just asked 'Where am I?'"

"I've got those dancing chickens, machine guns, this and that and... ha-ha-ha, how did I get here? It was like closing your eyes and driving somewhere, then opening them and not knowing where you are."

And two decades after that interview, he remained unhappy. "The band plays great on it," Alice mused sadly, reflecting on the stellar line-up of Steve Hunter, Dick Wagner, Prakash John, Fred Mandel and Whitey Glan. "The live album we did in Vegas, some of the guitar work on that goes crazy, it goes on for eight hours of them playing against each other going back and forth and you listen to it and you go geez, this stuff is amazing."

He, on the other hand, was "fine... I suppose". Later he claimed he was unable to recall recording *Lace And Whiskey*. This time around, reflecting on *The Alice Cooper Show*, the recordings were all too painful to recollect.

Chapter Thirteen

Whiskey Please, And Hold The Lace

A lice charts his decline by the amount of money he spent on alcohol, the number of memories that deteriorated into a grey haze, and the number of so-called friends who seemed to flock to his table at the Rainbow Bar & Grill on Sunset Boulevard and milk him for every ounce of reflected glory that they could.

He kept his own associates tight around him, the Hollywood Vampire set that shared both his fame and his demons, and he relied on his instinctive professionalism to keep him going, even when every fibre of his being was rebelling against the discipline.

In the past he had jokingly referred to himself as a Jekyll and Hyde character; Killer Alice by night, mild-mannered Vince Furnier by day. Now his friends were discovering just how true that analogy was, but it was not the difference between his on and offstage personas that brought it to life. It was the fact that on stage, he was on autopilot, and off it, he was a mess. And the only person who didn't realise that was Alice himself, as he continued to convince himself that his drinking was not a problem, and kidded himself that nobody would have noticed if it were.

He prided himself on appearing normal even when he was completely gone; even today, he can honestly say "you'd never imagine I was a drunk. Those closest to me didn't realise how much I was drinking."

"When I was 16 and dreaming about being a big rock star," he told *Classic Rock* in 1999, "getting money and cars, I never included being an alcoholic. It sneaked up on me. I liked drinking and hanging out with the guys who were drinking. We'd have these long drives in the States, so I'd have a beer or three and some more after the show. Pretty soon I was having a beer in the morning, too. But I didn't feel like an alcoholic. Then I found that the beer was gone and I was drinking whisky in the morning and more whisky in the afternoon. And more before the show, and then more after the show – it wasn't fun anymore – it was like medicine.

"It didn't change my personality drastically. If you'd met me at the time you wouldn't have known I had a problem. I never missed a show or even a lyric." Echoing Suzi Quatro's description of the man she toured with two years before, he concluded, "I was what I called a 'functional alcoholic'."

Yet how functional was he really? He was no longer enjoying the performance. He was no longer enjoying the tours. Writing new songs was a chore, rehearsing was a pain. Backstage before a show, even the sight of the outfit he would soon be changing into made him feel physically sick, and so he'd reach for the whisky once again, down half a bottle and then he'd get dressed.

And still he insisted that nobody knew.

But of course, people did know. It is hard to live with somebody and not be aware that they are throwing up blood every morning when they wake; nor that the whisky bottles that were on the table in the morning were in the trash by mid-afternoon. Daily, Sheryl and Shep would compare notes. The empty cases of beer that piled up in the garbage, the fact that every performance seemed a little less spontaneous as the autopilot kicked in earlier and earlier. And daily, Alice would blithely carry on destroying himself. "You hear about the dangers of heroin and cocaine," he cautioned *Kerrang!* in 1982. "But alcohol is the perfect killer. It's the worst drug in the world and I took it too far. It reached the stage where I was convinced that there was no way I could live without a drink."

He allowed alcohol to dictate his friends; he allowed it to flavour his career, too. It may have come to naught in the end, battered down by record company politics, but Alice and Aerosmith's Steve Tyler were close friends, and often talked about recording something together. "I've wanted to work with [him] for so long," Alice reflected to *Kerrang!* in 1989. "[But] Steve and I were so out of it we could never get it together.

It'd be a situation where we'd meet up, say we have to do it, and a year'd pass by because we were so out there.

"The last time I saw Steve, we were driving around Beverly Hills in my Rolls. I had a bottle of whiskey and he had a gun.... I don't remember what happened. When I saw him recently I reminded him about it, and he couldn't remember a thing either. What did we do, rob a grocery store or something?"

Like Sheryl, Shep Gordon was under no illusions of what Alice was going through, although for him, the situation was more difficult, attempting to balance the star's career demands with his concern for his best friend's health, and being shot down by Alice himself every time he suggested maybe taking things easy. Warner Brothers had a contract that it demanded be fulfilled. There were promoters and backers, all as insistent as one another. Gordon wanted more than anything to give Alice a break, but Alice refused to take one.

Because he was in demand. Even with sinking record sales, Alice had transcended the mere rock stardom he once laid claim to, and had moved to the next level of being a celebrity; a character whose larger than life persona shunted even his music and art into a corner, and allowed him to glory in simply being Alice Cooper.

It was a role that precious few people from the rock milieu had ever achieved. Elvis Presley, were he not so reclusive, was certainly among them, and the near-universal mourning that greeted his death in August 1977 showed just how deeply the old pelvis had engrained itself in American culture.

Paul McCartney and John Lennon were there; and so were Mick Jagger and Keith Richards, who even wrote a song about their new-found status, the rocking 'Respectable' on 1978's *Some Girls* album. No longer the demons that once shocked and mortified middle America, rock'n'rollers were now being accepted into the heart of showbiz society and who should be at the door to greet them, to welcome them into this new plateau of achievement? Alice Cooper.

He gloried in his reputation. Across the Atlantic, a new musical movement had arisen that declared Alice Cooper among its founding fathers. Punk rock may have had no time for the more overt theatrics of its idol, but the moods that percolated across the best Alice Cooper albums packed a sense of drama that the punks could effortlessly identify with.

Johnny Rotten, frontman with the Sex Pistols, auditioned for that band by miming to 'I'm Eighteen', one of the myriad Alice Cooper singles stuffed inside the jukebox at Malcolm McLaren's Let It Rock store – the same Let It Rock that Alice had visited on his first visit to London. And when Alice met his green-toothed acolyte, "[Johnny] actually told me that before the Sex Pistols took off he and Sid Vicious used to go down the London Tube station with an old violin and guitar and busk my song 'I Love The Dead', even though they couldn't play," Alice told the *Sunday Herald Sun* newspaper. "I think I came along at the time when a lot of the newer breed of rock performers were looking for some inspiration. I could say the same nice things about my prime influences and gush for hours about acts like the Yardbirds, the Rolling Stones, Salvador Dali, the Who and T-Rex."

Dave Vanian, singer with the Damned, had a vocal technique that was so obviously modelled on 'I Love The Dead' that, when his band recorded their own 'Feel The Pain' on their debut album, it was hard to believe you were not listening to a hitherto unknown Billion Dollar Babies out-take.

A schoolboy band called Eater let their Alice worship out in a stage routine that included the ritual destruction of a severed pig's head, purchased from a local butcher's store before the show.

Gaye Advert, bassist with the Adverts, captures Alice's appeal for their generation – kids who had grown up listening to Alice Cooper, and were now making music of their own. "Hearing Alice Cooper for the first time was really exciting, I can remember buying two copies of 'School's Out', one for me and one for my friend's birthday present. They had the power to shock back then, yet were accessible enough to get on *Top Of The Pops*."

That was the dichotomy that the punks sought to replicate, to horrify one side of society, while enthralling another, and it was one that the Adverts in particular pursued. The tale of an eye transplant going horribly wrong, their first hit single 'Gary Gilmore's Eyes' was easily as macabre as any Cooper classic, and not only did they perform it on *Top Of The Pops*, they also became the first punk band to appear on Alice Cooper's old stomping ground, the *Old Grey Whistle Test*. The four foot high, whip-flicking Alice cut-out that once adorned the teenaged Gaye's bedroom would have been so proud.

The action was not confined to the UK either. From New York out of Cleveland, Stiv Bators & the Dead Boys pursued their own teenaged love of Alice by befriending Glen Buxton, and pulling him on stage to jam with them at CBGBs.

In general Alice kept his admirers at arm's length, particularly when the panegyrics grew so loud that he started hearing himself proclaimed a prototype punk rocker. Even if there was truth in such comments, which he doubted, those honours, he insisted, belonged to the acts who had inspired him in the first place – the Rolling Stones, the Who, Them and the Pretty Things. But he did concede, talking with *Circus* in late 1977, "What's similar about me and the punks is that the whole thing is McLuhanism. Shock value. Like me in the old days, the punk rockers want to have the most erratic, difficult behaviour to attract your attention. These guys might slash themselves on stage but when they go home they listen to the Archies.

"Punk is a fad. I'll say it. But at the same time anybody who doesn't have fun with it is crazy, because fads are neat. And it's the American way of life to cash in on a fad. I want to start a punk rock band called The Anita Bryant."

Throughout 1977-1978, as he stared his own most private nightmare in the face, Alice seemed to be in constant demand. Of course he repaid the favour by giving his all. He appeared on *The Gong Show* and guested on Dinah Shore's chat show. Soon, he would be on *The Muppet Show*. He completed the King Of The Silver Screen US tour and he looked forward to introducing Maurice Escargot to Europe. He was planning a new album, and when he threw up in the mornings (or later in the day as well, now), he was always very careful to wipe away even the tiniest drop of blood, so that Sheryl would not suspect that he might not survive long enough to do any of those things.

Which was when, in the midst of all this, she and Shep scooped him up and deposited him, almost literally kicking and screaming, in a sanatorium, the Cornell Medical Centre in White Plains, New York. The night before his admission, he went out and got royally pissed.

The *Arizona Republic* broke the news to his old friends and family. "Alice Cooper, lead singer in the rock band of the same name, is in a New York sanatorium recovering from a bout of alcoholism, a spokeswoman for the entertainer said Monday. Barbara Pepe, the Cooper spokeswoman, said that after failing to overcome his drinking problem through private, out-patient treatment, Cooper decided to take advantage of a break in his schedule to undergo a hospital program of treatment. She said she was not told where he was getting treatment."

Celebrity rehab was an unknown beast at that time. As far back as 1970, Congress passed the "Comprehensive Alcohol Abuse and Alcoholism Prevention Treatment and Rehabilitation Act" which in turn established the National Institute on Alcohol Abuse and Alcoholism (NIAAA). But to most people, alcoholism was a problem that affected the elderly poor, and the homeless – the popular image of the drunken bum panhandling for small change that he would spend on methylated spirits was a pernicious one.

It would be another year before Betty Ford, wife of the former President Gerald, acknowledged her alcoholism after her family staged an intervention of their own, and forced to face up to her problems, and several years more before she opened the first of the treatment centres that bear her name. The idea that going into rehab could become a badge of pride (and a neat marketing tool) to be worn by the nineties generation of self-confessional rockers was one that even the most fevered campaigner could never imagine.

In 1977, the only "rehab" most people had heard of was the persistent legend of Keith Richards flying to Switzerland every year to have his blood changed, and the idea that anybody, least of all one of the most famous faces in America, should need to seek treatment because he liked the odd drink was one that even hardened addicts and alcoholics apparently had trouble getting their heads around. Alcoholism elicited little more concern than a confirmed smoker might receive; the notion that it could be as real a disease as cancer or the common cold was one that even drinkers scoffed at. It certainly wasn't like the drugs that bedevilled so many other members of Alice's trade.

Only to those who were close to the alcoholic, who could see the torment that the drink was inflicting (and who then experienced that torment themselves) were truly aware of just how crippling alcoholism could be; them and the staff at the handful of clinics that were actually equipped to deal with alcoholics.

And that equipment, as Alice later shuddered, was primitive, at least by modern standards. The centre itself was well-appointed, a vast structure whose campus on Bloomingdale Road was one of the most familiar landmarks in the city. Inside, however, Alice experienced first hand the kind of icy deprivation that he had toyed with only on his own musical path, wrapping himself in the straitjacket every night to ham out the decline of poor Dwight Fry. "I was in a cold and severe lockdown ward for drug addicts, alcoholics and people with severe mental disorders," he wrote in his *Golf Monster* autobiography.

He awoke and slept to the clinic's own schedule, a harsh routine that saw him eating breakfast at the same time as he had once gone to bed. Neither (again by today's standards) was there much psychological or psychiatric finesse to the treatment. "Drying out" meant exactly that, a regimen that snatched away even the smell of alcohol, and replaced it with exercise and food, and sufficient drugs to dull the inevitable comedown. The only advantage was, it seemed quick. After just three days of enforced sobriety, he realised that he was feeling better than he had in years. "And that was a big deal."

He consorted with the inmates; of course he did. They were the only thing that stood between him and absolute isolation. Nobody knew who he was; or if they did, the reasons, they were too bound up in their own problems and realities to care. And he was likewise so embalmed within his struggle that he didn't even notice. For the first time in a decade, he was Vincent Furnier again, just another guy, just another loser, just another bum. And then one day, his therapist, a doctor whom he had rechristened Dr Bacharach because he looked just like the legendary songwriter, asked him how much Alice drank.

"On stage?"

"Yes. How much does Alice Cooper drink?"

Vince thought about it for a moment. "Nothing. I never drink on stage."

He'd never thought about that before, and he'd never thought about the doctor's next revelation, either. "Alice Cooper doesn't drink. It is Vince Furnier who drinks."

All of these years, Alice had convinced himself that it was the monster he became who insisted on sinking the booze. In fact, it was the monster who tried to stop it. The monster was the professional. It was Vince who was the loser, and Vince at whom the treatment was targeted. Once he understood that, one associate from this time reveals, he understood what he needed to do.

Vince was hospitalised, but Alice still had his liberty, grabbing a few days release to shoot a cameo role in the then-gestating movie version of the Beatles' *Sergeant Pepper's Lonely Hearts Club Band*, before heading back to Cornell. And two weeks into the treatment, Vince was proclaimed alcohol free, and was asked if he wanted to leave the clinic. He turned the opportunity down, voluntarily committing himself to another fortnight of treatment. That was how determined he was to break the self-destructive cycle, he reasoned. That was how much he wanted to be cured. And that is how dedicated he was to the concept that he had decided would frame his next album.

He'd already made it through the hardest part of his own treatment. Now he wanted to watch everybody else as they went through theirs, and translate his observations into a new album. In 2011 he explained to *Classic Rock* magazine, "I was thinking of it as a diary of what goes on in a mental hospital. As a lyricist you're always looking for subject matter. You can't help it. So I always carried a little pen and paper."

Random remarks from his fellow inmates would be noted down. The staff's methods of dealing with difficult patients would be recorded. He hung with the criminally insane and the mentally unstable; one inmate, he heard, had hacked an uncle to pieces and stowed them in the trunk of his car. Another talked of nothing but his pet dog, Veronica, and Alice quickly immortalised him in the germ of a new song, 'For Veronica's Sake'.

He met Jackknife Johnny, a Vietnam vet who had found love while on duty, and brought his wife home, only to encounter the rampant racism that was so much a part of small town American life at that time. And he visited the Quiet Room, the padded cell where over-stimulated patients would be placed with just a shot of the psychiatric drug Thorazine for company. Alice himself sat in that same room a few times, although not because he was forced to. "It was just a nice quiet place to write lyrics."

It would be November 1977 before Alice finally left Cornell, clean and resolving to stay that way, by keeping company with one of the few people he knew who had also beaten a drinking problem, his old Hollywood Vampire friend Bernie Taupin.

Taupin was, and remains, one of rock's most inspired and inspirational lyricists. In tandem with Elton John, Taupin was the English lyricist who succeeded in selling Americana back to America, by taking his own cinematic obsessions with the culture and setting them to Elton's extraordinary melodies. Indeed, many people simply assumed that Taupin was American, and were surprised to discover that he was born no place more romantic than Flatters Farmhouse, an isolated farm in southern Lincolnshire, England.

Leaving school aged 15 to work in the print room of the local newspaper *The Lincolnshire Standard*, Taupin's sights were originally set on a career in journalism. But he also wrote poetry which he dreamed of seeing set to music, an ambition that was realised when he met Elton John – a remarkable tunesmith with precious little lyrical ability.

In 1967 Taupin answered an ad placed in *New Musical Express* by Ray Williams, an A&R man at Liberty Records. It called simply for talent, and both Taupin and John (or Reginald Dwight as he then was) were among the respondents. Williams introduced them and set in motion a partnership that, over the next decade, would be responsible for some of the most memorable hits, and best selling albums, of the era. By 1977, however, the partnership had apparently run its course. Three successive albums, *Caribou, Rock Of The Westies* and the sprawling double *Blue Moves* had barely flickered with the fire that once hallmarked the duo's collaborations, and the distance between the pair had grown geographically too.

Elton still lived in England, refusing to leave the land of his birth simply to avoid the taxes that were then levied on his income. Taupin, however, was living in Los Angeles now; it was there that he first encountered Alice, and so vivaciously did he enter into the spirit of the Hollywood Vampires that he soon joined Keith Moon as the resident English drunk.

He told author Philip Norman, "I used to wake up in the morning in my house on North Doheny Drive, the rock star's empty house, and the first thing I'd do would be to reach over to the refrigerator by my bed. I'd take out a beer, empty half of it away then fill it up with vodka. I'd drink that every morning before I got up. When I went anywhere in a limo, I'd take a gallon jug full of vodka and orange juice. People were starting to say, 'Hey, you've got a problem.' But I wouldn't believe them. I said, 'No, I'm just having a good time.'"

He and Alice were soon palling around regularly, not only to the bars and clubs but also to shows. One night, according to Alice, they went to see Frank Sinatra, and were astonished when one of old Blue Eyes' handlers walked over to their seats and told them, "Mr. Sinatra would like to see ya in his dressing room."

Astounded, they followed him. The offer, Alice joked later, did not feel like one they could easily refuse, and so they waited nervously to be summonsed into the Great Man's presence, both turning over in their minds the range of fates that might be awaiting them for some unintended slight to Sinatra's alleged Mob connections.

Instead, they were greeted effusively and with thanks as well. Sinatra was intending to perform a song apiece by Alice (*Goes To Hell*'s 'You And Me') and Taupin in his set that night, and just wanted to thank them for writing them. "So we told him it was a great honour to have him sing our songs," concluded Alice, "and he said: 'That's OK, you keep writing 'em and I'll keep singin' 'em!' Ha!"

On another occasion, the pair read and fell in love with *Interview With The Vampire*, author Ann Rice's newly published reinvention of the vampire myth. The idea hit them simultaneously – they should become movie producers, and this would be their first project. They were even working out the casting as they figured out how much money they should offer for the rights; Peter O'Toole, they decided, would make the perfect Lestat, and $500,000 should be enough to buy the movie rights.

They were too late. Somebody else had already purchased them for little more than half of that.

But that was the relationship that Alice and Taupin had, "always sparking one another's creativity", as Dee Murray, bassist in Elton John's band through his years of greatest chart success, put it. "Every time I saw them together they were cooking up something else, so it was no surprise when they started writing together. They probably should have done it years before."

Taupin entered his own style of rehab shortly before Alice was admitted to Cornell, renting a house in Acapulco and drying himself out. Then, he called Alice to ask whether he was interested in making an album about their shared experiences, a cautionary saga of the demon alcohol.

Alice agreed, and together the pair embarked upon one of the most rewarding songwriting sessions that Alice had ever been a part of, and one that would take on even greater resonance the following September, following the overdose death of fellow Vampire Keith Moon. If the irrepressible, indestructible Moon could be blanked out, what hope did anybody else have?

No matter that both men were primarily lyricists. Alice would pull a lyric from his notebook and Taupin would promptly answer it, and that was how they worked, bouncing ideas and notions off one another, and doing so with such productivity that "in the end, we came up with a really great album".

They were still writing when Alice found himself back in the headlines, as one of the stars of the long-awaited and much anticipated *Sergeant Pepper* movie. Produced by Robert Stigwood, whose last movie, *Saturday Night Fever*, had proved such a massive success, *Sergeant Pepper* threatened to be even bigger. Like *Flash Fearless* in the past, it called upon a host of different singers and performers. Unlike *Flash Fearless*, it mopped up the superstars of the age. Alice was just one in a galaxy that flickered with brilliance.

Peter Frampton was still riding the record-breaking success of *Frampton Comes Alice*. The Bee Gees were the unstoppable soundtrack to both *Saturday Night Fever* and the world disco scene in general. At the same time as the movie came out, the brothers Gibb were about to launch into an unprecedented run of five solid months at the top of the American singles chart, as performers, composers or simply undeniable influences on no less than six separate singles. Aerosmith were one of America's hottest rock bands; Earth Wind and Fire likewise in the R&B stakes. Top ranking comedians from both sides of the Atlantic filed in, and so did George Martin, the man who produced the original album. And while Alice's role was brief, it was also significant. He played Father Sun, a Machiavellian fiend devoted to brainwashing the kids and turning them onto something called the Future Villain Band (played with swaggering aplomb by Aerosmith). The role also gave him the opportunity to voice a Beatles song for the first time since the days of the Spiders, and he wrapped a decidedly sinister throat around the Fab Four's hitherto charming 'Because'.

It was difficult to imagine any way the movie could fail.

But it did, and Peter Frampton speaks for most involved parties when he shudders, "I've watched it [and] every time I put a new record out, Robert Stigwood puts it out on TV somewhere. 'You want to try a new record? Hold on while we put this out. We'll destroy you again.'

"I'm hearing now that it's becoming almost a cult movie, and it's nowhere near as bad as it was made out to be at the time. It's just... you had the Bee Gees in it, and *Saturday Night Fever* was zooming up the chart at the time we were making it; you had me, who was at the top of the chart; we had the cover of *Time*, *Newsweek*, everyone going, 'Oh this is going to be a blockbuster movie,' and it was useless! It was a piece of crap, it was horrible. The only thing the director had ever directed before was *Car Wash*, and I don't think he'd ever heard of the Beatles!

"We were up the creek without a paddle, definitely. I always said it wasn't that bad; Steve McQueen was in *The Blob*, and it didn't hurt him. But, I've made many albums and I've made some stinkers, and people bring them up with the good ones. I only made one movie, and people jump on it, and rightly so, because I don't like it either. I think I took the rap for everybody. No-one ever mentions it to the Bee Gees!"

Or to Alice Cooper. Well, not very often, anyway.

In 1999, he explained to *Wall Of Sound* magazine, "You know, when you were asked to do the Beatles, and George Martin was going to produce it, what could you say? 'And I get to beat up the Bee Gees in this movie?' It was perfect. When I heard what the whole deal was, and Aerosmith was gonna be in it, and Steve Martin was gonna be in it, I said, 'What's not to do?' Right there, that was enough for me to do it. Nobody knew it was going to be the stinker that it was."

For now, Alice was happy to simply close his eyes and pretend the movie hadn't happened. Booking themselves into Cherokee studios in Hollywood, Alice and Bernie Taupin were pulling together the band that would bring their songwriting efforts to fruition. They chose players with whom they had worked most successfully in the past: Taupin called in Dee Murray, and another Elton John Band veteran, guitarist Davey Johnstone. Singer Kiki Dee, another Elton associate, followed. Alice called in Dick Wagner, and then extended invitations to Steve Lukather of Toto, Rick Nielsen of Cheap Trick and his old buddies Flo & Eddie. Other session players were rounded up by producer David Foster.

For Flo & Eddie, the offer to reunite came as a surprise. But not as big of a shock as they'd experience once they actually arrived in the studio.

Alice in 1978 was a somewhat different character to the man they had known in the past, a lot less driven and a lot less secure. In the studio, he had taken to building himself a tent out of mike stands and baffle blankets, and staying inside while everything else was recorded. "Then," Howard Kaylan recalls, "when it came time for him to begrudgingly leave, step outside of it for the two or three minutes it would take for him to lay down the vocals, he wasn't very happy about it. So Shep and the people involved with the production knew what we were capable of in the studio and how Alice liked us being around, and they called us in.

"First we'd do our background parts, then we'd sing leads along with Alice, to guide him along, help him get to notes he wouldn't have been able to otherwise. Then, they'd take us out of the final mix and leave Alice's voice in on its own. Of course, that meant we had to learn the entire song, but we didn't mind – this was Alice, he was our buddy and it made the record sound OK. Now he's back on the other side, I'm sure he looks back on those records in horror. For me, though, it was just like helping out a pal."

Dee Murray, too, recalled the sessions as fraught. "Bernie was the motivating force. Alice had stopped drinking, they both had, but he was still weak. He wasn't the old Alice, he just didn't have the confidence, not even when he was singing."

Matters did improve as the sessions progressed, and all concerned are adamant that the album emerged sounding a lot better than perhaps they expected it to. But Alice's own subsequent rehabilitation of songs and characters from this most harrowing of all his records perhaps testifies to the emotional depths that he needed to sink to in order to create the record he would call *From The Inside*. Understandably aware that the album was very much a solid swerve in direction, Alice prepared for its release with a tour designed, with almost callous calculation, to reminding people exactly who he was. 1978's *School's Out* Summer Tour was little short of a greatest hits outing, more or less restating the previous year's *King Of The Silver Screen* misadventure in terms of musicians and material, but playing down any song that the audience would not instantly greet with a roar. Thus, it would be February 1979 before Alice would go out with the stage show he had schemed around the new album, by which time the record's fate had already been determined.

From The Inside was released shortly before Christmas 1978 and it proved instantly divisive. Its cover, recapturing the ghoulish Cooper of old, had little in common with its contents, as producer Foster pushed the proceedings into a slick, almost AOR vein; a commercial brainwave in an age when the US charts were being overtaken by the soulless flab of Lukather's Toto, Foreigner, Journey, Styx and so many more, but a betrayal too of all that Alice had represented in the days when he stood as an antidote to the kind of slush that generally filled the airwaves.

Lyrically, the album was as strong as it needed to be, and if its confessional edge grew wearing after a time, then that was the listener's problem, not the songs'. Sonic flashes that sounded like Queen add quirk, spray-painting the album's ambition over pastures that Alice did not habitually fly, at the same time as fears of rampant Elton Johnisms were largely confined to just the brief piano-led 'In The Quiet Room' and 'Jackknife Johnny', and even there, there was an edge of menace. Two years later, Peter Gabriel's 'Lead A Normal Life' would segue so effortlessly from 'In The Quiet Room' that they could almost have been twins.

Elsewhere, however, 'Millie And Billie' was a gruelling duet with former Eric Clapton vocalist Marcy Levy, but too many of the album's heavier numbers ('Serious', 'For Veronica's Sake') were simply riff-by-numbers rockers that sounded more like latterday Sweet than anything else.

Billboard seemed impressed despite all such misgivings. "This concept album... chronicl[ing] Cooper's self-imposed stay in a rehabilitation centre... is without a doubt his most ambitious statement to date. The subject is not an easy thing to publicise, yet Cooper... has come up with a moving, often emotional autobiographical rock record with more lyrical sting than anything he's ever done."

Indeed, the album's first single, the ballad 'How You Gonna See Me Now', surely ranks among the most naked songs any performer has confessed to, a dedication to wife Sheryl that wonders how she would respond, or even relate, to the suddenly sober man she now found herself married to. In the three years the couple had spent together, Alice wondered whether she had once seem him stone cold sober. In terms of catharsis and, perhaps, the slaying of personal demons, *From The Inside* could be regarded as a triumph. But it was not an especially well-starred move commercially.

'How You Gonna See Me Now' received some airplay but little more than that; *From The Inside* itself barely bothered the chart. But the old trouper was not discouraged. With a band that saw Davey Johnstone stepping in for Dick Wagner alongside the ever present Steve Hunter, plus fellow Ezrin alumni Prakash John and Whitey Glan, the three-month Madhouse Rock tour was swiftly revealed as Alice's most visually extravagant since *Welcome To My Nightmare*, a plaudit that was only amplified when the San Diego show on April 9 was filmed for the *Strange Case Of Alice Cooper* home video release.

Sheryl Cooper's choreography was astonishing, and the appearance of dancers disguised as bottles of alcohol and a dancing pink poodle led exquisitely into what remains one of Alice's most theatrically moving death scenes yet, the suicide attempt in the Quiet Room. And he was fighting his own corner, too.

"I'm back in rock'n'roll now," he told *Creem*. "I've got my desire back. These young bands like Kiss, they're great, but what can they do for an encore? I'm gonna burn them all, blow them off the stage. I hope the kids think Kiss is the ultimate show. That way when they see me, we'll look that much better. I can work it out. They'll think I had four lungs put in. You see, it's a whole different audience. I'm playing to kids who've never seen Alice before. And I can't wait to shock 'em."

For all its musical failings, then, *From The Inside* was an album of triumph, and the live show likewise. The neo-funk groove with which flared the opening 'From The Inside' was an electrifying overture long before the song itself got going, and learning from the mistakes made on the 1977 tour, this time the new songs were largely corralled at the beginning of the show. But while the remainder of the set adhered to the hits routine, it packed its own surprises; the effortless manner in which 'Go To Hell' medleyed with 'It's Hot Tonight' was a highlight that few Alice performances have matched, and closing the main set with 'How You Gonna See Me Now' was an act of boldness that, again, he has never returned to.

Behind the scenes, however, Alice – or Vince – had not come as far as he thought. Unthinkingly taking a sip of wine while he sat eating dinner with Sheryl one evening, he relapsed so hard into alcoholism that the next three years barely even register in his memory today; and the three albums that he produced during that span are likewise all-but-forgotten.

It's called self-defence.

Three albums had now crashed and more-or-less burned in the years since *Welcome To My Nightmare*, four if one counted the live record, and while Alice was scarcely the first or only seventies idol to be cast adrift as one decade moved towards another, the heights from which he had fallen, and the speed with which he had done so, were alarming. How to arrest that fall, though; that was the question. For Alice, the alcohol helped deaden the daily impact of another year off the top. For his friends and associates, it was a tougher call.

"The first we knew about a new album was when we got the call to go back to Cherokee to meet with Roy Thomas Baker," Dee Murray recalled a decade later. "And I think it was Roy who impressed upon us what this was, ie less of an album and more of a rescue mission." Murray would not, ultimately, appear on the album, as he opted instead to return to England to live. But his impressions were not that far removed from the truth.

Best known at the time as the producer of Queen during their pomp, but more recently thrust into renewed fashion as the man behind the debut album by Boston power-poppers the Cars, Roy Thomas Baker was an intriguing choice to produce Alice Cooper and not necessarily a successful one. He and Alice had been friends since they met at Bernie Taupin's birthday party three years earlier, but he was scarcely unaware of the fact that it was his track record, as opposed to musical compatibility, that recommended him for the gig. For his own part, however, the success or failure of *Flush The Fashion* as an artistic venture was secondary to its humanitarian goals.

At the same time as Baker entered the studio with Alice, he was also producing Hilly Michaels, a former member of Alice Cooper's old sparring partners Sparks, but more recently the engine room behind Ian Hunter and Mick Ronson's eponymous band. Michaels was striking out now on what would become a very successful solo career, and while he does not recollect too many conversations about Baker's other projects, one thing was clear.

"Roy was trying to save Alice's entire life, career. He had heard that Alice was going on these week-at-a-time binges, spending at least $5,000.00 a week. In a nut shell, Alice was killing himself, Roy tried helping him every way he possibly could but all in all, there was a vibe in the air, 'save Alice, save Alice'. Roy looked like he had seen a ghost the first time he came back from talking with Alice. He was so on the verge of slipping, letting go.....very very ill."

It has since become routine to describe *Flush The Fashion*, recorded back at Cherokee Studios in 1980, as Alice's riposte to the growing swirl of keyboard and synth driven bands moving into view on the shirt tails of the New Wave, with the Cars just one of the touchstones. Hanging over the sessions, too, was the recent success of English synth maven Gary Numan, whose stripped back rhythms and icy key lines seemed, for a few moments there, to posit an entire new direction for rock'n'roll to explore. In fact, it is unlikely whether Alice even gave it that much thought at the time, although he has since come to acknowledge a certain slavishness.

"I think when I worked with Roy, we went in a really crazy direction because Roy did the Cars and he did Queen, and we were sitting there going, 'I have no problem doing a New Wave album as long as it has Alice's attitude and as long it has some teeth.' I kind of liked doing songs like 'Leather Boots', because they were weird little songs, [because] I think as long as Alice is singing them, they are still Alice songs." Where matters went off the boil was in the fast growing awareness that Alice probably wouldn't have recognised an Alice song if it was transplanted into his brain.

Flush The Fashion emerged a desperate album. "Roy, Alice, and the record company were all crossing their fingers that Roy could deliver a number one smash hit....get Alice in the limelight again," says Hilly Michaels. But neither the album's key cut, 'Clones (We're All)', introduced to the proceedings by Davey Johnstone, a friend of its composer David Carron, nor its most successful inclusion, an edgy grind through the Music Machine's 'Talk Talk', were Cooper originals, but they were the strongest tracks on what swiftly proved a very one dimensional disc, an album that attempted to mask its deficiencies behind the production, and failed almost every time. Alice Cooper was a lot of things, but he was not the new Gary Numan.

The failure of 'Clones' in particular hurt Baker. The most potently Numanesque of the album's futuristic contents, and matched by a video that spelled the debt even louder, Michaels recalls, "Roy wasn't too excited about the single, Alice's voice was way off the mark, and the track came out below par for an Alice Cooper/Roy Thomas Baker record. But Roy seemed distraught at not being able to wave his magic wand over Alice and give him his desperately needed hit single."

In fact there were several better choices for singles on board, beginning with the melodramatic sturm–und–drang of 'Pain' and the brooding guitar storm of 'Grim Facts', while producer Baker did his best to paper over the record's deficiencies. "Alice is bright, astute and really nice and we decided to put together an album," he explained. "He said to me, 'It's just as much your album as mine, so get on with it.' So I did."

Yet although it was a collaborative effort, it was not a meeting of equals.

Alice was scarcely in the room. As usual he took his best titles from the tabloids, and there was indeed something exquisitely *National Enquirer*-esque about such songs as the metal growling 'Nuclear Infected', the electropunch of 'Aspirin Damage' and the Stonesy 'Start Me Up'-isms of

'Dance Yourself To Death'. Unfortunately, the inspiration ran out there in a lot of cases, as Howard Kaylan, recalled once more to the studio, quickly realised.

"The eighties blur because, very often, the artists themselves weren't even in the studio, they had it done for them by their producers... or, the artists had become so corporate minded that a lot of the personality had left the arena. It used to be, if you were gonna have somebody come in and sing your backgrounds with you, you want to know those people, you want to include them as part of your album, you'd have a little family going.

"But in these later days, there wasn't any input from anywhere else – it might as well have been a Pepsi commercial. And if the personality is gone from the thing and the entertainment value of doing it is gone, then the only reason you have to do it is for the very small cheque you get from doing that sort of thing, or the satisfaction of saying 'I'm on that record'."

Roy Thomas Baker agreed. "[Alice] said he didn't care about the studio end of things, and that it was my job and just to tell him when to put the vocal on. So I'd call him when I needed him, he'd come down and sing, and then go away again and that was all we saw of him. His overall attitude was that he was paying me a lot of money to do it, so why did he need to be there all the time?"

Because it was his record? Apparently not. According to Baker, Alice never heard the finished LP in its entirety until the press playback, a few weeks before its April release.

In the event, *Creem*'s Jeffrey Morgan found a lot to love about an album that, he said, was "gonna stick to the roof of your skull like a web gob of Double-Bubble." The sleeve kicked it off, "a brilliant work hailing from the 'who-gives-a-shit' school of design... etched in fury with a rusty nail by old Salvadork A. C. himself." 'Clones', the first single, "out-replicas Gary Numan by adding a sense of humour tempered with a streak of masculinity... 'Leather Boots' sounds like epileptic Warriors on speed-balls... 'Pain' contains some of Alice's best lines since 'Second Coming' [and] when he snarls 'I'm the burnin' sensation when the convict fries,' he sounds just exactly like you'd want him to sound. It's 1980. Do you know where your heroes are?"

It was a question that Alice, as one of those heroes, desperately needed to answer.

Chapter Fourteen

Special Forces

For a time at the dawn of the seventies, it rather looked as though Blues Image were destined for the top. No longer the house band at Thee Experience in Los Angeles, where their frontman hung out with the unknown Alice Cooper group, an under-achieving debut album had been followed by a smash hit single. 'Ride Captain Ride' was written in about 15 minutes, guitarist Mike Pinera laughingly admits, yet it rose to number four on the *Billboard* chart, and number one in several regional markets. Quite simply, it became one of the defining smashes of the year, and Blues Image were set to soar.

Instead....

"In retrospect, we probably would still be together had we said no to the managers who had us touring non-stop, so the guys who had families could have time to be with them, and also so I could have had a little more time to write new songs. We would come home from months of touring and our managers would put us right into the recording studio, so they could hurry and have the label release a new album. The new songs I was writing were rushed onto tape, and before we knew it, we were back on the road.

"Our music suffered a great deal due to the managers' belief that a rock band had a life expectancy of a couple of years, so they were going to milk us for all we were worth." Battered and bruised by their sudden exposure to the true demands of the music industry, tension and fatigue contributing to the band members not getting along, Pinera quit. His bandmates continued on for a while, so Blues Image did not strictly break up. But their main muse was gone, and now it was management stablemates Iron Butterfly, one of the solid superstars of the previous few years, who welcomed Pinera on board in summer 1970.

A decade later, Pinera was still in demand. His career since then had taken him through a succession of fresh bands; Ramatan, with former Jimi Hendrix Experience drummer Mitch Mitchell; the New Cactus revision of Tim Bogert and Carmine Appice's post-Vanilla Fudge behemoth; a step back towards his own nomenclatural past with Thee Image, the first American band to be signed to ELP's Manticore label; and now a solo career with the Capricorn label. One album, *Isla*, had already come and gone and now Pinera was getting ready for his follow-up, *Forever*. "And that's when Alice called me and asked me to join his band.

"He called me up and said, 'Let's do a band, I want to put together a new band'. And I'll never forget this, but he said, 'I don't know if you know this, but I've actually done quite well since the last time you saw me....'

"Anyway, it sounded good for me except for one thing. *Forever* had just been released, and I couldn't really not promote it. It was part of my contract that I would go out and support *Forever*, so I said, 'Alice, if we can work out the tours when you tour and I have to tour, we can definitely put this together.' And he said, 'I have an even better idea. Why don't you open the shows with your band, and then come back on and play with me? And that's what happened. I would play my show, promote my album, then come back on with him." Alice even thought up a name for his new guitarist. "He called me 'the Mr Rogers of rock'n'roll'."

A three month tour loomed, but Pinera was not daunted. He was joined in the new-look Cooper band by Duane Hitchings, his bandmate since the New Cactus days and a key player on the *Forever* tour too, and he explains, "We were not on the *Flush The Fashion* album, but learning the songs was OK because the songs were very easy to play, things like 'Clones', and we had a great time. It was a good band, everybody was friends...."

The musicians had all the freedom they could desire. "We had complete free will. Alice said, 'Play whatever you want on this stuff. Keep the integrity of the arrangement of the verse and chorus when I'm singing, but when it comes to your solo don't think you have to play the solo that's on the record, you can play what you want.' So, knowing what the fans like, they like to hear certain lines from different solos, there are bits you have to play for them, the signature lines, so I would do that, on 'School's Out' and 'I'm Eighteen' I would do those double string bends and then go into my own things."

The tour kicked off in El Paso on June 4, 1980, with Alice in a very militaristic frame of mind. Shortly before the outing began, he heard that the White House was preparing to sell off a set of uniforms worn by the presidential security guards. The idea of kitting his band out in something similar was one that haunted him even after the uniforms were ultimately donated to a California marching band, an idea that clung in his mind throughout the tour and would ultimately do much to flavour his next LP.

For now, he contented himself with tormenting Mike Pinera. "Alice liked to ad lib and be very spontaneous and one night we were doing 'Billion Dollar Babies' and someone gave him some ice picks, or he found them somewhere. So he had three or four ice picks in one hand and three or four in the other and one night as I'm doing my solo, he comes up to me and says, 'I want to see you dance, Mike,' right over the microphone. So I said 'OK' and started jumping up and down and he goes, 'No, I want to see you really dance.' And he starts throwing these ice picks at my feet, and he was throwing them hard and fast. Thank God I was in good shape, so I started dancing faster and when he was done, there they all were, stuck in the stage. And he liked it so much that he started doing it every night."

Pinera, however, was not going to remain Alice's straight guy for long. "It became the new bit in 'Billion Dollar Babies', so one night I said, 'I'm going to play a little joke on him,' so I went to a joke shop and got a fake knife, one of those ones where the rubber blade goes into the sheath when you press it against your body, and I got a bottle of fake blood. I had the blood in my hand and the knife in my hand, so when he started throwing the ice picks at me, I said, 'is that all you got?'"

Alice looked at him in wonder. "Alice is like, 'Wow what's this, this isn't part of the show,' so I repeat, 'Is that all you got?' Then I took the knife out and started stabbing myself in the head and neck and my throat, and you're seeing the blade going in and out and there's blood going everywhere, and the people in the front row actually gasped and Alice lost it. He just stared, his jaw dropped, he didn't know what to do. He told me later that was the first time in his career that he had ever gone out of character onstage."

What Pinera is adamant that he did not witness was alcohol abuse, and that despite Alice subsequently admitting that this entire period of his life was spent blotted out by the bottle. "Alcohol... no. I never saw it. And Valerie my wife was doing his make-up before the shows and no, no alcohol. He must have been a master magician because we were in a tour bus all through the summer, riding together and he was in the back room, the state room, but the door was always open. He never locked it and anyone could go in and sit down to talk... and I never saw anything."

Road manager Damien Bragdon, too, insisted that Alice kept a clean ship, even after the band's August 19 appearance at the Canadian Rock festival in Toronto was cancelled because of the star's "ill health" – an explanation that promptly ignited a slew of rumours regarding Alice's old alcoholism. His relapse was not public, not yet. But a star falling off the wagon will always be a welcome story for some segments of the media, and Bragdon battled to disprove them. The singer was suffering from bronchial asthma, he explained, and missed two flights from New York to Toronto as he fought for a swift recovery.

But when he did arrive "he looked awful and he was burning up from fever. I would not put such a human being on stage. He was so sick he could hardly stand up."

A doctor was called to the band's downtown Holiday Inn and confirmed Alice's ailment. And Bragdon could only reiterate, "There was absolutely no drugs, no booze and no heroin involved. He's just a very sick man."

Back at the venue, however, the news of the cancellation, delivered just an hour before show time, was not taken so calmly. The *Toronto Star* reported, "Thousands of rioting rock fans tried to wreck the Grandstand last night. They bombarded 268 policemen with bottles, chains and other missiles during a 30-minute rampage that will cost at least $175,000 to repair... they tore out 200 seats welded to steel posts and bolted to concrete. They heaved scores of metal chairs on stage. They didn't brain anybody, but they ruined a public address system and an expensive set of drums. They ripped out steel turnstiles, smashed windows in ticket booths and the Grandstand restaurant, and damaged several cars outside the stadium." Twelve fans, five policemen and a security officer were injured, 31 fans were arrested and the following day's festival events were cancelled as the damage was repaired.

Off the road in October 1980, the band reconvened in the new year to begin work on Alice's next album. *Special Forces* was conceived around the singer's uniformed dreams of the previous year; guerrilla chic, he determined, was the look he wanted the band to adopt, and it was the sound he required as well.

Mike Pinera explains, "Alice would listen here locally to a station called KROQ that was playing really progressive punk, speed punk, heavy metal rap, completely different to any other station. So he would say to the guys in the band, 'This is the kind of stuff I want you to write, really cutting edge, out there, different, never before heard type stuff.' And that's what he told me, he said, 'Mike, I wanna do this but I want to do it better. When everybody's normal I'm weird, and when everybody's weird I'm weirder.'

"So I said OK, and I started writing stuff like 'Vicious Rumours' and things like that, in different time changes, a real throbbing type of punk edge guitar, and so the album started to manifest itself."

An underground LA vibe percolated to the surface as Alice dug back into the closet and unearthed his old Love and Doors albums. For a time, a new concept presented itself, a virtual history of Los Angeles rock, from the garage blast of the mid-sixties, full circle to the punk noise of the eighties. Pinera: "Alice really liked Arthur Lee and he liked a lot of those guys from that era, and there were a lot of songs we were looking at doing from that era. Then he changed his mind and said he didn't want to do too many covers. But he definitely wanted to do Love's 'Seven And Seven Is'."

The key to the album's eventual direction lay in a song that Duane Hitchings contributed to the proceedings, the snarling discombobulation of 'Who Do You Think We Are', riding in on Francis Ford Coppola-shaped chopper blades and scything down the gooks with a guitar as sharp as a switchblade. Another element, however, resonated. Alice explained, "The early Alice was a victim and a lot of that had to do with the alcohol. I always was the whipping boy, the world was against Alice, he was an outcast, a real odd man out and that was my attitude as well." By the time of *Special Forces*, however, he had "a whole different attitude. Alice was not a whipping boy any more, Alice had now become this arrogant villain and he had transformed himself into this total control freak and I liked that, it was really important to me."

Special Forces continued on. Into the studio, there was a welcome reunion awaiting Pinera as he walked in to shake hands for the first time in a long time with producer Richard Podolor, a veteran whose track record included hits for Steppenwolf, Iron Butterfly, Three Dog Night and Mike Pinera's old band, Blues Image. It was Podolor, the guitarist laughs, who spent the entire session for that band's second album demanding, "Make it more commercial."

"Well, we got to the end of the sessions, we only had another day left in the studio, and the producer took me aside, looked at me and sadly said, 'I've got to be honest here, you guys haven't come up with a hit single, or anything that has the potential to be one, and this is your last day to record. I don't know if you can pull out a miracle, but do you think you might have anything with hit potential you can play me?' And I said, 'Oh yeah, I think I remember something', so I went and told the rest of the band what he had just said and our keyboard player, Skip, said he had this little chorus idea he'd been playing with that went, 'Ride captain ride upon your mystery ship be amazed at the friends you have here on your trip' and not much else.

"But that little bit inspired me and so I went into a back room, I locked myself in, cleared my mind and meditated a bit and all of a sudden the words and the melody started flowing all at the same time. I ran out and went to the piano, wrote the rest of the song, then went and got the producer and said, 'OK, you have to hear this!'

"Skip and I started playing 'Ride Captain Ride' to him and he said, 'Oh my God, this is it, this is the one we've been waiting for.' It was written in about 15 minutes. We cut it right that day."

A similar sense of invention overhung the *Special Forces* sessions; invention and intensity that finally coalesced into an album poised effortlessly between the energies of punk rock and the traditions of hard rock, metallic in sheen but antagonistic too. A new album for an era.

'Prettiest Cop On The Block' merged guitars like sirens and prison-break rhythms over a lyric that flirted with the same gender bending defiance that flavoured 'The King Of The Silver Screen'; 'Don't Talk Old To Me' drove discordant drum patterns beneath a vocal that verged on the robotic; and when 'You Want It, You Got It' pouted over handclap and purr, it left you feeling like you'd just walked three blocks with every hooker on the strip sniffing the air.

But it was classic Alice, too. 'Skeletons In The Closet' rode in on the sound of Duane Hitchings' tinkling keys and could have been plucked bodily from *Welcome To My Nightmare*, while the staccato guitars of 'You Look Good In Rags' only updated a melody that felt as old as 'Love It To Death'. 'You're A Movie' was stentorian braggadocio, a hysterical call and response ring-mastered by a starch-shirted Anglophile luvvie; and absent from the album but a touchstone for the rest of the sessions, the immortally titled 'Look At You Over There, Ripping The Sawdust From My Teddy Bear' took the best ballad instincts from the past three or four LPs and transformed them into a whole new lyric for 'Go To Hell'.

On the road, however, it proved a hard sell. Pinera: "We'd go on stage and whenever we'd do the hits it was all great, and the minute we'd do one of these obscure songs from *Special Forces*, all the people would look at one another and go 'Huh? What's that?' But Alice didn't care. He was enjoying himself."

And doing so for the first time, it seemed, in a long time.

Just two of the new album's 10 songs made it into the live show – Hitchings' 'Who Do You Think We Are', which had in any case been worked up for the previous outing; and a rambunctious 'Seven And Seven Is' which was added to the repertoire once the tour hit Europe in 1982. There it was joined by the old *Billion Dollar Babies* standby 'Generation Landslide', rerecorded live in the studio for inclusion on *Special Forces*, and suddenly seeing strangely prescient as the eighties reflected back on the punk explosion that was their birthright.

Oldies heavy it may have been, then, but it was a memorable outing. Smoke choked the stage as a pair of camouflaged figures emerged into view, shining flashlights out into the audience like troops on a midnight reconnaissance mission. Trashed cars, buildings and bodies littered the surroundings, spotlights flashed like dying big rigs; even the amplifiers looked like something out of an urban cataclysm. The beams searched and then settled upon Apocalypse Alice, gaunt and leather clad, a whip in one hand, his hair tugged so tightly back that it looked as though he had cut it all off. A futuristic urban jungle unfolded, musically and visually, jangling and furious, the sound of a well drilled rock band letting its hair down in the bush, terrorising the foe with rock'n'roll.

"Special Forces are Alice's band these days, and an unlikely-looking crew of desperadoes they are," gasped *Kerrang!*. "They all sport combat gear, apt enough as they are obviously musical mercenaries – the very best, hardest and tightest rock players money can buy."

On form, as he seemed every night, Alice was priceless. His stage make-up had undergone a total revision. No longer something stepping out of a horror movie, now he was a horror full stop, a chicken liver sculpture disguised as an addled, aged prostitute, his make-up a mess, his hair tugged back and tattered, his eyes mascara'd slits. There was no beauty, no elegance, no class. The man who had once hung on the end of a rope now looked a man at the end of his rope. And he played the part to perfection, even bringing out a crutch for 'I'm Eighteen', as if to emphasise that he no longer was, before the requisite boa took her serpentine bow. Later, 'Billion Dollar Babies' caught him French kissing a disembodied doll's head, while 'School's Out' dropped him into a classroom, zombie pupils and all.

Pinera recalls, "We did the Tom Snyder TV show, we played real well and then it went into the break and Tom says, 'OK, when we come back we'll be talking to Alice Cooper,' and we knew the show, the way it worked, so we all said, 'Be careful, this guy's going to try and embarrass you or say something stupid,' and Alice goes, 'I got it, I got it.' So he goes over there and sits down, still out of breath, sweating, the paint is melting off his head, and Tom turns to him and says, 'So Alice, is it true you kill chickens on stage?' That was the opening question, and Alice looks at him real serious and goes, 'Oh no, no, no. That's Colonel Sanders. Colonel Sanders kills chickens.'"

Most of 1981 was spent on the road, but it was the tour's climax that remains most fondly remembered. Pinera: "We got to France in December, and they wanted us to do a one-hour special for French TV. It was so funny how it happened, because the French government brought out a director and a whole TV crew and put them at our disposal, and Alice said, 'OK, I'll come up with the stuff, the bits and pieces that we will do,' and it was so far out that the director said, 'You know what? Why don't you go ahead and produce it? You keep the crew and I'll exit.' So it ended up that Alice was the producer and director, with a little help from me, and wow what a trip."

The team, he explains, "had all of France at our disposal and this whole production crew, and Alice would come up with some pretty far out stuff. An old junkyard, an abandoned subway station where they had all these cars with graffiti on them, Alice would find these places," and shooting would commence.

The band in full urban guerrilla chic, striking menacing poses and pouting snarls, Alice in his own take on zombiefied mutant militaria, the hour-long presentation delved back as far as *Love It To Death* in search of material, the soundtrack a brittle mash of the original recording and latter-day overdubs, and always taking the best advantage of the surroundings.

'Under My Wheels' in a scrapyard; 'Seven and Seven Is' in a vandalised Metro carriage, with "boom bam bam" martial art strokes for emphasis; 'Prettiest Cop On The Block' on a deserted midnight street; and 'Cold Ethyl', of course, in a meat refrigerator, Alice and his tattered dolly date grinding among the carved open carcases, before transforming into an aching 'Only Women Bleed', which might well have been taking the song's title just a little too much to heart.

"But the heaviest part of this whole situation," laughs Pinera, "was when Alice came and sat down with me and said, 'Listen, tell me if you like this idea. We're going to do the song 'Go To Hell', and we're going to dress the band up as nuns and put the black make-up under their eyes, and I'll dress up in leather with my riding crop, and we'll go to the steps of Notre Dame Cathedral at night time on the full moon, and I wanna bring a smoke machine and strobe light.' We'd set up on the stairs and we'd play 'Go To Hell'.

"I said, 'I love the idea, but I don't know if the people going in and out of church will like it,' and he said, 'Well, I'll worry about that when the time comes.' So there we were, full moon, smoke machine, doing these steps in unison, looking like ghouls and the priest came out and said, 'Look, I know I gave my permission for this, but I want to know what exactly are you singing? What are the words to this song?'

"And Alice said, 'Father, I'm saying the same things that you say every Sunday in church. I'm saying if you're bad, if you treat people badly, you might go to Hell. And he said, 'OK good, continue'."

In truth, the finished footage utilised those august and evocative surroundings a lot less than they might have. But still 'Go To Hell' emerged one more triumph in a television special that was overflowing with them, as the European tour turned into the kind of victory Alice had not enjoyed in over half a decade.

With the country having been deprived of Alice for so many years, the UK dates in particular proved so successful, and so well-subscribed, that Alice rewarded his British audience with a new single, suitably titled 'For Britain Only'. Rumour swirled that he was also about to go into the studio to rerecord 'School's Out' with Adam Ant, the latest of the pop heroes to have emerged with a taste for old Alice in his valise (famously Ant gives a brief impersonation of the classic seventies Alice at the tail end of his 'Stand And Deliver' video), and fresh British dates seemed to be added daily, as the prearranged gigs sold out.

Yet, despite such successes, and despite the fact that Alice Cooper was still selling out any venue he cast his eyes over, 1981 and 1982 remain among the most misunderstood and, for the most part, poorly documented years of Alice's entire career, at least in terms of media interest.

In some ways, that is understandable. A new decade had ignited new concerns; the synthesized future that Alice had played with on *Flush The Fashion* had taken hold now, together with the whole new wave of musical nuances that formed the staple diet of the fledgling MTV video network. Today's heroes were the likes of Duran Duran and Culture Club, Joan Jett and Tommy Tutone.

But it was not so vast a sea change that the old guard had been exterminated. In 1982, David Bowie was less than a year from releasing the biggest-selling album of his career so far, *Let's Dance*. Michael Jackson, whose hit-making career was two years older than Alice's, was still on top. Bruce Springsteen was still making monsters, as *The River* spent a month at number one; Bob Dylan was still making headlines, as he toured his Born Again gospel show. Even Kiss, whose unmasking the previous year had revealed they looked even more grotesque sans make-up than they ever did while they were wearing it... even Kiss were still selling records.

So why wasn't Alice?

With hindsight, he took some of the blame upon himself. "We went through some changes in the early eighties, where we took it in different directions, and I think that confused people. We did the *Special Forces* thing and that was without the make-up – well, the heavy make-up – and without a lot of props, but it was still about the music."

But there were more pointed reasons too. Five years after the *Welcome To My Nightmare* debacle, when he outraged his record label by giving the soundtrack to another company, he had done it again. Mike

Pinera explains, "Alice produced and financed the movie *Roadie* and Warner Brothers automatically assumed that he was going to give the rights to them for distribution. But he did not, he gave them to another company and Warners literally came up to him and said if we don't have this, we're going to stop all promotion and block your albums from ever getting any kind of exposure.' Alice said, 'Well hit me with your best shot,' and they did.

"A lot of the big shots at Warners said, 'OK let's put him in the black book,' and sure enough, there was no co-operation from the label whatsoever."

Special Forces peaked in America at number 125, Alice's first studio album to fail to make the Top 60 (at the least) since *Pretties For You* in 1969. Only the makeweight live album five years earlier sold less copies than *Special Forces*; and panic hit Shep Gordon's offices like a tsunami. Yes, they could keep Alice on the road forever, and garner their income that way. But at the same time as Warners was refusing to promote the singer, it continued to demand new product.

It was as if the music industry had finally tired of artists complaining that record companies did nothing for them, and decided to show an artist what might happen if that really were the case. *Special Forces* arguably climbed as high up the chart as it did on the back of the momentum left behind by *Flush The Fashion* – which, for all its failings, at least reached number 44. Now it was time to see what would happen if a new album was following a flop.

Pinera sighs. "The moment we got back from the *Special Forces* tour, management told us, 'You need to go back into the studio, we need to get another album out there, we need to get some radio airplay.' Just the whole showbiz hoopla. We didn't have time to come down from the tour, we just found ourselves sitting there, Alice with a blank notepad and the rest of us with no idea of what we should do. And that is the way it began."

Last time out, he recalled, the album grew of its own volition. "Alice liked to take his time writing. He would get a lot of his ideas from reading newspaper ads and articles, the *Enquirer* 'boy born with alien head' sort of story. That's where he got a lot of his lyrical ideas, and as far as the music went, he would rely on the band to bring musical changes, chord changes and feels. We would rehearse at my house a lot in the Hollywood Hills, I had a studio and he would come over and different people from the band would come over and we would work everything out. So when we recorded *Special Forces*, we were already rehearsed and when we went into the studio we pretty much had the arrangements marked out.

"Whereas for this new album, a lot of that stuff was being written and completed in the studio, and it's no good to do that because you feel the pressure all the time, an enormous amount of money per hour, and I just kept saying, 'Man, I wish we could have more time to prepare and go over this stuff.'

"But we just did it the best we could and I think all that was a trickle down from Warners putting up that red flag for *Special Forces*, not letting the album be promoted."

Encouraged by the productivity of the *Special Forces* sessions, the band originally intended returning to producer Richard Podolar. He and they would, however, be waiting a long time for similar inspiration to strike this time. "In hindsight, I don't think Richard was the right producer for this job," Pinera acknowledges. "I think management made this call very predictably because Alice needed a hit single and Richard was known for finding hit singles and producing hit singles. But his forte was to go out and find songs from outside writers like 'Born To Be Wild' and 'Joy To The World'. He was trying to produce it like he would a pop session, and boy was he surprised.

"Alice would lock himself up in a room because he wanted to work on his lyrics and he didn't want to be distracted and Richard didn't really have access to him, until Alice would come out and say, 'OK here's the words to a new song' and we'd do it."

The end result was inevitable. "We started rehearsing the album there," says Pinera, "but went to record at another studio, with Alice and Erik [bassist Scott] producing." Unfortunately, even their best efforts simply weren't good enough. Scott and guitarist John Nitzinger were Alice's favoured writing partners, but either their melodies did not draw the best from his pen, or nobody cared what they came up with.

Ideas seemed half-formed if not half-baked. 'I Better Be Good', 'Zorro's Ascent' and 'No Baloney Homosapiens' all felt unfinished in the same way, oddly, as recent albums by Alice's old Detroit sparring partner Iggy Pop felt unfinished; and sadly, nobody has ever written a good song titled 'I Like Girls', though many (Sparks and, again, Iggy Pop among them) have tried. 'I'm Alive' intrigued with a truly inventive subtitle, 'That

Was The Day My Dead Pet Returned To Save My Life', but once again the song simply didn't live up to the promise. When the best original was 'Make That Money (Scrooge's Song)', a Dick Wagner co-write that effectively detuned 'Black Widow', and the finest melody was the Lalo Schifrin-penned theme to the movie *Class Of 1984*, it was clear the album was struggling.

Worse was to come. Blessed with a peculiarly Zappa-esque title (shades of *Weasel Ripped My Flesh*), *Zipper Catches Skin* was completed and everybody waited anxiously, if still trepidatiously, for the call to tour. Exhaustion was still dominating their lives, but like Warren Zevon liked to say, they could sleep when they were dead. For now, they had a record to promote.

Didn't they?

No, they didn't.

Pinera: "We didn't know there would not be a tour. It just came down as total exhaustion and I could dig it, I know I was exhausted; a lot of guys in the band were exhausted; and I could only imagine how Alice felt, because he was constantly doing interviews and working on other things and flying to the White House to play golf, so we were exhausted and it didn't surprise me when they said, 'Guys, we're not going to tour right now'."

What was more of a shock was the rest of the sentence. "In fact we're going to go into a holding pattern now, so if there's anything you guys want to do to make money, you should go and do it. So I kinda got the vibe that that was it, and Alice wasn't much for a lot of words, he just came and said, 'OK well I hope to see you guys in a bit, down the road,' and that was it."

The pervading notion that Alice was somehow out of touch with both his core constituency and the music scene in general was confirmed by the fate of *Zipper Catches Skin*. Not only was there no accompanying tour, there was no chart action either – Alice Cooper was, as a commercial prospect, a thing of the past.

One final album was demanded by Alice's Warner Brothers contract; *Dada* brought a reunion with Bob Ezrin for the first time in the studio since *Lace And Whiskey*, and a wholesale embracing of the much vaunted "new technology" in the shape of a CMJ Fairlight computer. But again there was no tour, and again there was no appetite for one. Staring a return to the sonics of *Pretties For You* in the face, and a clutch of 10 songs that bore little semblance to anything that Alice could have convincingly wrought on stage, *Dada* was left to languish, unheard by all but his staunchest supporters.

Which was sad because once expectations have been checked at the door, *Dada* stands at a stylistic crossroads that Alice had not visited in a decade; since that moment when the band stood poised between *Easy Action* and *Love It To Death*, or maybe *Killer* and *School's Out*. 'I Love America' even sounds like a *Billion Dollar Babies* out-take.

The opening title track is nothing less than a visit to the psychiatrist, set to an eerie electronic rumble, and the relentless cry of a talking baby doll; and if 'Enough's Enough' is a direct descendent of the last couple of albums, Ezrin's return grants it an epic frame that simply tastes like classic Cooper.

The mysteriously titled 'Formerly Lee Warmer' borrows its melody from the Bee Gees' 'Holiday', but is a labyrinthine examination of insanity regardless; while the BDSM-battered 'Scarlet And Sheba' is sheer grandiosity, so cinematic in its soundscapes that when Alice's vocal finally kicks in, everything has to rise up a few notches simply to make it count.

'Fresh Blood' isn't as evocative as its title, although it does pack one of Alice's most picturesque lyrics, "we're like a couplet out of 'Desolation Row'," and the song's serial killer protagonist was, of course, one to whom he would frequently return in the future. And then there's 'Pass The Gun Around', which is almost Dylanesque in its portrait of the last legs of a loser, and might well have been the most electrifyingly personal song on this most remarkable of albums.

But no matter how entertaining *Dada* emerged, just one thing was clear. Alice's life was falling apart, and with the Warners contract now discharged, and his career at apparently rock bottom, all agreed that it was time to stop.

"Those two albums are kinda avant-garde stuff," Alice mused to *Kerrang!* a decade after *Zipper Catches Skin* and *Dada*. "It was a time when I was doing exactly what I wanted to." On other occasions, however, he was more reflective. "I made six albums that no one ever heard of. That started to kill me."

The fact that *Dada* in particular can be ranked alongside any of the records that are habitually termed his greatest was no consolation.

He had just one source of solace. His family. Daughter Calico was born in Beverly Hills at the height of *Special Forces*, in 1981, and no matter what else befell Alice, she and Sheryl were always there. Until the day they weren't.

On September 30, 1983, her life shattered and inverted by her husband's drinking, Sheryl moved out of the family home, scooping up two-year-old daughter Calico and returning to her parents' home in Oak Park, Illinois. Six weeks later, on November 15, she filed for the dissolution of their marriage, asking $5,000 a month in temporary spousal maintenance and $2,240 a month in temporary child support. An affidavit filed listed her monthly expenses as $1,200 for a housekeeper; $1,300 for food and supplies; $1,200 for car repairs, maintenance and gas; $1,000 for entertainment; $400 for clothing for herself and her baby and $400 for beauty shop bills. She also requested temporary custody of Calico. The marriage, her petition contended, was irretrievably broken with no prospect for reconciliation.

Now Alice was back in the headlines. When he and girlfriend Cindy parted back in 1975, and an ugly palimony suit seemed imminent, attorney Marvin Mitchelson estimated the singer's worth at $10 million. Maybe Alice's earning powers had declined since then, but he was an astute investor. His value must have been several times that amount, and lawyers and tabloid journalists alike licked their lips at the prospect of what the courts might award.

There was just one cloud on the vultures' horizon. The fact that Alice and Sheryl really didn't want to divorce. Not really. All it would take for the whole thing to go away would be for Alice to say the words that Sheryl needed him to speak, and this time, to mean them. He needed to promise to give up drinking, and this time, he needed to say it himself and not wait for somebody else to force his arm.

He said it. They were actually in the court house, awaiting their appearance and the granting of the dissolution, when Alice finally pledged to stop drinking, without prompting, without nudging, without an arm being twisted behind his back.

He was true to his word, too, although he didn't only have Sheryl and Calico by his side.

Throughout his career, Alice had steadfastly avoided any onstage antics that he knew might embarrass either his father or his father's Church;

had often spoken, too, of his belief that his version of entertainment was, ultimately, as harmless as any other actor or performer's. It was a matter of familial pride for him, of course, but it also came from deeper-seated convictions, impressed upon him as a child and forever percolating at the back of his mind.

He laughed, for example, when the firebrand evangelists Dan and Steve Peters began publicising their Truth About Rock Ministry in 1979, dedicated to alerting responsible Americans to the evils embodied in their children's favourite music; as they gathered support for their message across the same televisual spectrum as had once publicised Alice Cooper; and as they published their hit list of the rockers most likely to burn in Hell.

There was Kiss – their name, it was now proclaimed, an acronym for Kids In Satan's Service. There was Ozzy Osbourne, of course, and Mick Jagger too. Any man who sang of giving sympathy to the Devil had to be a bad one. And there was Alice, who would not have argued with the Peters' suggestion that "his ominous lyrics and music are designed specifically to create a frightening atmosphere".

It was laughable; as ridiculous as the older insistence that if you played certain rock records backwards, subliminal messages would reach out to snare you, to drive you to suicide or into the arms of a waiting Lucifer. But that belief was still current in the early eighties, and the Peters' mission, too, swiftly found fertile soil, wildfiring across the American heartland, appealing to an increasingly vast cross-section of so-called Christians who based their faith not on the tolerant tenets of the religion itself, but on their intolerance of any life or lifestyle that did not fit their own narrow view of righteousness. Rock did not fit, and so the Peters' Ministry was born – ironically around the same time as one of its earliest targets, Bob Dylan, announced his own conversion to Christianity.

Soon, the brothers were overseeing public record burnings, inspired by the Biblical destruction of sundry occult books at Ephesus, as recounted in Acts 19. The media pricked up its ears, and the brothers were soon a nationwide phenomenon; in their first major television interview, they confronted the head of Elektra Records on the evils that his artists fed their guileless followers; by 1983, they were head to head with Gene Simmons, and publishing books that are, in fact, masterpieces of misconstrued research, pinpointing practically every topic in rock as another step down the road to damnation. Alice, "[a] monster rock ribald [who] sings an anthem of necrophilia" – "sexual intercourse with a dead person", they helpfully interject – was a natural target.

Other preachers took up the Peters' battle flag. Even more vehement an anti-rock crusader, Louisiana-based Jacob Aranza, publicly declared "[the] hellish and sexual overtones that Alice uses don't make it very hard to believe that he is going to hell, and leading many [of his fans] there with him." And that is where Alice drew the line. Although he believed it was nobody's business but his own, Alice himself was as fervent a Christian as any of his zealous foes, and probably more honest in his understanding of what that faith portended, as well. "I started thinking about Christianity," he told writer Danny Scott in 2001, around the same time as he dried out.

"The doctors told me that if I had been drunk another week, I would have joined the guys upstairs. When you get that close to dying, you come back looking for something more than limos and mansions. I guess it's not too surprising I turned to Christianity. My father was a pastor."

Alice does not preach and he does not proselytise. He does not lace his lyrics with religious imagery, or deck his artwork in symbols and iconography. In fact, the only time he really mentions his faith is when he feels the needs to defend himself against another knee-jerk rock assassin, accusing him of Satanism and of leading the children astray. To a man of his beliefs and faith, that is one of the cruellest insults of all.

"You could call me untalented and boring," he said. "OK, I can live with that. But call me Satanic and you're stepping on what I really believe in.

"I spent a lot of time in my lyrics warning against Satanism, because I don't believe in the concept of Satan, I believe in the being of Satan. I believe in the being of God. And I think that we're in the middle. We're being pulled this way, and we're being pulled this way... Satan offers us everything we want, God is offering us everything we need. So when people start playing around with the 666 and the upside down crosses and all the blasphemy – I'm at a point in my life where I can go, 'Be careful, you're inviting something in and you don't know what you're playing with.'

"So I do lyrics that say, 'Be careful.' He's here, he's right here and he's going for your throat, and it doesn't look like it but in the end he wants to own you. And that's pretty horrific, that's real horror when you think of it. If you believe in a real Satan, then you believe in a real character that's trying to destroy your eternity. What's more horrific than that?"

Chapter Fifteen

The Day My Dead Pet Returned

While Vince took the cure, and this time kicked the booze, Alice slept. Occasionally word would seep out of a new project. Alongside the towering presence of Grace Jones, he co-presented the Grammys in February 1984, and barely batted an eyelid when *The Nightmare*, his latest video concert release, was passed over by the judging committee.

He spent some time with guitarist Joe Perry, working towards what might have been a new album at a time, he told *Metal Hammer*, "when we were [both] on the verge of giving up drink and drugs, so we had bad withdrawal symptoms, and that was reflected in our attempts to get a song together. We were still shaking all over, and had wobbly knees all the time. It was just impossible to play music or anything. We couldn't have written a tune to save our lives, and in the end I had to say to Joe, 'OK, come on man, forget it. We just can't do it'."

In fact, the pair were six songs into the process when Alice was called to Spain in March, to shoot the leading role in a new movie, *Monster Dog*. By the time he returned to the US three months later, Perry had reconciled with his former bandmates in Aerosmith, and was fired up about a whole new project. His work with Alice stalled, but was not completely wasted. Two of the songs they worked on together would appear on the *Monster Dog* soundtrack.

Destined to go straight to video, *Monster Dog* was, quite simply, the tale of a man, a rock star, who is transformed into what else but a monster dog.

He'd been on a binge of watching Dario Argento splatter movies when he was offered the part, and that combined with three months in Spain rendered the whole thing irresistible. Neither was he under any illusions as to the kind of movie it was. He'd grown up watching B-movies, and he knew that *Monster Dog* wasn't even that proficient. Never mind, Alice shrugged. "I love C-movies."

That was finished, and now he started talking about a new project. *The Magnificent Seven Of Rock'n'Roll*, a loosely conceived video collection that would allow Alice to strut his stuff alongside an unspecified half dozen other artists, hand-picked metal bands who grew up on Alice Cooper. He would be playing the Yul Brynner role.

Hanoi Rocks, the super flash Finnish outfit fronted by the platinum beauty of Mike Monroe, came on board and Monroe, in London that summer, was effusive. "It's a total fantasy, the wild west meets Alice, *Westworld* meets Freddie Kruger. We're going to be working on a bunch of the songs with him and it's going to kick everything into a whole new gear." Bandmate Andy McCoy was already penning material with Alice, and Monroe was adamant. "You think you've heard Hanoi Rocks in the past? You don't even know what you're listening to."

Mötley Crüe were recruited and, with them, the financial clout of Elektra Records. Def Leppard were involved and so were Twisted Sister. And then disaster struck. By early December 1984, some 20 songs had been written and were ready to record. And then Mötley Crüe's Vince Neil and Hanoi Rocks' drummer Razzle decided to make a run to the liquor store to replenish the mid-tour party they were celebrating. Drunk, Neil lost control of the vehicle, and Razzle lost his life.

Mötley Crüe were in disarray; Hanoi Rocks too. Elektra Records pulled its funding from Alice's venture, and fate was still not finished with *The Magnificent Seven Of Rock'n'Roll*. Just three weeks after Neil's accident, on New Year's Eve 1984, Def Leppard drummer Rick Allen was involved in a highway smash in England. He lost his arm, and Alice lost all appetite for a project that was already so ill-starred.

Seven months of work and planning were scrapped, and so was Alice's deal with Warner Brothers, a severance announced to the world in a tersely worded corporate press release that stated, simply, "He has fulfilled his contractual obligations to the company and is now negotiating a new deal which should be announced within the next few weeks."

But a few weeks quickly became a few years. Right now he was more interested in Vince.

Journalist Bob Greene, one of the reporters who had followed the *Billion Dollar Babies* tour around a decade earlier, and who had grown closer than most to Alice in the process, caught up with him shortly after the reconciled Furniers moved to Chicago in 1984.

Sheryl was already pregnant with their second child; the following June, daughter Calico would have a brother, named Dashiell – Dash for short. He was named for one of Alice's favourite authors, the hardboiled American detective novelist Dashiell Hammett, author of *The Maltese Falcon* among others.

But Alice, as Greene's *Esquire* article was appropriately titled, did not live there any more.

"We were living in Beverly Hills, but we just decided that is no environment to bring up children. It's crazy in Los Angeles – the drugs, the fast life. There are too many negative temptations. I just couldn't see risking bringing my children up in that kind of atmosphere." Now they were close to Sheryl's parents, and living the life of any suburban couple. Occasionally he would show three-year-old Calico one of his old videos, so she knew what her daddy did for a living. But she also knew that daddy took her to Sunday School every week, and was there in the house for the rest of the week.

For now, anyway. But restlessness was never far away, especially now that he did not have the booze to cushion the boredom of inactivity.

"Alice took three years off in the early eighties," the singer explained to writer John Burnes, "because it sounded good at the time. After a while, though, I discovered that I was retiring way too soon. I was looking at a magazine one day, seeing which bands were hot at the time, and they were all doing Alice. They were imitating the act I had done for so long." And that, he said, was all the urging he needed.

He had long since grown accustomed to seeing elements of his act lifted and filtered by other performers; the rise of Kiss was proof enough of that. By 1984, however, an entire generation had arisen who not only grew up aping Alice in their bedroom mirror, just as he had grown up aping Elvis, but they were still doing it now.

Twisted Sister, for example.

Yes, Dee Snider was as great a showman in his own way as Alice ever had been. And yes, his band of ultra-glammed New Yorkers kicked out an unholy racket that at least matched the classic Coopers in terms of decibel damage. That was why he had recruited them to the Magnificent Seven.

But there is such a fine line between inspiration and imitation and, though Twisted Sister walked that line with dazzling finesse, the media had no hesitation in trying to shove them over it.

So both sides of the mirror, Twisted Sister on one side and Alice on the other, decided to nail the nastiness for good. A new Twisted Sister song, the anthemic 'Be Chrool To Your Scuel', had drawn comparisons with 'School's Out' before it even left the rehearsal room. How great would it be to have Alice Cooper guest on it, conferring his approval on the antics of his offspring, at the same time as reminding the world what made Alice so great in the first place?

Brian Setzer of the Stray Cats, Billy Joel, the Uptown Horns and Clarence Clemons piled into the sessions too; in the age of Live Aid and Band Aid and so-many-superstars singing together, 'Be Chrool To Your Scuel' wasn't simply a great rock song, it was also a reminder that rock'n'roll had an import far beyond fund raising for African disasters. To some people, at least, it still represented rebellion and maybe Twisted Sister's call for contributors was less well-heeded (and certainly less fashionable) than Bob Geldof's. It was a clarion call regardless.

'Be Chrool To Your Scuel' would not be a hit; indeed, MTV took one look at the accompanying video and proclaimed the Sister's chosen cast of decaying zombies, casual cannibalism and a wryly Cooper-esque near-decapitation as "too graphic" for broadcast. Presumably the living dead could only be screened if they were dancing through a Michael Jackson video, and Twisted Sister were horrified at the decision.

But Alice celebrated the censorship. "I thought it was great. I figured it this way: If the only video I'd ever done ended up getting banned, then I must have done something right. I kind of like the idea."

After all, 'Be Chrool To Your Scuel' had another purpose, beyond simply paying off Twisted Sister's debt to the old shockmeister. It allowed Alice to make the pronouncement that Vince Furnier and all his real life problems had kept him from speaking for too long. He was back. And he was nastier than ever.

He needed to be.

The early eighties were the golden age of slasher horror movies. Of course they'd existed since long before that, and of course there have been better ones made since then. But if any genre that has essentially remained unchanged since it was first formulated can be said to have enjoyed a purple patch, it was that half-decade that yawned between John Carpenter's first *Halloween* movie and the debut *Nightmare On Elm Street* in 1984, and which essentially broke down every last gore taboo that mainstream Hollywood had ever held sacred.

No longer confined to the B-movie backlots that stuck two fingers up at the biggest studios; no longer sent out on the midnight mania circuit to play to insomniacs, sickos and the homeless alone. The movies that swamped the theatres of the eighties were big business and whether it was Alice who drew the first parallel, or somebody in his entourage, prophesies that he had been making since the early seventies were finally being proved true.

"We did the hanging when we first came out," he told *Music Express*. "It was done as morality play. Alice always had to pay for what he did onstage, then he'd come back out with the message that 'Everything's O.K., it didn't really happen.' Then I saw *Halloween* and the character Michael Myers, and Jason, who couldn't be killed. I thought, 'That's vaguely familiar.' There was a rock 'n' roll aura to those guys; people looked as them the same way they looked at Alice.

"They were villains, but somehow heroes, because their victims were such despicable characters, like the kids in school you hated. I think there was a lot of influence in *A Clockwork Orange*. His name was Alex, he had make-up under one eye, and a boa constrictor in his drawer. I kept going, 'Wait a minute! Where have I seen this before?'"

Alice Cooper had always insisted that he soundtracked exactly what America really wanted. And right now, it seemed, America wanted gore. Or, as he put it, "putting music to *Nightmare On Elm Street*". Yes, it did rankle to have to look at it like that, when it was far more accurate to say that many of these movies were simply putting visuals to *Love It To Death*. But the symbiosis had been pinpointed and all Alice needed now was to place his music where his mouth was. And dream up a stage show to match.

"I didn't waste the three years I took off," he told *Kerrang!* in 1986. He devoted it to research, devouring the horror shelves at his local movie rental store three movies at a time, and returning them the following morning to pick up another three. He wasn't even bothered by the fact that a lot of the movies were rubbish; that the special effects might have improved since the creature features of the fifties, but the dialogue, scripting and acting had not. It was, he insisted when anybody asked, research work. "In the last three years I've actually gotten more knowledge of what Alice should be doing on stage.

"I'm convinced that there's a connection between the popularity of splatter movies and that of heavy metal music. The trick is being able to get away with stage-splatter. It's very hard to put over something like *Night Of The Living Dead* – if I cut off somebody's head, you can only get the point across live if it's a 15-foot monster and the head is three feet in diameter! That's the only problem I'm coming across when projecting this thing... it just takes some technical stuff to get it to work."

But he also knew that visual technology had improved manifold in the decade since he last seriously investigated it, back in the planning stages of *Welcome To My Nightmare*, and though audiences had certainly grown more sophisticated across that last decade, they had contrarily become more susceptible too, more willing to suspend credulity and belief as the battle lines drawn by the likes of Truth Against Rock hardened not into the theological battle that the Peters were prepared for, but a simple war of wills, and the unexpectedly unstoppable force of sheer bloody-mindedness.

Bob Ezrin laughed. Back when he was first approached to produce Kiss, it was not their music that swayed him, nor even the popularity. It was a conversation that he had with a high school kid. "Kiss? Oh man, they're great. The kids at school love them. The only problem is, their records are so shitty. But we buy them anyway, simply cos they look good."

That was Kiss' secret. Musically they were little more than another stultifying heavy metal band, singing about sex, sex and more sex and partying all night. Nothing special there. But visually they were the tops... they were Over The Tops. And that remained the key to great rock'n'roll. It wasn't enough to put on a show. You needed to put on an unforgettable show, and throw in everything you could possibly find.

The most obvious move for Alice, all agreed, was for him to be relaunched with something that everybody would recognise. A decade had now passed since the original *Welcome To My Nightmare* and, in strict commercial terms, he still hadn't followed it up. Not one, or even all, of the albums he'd released since then had made even a fraction of the impact that *Welcome To My Nightmare* had, and yes there were any number of extenuating circumstances. But the fact was... well, he'd already said it. He'd made six albums that nobody had even heard of, and that showed how bad things had got, because there were actually seven, and one can only wonder which one even he had forgotten: *Goes To Hell, Lace And Whiskey, From The Inside, Flush The Fashion, Special Forces, Zipper Catches Skin...* or *Dada*? Poor unloved, unheard, *Dada*.

If Alice Cooper was going to come back, then, he needed to come back big. Bigger than he was in the seventies, and bigger than the reputation he had garnered back then. Bigger than the movies that now placed on screen the vicarious viciousness that was once his world alone, bigger than all the alternative Alices that haunted the world he had left behind.

He started making calls. Dick Wagner, his co-writer across so much of his past, came back on board. So did Joe Perry, fresh from the Aerosmith reunion album, *Done With Mirrors*. Alice dug into his closet and pulled out all the old props that had made the original *Nightmare* so enchanting, and when he talked of his plans for the immediate future, he was hopeful that he'd be able to begin his comeback in Britain.

The key to his musical resurrection, however, would turn out to be somebody none of his admirers had even heard of, a walking brick shithouse who seemed more muscle than man, whose custom guitar was the shape of an M60 machine gun, and who looked like he could eat Rambo for breakfast. His name was Kane Roberts and when *Kerrang!* asked him what the deal was, Roberts didn't even pause before answering. "I just became a flesh and blood version of what I feel about rock'n'roll. I kinda look like a power chord!"

Roberts was playing in a band called Criminal Justice when he met Alice, but it wasn't the band that caught the singer's eye first. Bob Ezrin had told him of Roberts' prowess and he wanted to check him out, only to walk into the club in the midst of a bar fight, with Roberts the star of the show. "As soon as I saw that," he told journalist Jon Sutherland, "I said 'I don't care if this guy can play, I want him.' Turns out he can play."

Days later, Roberts and Alice were writing their first song together; suitably, it was titled 'Step On You'. And the longer they hung out together, the more new songs they found themselves writing. From doing nothing but dreaming a few months before, Alice now had two whole new albums gestating, the *Nightmare* revision and the Roberts-fired rebirth, and the only question was, which one would he follow?

Sessions in New York in January with Roberts, bassist Kip Winger and producer Beau Hill solved that dilemma. Hill was best known for his work with Ratt, a metal band of such preposterous imagery that it was easy to forget they even made records or gigged; you could simply show your devotion by collecting the merchandise. And that seemed somehow appropriate for an act that itself would demand an image that devoured all in its path.

With a new deal with MCA in place, Alice started looking towards a whole new LP. It would be called *Constrictor* and if anybody doubted Alice's commitment to the new musical/slasher movie hybrid, the latest instalment in the *Friday The 13th* saga, *Part VI: Jason Lives*, resolved the dilemma. The first single from the new album, 'He's Back (The Man Behind the Mask)', doubled as the theme song for the flick.

The sessions were not plain sailing. While Alice and Roberts swiftly bonded with Michael Wagener, in his role of Beau Hill's assistant, Hill proved less pliable. "Everything that Beau did or wanted to do was completely the opposite of what I wanted to do," Alice would complain to *Metal Hammer* later. "He's one of these guys who'll use up every track on the tape to get a big fat sound. [But] that kind of production really messes up what a band really sounds like, it gives a false impression."

It was Hill, too, who insisted on the Simmons drum sound that today cements *Constrictor* firmly into the mid-eighties, a sound that was just so cutting edge in 1986 that today it sounds horrifically dated. But the album was completed, a Dreadnought packed with dramatic loud riffery, and Alice would not say a word against it at the time. For now, it was enough simply to revel in all the attention it was receiving. The eminently singable 'Teenage Frankenstein' followed as a second single; *Constrictor* itself scratched the US Top 60, Alice's first chart entry since *Flush The Fashion*. And the old *Welcome To My Nightmare* theme was revisited after all, in a tour that was so fittingly billed The Nightmare Returns.

It was, Alice knew, at least partially a shameless nostalgia trip. "This current show has got to get everyone back into the Alice Cooper thing," he admitted to *Kerrang!* that autumn. "That's why it has to rely a lot on the older songs; it's gotta be like a refresher course."

He pointed to the return of the guillotine, itself as iconic as any of the songs in the set, and he was adamant. "Before I go on to the next thing, I want everybody to understand the basic idea behind Alice Cooper, especially the kids who haven't seen it, because then they'll have a reference point. The object is to do the definitive show! It seems to me that everybody's been hitting all around it, Ozzy Osbourne and all those people, but no-one's produced the definitive show... but that's what the new Alice Cooper show will be."

But there was a timelessness to the unfolding concept, a sense of expectation that rose from the audience, to be coupled with a sense of the familiar. Alice Cooper, he reasoned, was like the old King Kong and Dracula movies; it didn't matter how many times you saw them, or how many years had passed since the last time, the same chills and thrills would always be there, and each time you would spot something different. "This show is like Nightmare 2," he enthused, in true horror-movie jargon. "This show is a lot more grotesque. We're using a lot more blood in this show. There's no dancers or distractions like that. The band are all street guys."

He admitted, of course, that the prospect of returning to the road made him nervous. The opening show on The Nightmare Returns, in Santa Barbara at the end of October 1986, would be his first full concert since the end of the Special Forces outing in early 1982 and he was very aware that a lot had changed in that time.

But they had changed, he believed, for the better. When he toured in 1982, the charts were still filled with that second wave of British Invaders who hit American shores in the wake of the synthesizer boom, so-called New Romantics named Duran Duran, Soft Cell and Culture Club.

Today they had all been pushed aside, and the heroes of 1986 were cut from a far harsher cloth: Beau Hills' Ratt; Guns 'N Roses, an LA band that had scarcely made a move out of the city, but had already been snapped up by Geffen, and were everyone's tip for the new year top; Mötley Crüe, recovering from that awful accident to find that the notoriety had just made them even more popular; a British band called the Cult; a reborn Aerosmith; thrashers Megadeth and Metallica; and the English trio Motörhead. And what did they all have in common?

They were all Alice Cooper fans, and spat out his influence in everything they did. Now it was time for the teacher to show them some new tricks.

Two months of rehearsal led up to the first dates; time spent both perfecting the musical side of things and working out the special effects too. Plans were put in place to film the Detroit homecoming for what would become the *Nightmare Returns* home video, and in and around all those preparations, Vince was working out his own effects as well. How he would again become Alice Cooper.

Back to the video machine. "Kane Roberts and I… all we did was watch every splatter movie there was," he laughed to *Rue Morgue*. "And our stage show was so bloody that people in the first two rows were literally soaked. But I think people got the idea of it. It was like *Evil Dead*. You know how the beginning of *Evil Dead* was so scary? Then it got so bloody that it got funny. You couldn't believe there could be any more blood, and then the pipes break and it covers everything."

He was right; it did. The tour, while scarcely opening any new windows into Alice's fantasy world, nevertheless re-established him as a performer, at the same time as confirming him, once more, as the hip name to drop by young metal and shock rockers as they set about establishing their own credentials. And, once again, as the nameless beast whose horror could be invoked by any crackpot organisation looking to grab some news stories for itself. According to Alice, one out of every three concerts on the tour was visited by pickets from one group or another, many of them so left-field and crackpot that it was hard to believe they had not simply been formed for that very purpose. "Mothers Against Lutherans Against Alice," he cracked. "Stuff like that."

Nowhere, however, was his return to form as the king of the bogeymen to be celebrated better than in the UK where, touring the following year's *Raise Your Fist And Yell* album, Alice found himself butting heads once again with the powers of British government. Although the story began, of course, back at home.

The new album's birth was difficult, early sessions with the returning Beau Hill being scrapped when it became clear the producer and the band were never going to agree on a sound. Hill's assistant, Michael Wagener, was pushed to the forefront instead, with a simple brief: to craft a sound that was at least as aggressive as the lyrics he was hearing. He succeeded, too, but nowhere was the furnace that burned beneath the album so pronounced as on 'Freedom', a song dedicated to the latest gang of scissor-happy censors to descend upon the American music industry, the Parents' Music Resource Centre, or PMRC.

The PMRC represented one of the periodic surges of righteous indignation that have stricken the American rock'n'roll music scene ever since television's *Ed Sullivan Show* in 1956 showed Elvis from the waist up only, for fear that his pelvic gyrations would transform a nation of impressionable teens into sex maniacs. Where it differed from these past guardians of morality was in the methods by which it approached its foe.

The group was founded in May 1985 when three women – Pam Howar, Susan Baker and Mary Elizabeth 'Tipper' Gore – quite independently caught themselves listening to the lyrics of songs that their children, their friends and, in Howar's case, their aerobics instructors were playing. Rude lyrics, shocking lyrics, coarse lyrics.

"We got together," Mrs. Gore explained, "and said, 'These things were happening to us in our homes'." They drafted a letter to sundry friends and associates, in the spirit of outraged women's groups the world over. The difference was, these women had some very powerful friends and associates. Gore was the wife of Tennessee Senator (and future Vice President) Al; Baker was married to President Reagan's treasury secretary, James; Howar was wed to the owner of a major Washington construction company.

"Some rock groups," their diatribe declared, "advocate satanic rituals... others sing of killing babies". And others recommended "open rebellion against parental... authority". The PMRC grew from there.

Lobbying the Recording Industry Association of America (RIAA), the umbrella organisation that represented the nation's major record labels, the PMRC demanded that all albums that could be considered 'objectionable' be prominently labelled according to the offence. An 'X' would indicate explicit sexual or violent content, an '0' condemned occultist material, a 'DIA' warned of songs glorifying drugs and alcohol – and so on until Frank Zappa, one of the PMRC's most vociferous critics, asked whether "the next bunch" would include "a large yellow J on material written or performed by Jews?"

Its confidence boosted by the apparent willingness of several RIAA members to go along with a modified version of those demands, and campaigning now for this initial victory to become an industry standard, the still predominantly female PMRC brought its battle into its fast-swelling membership's own backyard, the halls of government wherein many of their husbands worked. In mid-September 1985, the Senate Committee on Commerce, Science and Transportation sat to consider the PMRC's requests, and specifically its insistence that a parent has a discretionary right over the music a child listens to and should be afforded some means of personally checking the record prior to purchase.

This was never challenged, even by the PMRC's opponents. Albums, cassettes and CDs are unique in the mass media in that they are seldom offered for sale unsealed; it was many years since record stores had afforded their customers the luxury of listening booths, in which to test drive potential purchases. "So why not reinstate them?" asked Twisted Sister frontman Dee Snider when he was called to appear before the committee, but of course few parents would have either the patience or the willpower to listen to an entire album in search of a single reference to having smacked-out anal sex with the devil. It was the record company's job to warn them about it,

Although the Senate committee was granted no powers of legislation, by November, 20 RIAA member labels were agreeing to print warning labels to alert consumers to potentially controversial subject matter. One, A&M, reversed its decision shortly afterward. The remainder, however, stayed meekly in line.

Throughout the first year of the PMRC's existence, the group's prime target was heavy metal, and its most vociferous opponents too. Most agreed, and posterity has proved, that Alice's own withering assessment of the PMRC was correct; "Awww, it's a lot of fart," he groaned to *Metal Hammer* in 1987. "Their whole organisation is a joke. Just like Gore himself. He's got about as much chance of being President as Donald Duck has.... or Alice Cooper!"

At the time, however, in the heat of the PMRC furnace, the movement was a threat, and it did need to be spoken out against. Alice responded with 'Freedom', one of his finest anthems since 'School's Out'.

He explained to *Faces* magazine, "When we started writing it, I said 'Somebody ought to give the PMRC both barrels.' Not just being subtle, let's just give 'em a shot of Alice in this thing. Because there's something real un-American about the PMRC. It starts out with the premise that every kid out there is so stupid that they don't know what they're listening to, that every kid that buys a record is too dumb to understand satire, or humour, or horror. That's where these people are missing it. Not that I'm against the PMRC. The PMRC for some reason is one of the most necessary evils I've seen in my life.

"They've really brought outlawism back to rock'n'roll, which I think is healthy. I can only criticise their philosophy, I don't criticise the fact that they exist. I kinda enjoy them. They're a burr under the saddle that gets you going." And spurred by that burr, he tossed more ammunition back to the Washington Wives, declaring that onstage performances of 'Freedom', alongside another new number, 'Prince Of Darkness' (the theme to the latest John Carpenter movie), would give the Gores all the gore they could stomach, and then some.

"[They are] the real theatre on the tour. The tracks are ideal to stage and are all about psycho-killers. It'll be a kind of concept show that I'd like to turn into a video – guaranteed to be banned by MTV! The effects are really bloody!"

Despite these highlights, the true key to the album, and to the controversies that were set to erupt around it, was what Alice called the "kind of autobiographical" sequence of songs that made up side two of the original vinyl. At a time when movies and television, too, were coming under the microscope as a cause of anti-social behaviour, Alice conceived the ultimate doomsday scenario for both sides of the argument, a horror movie fan who spends so much time watching slasher movies that he is finally aroused to start living them out, without ever differentiating between film and reality. Is he really killing all these women? Or is he watching someone else do it?

He is the killer, although he is selective. He only kills women named Gail. "And at the end, when he's killed this girl in the song 'Gail', and he's thinking about her bones in the ground and about how the bugs are inside her ribcage, and the dog is digging up the bones – he wonders how the dog remembers Gail. And he sees this wedding dress and it's got blood-stains on it everywhere – but he doesn't see the blood-stains, he sees roses! This guy's a romantic y'know? He's so crazy, he looks at this blood and all he sees are roses. 'Roses On White Lace' is this whole thing about him not knowing that it's really blood. For him, he's painted these lovely roses on this white dress. So he's really a psycho.

"I don't really know how we're going to do it, we're working on that now. But I can picture some great stuff with the wedding dress all splattered... and all the Gail creatures, they can come up on stage at different times – they can keep on coming up! All we have to do is train a dog..."

Even by past standards, then, the latest tour had taken on a whole new realm of realism, a consequence of course of the availability of better quality props. The old intent was still there; and that had not changed. But the blood looked bloodier, the mannequins seemed more man-like, and if the dead babies didn't quite scream when he stuck them, who was to say that wasn't because the band was playing so loud?

"The new stage show is even more horrible than I thought it would be," Alice cackled to *Metal Edge* magazine. "We're doing 'Dead Babies' again, we've got a big black widow spider, we're taking the old classic stuff and bringing them up to date."

The guillotine had been replaced by the gallows, but confidence in both *Raise Your Fist And Yell* and Alice's own in-concert drawing power saw five songs from the new album built into the set, "gut level rock'n'roll" that he wrote with Roberts while they toured *Constrictor*, and then recorded with the same band once the touring was over.

He made no secret that the songs were basic. "Let's face it, politics and religion are boring. They're dead subjects. Most people don't really care about them. The only things that matter to people are death, sex and money. So we write songs mostly concerning those subjects." You would not, he laughed, find any socio-political commentary on his new album.

So socio-political commentary came looking for him, the moment the tour touched down in England.

This time around, it was a Labour MP who raised his fists and yelled; David Blunkett, the Member of Parliament for Sheffield, attended one of the performances and instantly called for the remainder of the tour to be cancelled.

"I'm horrified by his behaviour. It goes beyond the bounds of entertainment," the morally incorruptible Blunkett raged. Indeed, the Alice Cooper show was "an indication of the sick society we're moving into and something drastic should be done to protect young people from paying for this sort of obscenity."

The press detailed the kind of sequences that so outraged the avuncular family man. A hanging sequence. The dismemberment of a baby. "A mother [is] sliced down the middle, and a beautiful girl has her throat cut. [And] at the climax of the one-and-a-half hour performance young fans in the front rows are soaked by gallons of theatrical blood."

Yet what exactly did Blunkett see?

AND HIS PERSONALISED BASEBALL BAT. JOHN LIVZEY/REDFERNS

ALICE WITH TV PRESENTER/QUIZMASTER NICHOLAS PARSONS ON THE *ALL NEW ALPHABET GAME*, 1987. ITV/REX FEATURES

ALICE IN DRAG, 1991. EUGENE ADEBARI/REX FEATURES

ALICE APPEARING AS FREDDY'S FATHER IN *NIGHTMARE ON ELM STREET FREDDY'S DEAD*, 1991. SNAP/REX FEATURES

ALICE COOPER AND HIS BAND, RECEIVING A STAR ON THE HOLLYWOOD WALK OF FAME, LOS ANGELES, DECEMBER 2003. PETER BROOKER/REX FEATURES

ALICE AND SHERYL ON THE WALK OF FAME. PRESS ASSOCIATION

ALICE AND DAUGHTER CALICO TAPING *THE LATE LATE SHOW WITH CRAIG FERGUSON* SEPTEMBER 2003, AT THE CBS TELEVISION STUDIOS IN LOS ANG
VINCE BUCCI/GETTY IMAGES

PRODUCER BOB EZRIN IS INDUCTED INTO THE CANADIAN MUSIC HALL OF FAME BY ALICE COOPER DURING THE JUNO GALA DINNER AND AWARDS CEREMONY, IN EDMONTON, CANADA, APRIL, 2004. DONALD WEBER/GETTY IMAGES

ROB ZOMBIE AND ALICE COOPER DURING THE 2007 SPIKE TV SCREAM AWARDS AT THE GREEK THEATER IN LOS ANGELES, OCTOBER 2007. JEFF KRAVITZ/FILMMAGIC

ALICE AND MANAGER SHEP GORDON ATTEND THE TASTE OF WAILEA DURING THE MAUI FILM FESTIVAL, IN HAWAII, JUNE 2008. MICHAEL BUCKNER/GETTY IMAGES

ALICE AND BERNIE TAUPIN DURING THE 4TH ANNUAL MUSICARES MAP FUND BENEFIT CONCERT AT THE MUSIC BOX, IN HOLLYWOOD, MAY 2008. LESTER COHEN/ WIREIMAGE

ALICE PERFORMS AT THE SONISPHERE FESTIVAL IN KNEBWORTH, ON JULY 30, 2010. PHOTO BY SAMIR HUSSEIN/GETTY IMAGES

JOHNNY DEPP AND ALICE PERFORM TOGETHER ON STAGE AT THE 100 CLUB ON IN LONDON, JUNE 2011. CHRISTIE GOODWIN/GETTYIMAGES

E ALICE COOPER BAND ARRIVE AT THE THIRD ANNUAL REVOLVER GOLDEN GOD AWARDS AT THE CLUB NOKIA IN LOS ANGELES, APRIL 2011. FRAZER HARRISON/GETTY IMAGES

NTHI, ALICE AND TOMMY HENRIKSEN ON STAGE DURING THE *NO MORE MR NICE GUY 2* TOUR IN ATLANTA, GEORGIA, JANUARY 2012. ADMEDIA/SIPA/REX FEATURES

ALICE ON HIS *NO MORE MISTER NICE GUY 2 TOUR*. DAN HARR/ ADMEDIA

Very little. He is blind.

Four years later, an astonished Alice was still exclaiming, "Two guys… came to see one of our '88 The Nightmare Returns gigs. And believe it or not, and this is the God's honest truth: one of the two guys was blind, so the other one kept having to tell him throughout the show what was going on. And the other one was stone-deaf – no kidding!"

Alice might have taken further grim satisfaction a few years later when Blunkett, having risen further up the ranks of British politics, was then himself held up for similar inspection when his private life turned out to be no less controversial than Alice's public persona. For now, however, he continued amazed as the controversy spread.

Alice told *Metal Hammer*, "The result were some wild press releases in England which some German politician happened to dig up. He was going to stop me from ripping a teddy bear apart on stage. I think in view of all that stuff that's going off [in Germany] with regard to attacks on political refugees and skinheads, my teddy bear should be the least of their problems…" And later, "It's hard for an American to imagine anything as too violent for Germany."

For all the enthusiasm and excitement that surrounded the last two albums, however, restlessness was not far behind. Both albums, as Alice had declared, were basic; hard-hitting metal with riffs the size of dinosaurs lumbering across the landscape. No matter how gratefully Alice accepted the Godfatherhood of the eighties metal scene, however, he also knew that he was one of the least likely musicians to be granted such an honour.

At no prior point in his musical career, not even in the hard rocking days of *Killer*, had Alice Cooper been considered even peripheral to the heavy metal scene; that was the preserve of Black Sabbath and Led Zeppelin, the Blue Öyster Cult and Blue Cheer; and all those other groups that the old Cooper outfit used to relish blowing off stage. No matter how grateful he was for the accolade now, Alice knew that his dalliance with the musical form was at best a passing fancy and, at worst, a helping hand, a hitch-hiked ride back to mass popularity. And now it was time to get out of the car.

Kane Roberts had a solo career now, and it was time for him to pursue it. Kip Winger, too, was launching a new band, an eponymous outfit who would soon be riding high on the chart with their peculiar brand of melodic hair metal, and how sad (but fitting, because they were a gutless noise) it was that *Kerrang!* would soon be labelling them "the wussiest band of the eighties" and reminding people that "the only person who wears a Winger T-shirt...is Stuart... in Beavis And Butt-head!" Neither musician would truly sever ties with Alice, but they had their own music to worry about now, and Alice was casting around for new playmates.

Briefly, Alice reunited with Bob Ezrin and Dick Wagner to cut a new single, Spirit's 'I Got A Line On You'. But behind the scenes, it was the musical present, not the glorious past that was exercising his advisors and that could only mean one thing. It was time to change record labels.

Alice and Sheryl were vacationing in Hawaii at the end of the Raise Your Fist tour, when an intriguing request came to his attention. It was delivered by Bob Pfeifer, an A&R man at Epic Records and the gist of it was, "If you ever think you need to look for a new record company, call me."

Alice raised his eyebrows. He had, in fact, been tiring of MCA; grateful for what it had done to encourage his comeback, but aware also that the label was a lessening force on the music scene as the era of the multinational conglomerate loomed ever larger and the old traditional powerbases were either swamped or subsumed. Even more damaging in Alice's eyes was the knowledge that even though MCA had some areas in which it was still a commercial force to be reckoned with, hard rock was not among them. That was the remit of other labels – Geffen, with its deft handling of the Guns 'N Roses soap opera; Mercury, home to Bon Jovi; Atlantic, where Kip Winger's band Winger was now just breaking through. And Epic.

While Shep Gordon worked to forge an amicable break with MCA (an accomplishment of which he remains justifiably proud), Alice asked what Epic could offer, and he was astonished at its response. "Whatever it may cost," he was told, "don't ever worry. Always do what you think needs doing. Don't worry, we'll pay! The only thing you have to do in return, is bring us the songs, bring us a finished album!" He could, he was told, have anything he wanted. And anyone.

Alice shrugged. Anyone? He asked

Anyone, Epic responded.

OK then. Get me Desmond Child.

In 1988, Desmond Child was one of the biggest songwriting names around. Indeed, he had been enjoying that role for most of the past decade, ever since he made his debut in the Kiss camp by co-writing the band's descent into disco-dom, 'I Was Made For Loving You'. Since then, he had worked alongside some of the hottest names in American rock. Bon Jovi had Child to thank for their first ever chart-topping single,'You Give Love A Bad Name' (he also co-wrote 'Living On A Prayer' and 'Bad Medicine'), and when Aerosmith launched their 1987 revival, Child was in on 'Dude (Looks Like A Lady)'.

"The guy's a fucking genius," Aerosmith frontman Steve Tyler exclaimed. "The first time we met, we wrote 'Angel' in about an hour and 45 minutes – and I'm not bullshitting."

Most recently, Child had been working with Joan Jett, as she bounced back from a couple of years in the commercial doldrums, and 'I Hate Myself For Loving You' became one of Jett's biggest selling records ever. So what could Child give Alice?

How about a hit single, for starters?

"The way I judge a record," Alice told *Raw* magazine, "is this: when I'm driving my Corvette, if I hear something that makes me want to turn up the radio – to me that's a great record. 'Beds Are Burning' by Midnight Oil. 'Dude (Looks Like A Lady)' by Aerosmith, and all the Bon Jovi singles were great – 'You Give Love A Bad Name' was unbelievable. 'Heaven's On Fire' by Kiss, 'I Hate Myself For Loving You' by Joan Jett. Eight out of 10 records I found myself turning up were co-written by Desmond Child. So I said, 'I've got to get in touch with this guy because he's writing the kind of music I would like to hear Alice doing on the radio'."

Forty songs were stockpiled for the album. A few were Kane Roberts co-writes. Joan Jett weighed in with 'House Of Fire'. 'Trash' was a gift from two acquaintances of Child's and slipped so neatly into the old Cooper ballad bag that it not only became the new project's title track, it also inspired him to call in a co-singer, Aerosmith's Steve Tyler.

Jon Bon Jovi and Richie Sambora handed over some new compositions, and Childs was simply a writing machine. It didn't even seem to matter that most of them sounded very much like one another, or that you could sit through all 40 of the songs on the tape and, after the first two or three, really have problems telling them apart. Childs' production made every single one of them sound like a major event, a fanfare of fabulousness, and besides – a hit's a hit, right?

Epic Records, to whom Alice was now signed, certainly thought so. Even before the new album was complete, word of its star studded gestation was spreading; how it was recorded in Woodstock and mixed in LA, how the guest musicians included Kip Winger, Kane Roberts, Jon Bon Jovi, Richie Sambora, Steve Tyler, Joe Perry, Joey Kramer, Tom Hamilton, Steve Lukather and Guy Mann-Dude; how the quality of songs was so strong that Alice only found space for one of three songs that Jon Bon Jovi wrote for him. Oh, and one more thing, from the ubiquitous management spokesperson. "Alice has picked the songs purely by how good they sounded. The direction is less gore, more MOR!"

A lot of ears turned away right there. But, strangely, even more tuned in.

Chapter Sixteen

Don't Talk Old To Me

"We gave the company exactly what they wanted, they got what they hoped. We've recorded three or four potential singles and we still didn't have to sell out. The singles aren't wimpy at all, they're all tracks that I am really proud of, they are real Alice Cooper classics!"

Thus spake Alice as he looked back on 1989-1990, the years in which the clock rolled back to the days when he ruled the American chart. But he also admitted, "I'm not stupid. I know exactly what I have to do to get my music [more] airplay than I got during the *Constrictor* and *Raise Your Fist...* times. So I wrote the songs accordingly."

Four singles spun off *Trash*, beginning with the summer 1989 'Poison' – destined not only to become his most successful American hit in 18 years, but his joint biggest ever. Like 'School's Out', it rose to number seven, while British fans sent it soaring even higher, all the way to number two, where only the then-mega-monstrosities of Jive Bunny and Black Box could keep it from emulating his biggest UK smash.

A UK only release of 'Bed Of Nails' made the Top 40; American singles 'House Of Fire' and 'Only My Heart Talkin'' charted too and while their eventual places (56 and 89) could be construed as disappointing, that was tradition talking, not the reality of the ever-fracturing singles market of the late eighties. Radio was shattering into a succession of formats, and each had its own chart. On the listings where Alice's music was expected to do well, the hard rock and metal charts, and on the stations that his music was being marketed towards, both were solid smashes, while the rise of *Trash* itself was stupendous, his biggest album since *Welcome To My Nightmare*.

Dissenting voices would not be stilled, of course. Childs was still fresh from engineering Joan Jett's comeback the previous year and more than one listener pointed out that, in sonic terms, the two albums dovetailed so exquisitely that an Alice Cooper version of 'I Hate Myself For Loving You' would have been no more out of place on *Trash* than a Jett take on 'Poison' would have felt wrong on her *Up Your Alley*. And while Alice was more than happy to shrug away the absence of his trademark gore, he did so with a signal lack of conviction.

He told journalist Edgar Klüsener, "There'll be quite a few classic horror scenes built into the new show. However they won't dominate the show. And why should they, after two albums and two tours, everything starts getting slightly boring and evolves into a stereotype for me as well as for the audience."

Or, "I really wanted to do two full world tours that were totally blood lust, and it was fun. Now a lot of people have asked me: 'Are you going to do that again?' and the answer is no, we're not, because I'm not going to turn into Slayer! Why should I keep on plagiarising myself?" he asked. "Alice Cooper has still got far too many other ideas than be forced to rely on clichés like that."

Alice had the ideas? Or was it a tidy line of advisors that reached from Desmond Childs, to the suits at Epic, and onto the bean counters who could not believe their luck? In the same interview, Alice claimed that the new album "delves into the whole subject of sex a lot more than previously". And somewhere on the back of a dusty record shelf, a few hundred thousand barely played copies of *Muscle Of Love* pricked up their ears and listened.

Alice continued to talk a convincing conversation. "*Trash* is the word I use for everything that excites me. *Trash* is the girl with an amazing body that walks past me on Sunset Boulevard, *Trash* is the fantastic feeling I get behind the steering wheel of a fast car while zooming down the highway, *Trash* is sensational and impressive, *Trash* is the best possible title for the album, and I think this LP is the best Alice Cooper [has] recorded in ages."

He felt, he insisted, "that the album is real 'nineties' Alice. I have people saying to me that they like the weirder stuff like *Zipper Catches Skin* and

Dada, but most of my requests are for *Love It To Death.* People wanna hear that kind of rock'n'roll, so I wanted to capture that and push it into the nineties. When Desmond and I were writing, we were listening to *Love It To Death* and the *Greatest Hits* LP. Not because I wanted to throw back to that. Just to find that vibe and match it to the present era."

Besides, no matter how cynically older fans and journalists regarded *Trash* and its success; no matter how commercially tainted they considered it to be; and no matter how many times another disbelieving critic rightfully compared 'Bed Of Nails' to Bon Jovi's 'You Give Love A Bad Name', it served a purpose that, for Alice, might well have been the most crucial yet. He had long since grown weary with seeing all the baby Alices scampering over the landscape, all of them taking another piece of the old machine and letting it carry them to glory. And he had long since stopped complaining about it too.

He knew his value, he knew his worth, and he had always known what the answer was. An artist is not guaranteed success because he has always enjoyed it; and although a record can sometimes be a hit because its predecessor was, that cycle will always run out in the end. In order to sustain success, an artist needed to sustain his push for success. Alice had maybe forgotten that over the years; become so bound up in his own vision of the cult of Alice Cooper that he didn't see how quickly the cult's outside membership was shrinking. Desmond Childs reminded him of it.

"When I meet new bands who tell me, 'I love your stuff, I own everything you've done, you're the reason I'm here', it's great. But now I tell them to get ready, because I'm competing again. Y'know ... if you think I showed you everything, wait until you see up my sleeve a bit more!"

"I don't wanna be Chuck Berry," he told *Sounds.* "I love Chuck Berry as an artist but I don't wanna be that kinda golden oldie figure. I wanna be at the front of all the innovations whilst I'm still doing things. Alice should always be there. And unless I kill 'em every night, I won't do it. I've never had mediocre reactions. If I did, then I'd stop. I'll physically shake people if I have to, they'll react to me!"

He meant it as well. Yet although *Trash* could not be considered a false dawn, it did mark the last time in which Alice Cooper, like so many others of his generation, could be considered a genuine competitor in the commercial stakes, as the nineties and emergent technologies and business models of that decade commenced sweeping so much of the traditional industry away.

It was a gradual process and one whose enactment is littered with so many exceptions that it was hard to perceive the creation of the rules that would eventually stifle the one thing that had always ensured rock'n'roll's health – its status as art's last great outsider.

The emergence of the PMRC had restated those battle lines just five years earlier, after all. But when history looks back and remarks on just how brief that organisation's active lifespan seemed, it was not because the opposing forces swept Ms Gore and her allies back into the trenches. It was because the opposition crumbled. Parental guidance stickers were a fact of life now, and so many other of the censors' demands, too, came to fruition as shareholders and accountants started to design record company policy, and the record companies themselves simply became one more facet of a multi-media conglomerate.

The creation and, more importantly, the promotion of music suffered accordingly. But there were other factors, too, at least for now. The drive for the absolute homogenisation of rock'n'roll still had one more drama to circumvent.

Alice followed *Trash* with *Hey Stoopid* in 1991. It was his 19th studio album, produced by Peter Collins of Queensrÿche and Gary Moore fame, and again laden with collaborators. In terms of radio friendliness, and media recognition, it should have been as big as its predecessor. Instead it was crushed by the same bad timing that demolished so many other artists' hopes at that time, regardless of vintage or popularity. *Hey Stoopid* was released in June and was marching slowly up the chart all summer. Then September brought Nirvana's *Nevermind* and everything else, it seemed, stopped selling.

Hey Stoopid stands now as the last gasp of the good ship glam metal. Slash, the top-hatted guitarist of Guns 'N Roses, Mötley Crüe's Nikki Sixx and Mick Mars, songwriter Jack Ponti, guitarist Steve Vai, living legends Ozzy Osbourne, Rob Halford and Joe Satriani, all piled into the sessions as they switched from Bearsville, New York, to Los Angeles; and, once again, the formula was as flash as its creators. The opening 'Hey Stoopid', an anti-suicide anthem from a man who'd been accused of encouraging more than his fair share of such tragedies, became another big hit single, and the remainder of the album was as slick and polished an addition to the canon as anybody could have hoped... any fan of that sound, at any rate.

But glam metal had already been on the wane for a while now; had been visibly flagging since the new decade was born. In adhering to much the same musical signposts as its predecessor, *Hey Stoopid* adhered to the same death wish that would cripple new releases by the rest of the pack. All Nirvana did in that instance was give a bored audience something new to get excited about, in exactly the same way as punk had revitalised the late seventies, and Alice had reinvented the dawn of that same decade.

But there was something so all-consuming about Nirvana's success, and that of the grunge bands who slavered in their footsteps; something so vast and unprecedented, that the industry itself did not know how to contend with it. Lessons learned by punk rock, which music historians always credit with having changed the face of the late seventies industry, were not applicable here. Yes Nirvana portrayed themselves as outsiders, and yes there were aspects of the attendant circus that were less than palatable from a mainstream perspective.

In the past, however, the music industry's excesses were policed by the music press, with the tabloids and the entertainment media really only dirtying their feet in the sink of rock'n'roll when an artist had truly risen to the status of the genuine superstars of Vegas, Hollywood and prime time TV.

Now Kurt Cobain's wife was on the cover of *Vanity Fair*; and that was only the most egregious of the manifold examples of the mainstream's co-opting of that old teen spirit. Rock'n'roll had weathered numerous crises in the past, of its own invention and from outsiders too. And it had danced around respectability for decades, as well.

Alice had played a role in that, with his superstar schmoozing, regular appearances on the TV quiz show *Celebrity Squares* and invitation golf matches. But Alice had been just one monster, and there were always more to fill his place, the bad boys of rock whose only brush with the tabloids would be a disapproving headline for their latest drug bust, arrest or the public evacuation of unwanted bodily substances.

Now, it was as though every artist's "struggle with drugs" (or booze or sex or any of the myriad other addictions and afflictions that seemed to be granted a medical or psychological basis) was as open to debate in the mainstream press as it had once been in the corridors of scurrilous rock'n'roll rumour; and those artists who had taken a cure of some sort and come through on the other side found themselves the willing or otherwise paragons of virtue to which all would-be recoverers were expected to pray.

The bad boys were good. And, once that one ticking bomb of public opprobrium had been defused, they were safe.

They were no longer rock stars, they were celebrities.

They were no longer dangerous, they were national treasures.

And they were no long competing, they were veterans.

Alice recalled the first time he heard 'Smells Like Teen Spirit' for *Metal Hammer*. "It was different than anything else. It's just a cracker. It's one that you turn up. It was just all out.... It wasn't grunge, it was a big, ragged rhythm guitar. It was just relentless all the way through. Very cool. It reminded me of very early seventies rock."

Yet it also posited a musical future that he knew he could not be a part of; a fact that a lot of his contemporaries would eventually come to understand, but which few turned to their advantage as swiftly as Alice.

The family was living in Phoenix now, in a Paradise Valley house that Alice had purchased as an investment back in 1973. Completely remodelled in the first years after they arrived there in 1985, it was the base from which he found himself becoming a true cause celebre in local circles.

He spoke light-heartedly of moving into local politics, but when real politics hit a long-time fan in the form of the imminent loss of his home, Alice arranged a fundraising benefit to beat out the forces of foreclosure.

The birth of his third child and second daughter, Sonora, in January 1993 was celebrated in the local Phoenix press, and three decades after Vince Furnier was threatened with expulsion from the local school system for the crime of not cutting his hair, his son Dash was preparing to enter it.

And Phoenix, the city he had called home longer, and with more passion, than any place else he had lived, was where he retired to as he considered how he was going to approach the latest challenge not simply to his commercial comeback, but to the musical landscape that was all he had ever known.

By changing the landscape himself.

Hey Stoopid was the last album Alice Cooper Rock Star would ever make. From hereon in, he would simply be Alice Cooper, and he didn't give a damn what the job description was. Because he would be changing it every time.

Alice had never mounted a conventional tour, even in the days when Alice Cooper plied the same circuit as a thousand other bands, all convinced that they were just one hit single away from grasping the golden ring. Now, however, he was determined to take it one step further. "The Alice show is an event, not just a rock concert," he bragged to *Hot Metal*. "It's like 'Alice is coming in four months!' – and so's Christmas! I want people to look forward to the fact that we're coming into town, not like 'Who we gonna see this week? OK, let's go and see Alice....' I want them to go, 'Wow, Alice is here! Boy, what's going to happen in the new show?!'"

He landed the role of Freddie Kruger's stepfather in the sixth *Nightmare On Elm Street* movie, *Freddy's Dead: The Final Nightmare*, and nobody batted an eyelid. Pop stars playing at movie actors was never a comfortable fit, but those rules did not apply to Alice. Like he'd been saying way back at the beginning, he'd been a movie star all along, who just happened to do something other than make movies.

Wayne's World, the movie length spin-off from what had been a mildly amusing skit on television's *Saturday Night Live* came calling, and Alice stepped into that as well, turning out a ferocious 'Feed My Frankenstein' for the occasion, and then looking on as the movie's main characters Wayne and Garth, kneel and bow before him chanting "We're not worthy! We're not worthy!" For the next few years, Alice laughed, he was getting that everywhere he went, although it was an improvement, he said, on what he'd been putting up with before that. "[My] last album was titled *Hey Stoopid*. So for a year I had to hear, 'Hey, stupid!' This is better."

For a year, too, he was looking again at *Welcome To My Nightmare* and the possibility of crafting a sequel. It seemed impossible to believe that 20 years had now elapsed since he first formed the visions that would become that record, but that was the anniversary that was looming, and just as 1974 had seen him surround himself with the best, and most relevant musicians he could find, so two decades later he would scheme the same dream.

Soundgarden were one of the myriad bands that rose up in the slipstream of Nirvana although, like Cobain and co, they had been around their hometown Seattle scene for a few years before the rest of America noticed them.

They were not necessarily the most inspirational of the grunge pack; muddy introspection was their most obvious calling card, cast over the even muddier soundtrack that, even in the age of digital sound, seemed to have been sucked bodily off the banks of the Puget Sound. One prominent music journalist recalled catching an early Soundgarden video on MTV a few weeks before she and her own family moved to the city. "I almost cancelled the movers on the spot."

Since that time, Soundgarden had proved adroit at confounding expectations. They were tarred with the grunge brush by geographical circumstance, but when *Kerrang!* went looking for "the future of metal" in 1992, Soundgarden graced the issue's cover. When *Spin* sought out "the metal band for people who hate metal", they picked up on Soundgarden. And when *Almost Live*, Seattle's infinitely funnier alternative to *Saturday Night Live* wanted somebody to represent America's head-banging community for its semi-regular "lame list" feature, they turned to Soundgarden too. So why shouldn't Alice?

With Soundgarden frontman Chris Cornell travelling out to Phoenix, he and Alice co-wrote two songs; 'Unholy War' and 'Stolen Prayer' were both scheduled for an album that Alice now intended journeying to Los Angeles to record. Other Seattle-ites Alice In Chains and the Screaming Trees were called in to the sessions, as Alice worked towards what was surely destined to be at least a contemporary-sounding record. But he had no intention of delivering one.

"Let's face it, Alice Cooper can't speak for the 15-year-old grunge kids," he told *HM* magazine. "Guys like Steve Tyler and Ozzy and myself are out of touch with those kids. Violence has become much more acceptable, and everyone's getting very dour." And it was that dourness, and the hopelessness that clung to it like the rain clouds that haunt the Seattle skyline, that he wanted to investigate. The result would be one of the most evocative albums of his career… even if its promise was mildly rebuked by the UK news report that described it as "his first concept album since *DaDa*."

The Last Temptation, Alice explained, "is my first concept album in a long time, because I came up with a good story this time". He told *Metal Hammer*, "I won't do a concept without a beginning and an end, a hero and a villain, and a believable situation; this one was either going to be a movie or an album. The basic theme is temptation. We all experience temptation every day."

He outlined the tale; the arrival in a small American mid-western town of the mysterious Showman, owner of a weird looking theatre that most of the kids in town are too scared to enter. Finally one does... Steven, the slightly older hero of the original *Welcome To My Nightmare* production. This time, however, Steven is not caught in a dream.

Inside the theatre, the Showman displays for him a wealth of wonderful things; and a series of performers, each one represented by a different song on the album. And slowly it dawns on his audience what really is on display in the theatre. Death.

Where *The Last Temptation* stepped away from *Welcome To My Nightmare*, at the same time, ironically, as reawakening memories of a slightly earlier Alice-related concept, was in its overall presentation. As shades of *Flash Fearless* fall across the Alice fan's eyes, sold separately but intrinsic to the story were three comic books depicting the album's story. "I wanted people to really be able to see what I had in mind, and short of 10 expensive videos or an actual movie, this was the way to do it. You need to see the tempter, The Showman. He's just like the old Alice, slick and glib and cool and funny."

The comic book medium slipped naturally into place. As a kid, Alice loved *Tales From The Crypt*. As a teen, he read the superhero comics, the Spidermans and Fantastic Fours that ushered in the so-called Marvel Age. Now, as an adult, he read adult-themed comic books, the work of Alan Moore and Neil Gaiman, and the newly launched line of titles by already prodigious Vertigo. Comics which asked, as the new songs were asking, what had happened to all the old monsters? Who or what were they now?

"The monsters aren't the thing that live under your bed in your imagination," he explained to *Faces* magazine. "The reality is much scarier than anything fantasy. The monsters are needles, heroin, gang warfare and guns – most of the things that are in your face everyday, especially for a Generation X-er." The overall vision, he suggested, combined Ray Bradbury's own tale of fiendish carnies, *Something Wicked This Way Comes*, with nothing less than the temptations of Christ, a vast palette that required vast talents to realise it.

Fascinating indeed was Alice's choice of collaborators. In the studio, he worked with latter-day greats like Jack Blades and Tommy Shaw, Don Fleming, Andy Wallace and the Duane Baron/John Purdell duo; on the comic book, he wrote with Neil Gaiman, the English born creator of some of the most inspired fantasy of the nineties, and artist Michael Zulli.

Born in Britain but now living in Minneapolis, Gaiman's speciality was the mining of childhood terrors, usually drawn from his own London upbringing: the vague dread conjured by the Punch & Judy puppet show; the saga of the Lancashire Witches; the wrinkly old guy who once paraded around the metropolis in his raincoat and cap, bearing a placard warning "less passion from less protein". Childhood obsessions with a certain brand of candy, a comic book or TV show that rose above the usual realm of self-conscious "I was there"-isms to emerge nostalgic touchstones with which to ground the electricity of fantasy. To allow reality to get a look-in when all else was turning to madness.

Now, Gaiman's *The Sandman* comic book was already compulsory reading for an army of adult comic book fans; upcoming, too, were the first in what has since developed into one of the most engrossing sequences of novels in recent times.

Although it was Bob Pfeifer who initiated contact with Gaiman, Alice explained his own introduction to the writer in the book *Hanging Out With The Dream King*, a collection of conversations with Gaiman and his collaborators. His son Dash was a keen collector of *Star Wars* memorabilia, and "every time you're either in a comic book store or you're at a sci-fi convention, I kept seeing Neil's name pop up. I finally picked up a couple of the comic books and that's when Bob Pfeifer came in and said, 'I know this guy named Neil Gaiman,' and I said, 'Oh yeah, I know who this is'."

"Neil did a spectacular job," Alice continued to *Metal Hammer*. "He filled in all the holes in my storyline. I brought him in as soon as I had the basic ideas down, and he helped a great deal with the songs themselves by filling in the gaps before I actually wrote the songs."

Gaiman himself was a longtime fan, which probably shouldn't surprise anybody, given the nature of his own remarkable talents. "I liked Alice Cooper," he wrote in the forward to the collected edition of the comic. "I liked 'School's Out' and 'Billion Dollar Babies' and 'Teenage Lament 74'. I thought *Welcome To My Nightmare* was one of the great rock'n'roll records. I thought *Trash* was a remarkable comeback album." As he spoke with Bob Pfeifer the first time he called, Gaiman admitted, "My head swam with snakes and swords, top hats and black-rimmed eyes."

He recalled, "We sat in the hotel room and I listened to the tapes of the first few songs he'd written, and I watched Alice and his collaborators write another three songs while I sat on the bed, occasionally making suggestions for lyrics and song titles."

It was not Alice's first brush with comic book immortality; 1979 saw Marvel's Stan Lee produce an Alice edition in its Marvel Premiere series, and ask the readers the pertinent question, "Should Alice be awarded his own Marvel title? Should we send him blasting through the Marvel Universe?" The answer, presumably, was no; or at least so undecided that no series emerged. But Marvel Premier 50 earned the star's full stamp of approval, even as he used it as another barb with which to jab his then arch-rivals Kiss. They too had a comic book and had requested a drop of each band members' blood be mixed into the printing ink. Alice went one further. He also requested that Kiss' blood be used, but that the printers should not confine themselves to a drop.

With Marvel again the publisher, the tie-in this time was seamless, although the marketing did experience a handful of hiccups as hopes to tie in a third strand, a virtual reality computer game, were finally abandoned when it became clear that it simply could not be completed. The album had already been delayed for four months as the designers worked to get the game up and running; finally, all had to concede defeat.

Yet the paraphernalia was never more than that. *The Last Temptation*, first and foremost, was a rock album, and one that touched upon some of the most primal sounds Alice had ever employed. One track, 'Lost In America', he even described as "bare bones Stooges", although it might also have been compared to Eddie Cochran's 'Summertime Blues', with its circular catalogue of juvenile deficiencies – I got no girl cos I got no car, I got no car cos I got no job, I got no job cos I got no car...

Dig deeper, however, and the theology would emerge; the belief that so nihilistic had the rock world become as it searched for ever darker, deeper, demons to dance with, in order to keep the accountants smiling, that the country had lost touch with its soul. Words like redemption and temptation, so much a part of Alice's own Biblical upbringing, were lost now to the common vernacular; either that, or wholly hijacked by a religious right wing whose sole purpose in life seemed to be the besmirching of religious belief in the eyes and hearts of anybody who didn't follow their own creed of righteous intolerance.

"It's very hard for Alice to be about shock rock any more, because I can't compete with CNN," Alice told the *Toronto Star*. "CNN is much more shocking than anything Alice Cooper could do. I don't think anybody is shocking any more. I don't think Madonna going on David Letterman and swearing is very shocking. So what? Everybody uses those words every day anyway."

For him, the greatest shocks were the things that the media now seemed to be accepting as simply everyday perils – guns, drugs, AIDS and violence. It was no coincidence that, as the album came together, Alice would be a witness to a restaurant shoot-out in Los Angeles, seated at his table eating as 15 bullets flew around the room ("They could have killed me, and they didn't even know who I was"); nor that the music industry itself would be stunned as Nirvana's Kurt Cobain committed suicide in April 1994, shortly before *The Last Temptation*'s completion. Events such as those, while he never referenced them directly in the music, shaped the course of the songwriting all the same, and the direction of the story too.

Even as he tried to avoid the circus, Alice realised, it had a way of drawing him back inside.

There would be no tour for *The Last Temptation*, just an endless routine of promotional appearances, and one off guest spots. In February 1994, he appeared alongside Roger Daltrey at Carnegie Hall's Celebration: The Music Of Pete Townshend And The Who spectacular, performing 'I'm A Boy' – a wry choice, of course, given the old gender confusion that he once provoked. He guest-hosted a week's worth of radio shows for Z-Rock, Alice's Attic, shot a blink-and-you'll-miss-him cameo in the movie *Maverick* and joined Neil Gaiman for an autograph session at London's Forbidden Planet sci-fi bookstore.

It would be September 1995 before he returned to the road, as he clambered aboard the Monster of Rock touring festival wagon, scouring South America alongside Ozzy Osbourne, Megadeth, and Faith No More. Yet things continued changing around him. The on-going "crisis" that the music industry complained was undermining it through the nineties was in full swing now. Of course, it was nothing compared to the even greater disasters it would inflict upon itself once downloading became a part of daily life, but cost cutting and belt tightening were the order of the day, as a gradual decline in overall CD sales first began to manifest itself.

Epic Records was no exception. Autumn 1994 saw the bean counters commence a slash through the company catalogue, taking out any number of lesser-regarded acts (Arcade, Infectious Grooves and Suicidal Tendencies all felt the axe), but some larger ones too as Alice was also released from his deal. They bade farewell with the distinctly mistitled *Classicks* compilation.

Hollywood Records, a relative upstart newcomer that was nevertheless sweeping up great swathes of the classic rock catalogue, was rumored to be his next port of call; Bob Pfeifer, the man who signed Alice to Epic in the first place, was the company's President, and his loyalty was never in doubt. Still rumour had it that the move was very dependent upon one condition – that Alice reform the old Alice Cooper group for the occasion.

Dennis Dunaway and Neal Smith were both said to be onboard already; Michael Bruce was considering the offer, and Dick Wagner had agreed to step in for Glen Buxton, whose health problems rendered his participation improbable. But rumour can rarely be believed and this one fizzled out as Alice simply continued to ride the celebrity-go-round. He was a presenter at the 1995 Grammy awards, guested in actor Gene Wilder's *Something Wilder* TV series... another year of frenetic activity could be rendered simply as a list of bullet points, and the musical rebirth of *The Last Temptation* was in danger of being lost beneath the poor reviews that reached up from the South American shows.

Steffan Chirazi from *Kerrang!* caught the Sao Paulo show, and shrugged, "Alice Cooper was, frankly, boring. Without being too callous, the stage schtick came across as dated, the songs uninspired and Alice's pink plastic pants quite fucking frightening... much more so than the whipping of the blow-up doll and the ol' *West Side Story* rucking routine. Once highly entertaining, nowadays Coop simply shows those laurels got a little too comfortable."

His uncertainty scarred his first album for Hollywood. Demoing in Phoenix with guitarist Stef Burns and drummer Jimmy DeGrasso, fresh from those South American dates, *Spirit Rebellious* was the working title of an album Alice began writing in 1996, a conceptual effort that he summed up as "a gang warfare thing, on three different levels, socially, spiritually and there's a romance in it". And he grasped his own changed role in the music industry by explaining, "I want to make Alice Cooper albums like Stephen King does books, not just a collection of songs. It should really say something."

"I've actually written two full albums lyrically," he told *Metal Edge*. "I just haven't put the music to them yet"; the other, *Alice's Deadly Seven*, paired him with Disney composer Alan Menken. "It's fun to work on, because this guy sits down at the piano and everything he plays is a hit. And all it really needs is for Alice to take it and warp it a little bit. I wrote all the lyrics; I took lust and sloth and all of that and wrote songs concerning those, and it really came out great. It'll be a rock'n'roll album – these seven different little stories all entwined with one guy telling the entire tale. It could be an album, a Broadway play, a cartoon, a movie. It's very visual, and it's full of hits, and when you have that, you can go in any direction with it."

Yet neither project would come off.

It was time to regroup. Alice would not return to the studio for six long years, instead allowing his back catalogue and his fame to keep the name alive. He reacted to Epic's release of *Classicks* by hitting back with a *Greatest Hits Live* set, *A Fistful of Alice*, recorded in Mexico and positively laden with guest superstars as Slash (Gun N' Roses), Sammy Hagar (ex-Van Halen Mark II) and Rob Zombie (White Zombie) filed onto the stage.

He turned down the chance to go out on the road with Kiss, a double header that both act's fans insisted would sort out who was the best once and for all; he went out instead with the Scorpions, alternating the headline spot nightly, and dumping the Germans in his dust, even after he left the theatrics at home. "I've known [the Scorpions] forever. I told them I'd do the tour as long as they didn't do the song with the whistling in it ['Winds Of Change']. Ever time I hear that song, I want to go and build the Berlin Wall back again," he cracked.

Instead, he contented himself with their nightly destruction, courtesy of a 12 song set that blazed with old masters. His band felt more anonymous than any past outfit, but still guitarists Reb Beach (ex-Kip Winger's Winger) and Ryan Roxie, keyboard player Paul Taylor, Y&T drummer Jimmy DeGrasso and the reformed Rainbow's bassist Greg Smith could do little wrong in a live set that positively ached glorious history.

In and around these activities, he dove, too, into a string of collaborations, cherry-picking his disciples with a sharp eye for their own ability to increase his audience, and perhaps to rub off some of their own reputations on him.

Insane Clown Posse, for example. Insane Clown Posse was a Detroit band who had been around since the early nineties, rap metal's self-styled most excessive, and long-running prank originating, they claimed, from a chance encounter with the sinister Carnival Spirit.

Like Alice two decades earlier, Insane Clown Posse knew how to rile up the locals and, after three albums, their notoriety had spread sufficiently for Hollywood Records to step in for their signature. Backed by a million dollar press campaign, Insane Clown Posse cut *The Great Milenko* with Alice a much-heralded guest on one song; and on the day of release, the Disney-owned Hollywood withdrew it. Instant notoriety was, of course, followed by instant acclaim. Island stepped in and released the album, and Insane Clown Posse were finally thrust onto the major stage. At least for a short time.

It is sad but true, however, that few rock stars ever see their musical progeny live to maturity. A Xerox is always a Xerox, of course, but even the finest reproductions seldom last for longer than they need to, because the originator is always still around. David Bowie has buried more cavorting little Ziggies than Ziggy himself spent days on this earth; Lou Reed and Iggy Pop can probably set their watches by the funerals of their legion imitators and spawn; and Alice had given up counting the number of performers to whom he'd been compared. "Call me in 20 years," he might have responded. "See if they're still comparable then."

Rob Zombie was different. Another acolyte, another horror buff, another name for the legions of decency to chastise from the soap box, Zombie could have been simply another nine day wonder, rising up in the early nineties with what the music press called the Industrial Revolution, and then sinking back down again the moment it became apparent that harsh, grinding vocals scraped out over the sound of haywire machinery was never going to displace melody from the top of the charts.

Unlike so many of the artists who floundered in the forthcoming wipe-out, however, Zombie had never placed all of his heads in one basket. Rather, alongside the musical reputation of his band, White Zombie, he simultaneously cultivated a persona that superficially may have owed much to Alice, but which was also capable of standing alone – a Frankenstein, perhaps, to Alice's Dracula, built on the visual imagery that he drew from the same wellspring of horror flick fodder that Alice was already so identified with.

Happily, Zombie acknowledged that influence. The first record he ever owned was 'School's Out', he said, and Alice returned the compliment when he described Zombie, in 1997, as the only artist who actually seemed to be having fun with his image. Because that, at the end of the day, was what being a performer was all about. Having fun, and drawing your audience into the circus alongside you.

He told *Pulse* magazine, "[Rob is]… the only person out there who's having any fun with this…. And it's clear when you listen to his albums, and when you see his show, that he's having a great time. …the other people look like they're just tortured souls up there, and you go, you know, 'Guys! Lighten up! The image is heavy and everything, but you don't have to really be that.' These guys are trying to live their lives the way their image is, and I'm going… The idea behind rock'n'roll is joy. It's joyful music. It's not a depressing thing.

"You know, the big difference between an Alice Cooper show and a lot of the shows you're talking about – I won't specifically say anyone – is that I always left the audience on an upper. I left them inspired rather than… They walk away going, 'Wow, I've got confetti in my hair and Alice has got a white tuxedo on, and he just did 'School's Out', and balloons are popping.' And then they remember back, and they go, 'Wow, he did a thing with a baby carriage, and he did this, and then he got his head cut off. What a great night!' They always walked out with big smiles on their faces. Whereas I know a lot of people walk out [of shows now], and they go, 'Wow, my life is over'."

It was inevitable that Alice and Zombie would meet and probably inevitable that they would become close friends – in 2011, it was Zombie who inducted the old Alice Cooper band into the Rock and Roll Hall of Fame, while the intervening years had seen Alice and Zombie alone collaborate on a variety of musical projects and tours.

"We both have an appreciation for the absurd," Alice explained to *Metal Edge*. "We both like horror movies but only the bad ones, the really stupid ones. We don't like the good ones. There's a certain common chord to what we do, we both see the comedy in horror and we both realise that it's a carnival ride and shouldn't be taken more seriously than that, a good comedy.

"When we work together it's very easy, there's a common respect. He does something totally different musically than I do, he creates a wall of sound and writes lyrics on top of that. I try to write more of a conventional song and my twists and turns come in the story line, whereas his come in what's going on in the sound, [whereas] Rob's whole thing is built on what the groove of the song is. I like Rob because he's in on his own joke. That's something a lot of people are afraid of. He knows that you have a certain amount of popularity for a certain length of time. He always makes fun of himself, his band, what he writes, he has the healthiest attitude in the world, he loves what he's doing. When you talk to him he's so self-effacing. I like that."

Initially, the pair cut just one song together, 'Hands Of Death (Burn Baby Burn)' for the *Songs In The Key Of X* album that tied into the *X Files* TV series. Soon, however, they were writing towards Alice's own new studio album. If it ever came.

But there was one artist with whom Alice would never see eye-to-eye. Speaking in 1996, he essentially predicted his own revival when he prophesied the arrival of a new metal superstar, "movie star-ish and over the top with cool music". He reflected on his own favourite bands – Soul Asylum, Collective Soul, White Zombie, Nine Inch Nails, and Soundgarden, but he also acknowledged "there's no-one out there who's really shocking". Back in the day, "We were the cutting edge, the scourge of rock'n'roll. We were scary because the seventies were pretty innocent. Now I'm not nearly as shocking as CNN."

Alice dreamed of rock receiving a new messiah. Instead, it got Marilyn Manson. "Hmmm. Where have I seen that before? Marilyn Manson. Even the names – Alice Cooper, Marilyn Manson – are pretty similar," Cooper told writer Mark Brown. "I don't agree with their whole satanic thing, this whole 'Antichrist Superstar' sort of thing. I know that's meant to irritate people, but I certainly don't want people to associate me with that. Alice was always more fun than that. Religion was much too personal, and politics was much too boring. Our three targets were sex, death and money."

Kerrang! probed deeper, but Alice remained coy. "Marilyn Manson and I have this agreement, I don't talk about him, and he doesn't talk about me!" And he then proceeded to talk about him. "I was reading an article about Marilyn the other day. He was disclaiming all these rumours, which I totally understand. I was reading the list of things he is supposed to have done, and you know what? He's living my life.

"Ninety per cent of what you hear about Marilyn Manson isn't true. Ninety per cent of what you heard about Alice Cooper wasn't true. I was called everything from a witch to a vampire. There's something sexy about being a vampire," he smiles, "but the occult? Alice Cooper was about as occult as Porky Pig!"

Which made his own next controversy all the more ironic, as Alice took it upon himself to land Pat Boone in trouble with the Christian Right. Boone had recently engineered a musical comeback of sorts by cutting a metal album, suitably titled *In A Metal Mood: No More Mr. Nice Guy*. The antidote to the fifties rock'n'roll hell-raisers, Boone took it on himself to record bland versions of some of rock's greatest early hits, softening them for the mainstream market and, of course, siphoning off sales that belonged to rock's true originators. A smooth, clean cut all-American figurehead for everything that is good and holy and mom's apple pie about Uncle Sam, Boone also had a massive following on Christian television. His weekly *Gospel America* show was one of the shining stars of the Trinity Broadcast Network, not only at home but around the world. And many of his loyal audience would have tuned in to see their idol at the American Music Awards on January 27, 1997.

Minutes later, the Trinity switchboards lit up like an electric chair.

It was presenter Dick Clark who came up with the idea, for Boone to appear on camera dressed as a hardcore rocker – bare chest festooned in temporary tattoos, leather and be-shaded, stud collar and wristbands; while Alice emerged with short hair and a cardigan, sensible slacks and white buckskin shoes.

Unfortunately, Boone explained, "He must have taken one look at those buckskin shoes and gotten sick to his stomach. He backed out at the last second. I walked onstage dressed like a heavy metal rocker and was fully expecting to see him dressed like Pat Boone. Instead, he was dressed like – well, Alice Cooper!"

Boone's loyal viewers flipped, bombarding the TBN switchboard with so many complaints that, incredibly, *Gospel America* was cancelled. Boone, however, refused to apologise. "It was all done as a joke. And as for my album, it has taken a major jump on the charts. It's the first time in 30 years I've been on the charts! I've been one of the biggest squares of all time. Now suddenly some people see a picture of me and think I look like a Kiss reject. I realise I'm now being judged like I used to judge these rockers. But God loves rockers too!"

That autumn, He had one more to love. On October 19, 1997, guitarist Glen Buxton died from pneumonia at his home in Clarion, Iowa, where he had lived since 1990.

Like Alice a born again Christian, Buxton had lived as far from his past as he could, a farmer whose place in rock history was known only to his friends and family; not only his years with Alice, but also with the clutch of later acts he led for shorter periods of time – Shrapnel, the New York act that toyed with the last ebbing of the city's late seventies punk scene, were the most fondly remembered; Virgin, a Phoenix covers band whose act mixed old Alice hits with more recent eighties fodder, the least.

Obituaries spoke of the last time he and Alice spent time together, after Alice's show in St Paul, Minnesota in August. Afterwards the pair spent an hour together talking and, in early October, Buxton reunited with Michael Bruce and drummer Neal Smith for a series of autograph shows and live performances in Houston. (Dennis Dunaway was ill and couldn't make it.) It was there that Buxton mentioned that he'd been suffering from a pain in his chest, and Smith joined the long line of friends and relations who asked him to visit his doctor and get it checked out. Which Buxton did, finally, do. But it was already too late.

Alice delivered his own tribute.

"I grew up with Glen, started the band with him and he was one of my best friends. I think I laughed more with him than anyone else. He was an underrated and influential guitarist, a genuine rock'n'roll rebel. Wherever he is now, I'm sure that there's a guitar, a cigarette and a switchblade nearby."

And it was Buxton's death, probably more than any other consideration, that finally reunited Alice with the remainder of the old band. It was a reunion that started on the telephone and though it would never become a full fledged return to past glories, somewhere in between those extremes, it found a comfortable place to live.

Chapter Seventeen

Candy Canes for Diabetics

Now a pillar of the community, Alice opened his own sports bar in Phoenix. Cooperstown, he insisted, was set to become the "Taj Mahal of sports bars". Of course his was simply the name over the door – like so many other celebrity endorsed venues around America, BB King's in New York for example, the artist had minimal involvement in the day-to-day running of the bar and a minimal investment too; in Alice's case, a reported $5,000, and the life-size cardboard cut-out that greeted visitors at the door.

He performed there too, opening the doors on December 19, 1998 by calling Neal Smith and Michael Bruce into town, and looking as though they all had just stepped in off the street, punching through a loose, laughing 'No More Mr Nice Guy', the first time they had played together in 24 years – and it showed. "Rehearsal at your house tomorrow night," Alice quipped to Bruce as they slipped into a scrappy 'Muscle Of Love'. Then, with time for a few more, 'Is It My Body' seemed to take Alice as much by surprise as the crowd, but the grins on his old bandmates' faces eased away any consternation. The whole thing was over in barely 20 minutes.

So it wasn't strictly his club but nevertheless the triumphs (and, sadly, the tribulations) of the bar would be gifted to Alice, just one more brick in the wall of solid local citizenship that he and Sheryl were constructing in Phoenix.

Sometimes it felt that the pair were as active in the local community as Alice had ever been on stage. They wrote and produced the annual Hopi

Variety Show for a nearby school; and they oversaw, too, the Solid Rock Foundation, a charitable organisation he launched in 1995 to financially aid Christian organisations and ministries that work with youths.

Annual Alice Cooper Celebrity Golf Tournaments were a feature of the landscape too, and he was as likely to be overheard discussing his treasured collection of vintage wristwatches as he was his musical ambitions. Specialising in the wonderfully sci-fi-like creations that adorned fashionable wrists during the fifties, Alice looked forward to touring as much for the chance to visit yard sales and junk stores, in search of new treasures, as he did any more traditional on-the-road pursuits.

By 2002, he was fronting another soon-to-be-annual event, the Christmas Pudding, taking over the Celebrity Theater (longtime supporters of the Solid Rock Foundation) and staging a full scale charity show that December 13. Peter Frampton, comedian John O'Hurley, Sam Moore and Nils Lofgren all slipped onto the bill, and Alice enthused, "It's a mix of stuff, like a Christmas pudding, so that's why we're calling it Pudding. And we're actually going to have pudding! [Restaurateur] Mark Tarbell is going to make pudding for 2,500 people. This is our first one," he said at the time. "But I think this is the kind of thing that's going to grow every year and get bigger and bigger and better and better."

And so was he.

For three or four years now, the grapevine had been rustling to rumours of an impending Alice Cooper box set, a sprawling beast whose fight for existence was fast becoming a legend in its own right, as the different labels that owned Alice's catalogue raised objections and obstacles in the path of the compilers, while all of them swore that they supported the project. Yet it would be late 1999 before they finally lived up to those pledges, and *The Life And Crimes Of Alice Cooper* was finally unveiled.

It was a joy to behold, a four-disc box set that lived up to its title, not only by rounding up the hits and bits that everybody expected, but also by digging deep for the odd little one-offs and surprises that were buried away on B-sides or deeper. Single mixes of the classic 45s, unheard since their day on the radio, were restored to life. The two *Flash Fearless* cuts were gloriously resurrected, alongside those early, pre-Alice sides that all but the most rabid collector had despaired of ever owning. There was even room for that *Special Forces* era jewel, 'Look At You Over There,

Ripping The Sawdust From My Teddy Bear', omitted from the original album because it didn't fit in with the rest of the tunes, but now revealed as one of the eighties Alice's most beautifully realised visions.

Disc by disc, the journey from the Spiders to Rob Zombie was undertaken with more shocks and surprises than even the most expectant fan could have imagined. But what was perhaps most important was the way in which the manifold delays ultimately worked in the box set's favour. Alice Cooper had soundtracked the last three decades of the 20th century as uniquely, and astonishingly, as any other artist of his generation. What better time could there have been to unleash the box than in the last months of the last year of the century?

And what better time could there be to follow it up than in the first weeks of the 21st, with the announcement that *Brutal Planet* was poised for release, a full fledged return to in-yer-face horror rock, shot through with a vision of an apocalyptic future shaped indeed by the brutality of the modern world itself: the continued growth of the political far right, with its own savage disregard for life and liberty; the emergence on the American home front of both domestic and imported terrorism; the expansion of banks into corporate megaliths with a scavenging claw in everybody's life; greed, rage, tragedy and death.

"There were some songs that I just didn't want to write," he told *Live Daily* in spring 2000. "But I couldn't let some of these things go by without writing about them. They're part of our society, and to me, they're part of Brutal Planet."

But so were a lot of other things; with a wit that surprised even Alice's most loyal supporters, when the *Brutal Planet* road show hit the tour circuit, pop singer Britney Spears (exquisitely portrayed by Alice's daughter, Calico), would be executed nightly for perpetrating "everything that my audience hates – the softening of rock'n'roll... the sweetness of it all."

Sometime Black Sabbath overseer Bob Marlette produced, Bob Ezrin was billed as Executive Producer, and even before the sessions began in earnest, Alice's intentions were clear, as he rounded up Marcus Blake and Jim Wilson, bassist and guitarist with the Rollins Band, to work with him on the demos.

Blake recalls, "It was Bob Ezrin who introduced us; originally he was going to be working with Billy Idol, and called us up for that, and then one day he called and said that project was off, but he had somebody else he wanted us to meet."

Linking up at Marlett's home studio, the pair ran through the tunes while Alice sat on a sofa with a notebook, sketching lyrics that very often became his final draft. "It was incredible watching him write," Blake enthuses, "because what he was coming up with was usually the final lyric." The pair also found themselves writing with him, as a piece of music that they conjured in the studio was grasped and transformed into the immortally titled 'Can't Sleep, Clowns Will Eat Me' – a title Alice heard on *The Simpsons* TV show one night, and had been wanting to borrow ever since. "I saw it as a Kinksy-sounding thing," Blake says of the leviathan riff that powers the song, "and Alice saw that right away."

Blake and Wilson would not be recalled for the actual sessions; their own commitments with Rollins ensured that. Instead, Alice and Ezrin rounded up a new crew, former Kiss drummer Eric Singer and guitarists Ryan Roxie, China and Phil X, all slammed together for four months spent cutting basic tracks at A&M Studios in Los Angeles before shifting to Marlett's digital home studio.

The end result, Alice celebrated, was "the heaviest album I've ever done. It's loud, tough, *big*! Sonically it's a monster. It's an absolutely Godless world, a place where it's just desolate and horrific. I wanna throw a scare into [people]. It's not going to be like I used to in the seventies, because the audience is shock-proof now. It's impossible to shock the audience now. Unless you go on stage, cut your arm off and eat it, you're not going to really shock an audience." But *Brutal Planet* would come close.

Neither did he expect everybody to understand. "The first review I read of *Brutal Planet* called it 'a tragic waste of plastic'. I have to laugh because 30 years ago, most of the press were saying, 'They'll last about three minutes', and here we are 24 albums later, still doing it."

Alice had never strayed this close to what could be described as overt social comment before; had never strived for anything more than what he called political incoherence. Even 'Elected', the single that had once been shunted to one side for fear that it might unfairly influence an election, had offered no solutions or suggestions for its listener's ills. And neither did *Brutal Planet*.

"[Alice] doesn't belong in politics," Alice explained to *Braveradio Plus*. "He doesn't belong in social events at all." But *Brutal Planet* demanded its existence, songs forcing themselves into his consciousness not necessarily so that Alice might condemn their subjects, but in order to make other people think about them. For that, Alice believed, was what was missing from this brave new world in which Alice found himself. People acting without thought.

"A song like 'Blow Me A Kiss', I'm talking about senseless killings. It's not like I could understand any killing at all, but if somebody is going out and saying, 'I'm going to go kill 20 abortion doctors' or something, then he has an agenda. People that just go into school and say, 'I'm going to kill you 'cause you're black, gay, you're afraid, because I saw you in biology class,' that song was hard to write for me because there's no rhyme or reason for these murders. You can't let that go by."

His own listening habits shifted with his method of writing. Bands like Rage Against The Machine, Limp Bizkit and Korn were the musical powers that fuelled his imagination; then there was Bob Ezrin's own solid grasp on what the overall vision should feel like. It was its own innate melodicism that saw 'Can't Sleep, Clowns Will Eat Me' omitted from the final album; it simply wasn't brutal enough (the song would appear as a bonus track on the Japanese edition). In its place lined up the heaviest artillery that Ezrin could coax from the players; all still recall how he thought nothing of simply halting the proceedings and telling the musicians outright, "Those chords are too gentle, that tune is too nice. It's not *Brutal Planet*." Then, with everybody suitably chastened, the mood would climb up another notch or four, and the next take would blaze with all the fury he demanded.

It was time to tour, and do so with the most extravagant stage set Alice had devised in some years. With the guillotine returning one more time, the set was created by an organisation called Distortions, who had already staged a show of their own in Denver, built around the *Brutal Planet* concept.

"[It] was a walk-through, but it was the best walk-through haunted house I've ever seen in my life," Alice raved to *Rue Morgue*. "You walked in, the doors close, you're standing on this steel grate and it was like being in the Nostromo from *Alien*.The floor started shaking, the heat for the lights was up – all your senses were attacked in the first five seconds and you really wanted to get out of there, and that was the beginning of the ride! They also had bodies that looked like they'd been nuked, bodies that had been melted into toxic waste cans. So when we decided to put *Brutal Planet* together as a show we went right to them and said, "OK, we want the stage to be like the haunted house."

Yet *Brutal Planet*, both the album and the show, was only the first stage in Alice's 21st century reinvention. Barely had the stages been cleaned from that tour than he was back in the studio, narrowing the last album's focus even further, and taking his listeners deeper inside, on a day trip to *Dragontown*.

Dragontown itself, he explained, was "the worst town on *Brutal Planet*", and with Bob Ezrin back in the production chair the wide open vistas of *Brutal Planet* were to become even more grandiose. He told *Get Rhythm*, "When I finished work on *Brutal Planet*, I was really pleased with the way it had turned out, but I sat back and thought the story was not finished. I could think of at least 10 or 11 more things I wanted to say to finish it all up, so when I started to write the next album it just sort of turned into part two." Dragontown itself was "like [*Brutal Planet's*] capital. It's a whole lot deeper and the whole *Dragontown* show will have a very different look, it will finish the story."

It would also people its streets with some surprising characters. He revived Nurse Rozetta from *From The Inside*, renaming her Sister Sara but really not altering her personality much; and created some new devils from archetypes that mainstream society had long since accepted, the opening Triggerman, the surreal Fantasy Man and the foreboding Sentinel.

He also toyed with rock mythology, and the cult of sentimentality that builds up around rock's tragic fallen. "I was tired of hearing things like, 'He died and went to rock'n'roll heaven.' I went, 'I don't think so'." Did John Lennon go to rock'n'roll heaven, he asked? Elvis? Janis Joplin? Jimi Hendrix? His own fallen friends Jim Morrison and Keith Moon?

He didn't think so. And so a swaggering, dissolute Elvis enters the picture for the buzzsaw rockabilly 'Disgraceland', a song that took the old 'Slick Black Limousine' and transformed it into a tabloid requiem for Presley's demise; Morrison drawls through the urban squalor of the title track, and there's a distinct Beatles bounce to 'It's Much Too Late'. "I did my own little impressions of them all," Alice smiled, although the latter pair, at least, were scarcely impressions that would be readily recognised.

Even as it retained its predecessor's dental drill guitars and a vocal on the far side of furious, however, *Dragontown* was also capable of surprises.

'Every Woman Has A Name' was a gorgeous ballad, up there with any of the more sainted love songs in Alice's repertoire (without really being the kind of love song you'd want to be the recipient of), while 'Sister Sara' slapped its metallic instincts with a mocking vocal straight out of the Beastie Boys. And for anybody who missed *Special Forces*, the closing 'I Am The Sentinel' opens his mad manifesto with a lyrical reminder of 'Model Citizen'.

The stage show, too, would draw in tighter. In his own mind, Alice pictured Cleveland "after it got hit by three or four atomic bombs. There's no morality or technology, just Roadwarriors." On stage, he took the costuming of some bizarre hybrid warrior, half samurai, half biker. The stage was strewn with rubble and wreckage. And if the parallels between that vision and the nightmare that unfolded over New York City just weeks before the album's November 2001 release were painful for the audience to contemplate, that did not make them any less real. The horror of 9/11 was not a touchstone for the decay of *Dragontown*. But perhaps, in its audience's mind, *Dragontown* was a reminder of that awful day.

Alice's own vision of that landscape remained cautionary. He did not celebrate the *Brutal Planet*'s brutality, he condemned it and, as the next decade progressed, so Alice became increasingly outspoken in his fight against his own reputation as a power of evil.

"I want people to worry about their soul," he told *Metal Edge* in 2002. "And not in a cheap way, not in a [singing] Oh Devil thing, with the two fingers sticking up – Ya' know, that black metal crap. I really want them to be very nervous about it on an *Exorcist* level. It presents a question where you can't really say, 'Well, it doesn't exist,' 'cause you don't know. I believe it. I believe there will be a Judgement Day. I think a great way to scare an audience is to present it to them. If I'm wrong, I'm wrong. What if I'm right?"

These thoughts were percolating as Alice considered his next move, a swift concluding third part to the *Brutal Planet* trilogy. It didn't happen. Other developments elsewhere in the rock underground instead sent his ideas soaring in a different direction entirely, and when a new Alice album did come along, it was the dawn of yet another new age, created by attempting to relive an older one.

The Eyes Of Alice Cooper, he admitted, was built around his own excitement when he switched on the radio and heard a new wave of what he considered garage bands coming through, the Hives, the White Stripes, the Vines, the Strokes and the Yeah Yeah Yeahs and so forth, It was stripped down, bare bones, undiluted rock'n'roll and he admitted that, by comparison with their primitive thrills, his last few discs had sounded bloated. Three major concept albums, three trips into the apocalypse, three questions, querulous examinations of what truly makes the modern world tick. It was time, he decided, to put all that behind him and just make a good old-fashioned rock'n'roll record again. Which meant making a good old fashioned Alice Cooper record.

For promotional photos and the album cover, Alice returned to the spider eye make-up that had once been his trademark, and in the studio he schooled his band in the art of making a rock record, 1971 style. "It was an idea that the only way to get that is to act like the old band," he told the *Boston Herald*. "The way we used to do it was, we would write a song, we would rehearse it for eight hours, take a dinner break and then record it. And then the band says, 'Well, I want to go back in and fix those two notes there,' and I'm going, 'No. You can't.' 'Why?' "Well, because the guitar's already leaked into the drum mikes, and it's in the tracks. You can't just go in and pull it out. It's too hard to do that. You can add to it, but we're not allowed to go back and mess around with the basic tracks.' Which means that bass, drums, guitars, everything is already there."

The whole thing seemed straightforward to Alice, but of course his reputation preceded him. Producer after producer, thrilled at being contacted in the name of Alice, then began planning what they could do with him; out-Ezrin-ing Ezrin with the bombast and barrage, because that's what Alice likes best. Isn't it?

Not this time. Alice wanted to be in and out of the studio lightning fast. Two weeks would be a long time, and he might even have been despairing before he finally met a producer who actually understood what he wanted. Andrew "Mudrock" Murdoch had worked with the likes of Godsmack and Linkin Park, he understood the value of the short sharp shock and he needed to listen to the material just once to know what it required.

"You should record this live in the studio," he said, and Alice just smiled. "That's exactly what we're going to do...."

The accompanying tour, suitably titled Bare Bones, followed a similar recipe, and sticking with his now established patterns of seemingly recording albums in pairs, Alice moved straight from the tour to the studio again, to cut *Dirty Diamonds*, a tightly wrought reminder of its predecessor's straight-edged slash that was destined to become his biggest American hit in a decade; at the same time as the *Nights With Alice Cooper* satellite radio show, broadcast for the first time on January 26, 2004, became one of that medium's greatest success stories.

Indeed, in an age when most artists of Alice's vintage were doing little more than treading musical water, Alice continued forging forward, with presentation and concepts if not commercial power. In fact, a DVD filmed on the Dirty Diamonds tour, *Alice Cooper: Live At Montreux 2005*, remains as powerful a document of an Alice Cooper concert as any vintage favourite from the back catalogue.

The drama doesn't change, even when the songs do. Touring in 2007, the show opened with the seldom-aired 'It's Hot Tonight' as two silhouetted Alices did battle behind the stage curtain, and a band of ridiculously young looking musos gurned and ground in the presence of a legend.

Alice moved as Alice always had, impossibly skinny, razor sharp movements, turning on a pin to raise his cane to the skies, as lean and lithe as performers half his age wish they could be, and still as dangerous as the dreams he danced through in his own youth, when the songs in the set were themselves in short trousers, and 'No More Mr Nice Guy' was less a statement of intent, and more a statement of fact.

The thought steamrollers your head, that the boys in the band probably weren't even born when 'Under My Wheels' was written and recorded. And then another one, that the AC monogram painted on the drummer's kit looks an awful lot like the anarchy symbol that Alice was once accused of propagating. One year short of his 60th birthday, he sings of being 18 as though he were still 21, and when he serenades his own corpse in 'Is It My Body' (get it?), you could even forgive the fact that the new material wasn't even half as catchy as the old, and the jokes aren't as funny either ('Woman Of Mass Distraction' indeed), because he put just as much energy and conviction into it as he ever did

But 'Lost In America' was pure Detroit rock'n'sweating roll, just like he always said it was, just like 'Be My Lover' always used to be, and half an hour into the show you realise that the only special effects of the night have been two guys with a gurney and you're utterly captivated

274

regardless. Like the song says though, we've still got a long way to go, and when darkness envelops the stage for a Spanish guitar solo, a cat with no ears could tell you that something dramatic is finally afoot, the deathless swagger of 'Desperado' – still the greatest western ever set to music, no matter how hard the Eagles tried to outgun it in their pomp.

He flexes his 'Muscle Of Love', and dons a 'Halo Of Flies', and if anyone ever asks what was so special about *Killer*, the fact that almost the entire album is dragged out every concert he plays should answer that question. To be fair, no new band has ever nailed it as neatly as the originals used to, and no drummer has ever captured the Neal Smith solo in all of its glory, where the silent strokes that he doesn't play are as much a part of the sound as the beats. But with the stroboscope dancing and your mind's eye still conjuring the images which filled your head as a teen, none of that matters.

We're into the final stretch now, fog choking the stage as we are welcomed to the nightmare, and a clutch of Alice's own nightmares emerge from the wings to hack and harass him. 'Cold Ethyl' is reheated, women bleed and a blonde ballerina is summarily smacked around the stage; and even after all these years, has rock ever schemed a more nightmarish lyric than 'Steven''s whispered promise to put pennies on your eyes, and hope you'll go away?

He brings out a pram for 'Dead Babies', a ratty, moth-eaten, old pram, and serenades its contents with a grimace and a growl... contents that are hauled out on the blade of a knife, held aloft for the audience's approval; and then the lunatic killer is bound in a straitjacket, and that voice pleads across the PA – "Mommy, where's daddy?"

Alice performs 'The Ballad Of Dwight Fry' on his knees, broken, and you can almost feel for him. But then you remember that yes, it is Alice, which means he has at least one more trick up his white-wrapped sleeve, no matter how eloquently he promises to return the little girl's toys. And now he's standing, swearing his escape, raving and drooling, and he's suddenly Harry Houdini, ripping off the straitjacket while his attendants hustle in search of him.

Captured again, bound again, he is led to his fate, a gallows whose shadow frames the drums. Hanged by the neck yet again, he is wheeled away, while the band celebrates his execution with a hamfistedly happy

'I Love The Dead', and the audience links hands above their heads to howl out the refrain alongside them.

It could have ended there; the show could have halted and we'd have all gone happy. But in top hat and tails, the monster is reborn, and 'School's Out' is a mass singalong too. 'Billion Dollar Babies' is a magnificent encore, 'Poison' is a soaring monster, and just when you think he has no hits left, the whole thing ends with 'Elected', and everything Alice sang back then was still true tonight. The kids still need a saviour, they don't need a fake. Alice Cooper for President!

Or not. He still hasn't run for political office, but the years since then can be read like a Powerpoint presentation regardless, a sequence of headlines underlining every new honour, every award, every new release. Or they can be seen as the steady and steadying output of an artist who suffers none of the pangs of regret that beset his peers; no need to constantly return to his past in order to validate his present.

Chapter Eighteen

Redemption For The Coop

As the 21st century got into its stride, so the rock industry was obliged to reinvent itself in the light of new technology and the realisation that things would never be the same again. In the early seventies, when Alice Cooper emerged into the popular consciousness, the record business was entering a period of growth that knew no precedent, and on and on it went, encompassing punk and new wave and all the other fads, until shiny silver CDs became the icing on the cake, the technology that enabled the industry to resell its wares again, at a higher price, to those who'd already bought it once. Then came the crunch – technology bit back in the shape of digital downloading and made records redundant.

Alice was lucky. He was of a generation of rockers who'd tasted the golden era, though like so many of his peers he'd seen the sales of his later work decline alarmingly. But he was a trooper – one of the best in the business – and therefore in a perfect position to take advantage of what was becoming known as Heritage Rock, a world where everyone was a 'legend', where deluxe upgraded box sets of cast-offs re-imagined as 'rarities' were the norm, and where huge tours were promoted on the unstated but implied threat that, in the words of the Stones' song, "This could be the last time".

Alice was feted by magazine writers not yet born when 'School's Out' first hit the charts and who knew nothing about how Alice Cooper was actually the name of a group he once fronted. He was a genuine icon and, because of his theatrics, a unique one at that. His make-up hid the scars of age and his sobriety fitted in well with the prevailing trend amongst so many surviving rockers with a taste for overindulgence in their glory days: Elton & Bernie, Ringo, Clapton, Townshend, even Ronnie Wood (though the jury is still out on whether he remains dry) are all now as sober as judges, and probably much wiser too.

Alice's professionalism stood him in good stead as touring became the principal source of income for rockers of his rank, and he didn't disappoint. His shows were extravaganzas, reviewed in glowing terms by quality broadsheets and the new monthly rock mags designed to appeal to the mature rock fan. His sins, such as they were, seemed to have been forgotten, or at least forgiven with the passing of time. No longer would politicians with an eye for a headline stoop to the level of Leo Abse and his ilk, and call for Alice's head on a plate. He never repented, of course – that wasn't Alice's style – but redemption had arrived on the back of recognition that Alice was really nothing more than a pantomime villain, fabulously wicked for the sake of the show but quite harmless, and actually quite charming, when the face paint was removed.

Unlike many, however, he didn't simply rest of his laurels, and 2008 brought another concept, another serial killer (or another arachnoid) in the shape of *Along Came A Spider* which emerged with a somewhat samey melange of alt-metal stylings. But still both the album and the accompanying Theatre Of Death (this time featuring four separate executions, and one of the greatest hats of Alice's entire career, unveiled for 'Go To Hell') were as vital and valuable in their own time and place as anything Alice had done since *Welcome To My Nightmare*, and the only reason that divide is drawn is that his earlier work, of course, was a five man effort and not one man's vision.

Yet that earlier work was not forgotten, and neither were its makers. In December 2006, the four surviving members of the original Alice Cooper band reunited to perform half a dozen classic oldies at the Christmas Pudding. "We played basically the greatest hits," Neal Smith says of that show. 'No More Mr Nice Guy', 'I'm Eighteen', 'School's Out', 'Billion Dollar Babies', 'Is It My Body' and 'Under My Wheels' tore out of the monitors and, though all may have been older and greyer, nobody would ever have accused them of being slower.

Originally they intended playing just two or three songs together. Instead, Alice marvelled, "We ended up playing for more than an hour, and it was just like the old days. I knew exactly where Dennis was going to be, I knew exactly what Neal's fills were going to be and I knew exactly how Mike was going to handle it. The only thing that was missing was that insane little guitar of Glen... but I'm sure he was there playing in spirit if no longer in person."

There would be no full-scale reunion, he insisted. "The worst thing I could ever do would be for Alice to go backwards."

That was true, but the occasional glance in the rear view mirror was permissible. Neal Smith: "We reunited again for a big autograph signing at the Monster Mania Con on the official birthday of the band. March 15, Mike Bruce's birthday, that was the first show we did under the name Alice Cooper." And after that, things really began to pick up pace.

A new Alice Cooper box set was mooted, a disc and souvenir-packed deluxe edition titled *Old School*, jammed with rarities, live cuts (the old 1971 St Louis bootleg was faithfully repackaged within) and unreleased material. Alice later admitted he did not have the courage to listen to the entire thing – "because I'm afraid to listen to the rehearsal tapes from high school". But it would turn out to be a godsend for fans, or at least those who had not already collected the large part of its contents on bootleg.

And even bigger dreams were on the horizon.

By mid-2010, plans for a new Alice album titled *The Night Shift*, for which he already had 10 new songs prepared, were abandoned in favour of a project that some people may have tired of hearing was about to be revisited, but that others had been gagging for for 35 years. It was time, finally, for Alice to have another nightmare.

Even in the planning stages, Alice's enthusiasm was contagious. "This one, it really is all about the songwriting. If the songs weren't flowing out the way they were, it wouldn't have happened. But these songs were coming out really good, so I knew we had something going on. Music has not changed since 1970; I listen to bands, the Foo Fighters, great guys, great energy, and they're playing early seventies hard rock. Same with Jack White. It's Detroit garage rock and there's nothing new under the sun. It's the attitude, the personality and the lyrics that turn it into whatever it is. And that's what makes the Nightmare work...

"It was going to be 35 years since the original *Nightmare* and I didn't want to just do 12 new songs, there's nothing special about that. So I said, 'Why don't we do something important and something that we do really well? Let's do another concept. Let's do another nightmare.' Let's give Alice a new nightmare. Who says he only gets one nightmare? Let's give him another one!"

The original album was not held sacred; themes and melodies from 1975 were reworked and reshaped into new material, until the opening 'I Am Made Of You' and the closing 'Underture' became historical book-ends as well as musical ones. It would, he told a French press conference, be "more bloody and more accomplished than the first. It sounds like the early years" – and if anybody doubted that, news that he was back in the studio with Dennis Dunaway, Neal Smith and Michael Bruce dispelled all doubts.

Alice explains, "[Bob and I] wrote the first song, then we wrote the disco song, because we decided Alice's nightmare would be disco, so let's write a really good disco song, and make it into a bloodbath." It was an old idea, of course; both *Goes To Hell* and *Lace And Whiskey* had driven down that particular road. But 'Disco Bloodbath Boogie Fever' was the one that he'd been wanting to write, an utterly unapologetic slaughterhouse set to the most pounding beat of the decade.

Alice continues: "Then we wrote two or three other songs, 'Caffeine' was one of them, and then what I decided was, I said, 'Bob, why don't we include the original band, Neil, Dennis and Mike, and have them play on the album? Why don't we write with them?'"

He elaborates: "Neal had this song that had a little section that was the feel of the whole song and I said, 'Let's get Neal in and we will rewrite this whole song.' The same with Mike on 'When Hell Comes Home' and the same with Dennis on 'Runaway Train'. That's the original band playing live in the studio and it does remind me of something that should be on *Love It To Death* or *Killer*."

Even more exhilarating, he admits, was the realisation that the band knew exactly what he wanted. "It was one of those times where I didn't have to go in and say, 'OK guys, let's get a live Alice seventies sound.' I didn't have to say that; they started playing that and Bob and I listened to the whole thing and at the end I said, 'This is exactly what I'm looking for'. At the end of the song, I didn't have to tell them to do that big ending where everything falls apart; that was just the way they would end, and it was very satisfying for me to hear that."

Welcome 2 My Nightmare came together effortlessly, both conceptually and musically. "The whole thing is pretty diverse; it goes in a lot of directions in the way a nightmare goes in a lot of directions and I think what we did, when we got something going in a certain direction we didn't try and change it. We let it have its own life. When we first listened to 'Bite Your Face Off', I thought, 'Wow we've really got that 1964 Rolling Stones sound, so let's keep that and make it that'. That's a part of Alice's background; that's how we learned to play, listening to the Rolling Stones, so let's make that a 1964 Rolling Stones song."

'Ghouls Gone Wild' could have come screaming off the Ramones' *Rock And Roll High School* movie soundtrack, and Alice delved into his own heritage too, with 'Disco Bloodbath Boogie Fever' emerging the kind of stomp that *Goes To Hell* would have loved to travel with, while Alice snarls like Heat Miser, that most delightfully vaudevillian of American animation's classic anti-heroes. 'What Baby Wants' even sounds like something that could have slipped out of *Trash*!

Alice: "'The Last Man On Earth,' it sounds like an old honky-tonk bum song so I said let's make it that. I don't want to put a square peg in a round hole, so let everything fit in the way it fits in and then we'll start connecting it up with little passages from the first album, bits from 'Steven' and 'Awakening' and things like that, and that will connect things up."

So did the announcement, on December 15, 2010, that Alice Cooper was to be inducted into the Rock And Roll Hall Of Fame. And not just Alice Cooper the man. Alice Cooper the band. The originals and the best.

Common sense shrugs and says, "What else did you expect? Of course it's the band, it could be nothing else." But as Neal Smith said when he first heard the news, common sense and the Hall Of Fame have not always marched hand in hand.

"It is the original band and not any of us on our own, and that's another thing I'm excited about. Because it could have been Alice by himself, and he certainly at this point deserves a nomination by himself. But first steps first, and I think it's the right thing to do. It's right that they go back to the original concept of the artist... like Iggy & the Stooges.... But then there was Patti Smith, who was nominated alone, without the band, and because of that, I was never sure what would happen until it occurred."

281

And afterwards? "We will play for the induction and we're talking about doing some shows post-induction, as well. It's all talk at this point, and we've been talking about it for the last 10 years, but this may be the boost that we've been needing. We all still have our solo careers, but I'm sure in some of the major cities, the fans will be able to come and see the original band play together again."

That prophecy has still to be realised. But in the meantime there was an unforgettable night when Alice Cooper took the national stage once again, the singer resplendent in blooded shirt and albino boa, his bandmates still like something that stepped out of *West Side Story*, and their sound a furious fire that not only rolled the years back, it kept them rolled back.

Rob Zombie introduced them, recalling a hypothetical night at the Cheetah Club when Frank Zappa signed the group on the spot, "and they went on to become the most rock star destroying band of all time, the most murderous gang of drag queens... in a good way. [And] all they wanted was Ferraris, switchblades and blondes. Before Alice Cooper there were no rock shows. Alice Cooper invented the rock show."

He recalled a photograph that impressed him as a kid growing up, Alice leaning on a bar in a jacket that spat out "Remember the Coop". "Forty years later, we fucking remember the Coop, all right." And it was only when the big screen scrolled through a bunch of vintage live footage that you realised just how much the American music industry had tried to forget him, because the best of the clips were all European: 'I'm Eighteen' from Germany's *Beat Club*, 'Under My Wheels' from the *Old Grey Whistle Test*, 'School's Out' from *Top Of The Pops*.

"The most disgusting, parent-terrorising band of all time," glowed Zombie, and there they were, Alice, Dennis, Neal and Mike... thanking Shep Gordon, remembering Glen Buxton, and taking us back exactly 40 years, to the single that shook through radio in March 1971, a still thumping, still thunderous and, most of all, still resonant 'I'm Eighteen'.

Zombie and a cosmetically enhanced kid's choir joined them for 'School's Out', but the point had already been made. The musicians were older, bulkier, greyer. But if any band truly represented everything that it meant to be young, loud, snotty and rebellious, and still represents those same qualities today (for they are qualities, no matter how big your mortgage or loud the grandkids), then this was it.

Because that, more than anything, is what Alice has always aspired to, and Alice Cooper always assumed would be true. Yes there would be missteps, yes there would be off nights and odd sideswipes and albums that didn't quite make the grade.

But on a good night, which is most nights, when everything falls into place, the passage of time does not mean a thing.

Alice: "When you're in front of an audience and you start one of those [old] songs, and I always tell the band when we're learning those songs, we're not going to do a new version of those songs. I hate to go see the Rolling Stones and see them do a reggae version of 'Brown Sugar'. I want to hear the song the way the record is, so that is how we do it, we absolutely do it like the record, and when you have an audience screaming for more and they hear the opening chords to this song or that song and they go crazy, it's impossible to get tired of it. You just can't.

"It's annoying to rehearse it, and I do have a hard time rehearsing. But to get it on stage in front of an audience, you just can't be tired with it."

So many gigs, so many great nights. On stage at the Rainbow in London in November 1971. The Kings of LA in 1973 and alone in that same city in 1975. Las Vegas in 1977, Philly in 1978. Manchester and Glasgow in 1982, and Manchester again in 1986. Pittsburgh in 1990. The Christmas Pudding in 2006. Alexandra Palace for Halloween 2011. There's a shelf of DVDs of a lifetime of shows, and another one of live performances, dating back to days when reel-to-reels were considered portable. And if you switch on your computer and dial up the virtual world of Second Life, you'll find an Alice Cooper tribute act there. Alice gets hanged by the neck until not-dead there as well.

Pick your own poison because the list could last forever. But one thing remains the same. On a night when everything falls into place, it's impossible to imagine that any time at all has passed since the first time you stood, sat or ran and hid behind the sofa while a hook nosed, black eyed, scraggly-haired half-man, half-Muppet arose from a pit of your own foulest nightmares to tell you what had happened to your school.

It is... "out".

Acknowledgements

Thanks to the small phone book full of people for contributing to this story, some anonymously, some accidentally, but all very valuably. At the heart of the story, of course, lie my own interviews, conversations and encounters with Alice, Neal Smith, Glen Buxton, Shep Gordon, Mike Pinera, Marcus Blake, Ray Manzarek, Hilly Michaels, Russell Mael, Harley Feinstein, Howard Kayman, Mark Volman, Tony Visconti, Harry Nilsson, Dee Murray, Jack Curtis, Dave Vanian, Stiv Bators, Cheetah Chrome, Kip Winger, Peter Frampton, Keith Boyce, Gary Holton, Suzi Quatro, Gaye Advert, Jim McCarty, Arthur Brown, John Donovan. But I am also indebted to the friends and associates who spoke to me off the record, and whose observations gave so much to the back story.

And to everybody else who threw something into the stew – Amy Hanson, Jo-Ann Greene, Toby, Oliver, Trevor, Jen, Gaye & Tim, Bateerz and family, Geoff Monmouth, Barb East, Karen and Todd, Linda and Larry, Deb and Roger, Dave and Sue, Mike Sharman, Chrissie Bentley, my agent Brandi Bowles, and all at Omnibus Press.

Discography

SINGLES
PRE-ALICE RELEASES

THE SPIDERS
Why Don't You Love Me/Hitch Hike
Mascot 112 (USA), 1965

THE SPIDERS
Don't Blow Your Mind/No Price Tag
Santa Cruz SCR 10.003 (USA), 1966

THE NAZZ
Wonder Who's Loving Her Now/Lay Down And Die, Goodbye
Very 001 (USA), 1967

THE SPIDERS
Why Don't You Love Me/Hitch Hike/Don't Blow Your Mind/Why Don't
You Love Me
Sundazed SEP 141 (USA), 1998

UK SINGLES DISCOGRAPHY
Unless otherwise noted, the discography notes UK vinyl releases only.

Reflected/Living
Straight ST 101 (USA), March 1969

Shoe Salesman/Return Of The Spiders
Warner Bros. 7398 (USA promo), 1970

I'm Eighteen/Is It My Body
Straight STR S 7209, August 1971

Under My Wheels/Desperado
Warner Bros K 16127, November 1971

Be My Lover/You Drive Me Nervous
Warner Bros. K 16154, March 1972

School's Out/Gutter Cat
Warner Bros. K 16188, June 1972

Elected/Luney Tune
Warner Bros. K 16214, September 1972

Hello Hurray/Generation Landslide
Warner Bros. K 16248, February 1973

Slick Black Limousine/Unfinished Sweet (Extract)/Elected (Extract)/No
More Mister Nice Guy (Extract)/Billion Dollar Babies (Extract)/I Love
The Dead (Extract)
Lyntone LYN 2585 (flexidisc), February 1973

No More Mr. Nice Guy/Raped And Freezin'
Warner Bros. K 16262, April 1973

School's Out/No More Mr. Nice Guy/Elected/Billion Dollar Babies
Warner Bros. K16409, 1974

Teenage Lament '74/Hard Hearted Alice
Warner Bros. K 16345, January 1974

Department Of Youth/Cold Ethyl
Anchor ANC 1012, February 1975

Only Women Bleed/Devil's Food
Anchor ANC 1018, June 1975

Welcome To My Nightmare/Black Widow
Anchor ANC 1025, November 1975

Welcome To My Nightmare/Department Of Youth/Black Widow/Only
Women Bleed
Anchor ANE 7001 (12-inch), 1976

I Never Cry/Go To Hell
Warner Bros. K 16792, July 1976

School's Out/Elected
Warner Bros. K 16287, November 1976

Love At Your Convenience/You And Me
Warner Bros. K 16914, March 1977 (withdrawn)

(No More) Love At Your Convenience/It's Hot Tonight
Warner Bros. K 16935, April 1977

You And Me/My God
Warner Bros. K 16984, July 1977

How You Gonna See Me Now/No Tricks
Warner Bros. K 17270, November 1978

Clones (We're All)/Model Citizen
Warner Bros. K 17598, May 1980

(No More) Love At Your Convenience/Generation Landslide
Warner Bros. K 17914, February 1982

Seven And Seven Is (Live)/Generation Landslide '81
Warner Bros. K 17924, February 1982

For Britain Only/Under My Wheels (Live)
Warner Bros. K 17940, May 1982

For Britain Only/Under My Wheels (Live)
Warner Bros. K 17940M (12-inch), May 1982

I Am The Future (Remix)/Zorro's Ascent
Warner Bros. K 15004, March 1983

School's Out/Elected
Old Gold OG 9519, September 1985

He's Back (The Man Behind The Mask)/Billion Dollar Babies
MCA MCA 1090, October 1986

Teenage Frankenstein/School's Out (Live)
MCA MCA 1113, April 1987

Freedom/Time To Kill
MCA MCA 1241, March 1988

Poison/Trash
Epic 655061 7, July 1989

Bed Of Nails/I'm Your Gun
Epic ALICE 3, September 1989

Bed Of Nails/I'm Your Gun
Epic ALICEB 3 (blue vinyl), September 1989

Bed Of Nails/I'm Your Gun
Epic ALICEG 3 (green vinyl), September 1989

Bed Of Nails/I'm Your Gun
Epic ALICER 3 (red vinyl), September 1989

House Of Fire/This Maniac's In Love With You
Epic ALICE 4, December 1989

House Of Fire/This Maniac's In Love With You
Epic ALICEP 4 (shaped picture disc), December 1989

Hey Stoopid/Wind Up Toy
Epic 656 983 7, June 1991

Love's A Loaded Gun/Fire
Epic 657438 7, September 1991

Feed My Frankenstein/Burning Our Bed
Epic 658092 7, June 1992

Lost In America/Hey Stoopid (live)/Billion Dollar Babies (live)/No More
Mr Nice Guy (B2)
Epic 660347-6 (12-inch), May 1994

It's Me/Bad Place Alone/Poison (live)/Sick Things (live)
Epic 660563-6 (12-inch), July 1994

UK LPs
(except where noted)

Alice Cooper At The Whisky A Go Go
No Longer Umpire (live)/Today Mueller (live)/Ten Minutes Before The
Worm (live)/Levity Ball (live)/Nobody Likes Me (live)/BB On Mars (live)/
Sing Low, Sweet Cheerio (live)/Changing Arranging (live)
Straight R2 70369, 1969 (1992 – USA)

The Toronto Rock'n'Roll Festival 1969
No Longer Umpire (live)/Lay Down and Die, Goodbye (live)/Don't Blow
Your Mind (live)/Nobody Likes Me (live)/Fields Of Regret (live)
(Alice Cooper performances only)
Accord SN 7162, 1982 (USA)

Pretties For You
Titanic Overture/Ten Minutes Before The Worm/Sing Low Sweet Cheerio/Today Mueller/Living/Fields Of Regret/No Longer Empire/ Levity Ball (live)/B.B. On Mars/Reflected/Apple Bush/Earwigs To Eternity/Changing Arranging
Straight STS 1051, 1969

Easy Action
Mr. And Misdemeanor/Shoe Salesman/Still No Air/Below Your Means/ Return Of The Spiders/Laughing At Me/Refrigerator Heaven/Beautiful Flyaway/Lay Down And Die, Goodbye
Straight STS 1061, 1970

Love It To Death
Caught In A Dream/I'm Eighteen/Long Way To Go/Black Juju/Is It My Body/Hallowed Be My Name/Second Coming/Ballad Of Dwight Fry/ Sun Arise
Straight 1065, 1971

Killer
Under My Wheels/Be My Lover/Halo Of Flies/Desperado/You Drive Me Nervous/Yeah, Yeah, Yeah/Dead Babies/Killer
Warner Bros. K56005, 1972

School's Out
School's Out/Luney Tune/Gutter Cat Vs. The Jets/Street Fight/Blue Turk/ My Stars/Public Animal No. 9/Alma Mater/Grande Finale
Warner Bros. K56007, 1972

Billion Dollar Babies
Hello Hooray/Raped And Freezin'/Elected/Billion Dollar Babies/ Unfinished Sweet/No More Mr. Nice Guy/Generation Landslide/Sick Things/Mary Ann/I Love The Dead
Warner Bros. K56013, 1973
(A remastered *Billion Dollar Babies* released in 2001 contained the following live bonus tracks and out-takes: Hello Hooray/Billion Dollar Babies/Elected/I'm Eighteen/Raped And Freezing/No More Mr Nice Guy/My Stars/Unfinished Sweet/Sick Things/Dead Babies/I Love The Dead/Coal Black Model T (out-take)/Son Of Billion Dollar Babies (out-take)/Slick Black Limousine (out-take)

School Days – The Early Recordings
Titanic Overture/Ten Minutes Before The Worm/Sing Low Sweet Cheerio/Today Mueller/Living/Fields Of Regret/No Longer Empire/Levity Ball (live)/B.B. On Mars/Reflected/Apple Bush/Earwigs To Eternity/Changing Arranging/Mr. And Misdemeanor/Shoe Salesman/Still No Air/Below Your Means/Return Of The Spiders/Laughing At Me/Refrigerator Heaven/Beautiful Flyaway/Lay Down And Die, Goodbye
Warner Bros. K66021, 1973

Muscle Of Love
Big Apple Dreamin' (Hippo)/Never Been Sold Before/Hard Hearted Alice/Crazy Little Child/Working Up A Sweat/Muscle Of Love/Man With A Golden Gun/Teenage Lament '74/Woman Machine
Warner Bros. K56018, 1973

Alice Cooper's Greatest Hits
I'm Eighteen/Is It My Body/Desperado/Under My Wheels/Be My Lover/School's Out/Hello Hooray/Elected/No More Mr. Nice Guy/Billion Dollar Babies/Teenage Lament '74/Muscle Of Love
Warner Bros. K56043, 1974 (These tracks were lightly remixed)

Welcome To My Nightmare
Welcome To My Nightmare/Devil's Food/The Black Widow/Some Folks/Only Women Bleed/Department Of Youth/Cold Ethyl/Years Ago/Steven/The Awakening/Escape
Anchor L2011, 1975
(A remastered *Welcome To My Nightmare* released in 2002 contained the following alternate versions as bonus tracks: Devil's Food/Cold Ethyl/The Awakening)

Alice Cooper Goes To Hell
Go To Hell/You Gotta Dance/I'm The Coolest/Didn't We Meet/I Never Cry/Give The Kid A Break/Guilty/Wake Me Gently/Wish You Were Here/I'm Always Chasing Rainbows/Going Home
Warner Bros. K56171, 1976

Lace And Whiskey
It's Hot Tonight/Lace And Whiskey/Road Rats/Damned If You Do/You And Me/King Of The Silver Screen/Ubangi Stomp/ (No More) Love At Your Convenience/I Never Wrote Those Songs/My God
(Warner Bros. K56365, 1977)

The Alice Cooper Show
Under My Wheels/I'm Eighteen/Only Women Bleed/Sick Things/Is It My Body/I Never Cry/Billion Dollar Babies/Devil's Food – The Black Widow/You And Me/I Love The Dead – Go To Hell – Wish You Were Here/School's Out
Warner Bros., K56439, 1977 (Recorded live)

From The Inside
From The Inside/Wish I Were Born In Beverly Hills/The Quiet Room/ Nurse Rozetta/Millie And Billie/Serious/How You Gonna See Me Now/ For Veronica's Sake/Jackknife Johnny/Inmates (We're All Crazy)
Warner Bros. K56577, 1978

Flush The Fashion
Talk Talk/Clones (We're All)/Pain/Leather Boots/Aspirin Damage/Nuclear Infected/Grim Facts/Model Citizen/Dance Yourself To Death/Headlines
Warner Bros. K56805, 1980

Special Forces
Who Do You Think We Are/Seven And Seven Is/Prettiest Cop On The Block/Don't Talk Old To Me/Generation Landslide '81/Skeletons In The Closet/You Want It, You Got It/You Look Good In Rags/You're A Movie/ Vicious Rumours/Look At You Over There, Ripping The Sawdust From My Teddybear (CD bonus track)
K56927, 1981

Zipper Catches Skin
Zorro's Ascent/Make That Money (Scrooge's Song)/I Am The Future/ No Baloney Homosapiens (For Steve And E.T.)/Adaptable (Anything For You)/I Like Girls/Remarkably Insincere/Tag, You're It/I Better Be Good/ I'm Alive (That Was The Day My Dead Pet Returned To Save My Life)
Warner Bros. K57021, 1982

DaDa
DaDa/Enough's Enough/Former Lee Warmer/No Man's Land/Dyslexia/ Scarlet And Sheba/I Love America/Fresh Blood/Pass The Gun Around
Warner Bros. 923969, 1983

Constrictor
Teenage Frankenstein/Give It Up/Thrill My Gorilla/Life And Death Of The Party/Simple Disobedience/The World Needs Guts/Trick Bag/Crawlin'/ Great American Success Story/He's Back (The Man Behind The Mask)
MCA MCF 3341, 1986

Raise Your Fist And Yell
Freedom/Lock Me Up/Give The Radio Back/Step On You/Not That Kind Of Love/Prince Of Darkness/Time To Kill/Chop, Chop, Chop/ Gail/Roses On White Lace
MCA MCF 3392, 1987

Trash
Poison/Spark In The Dark/House Of Fire/Why Trust You/Only My Heart Talkin'/Bed Of Nails/This Maniac's In Love With You/Trash/Hell Is Living Without You/I'm Your Gun
Epic 465130, 1989

Hey Stoopid
Hey Stoopid/Love's A Loaded Gun/Snakebite/Burning Our Bed/ Dangerous Tonight/Might As Well Be On Mars/Feed My Frankenstein/ Hurricane Years/Little By Little/Die For You/Dirty Dreams/Wind Up Toy
Epic 656983-7, 1991

The Last Temptation
Sideshow/Nothing's Free/Lost In America/Bad Place Alone/You're My Temptation/Stolen Prayer/Unholy War/Lullaby/It's Me/Cleansed By Fire
Epic 476594-2, 1994

Classicks
Poison/Hey Stoopid/Feed My Frankenstein/Love's A Loaded Gun/Stolen Prayer/House Of Fire/It's Me/Under My Wheels/Billion Dollar Babies/ I'm Eighteen/No More Mr. Nice Guy/Only Women Bleed/School's Out/ Lost In America/Fire
Epic 480845, 1995. (Tracks 8-13 recorded live Birmingham NEC, England, December 1989)

A Fistful Of Alice
School's Out/Under My Wheels/I'm Eighteen/Desperado/Lost In America/Teenage Lament '74/I Never Cry/Poison/No More Mr

Nice Guy/Welcome To My Nightmare/Only Women Bleed/Feed My Frankenstein/Elected/Is Anyone Home
EMI CTM 331, 1997 (All tracks live)

The Life And Crimes Of Alice Cooper
Disc One: Don't Blow Your Mind – The Spiders (1966)/Hitch Hike – The Spiders (1965)/Why Don't You Love Me – The Spiders (1965)/Lay Down And Die, Goodbye – (OriginalVersion) The Nazz (1967)/Nobody Likes Me (demo version – 1968)/Levity Ball (studio version – 1968)/Reflected (*Pretties For You* – 1969)/Mr. And Misdemeanor (*Easy Action* – 1970)/Refrigerator Heaven (*Easy Action* – 1970)/Caught In A Dream (*Love It To Death* – 1971)/I'm Eighteen (*Love It To Death* – 1971)/Is It My Body (*Love It To Death* – 1971)/Ballad Of Dwight Fry (*Love It To Death* – 1971)/Under My Wheels (*Killer* – 1971)/Be My Lover (*Killer* – 1971)/Desperado (*Killer* – 1971)/Dead Babies (*Killer* – 1971)/Killer (*Killer* – 1971)/Call It Evil (demo – 1971)/Gutter Cat vs The Jets (*School's Out* – 1972)/School's Out (*School's Out* – 1972)
Disc Two: Hello Hooray (*Billion Dollar Babies* – 1973)/Elected (*Billion Dollar Babies* – 1973)/Billion Dollar Babies (*Billion Dollar Babies* – 1973)/No More Mr. Nice Guy (*Billion Dollar Babies* – 1973)/I Love The Dead (*Billion Dollar Babies* – 1973)/Slick Black Limousine (Flexi-disc from *New Musical Express* 1973)/Respect For The Sleepers (demo – 1973)/Muscle Of Love (*Muscle Of Love* – 1973)/Teenage Lament '74 (*Muscle Of Love* – 1973)/Working Up A Sweat (*Muscle Of Love* – 1973)/Man With The Golden Gun (*Muscle Of Love* – 1973)/I'm Flash (*Flash Fearless Versus The Zorg Women* – 1975)/Space Pirates (*Flash Fearless Versus The Zorg Women* – 1975)/Welcome To My Nightmare (*Welcome To My Nightmare* – 1975)/Only Women Bleed (single version)/Cold Ethyl (*Welcome To My Nightmare* – 1975)/Department Of Youth (*Welcome To My Nightmare* – 1975)/Escape (*Welcome To My Nightmare* – 1975)/I Never Cry (*Alice Cooper Goes To Hell* – 1976)/Go To Hell (*Alice Cooper Goes To Hell* – 1976)
Disc Three: It's Hot Tonight (*Lace And Whiskey* – 1977)/You And Me (*Lace And Whiskey* – 1977)/I Miss You (*Battle Axe* – 1977)/No Time For Tears (*Sextette* out-take – 1977)/Because – With The Bee Gees (*Sgt. Pepper's Lonely Hearts Club Band* – 1978)/From The Inside (*From The Inside* – 1978)/How You Gonna See Me Now (*From The Inside* – 1978)/Serious (*From The Inside* – 1978)/No Tricks (Single B-side – 1978)/Road Rats (*Roadie* – 1980)/Clones (We're All) (*Flush The Fashion* – 1980)/Pain (*Flush The Fashion* – 1980)/Who Do You Think We Are (*Special Forces* – 1980)/Look At You Over There, Ripping

The Sawdust From My Teddybear (Out-take – 1980)/For Britain Only (UK only single – 1982)/I Am The Future (*Zipper Catches Skin* – 1982)/Tag, You're It (*Zipper Catches Skin* – 1982)/Former Lee Warmer (*DaDa* - 1983)/I Love America (*DaDa* - 1983)/Identity Crisis (*Monster Dog* – 1984)/See Me In The Mirror (*Monster Dog* – 1984)/Hard Rock Summer *(Friday The 13th* – 1986) Disc Four: He's Back (The Man Behind The Mask) (Demo with music from *Trick Bag* – 1986)/He's Back (The Man Behind The Mask) (*Constrictor* – 1986)/Teenage Frankenstein (*Constrictor* – 1986)/Freedom (*Raise Your Fist And Yell* – 1987)/Prince Of Darkness (*Raise Your Fist And Yell* – 1987)/Under My Wheels (*The Decline Of Western Civilization* – 1988)/I Got A Line On You (*Iron Eagle II* - 1988)/Poison (*Trash* – 1989)/Trash (*Trash* – 1989)/Only My Heart Talkin' (*Trash* – 1989)/Hey Stoopid (*Hey Stoopid* – 1991)/Feed My Frankenstein (*Hey Stoopid* – 1991)/Fire (Single B-side)/Lost In America (*The Last Temptation* – 1994)/It's Me (*The Last Temptation* – 1994)/Hands Of Death (with Rob Zombie, remix of the track from *The X Files* – 1996)/Is Anyone Home? (*A Fistful Of Alice* – 1997)/Stolen Prayer (*The Last Temptation* – 1994) Rhino R2 75580, 1999

Brutal Planet
Brutal Planet/Wicked Young Man/Sanctuary/Blow Me A Kiss/Eat Some More/Pick Up The Bones/Pessi-Mystic/Gimme/It's The Little Things/Take It Like A Woman/Cold Machines/It's The Little Things/Wicked Young Man/Poison/My Generation/Total Rock Rockumentary (Radio show bonus track) Eagle CDE 115, 2000 (Tracks 11-15 are live bonus tracks with the album's tour edition)

Brutally Live
Brutal Planet/Gimme/Go To Hell/Blow Me A Kiss/I'm Eighteen/Feed My Frankenstein/Wicked Young Man/No More Mr Nice Guy/It's Hot Tonight/Caught In A Dream/It's The Little Things/Poison/Take It Like A Woman/Only Women Bleed/You Drive Me Nervous/Under My Wheels/School's Out/Billion Dollar Babies/My Generation/Elected Eagle DVD + CD, 2000 (Recorded live)

Dragontown
Triggerman/Deeper/Dragontown/Sex, Death And Money/Fantasy Man/Somewhere In The Jungle/Disgraceland/Sister Sara/Every Woman Has A Name/I Just Wanna Be God/It's Much Too Late/The Sentinel/Can't Sleep,

Clowns Will Eat Me/Go To Hell (live)/Ballad Of Dwight Fry (live)/Brutal Planet (Remix)/Gimme (Enhanced video)/It's the Little Things (Enhanced video)
Eagle CD 181, 2001 (Tracks 13-18 are tour edition bonus tracks)

The Eyes Of Alice Cooper
What Do You Want From Me?/Between High School And Old School/Man Of The Year/Novocaine/Bye Bye, Baby/Be With You Awhile/Detroit City/Spirits Rebellious/This House Is Haunted/Love Should Never Feel Like This/The Song That Didn't Rhyme/I'm So Angry/Backyard Brawl
Spitfire CD090, 2003

Dirty Diamonds
Woman Of Mass Distraction/You Make Me Wanna/Perfect/Dirty Diamonds/Pretty Ballerina/Sunset Babies (All Got Rabies)/Zombie Dance/The Saga Of Jesse Jane/Six Hours/Steal That Car/Run Down The Devil/Your Own Worst Enemy
Spitfire CD 257, 2005

Live At Montreux 2005
Department Of Youth/No More Mr Nice Guy/Dirty Diamonds/Billion Dollar Babies/Be My Lover/Lost In America/I Never Cry/Woman Of Mass Distraction/I'm Eighteen/Between High School And Old School/What Do You Want From Me/Is It My Body/Gimme/Feed My Frankenstein/Welcome To My Nightmare/School's Out/Poison/Wish I Were Born In Beverly Hills/Under My Wheels
Spitfire DVD + CD, 2006

Along Came A Spider
I Know Where You Live (Prologue)/Vengeance Is Mine/Wake The Dead/Catch Me If You Can/(In Touch With) Your Feminine Side/Wrapped In Silk/Killed By Love/I'm Hungry/The One That Got Away/Salvation/I Am The Spider (Epilogue)
(SPV 90602, 2008)

Theatre Of Death
School's Out (Short version)/Department Of Youth/I'm Eighteen/Wicked Young Man/Ballad Of Dwight Fry/Go To Hell/Guilty/Welcome To My Nightmare/Cold Ethyl/Poison/The Awakening/From The Inside/Nurse

Rozetta/Is It My Body/Be My Lover/Only Women Bleed – I Never Cry/Black Widow (instrumental)/Vengeance Is Mine/Devil's Food/Dirty Diamonds/Billion Dollar Babies/Killer/I Love The Dead/No More Mr Nice Guy/Under My Wheels/School's Out (Long version)
BGP 2525591, 2009

Old School
Disc One: No Price Tag (Spiders)/Nobody Likes Me (Demo)/On A Train Trip (Sing Low Sweet Cheerio) (Demo)/Reflected (Demo)/ Easy Action Version Two (Radio ad)/Mr and Misdemeanor (Chicago Underground)/Fields of Regret (Chicago Underground)/I'm Eighteen (Chicago Underground)/Love It To Death (Radio ad)/I'm Eighteen (Pre-production)/Be My Lover (Demo)/Killer (Demo)/Halo Of Flies (Demo)/ Tornado Warning (Desperado) (Demo)/Killer (Radio Ad)/Is It My Body (Live in Seattle, 1971)
Disc Two: Akron Rubber Bowl Ad (Radio Ad)/School's Out (Mar Y Sol, Puerto Rico)/Kids Session (School's Out Kids Session)/Outtakes – Luney Tune (Pre-production)/Outtakes – My Stars (Pre-production)/School's Out (Demo)/Under My Wheels (Live at Madison Square Garden)/ Teenage Lament '74 (Demo)/Never Been Sold Before (Demo)/Working Up A Sweat (Demo)/Muscle Of Love (Pre-production)/Teenage Lament '74 (Pre-production)/Muscle Of Love (Radio Ad)/Good To See You Alice Cooper (Radio Ad)/Muscle Of Love (Rio)/Greatest Hits (Radio Ad)
Disc Three: In Their Own Words
Disc Four: Intro/Be My Lover (Intro)/Be My Lover/You Drive Me Nervous/Yeah, Yeah, Yeah/I'm Eighteen/Halo Of Flies/Is It My Body/ Dead Babies/Killer/Long Way To Go (All tracks on disc four recorded on the Killer Live tour from St Louis, 1971)
Universal B004X96IZA, 2011

Welcome 2 My Nightmare
I Am Made Of You/Caffeine/The Nightmare Returns/A Runaway Train/ Last Man On Earth/The Congregation/Disco Bloodbath Boogie Fever/I'll Bite Your Face Off/Ghouls Gone Wild/Something To Remember Me By/ When Hell Comes Home/What Baby Wants/I Gotta Get Outta Here/The Underture/Under The Bed (bonus track with *Classic Rock* magazine CD)/ Poison (Live at Download 2011) (bonus track with *Classic Rock* magazine CD)/We Gotta Get Out Of This Place (bonus track with Limited Edition

digipack)/No More Mr Nice Guy (Live At Download) (bonus track with Limited Edition digipack)/The Black Widow (Live At Download) (bonus track with Limited Edition digipack)/Flatline (bonus track with iTunes version)/A Bad Situation (bonus track with vinyl)
Spinefarm Records B005F908W6, 2011

Index

299